Communism Unwrapped

Communism Unwrapped

Consumption in Cold War Eastern Europe

EDITED BY

PAULINA BREN AND MARY NEUBURGER

OXFORD
UNIVERSITY PRESS

OXFORD
UNIVERSITY PRESS

Oxford University Press is a department of the University of Oxford.
It furthers the University's objective of excellence in research,
scholarship, and education by publishing worldwide.

Oxford   New York
Auckland   Cape Town   Dar es Salaam   Hong Kong   Karachi
Kuala Lumpur   Madrid   Melbourne   Mexico City   Nairobi
New Delhi   Shanghai   Taipei   Toronto

With offices in
Argentina   Austria   Brazil   Chile   Czech Republic   France   Greece
Guatemala   Hungary   Italy   Japan   Poland   Portugal   Singapore
South Korea   Switzerland   Thailand   Turkey   Ukraine   Vietnam

Oxford is a registered trade mark of Oxford University Press in the UK and certain other countries.

Published in the United States of America by Oxford University Press
198 Madison Avenue, New York, NY 10016

© Oxford University Press 2012

Library of Congress Cataloging-in-Publication Data
Communism unwrapped : consumption in Cold War Eastern Europe / edited by Paulina Bren and
Mary Neuburger.
    p.   cm.
Includes bibliographical references and index.
ISBN 978-0-19-982767-1 (pbk. : alk. paper)—ISBN 978-0-19-982765-7 (hardcover : alk. paper)
1. Communism—Europe, Eastern. 2. Consumption (Economics) 3. Lifestyles—Europe, Eastern.
I. Bren, Paulina. II. Neuburger, Mary, 1966–
HX240.7.A6C576   2012
339.4'709409045—dc23   2012015112

To the memory of Jacqueline Lucas Rocks,
who spent much of the 1990s in Prague "unwrapping communism"

Contents

Acknowledgments

Paulina Bren would like to thank the Collegium Budapest Institute for Advanced Study, where she spent a most pleasant and industrious 2009–10 academic year as a Senior Fellow. Mary Neuburger would like to thank the University of Texas Department of History and the Center for Russian, East European, and Eurasian Studies for offering support and an intellectually stimulating environment. She would also like to thank the American Council of Learned Societies, the International Research and Exchanges Board, and the National Council for Eurasian and East European Research, whose support facilitated research and collaborative work on this project.

Contributors

Wendy Bracewell is professor of Southeast European history at the School of Slavonic and East European Studies at University College London (UCL). She is the author of *The Uskoks of Senj: Piracy, Banditry, and Holy War in the Sixteenth-Century Adriatic* (1992). More recently, she has directed a research project on East European travel writing, the results of which have been published in a three-volume set, *East Looks West* (2008–09) and an additional volume, *Balkan Departures: Travel Writing from Southeastern Europe* (Oxford, 2009), edited together with Alex Drace-Francis.

Paulina Bren teaches in history and various multidisciplinary programs at Vassar College. She is the author of *The Greengrocer and His TV: The Culture of Communism After the 1968 Prague Spring*, which won the 2012 Council for European Studies Book Prize and was short-listed for the 2011 ASEEES Wayne S. Vucinich Prize for the most important contribution to Russian, Eurasian, and East European studies. In addition, she has written a wide range of articles on the politics of everyday life in the Eastern Bloc.

Karl Brown received his Ph.D. in history from the University of Texas at Austin. A former Fulbright Scholar to Hungary, he is currently a visiting assistant professor at James Madison University. His research focuses on communism, crime, revolution, and transnational media. He has also published on jazz and hooliganism in communist Hungary and is currently working on a monograph entitled *Regulating Bodies: Everyday Crime and Popular Resistance in Communist Hungary, 1948–1956*.

Kate Brown is an associate professor of history at the University of Maryland Baltimore County. She is the author of *A Biography of No Place: From Ethnic Borderland to Soviet Heartland* (2004), which won the American Historical Association's George Louis Beer Prize for the Best Book in International European History. Brown is a 2009 Guggenheim Fellow and is working on a book called *Plutopolia*, a tandem history of the world's first plutonium cities, to be published by Oxford University Press in 2013.

Tamas Dombos is a Ph.D. student in the Department of Sociology and Social Anthropology at Central European University, Budapest, where he focuses on ethical consumption in Hungary. He is also a junior research fellow at the Center for Policy Studies at Central European University, an editor of the quarterly interdisciplinary journal *Café Bábel*, and an occasional lecturer at the College for Social Theory at the Corvinus University of Budapest.

Rossitza Guentcheva is assistant professor in the Department of Anthropology of the New Bulgarian University, Sofia. She has a Ph.D. in history from the University of Cambridge and an M.A. in history from the Central European University in Budapest. Her research interests are in the fields of social and cultural history of communism, anthropology of memory and consumption, and migration and mobility.

Mark Keck-Szajbel is currently a Ph.D. candidate at the University of California, Berkeley, and an associate professor at the Institute for East European History and Geography at Eberhard Karls Universität Tübingen. A recipient of numerous awards, Keck-Szajbel is author and translator of several articles on East European history and culture. He is writing his dissertation on travel and tourism in the Eastern Bloc.

Brigitte Le Normand received her Ph.D. in history from the University of California Los Angeles. She has written several pieces on urban planning in socialist Yugoslavia, including most recently a chapter in *The Socialist Car: Automobility in the Eastern Bloc*. Her research was supported by a doctoral fellowship from the Social Science and Humanities Research Council of Canada and a Max Weber fellowship at the European University Institute. She most recently taught history at Indiana University Southeast.

Jill Massino is assistant professor of history at the University of North Carolina-Charlotte, where she teaches courses on modern Europe. She has published a number of articles on gender in socialist Romania and co-edited (with Shana Penn) the collected volume *Gender Politics and Everyday Life in State Socialist Eastern and Central Europe*. Her current project explores the interplay between state constructions of gender and citizenship and the everyday lives of women and men in socialist and postsocialist Romania.

Małgorzata Mazurek is a postdoctoral fellow at the Center for Contemporary History in Potsdam. She graduated from Warsaw University and the Graduate School for Social Research at the Polish Academy of Sciences. She is the author of two monographs in Polish, titled *The Socialist Factory: Workers in Communist Poland and the GDR on the Eve of the 1960s* (2005) and *Society in Waiting Lines: On Experiences of Shortages in Postwar Poland* (2010). She has also written several articles on the comparative and social history of communist Poland and is currently working on a new book project entitled *Reconfiguring Backwardness: Polish Social Scientists and the Making of the Third World*.

Mary Neuburger is the author of *The Orient Within: Muslim Minorities and the Negotiation of Nationhood in Modern Bulgaria*. Her second book, a cultural history of tobacco in Bulgaria, is currently in production. Neuburger is an associate professor of history; director of the Center for Russian, East European and Eurasian Studies; chair of Slavic and Eurasian Studies; and associate director of the European Union Center for Excellence at the University of Texas, Austin.

Patrick Hyder Patterson is the author of *Bought and Sold: Living and Losing the Good Life in Socialist Yugoslavia*. An associate professor in the Department of History at the University of California, San Diego, he is currently at work on a large-scale comparative study of market culture and the consumer experience in socialist Eastern Europe.

Lena Pellandini-Simanyi obtained her Ph.D. in sociology from the London School of Economics and Political Science in 2009 and currently works as an assistant professor in the Department of Media and Communication of ELTE University, Budapest. Pellandini-Simanyi's recent work has focused on changes in consumption norms in Hungary. Her current research is in the sociology of morality, exploring the relationship between ethics and practice.

Katherine Pence is an associate professor, chair of the History Department, and director of Women's Studies at Baruch College of the City University of New

York. Alongside publishing numerous articles on consumer culture in East and West Germany, she has co-edited a volume of essays with Paul Betts entitled *Socialist Modern: East German Everyday Culture and Politics* and is publishing *Gender and Consumer Politics in Cold War Germany*. Her current research, entitled *The East and West German Scramble for Africa: Exhibiting Cold War Competition in the Age of Decolonization*, examines German trade and political exhibitions in early 1960s Africa.

Kacper Pobłocki is an assistant professor of anthropology and urban studies at the University of Poznan. He is a graduate of the Central European University. In 2009, he was a fellow at the Center for Place, Culture and Politics (CUNY Graduate Center) and in 2010 taught urban studies at Utrecht University. Currently he is preparing a book manuscript titled *The Cunning of Class: Urbanization of Inequality in Postwar Poland*.

Narcis Tulbure is a doctoral candidate in social anthropology at the University of Pittsburgh. His thesis analyzes the changing notions of money and value in postsocialist Romania. Tulbure has conducted research and published articles on work, leisure, and the second economy in Romania; social drinking and informal exchange under socialism; and contemporary meanings of money and their regulation in postsocialist Eastern Europe. In the last few years, he has held various research and teaching assignments at the New Europe College, Institute for Advanced Studies, at the Bucharest Academy of Economic Studies and at the University of Bucharest.

Communism Unwrapped

Introduction

Paulina Bren and Mary Neuburger

Today, if you pass through Krakow as a tourist, you can forgo the lively cafes and standard historic sites in favor of revisiting "communism"— an experience that can be booked online before you leave home.[1] Your tour of communism, set against the cityscape of Krakow, can be standard or luxury, depending on your budget; or, as the tour website cheekily admits, "All of our customers are equal, but some are more equal than others." The deluxe package includes a four-hour tour that showcases not the world of communist elites but that of ordinary communist citizens in Poland. Chauffeured around in a vintage Trabant (the ubiquitous car of the Eastern Bloc), clients can be picked up at the airport by a "typical Polish worker," stop for refreshments at a "communist-style restaurant," and finish up in a "communist apartment," where time seemingly stands still. The tour would not be complete, notes the website, without a side trip to "Stalin's gift to Krakow," the industrialized communist mecca known as Nowa Huta. To the uninitiated, the tour sounds like good fun; to insiders, subtle jokes abound as does the nostalgic fetishization of the not-so-distant past. With customers paying for a "taste of everyday life in Poland during the 1970s," the commodification of communism itself is the ultimate irony. It is food and drink, cars and houses—all manner of consumables—that recall the communist past, a past that is experienced through the senses and sensibilities of the consumer.

It might be surprising that this face of the communist past, so often associated with poor quality and scarcity, could tantalize. Yet with its many wrinkles and flaws, the consumer experience under communism continues to attract the attention of locals, tourists, and scholars on the region. Consumption in communist Eastern Europe followed its own rhythm and logic.[2] In other words, consumer experiments and

FIGURE O.I.   A screen shot from "Crazy Guides," the "communism tours" company based in Krakow, Poland. Here one sees a "time warp apartment" with communist-era furnishings, one of the featured attractions on the tour. Courtesy of Crazy Tours, Krakow.

experiences in Cold War Eastern Europe by no means constituted mere imitations or reactions to capitalist patterns of consumption. While not disclaiming the deprivations of the Cold War period, this book explores consumption beyond the one-dimensional images of long shopping lines, shabby apartment blocks, bare shelves, and outdated fashions. We do not abandon these "commonplaces" of communism; rather, the essays here view them from various (and in many cases surprising) angles. *Communism Unwrapped* builds upon a new body of work that has emerged in the last decade that seeks to unpack the experience of consumption under the unique constraints of socialism.[3]

Yet despite a proliferation of work on Soviet Russia and East Germany, the rest of Eastern Europe—that complicated multilingual, multi-ethnic swath of nation states in between—has received short shrift. This is despite (or perhaps because of) the much wider spectrum of responses to consumption that it pursued. This volume brings together scholars of various disciplines working on socialist and postsocialist Eastern Europe whose work intersects with questions of consumption—from illegal pig killings in Stalinist Hungary to plutonium cities in the Soviet Union and the United States, coffee drinking in East Germany, smoking in Bulgaria, cooking in Yugoslavia, and hustling in Prague. This book might be understood as a collection of individual but interlinked tours through communism's past, with consumption as its gateway—but, unlike the Krakow tours, bypassing nostalgia.

Importantly, we want to clarify that the category of "consumption" employed here is distinct from "consumerism," which has become the operative category in the study of the postwar "West." Consumerism, although it has a plethora of meanings, generally assumes a society that is driven and mobilized by marketing and corporate strategies that stimulate and then fulfill ever more unquenchable desires. In the United States, in particular, consumerism was not only embraced and normalized as never before in the postwar period but elevated to a patriotic duty, analogous with citizenship.[4] Consumption is a far broader term that encompasses a range of phenomena connected to the appraisal, procurement, distribution, and even production of goods and services—whether ingested (literally consumed), used, or experienced. For postwar Eastern Europe, as for much of the world, consumption is a far more useful and value-neutral category of analysis that does not necessarily presuppose a Western teleology, or privilege presumably Western forms.[5]

At the same time, histories of consumption in the West are relevant to the story of Eastern Europe. Scholarship on the processes in the West has drawn important analytical connections, such as the historical role of consumption as a driving force of industrialization and modernity.[6] It has mapped the role of consumption as a critical factor in a wide range of phenomena including power relations, group identity formation, and individual subjectivities.[7] But, until recently, consumption under communism had received little attention beyond generalized works on its "failure," whether in reference to *pax Americana* or its stated Marxist ideals.[8] Yet the story of postwar Eastern European consumption is a critical chapter in the larger history of global consumption, and indeed modernity. As in the West, consumption practices in communist societies were related to social status, gender, sociability, leisure, individual agency, and popular discontent, but in decidedly different ways. They were intimately tied, for example, to socialist notions of modernity and progress; that is, consumption of "modern" goods was part and parcel of the making of a modern *socialist* citizen-consumer.[9] In addition, because of the centrally planned economies of communist regimes, Eastern European consumption was closely interwoven with the state realm of supply and retail as well as the subterranean worlds of commerce, which formed complex and interconnected webs of consumption and trade. Confounding binaries of "official" and "unofficial," the interweaving of state and popular consumption and exchange was in many respects far more complex than under capitalism, and certainly more overtly political. Consumption, we propose, offers a window into these still shadowy interiors of everyday life and state-society negotiations in Cold War Eastern Europe.

It also promises to illuminate the region's complicated engagement with the "West"—a West both real and imagined—and elevate it beyond the merely reactive. The ever-increasing desire for and consumption of Western items in the later decades of socialism has been interpreted by many as "resistance," or else as erosive to the ideology and legitimacy of socialism. These goods, as many from within and outside the region argue, represented unparalleled propaganda for the West and capitalism; just compare, for example, the West German Mercedes to the East German Trabant. But it could also be a mixed bag: as the Croatian writer Slavenka Drakulić has recalled, *Vogue* magazine was the best advertisement for the material superiority of the West, while Barbie was indicative of all that was wrong.[10] Even for those who were wholly seduced, it was by an "imagined West," no less utopian and out of reach than the bountiful "ripe communism" perpetually promised to citizens of Eastern Europe.[11]

At the same time, for those who integrated artifacts of this "imagined West" into their daily lives, it is not a foregone conclusion that the desire for and possession of such things undermined their belief (however vague) in socialism. For many, the clothes, music, and trinkets of the West were woven seamlessly into their normalized and seemingly stable lives under communism. As anthropologist Alexei Yurchak persuasively argues, even for outwardly "rebellious" youth, Western music, clothing, and styles did not contradict their commitment to the Komsomol, the Soviet communist youth organization. Instead, this assimilation was constitutive of Soviet life, in which most were able to integrate Western forms and goods into their everyday lives without apparent ideological contradictions.[12] Although ideological faith had a much shorter (and pricklier) lifespan in the Eastern Bloc and Yugoslavia compared to the Soviet Union, there too similar contradictions ran rampant in the details of everyday life.

The major issue with consumption during communism was the ideological juggernaut it represented; that is, it was both needed, given the pursuit of a communist utopia, and endlessly problematic. In practice, this meant considerable ambiguity. But born of this ambiguity was also a certain flexibility, even creativity, in a system that is by contrast generally seen as stagnant and stultified. Historian Jonathan Zatlin, for example, suggests that the East German leadership, when faced with a thriving illegal trade in sought-after goods from which the state was not profiting, expanded its state-owned hard currency shops as a way to co-opt and monopolize the black market. In effect, hard currency shops across the Bloc might be best understood as indoor, state-sponsored, state-run, and state-profiting black markets.[13] Nor was the system's elasticity always a defensive strategy. Given the complex engagement with Western technologies, methods, and aesthetics in this period, late socialist consumer cultures were not simply a failed attempt to "imitate" Western forms. Certainly, some Western technologies and aesthetic forms were appropriated during the post-Stalinist period of détente. But, just as often, they were domesticated and tamed, woven tightly into local innovations and techniques as well as visions of communist futures. Certain industries in the region employed market research of their own, expending vast resources in pursuit of quality products and consumer satisfaction. This is something often overlooked in assumptions that these systems were defined solely by a "dictatorship of needs." Indeed, socialist regimes and some industries were quite attuned to desires, stimulating them through such institutions as the department store. And socialist consumers—revealing vast reservoirs of flexibility and creativity themselves—readily expressed such desires, exercising agency through choices, strategies, and refusals.[14]

Exploration into consumption under communism does not mean downplaying "shortage economies" and "societies of scarcity," which were a basic fact of life in postwar Eastern Europe.[15] One was often hard-pressed to find toilet paper in much of the Eastern Bloc in the 1980s; or, if available, it was most likely of the type more akin to institutional paper towels in the West. But putting the infamous production and distribution glitches aside, it was never the ideological aim of the system to produce fifty-five varieties of toilet paper in every conceivable texture, thickness, and color. Moreover, such consumer "successes," though pleasurable, have always been controversial, more so now given the recent cycle of economic crises, largely based on the overconsumption of "supply economies."[16] The history of the region should not be defined by "Western" narratives of the consumer experience, in other words, or by a "modernization theory" that assumes all societies develop along the lines of a familiar American consumerist model.[17] Instead of how it should have been, we are interested in how it *was*: the forms, meanings, and myriad paths of consumption in postwar Eastern Europe. It is here that socialist citizens, just like their Western counterparts, learned to be consumers.

The recent surge of interest in everyday life in socialist Eastern Europe is in part an antidote to a previous body of scholarship bogged down by Cold War politics and stymied by limited access to archival materials. But everyday life as a category has its own dangers; the search for specificities can overlook the commonalities. Turning the spotlight on consumption, however, allows a common thread to emerge, and with it a new history that is mindful of the region's similarities and yet careful not to shatter the differences. We have organized the essays in this volume around this principle, with themes rather than places or timelines dominating. These shared themes, on which we further elaborate in short introductions for each section, include consumer elites ("Living Large"), production of desire ("Quality Control"), gender and consumption ("Kitchen Talk"), black markets ("To Market, to Market . . ."), and state-generated critiques of consumption ("Constructive Criticism").

A Short History of Communist Consumption

In the immediate postwar period, as communists consolidated power through-out Eastern Europe, production, distribution, and various modes of consump-tion became instruments for imposing and negotiating political control. The message was clear to all: the bourgeoisie was out, the working classes in. Yet by the mid- to late 1950s, a decade following the communist parties' consolidation of power, these same regimes began to openly embrace many aspects of "bourgeois consumption," though now in a socialist guise. Invariably, this turn is associated with the death of Stalin in 1953 and Khrushchev's rise to power in 1956 and his denunciation of Stalinist crimes, followed by a reorientation of resources from heavy to light industry and agriculture. In other words, the of-ficial call that socialist societies must pay greater attention to consumer needs is deemed to be inextricable from de-Stalinization and the consequent need to find other avenues of legitimacy after the relaxation of more draconian measures of control. But was the consumer "turn" really as reactive, abrupt, or anomalous as is assumed?

The possibilities for the "consumerist turn" in fact were very much built on the foundation of Eastern European postwar recovery. Much of the region, after all, lay in ruins at the end of World War II, surrounded by unimaginable losses of life and property and mass dislocation. Imposition of communist regimes created even greater dislocation, but simultaneously it brought about a mass mobilization of physical and human resources for rebuilding war-torn landscapes and infrastructures. Much as in Western Europe, it took many years for the reconstruction to be complete. Even in parts of Western Europe—such as the United Kingdom, which remained on rations until 1955—consumer austerity was an integral part of that process.[18] With reconstruction and the imperative of communist modernization in mind, Eastern European state resources directed funds and materials toward rebuilding and, especially for lesser-developed states, industrializing.

In many ways the centrally planned economies of the region, with their far-reaching, redistributive powers, were well equipped to engineer the necessary rebuilding as well as the mobilization of populations for the con-struction of new industrial bases. As historian Tony Judt pointed out, "there are some things that command economies can manage quite well."[19] Having forced former peasants and small business owners into the new industries, growth rates in these early years were notable—particularly in places like Bul-garia and Romania "which had started from virtually nothing."[20] Along with Yugoslavia, they enjoyed some of the highest growth for their region during the 1940s and early 1950s, far outstripping nearby Western-oriented Greece and

Turkey.[21] In the northern tier of Eastern Europe, the largely agricultural coun-tries of Poland and Hungary rapidly expanded their industrial base; even Czechoslovakia, already an industrial powerhouse during the interwar years, registered a decrease in agricultural workers and attendant industrial growth.[22] Of course, in hindsight the nature and long-term efficacy of such developments are questionable, but at the time recovery moved forward apace, creating the foundation for consumer societies to develop. Finally, the fact that nonaligned Yugoslavia—out of the Bloc since 1948—experienced the consumer turn at pre-cisely the same time bolsters the contention that shifts in Soviet ideology, to which Yugoslavia was largely impervious, may have had less impact than imagined.

What Khrushchev advocated, once given the chance, was a Stalinist-Leninist hybrid of consumer practices, where abundance (and even luxury) for workers was embraced, but amid official pronouncements of austerity and at-tempts to "manage" needs and desires through "rational" consumption.[23] This synthesis required constant negotiation of the boundaries of the ideologically and morally acceptable. In the Soviet Union and even more so in East-Central and Southeastern Europe, this negotiation led to a spectrum of regimes of con-sumption across the region after 1953. Providing goods to new socialist con-sumers was especially critical in many of the East European satellites, where the revelation of Stalinist "mistakes" brought a wave of revolts against local leaders, the "little Stalins" who still held power. The eruption of mass discon-tent in the midst of this de-Stalinization—namely, in East Germany and Poland in 1953 (and on a smaller scale Bulgaria and Romania, and Pilsen, Czechoslo-vakia) and Hungary in 1956—is often cited as a major factor in the decision by socialist regimes to stabilize by expanding their offerings in consumer goods.[24] As Khrushchev gave a green light to Bloc satellites to pursue various "roads to socialism," Yugoslavia—and its independent path toward socialism—became an inspiration for communist-led resistance movements that rocked the region in this period. Yugoslavia's relatively humane approach to its population, its openness to the West, and its still nascent "mixed economy" were highly at-tractive to communist leaderships for a variety of reasons. Even after the various resistance movements were crushed, a modified Yugoslav model of "mixed" forms and permeable trans-Bloc borders became part and parcel of the consumerist turn.

Moreover, by the early 1960s these countries saw their economic growth decline considerably, which necessitated restructuring.[25] The 1968 Prague Spring is best remembered for "socialism with a human face," jazz clubs, and miniskirts, but the movement for political reform originated in economics with the recognition in 1963 that the Czechoslovak economy was faltering and something had to be done. Czechoslovakia's short-lived Action Program, rolled out by the Prague Spring government in April 1968, proposed mixing aspects of planned and market economies. The same year, Hungarian Party leader János Kádár launched the NEM program (the New Economic Mechanism), which similarly decentralized Hungary's planned economy, bringing market mechanisms and profits into the picture. Unlike the Action Program, which was never enacted, the NEM contributed to what became known popularly as "goulash communism"—an eclectic economic mix in part meant to curry favor with a still-disgruntled post-1956 public. With NEM, Hungary became known as the "happiest barracks in the communist camp." Poland, whose receptivity to communist rule Stalin once described on par with attempting to saddle a cow, was perhaps best known for its consumer-related volatility. Here, communist leaders came and went in rhythm to price hikes followed by worker uprisings.[26] But since deeply subsidized basic consumption had been propagated as a socialist citizen's right, not just shortages but even the most reasonable price hikes incited anger. Cheap food, housing, education, and health care became common features of socialist societies in this period and were taken for granted. When prices on any such items were raised, citizen rights were seen as threatened, and riots ensued.

Not coincidentally, the major explosions of unrest in the region occurred mostly in the "northern tier" countries, where there was a comparatively high standard of living in the prewar period, lower growth in the postwar period, and proximity to more successful West European states. Comparative (though not complete) lack of unrest did not mean, however, that the Balkan states did not pursue their own consumer-oriented paths to socialism, with the intention of evading potential instability. While Yugoslavia continued to liberalize, Romania and Bulgaria also moved toward providing abundance for their populations, with various reform programs throughout this period. In both states, however, a short-lived political "thaw" was accompanied by an increasingly, or at least intermittently, harsh political environment. Romania, like Albania, reacted viscerally to Soviet demands for further Bloc integration and specialization in the 1950s—intended, among other things, to bolster the variety, quality, and availability of consumer goods. But even though this pushed Romania "west," at least in terms of diplomatic and trade policies, Albania moved "east," out of the Bloc entirely and into a relationship with China in 1960.[27] This, as well as the policy of building four hundred thousand "pillbox" concrete bunkers against "enemy" invasions, made Albania easily the poorest country in Eastern Europe and the most challenged when it came to provisioning consumer goods.[28] In the Balkans, only Bulgaria embraced its role in Comecon (Eastern Europe's answer to the European Economic Co-Operation) specialization.[29] Hence, in the Balkan context alone, there was a vast range of orientations toward both

West and East. Indeed, diversity of orientation was the rule, with profound implications for the regimes' cultures of consumption.

In all cases, economic decisions related to consumption were made either as the result of public political flare-ups or in anticipation of them—even though at no time did political uprisings in the region demand the adoption of capitalist systems as such. Consumption issues not only ignited revolt, they also served as the healing salve for failed revolutions. In Czechoslovakia, where the 1968 Soviet-led invasion delivered a fatal blow to the Prague Spring, price subsidies on food, including meat, were used specifically to appease an angry public. As the leader of Czechoslovakia's subsequent "normalization" saw it, once people "have their creature comforts, they won't want to lose them."[30] Hence both reform *and* anti-reform often meant lowering prices on an ever wider variety of subsidized basic goods and services.[31] Gradually, these lower prices were accompanied by ever greater consumer abundance, although perpetually trailed by ideological concerns. That is, the unfurling of colorful advertising was offset by stern advice on how to be responsible socialist consumers.[32]

The push and pull between desire and ideology was most clearly on display in East Germany, the only Bloc state that had to contend with an ever-present prettier cousin (West Germany). Before the Berlin Wall was erected in 1961, East Germans could still travel west to see for themselves the postwar "economic miracle" laid out attractively in shop windows across the Iron Curtain. Afterward, this possibility was blocked off, but images of West German lifestyles continued to be beamed in daily through the television screen, with only the city of Dresden, where West German television signals did not reach, left "untainted." Because of its "virtual" proximity to capitalism, the GDR was, according to one scholar, forced to compete—unlike elsewhere in Eastern Europe—"with the West on capitalism's own terms."[33]

But whether in East Germany or Poland, political reform, revolt, and acquiescence took place against the parallel emergence of a new category of comfortable consumers, whose presence was palpable by the late 1950s and on view by the 1960s.[34] Stepped-up industrialization as well as forced agricultural collectivization—though this was eventually shelved in Yugoslavia and Poland—urbanized Eastern Europe to an unprecedented degree. Rural migrants often took the place, and literally the apartments, of old urban elites and professionals who had been largely pauperized and even exiled from cities by communist regimes as politically objectionable.[35] In the course of the 1950s, the ability of the socialist states to provide housing, food, and other material comforts for these populations gradually improved.[36] More pointedly, educating and training significant numbers of this population to form a new army of technocrats created a segment of society with rising expectations and consumer desires.

By the 1960s, as this new class continued to expand, regimes across the region began to openly cater to consumer anticipation. As many scholars argue, by the 1960s this rising standard of living had contributed to a new kind of stability, political consensus, and normality to everyday life under communism. Part of this consensus, what many scholars have dubbed a "social contract," seemed to rest on the ever wider availability of consumer goods, retail outlets, and leisure venues.[37] The social contract was used in varying forms across the Bloc, but in large part it came to define the 1970s and 1980s, what Václav Havel called "post-totalitarianism." Indeed Havel, even as he was glad to see Stalinist forms of repression go, had little good to say about this new era in which socialist citizens made Faustian deals for increased consumption in return for ideological compliance and social order. For this reason, he argued that the Bloc's post-totalitarianism did not differ as much as one might think from the spiritually bankrupt overconsumerist democracies on the other side of the Iron Curtain.[38]

The social contract, or certainly the consumption associated with it, flourished not only in Gustáv Husák's post-1968 Czechoslovakia but also in Josip Tito's Yugoslavia, János Kádár's post-1956 Hungary, Edward Gierek's Poland of the 1970s, and even in places like Bulgaria and Romania, where local and outside observers reported the appearance of new communist consumers at restaurants, shops, and newly built resorts and leisure complexes. Indeed, in the 1960s Romania was very much at the forefront of actively responding to, if not stimulating, the desires of domestic consumers. After coming to power in 1965, Nicolae Ceaușescu pursued the region's most aggressive trade and diplomatic relations with the West and in so doing became (like Yugoslavia) the darling of the West. Ceaușescu, who was on the cover of *Time* magazine in 1966 along with the headline "Life Under a Relaxed Communism," was reputed to have "set the pace" for a new kind of "European communism" behind a "rusting Curtain."[39] Real wages and consumption of basic foodstuffs rose dramatically for most throughout the period, especially during the "consumer golden age" of the 1960s and 1970s that resulted from restructuring and loans. The significant expansion of available goods and services had a ready army of consumers throughout the region.

But even in the thick of the consumer golden age, East European regimes continued to perceive consumption in the larger framework of "collective" good. Though a variety of new luxury goods were offered (some at prohibitive prices), in the case of staples prices were actually lowered to be affordable to almost all consumer-citizens.[40] The relationship this set up between consumers and consumption became problematic for the very regimes that incited it: the socialist consumer had an ever greater expectation of luxury goods but also assumed that staples would be offered at extremely low prices. This was exceedingly hard for the regimes of Eastern Europe to sustain, and they did so with varying degrees of gusto and success. What were the acceptable levels and parameters of consumption in a socialist society? It was a conundrum that plagued Bloc leaders, for socialism was built on the idea of progress toward the Eden known as ripe communism, and not late capitalism; many Bloc citizens, however, even though they did not call for capitalism, came to see abundant consumption as the primary signifier of progress.[41]

The golden years of these decades, however, were soon forgotten during the relatively lean 1980s, which for many inside and outside the region became emblematic of the failure of the system. The inability of regimes to sustain the relative plenty of earlier decades was in large part due to their vulnerability to the world economy: Eastern European exposure to the world economy through loans from Western creditors in the 1960s and 1970s, which had propped up the consumer golden age, now sent Eastern European economies into a tail spin as the global recession hit in the mid-1970s. As those debtors were cut off by their Western creditors, exports were heightened to fill the credit gap and mass shortages ensued. By the 1980s, in some places there was hardly anything left on the shelves. Nowhere was this more acute than in Romania (except possibly Albania), where Ceauşescu's independent road now translated into almost surreal austerity measures: bread rations were reinstated, electricity supplies were cut off without warning, and citizens were encouraged to save resources by abandoning all the markers of their earlier modernity such as refrigerators, vacuum cleaners, and use of elevators.[42]

As belts were tightened out of necessity, women and men displayed impressive creativity to make ends meet and even to go beyond the basics, as many managed to do. New skills were learned, innovation was reinvigorated, and personal relationships took center stage—all in the name of getting food on the table and clothes on one's back. Even as saving up was derided in economies having more cash than things to spend it on,[43] thinking ahead in other ways was necessary: if one saw a queue, one usually went to stand in it—it did not matter what was on offer because it could always be exchanged for something else. Professional queuers, mostly the retired, helped the process along.[44] Housing shortages meant that parents and grandparents often had no choice but to share households, putting three generations under one roof. Early marriages, partially encouraged by the state and partially the result of the limited availability of prophylactics, also meant an army of grandparents stepping in when the state failed: taking care of children when the state nursery school was full, standing in line when parents had to be at work, cooking during the day so dinner was on the table in the evening.[45]

What is certain is that by the 1980s, East European's ruling regimes—and not just their citizens—had to find creative means to shore up the losses. In the case of Poland, it meant allowing Poles to make their way through Europe,

Eastern and Western, to trade and moonlight.[46] In Hungary, which had experienced relative prosperity under early "goulash communism" and where appetites were thus whetted, citizens took on extra shifts and second jobs, forever adding hours to their work days so as to afford the increasingly available goods but with ever rising prices. By the 1980s much of the region was sitting on a real rust belt in a quickly changing global economy: earlier mass investments in heavy industry were now obsolete; high hopes for consumer goods developed in the 1960s and 1970s were dashed. But the fact remains that consumer expectations were there, as well as diverse experiences with consumption.

If nothing else, communism was a testament to the fact that the dream of a perfect future is utterly seductive, and its failure equally demoralizing. Just as "real socialism" proved to be less than its promise, the post-1989 confrontation with "real capitalism" was (and in many cases continues to be) complicated and in some cases downright disappointing. As one former communist citizen recalled: "To have [the West German brand] Fa shampoo, that was something! It smelled so fine!" But after 1989, the "Fa shampoo does not smell so fine any more and it is only an ordinary shampoo!"[47] Endless rows of colorful Fa bottles became just that—shampoo—and no longer a repository for unlimited fantasies. In the same way that shampoo bottles, and not parliaments and congresses, embodied critical East-West identity issues during communism, so today it is again not "state architecture, monuments, paintings, or even literature" but "mass-produced subpar consumer items" and out-of-reach designer items that bolster the world of *Ostalgie*, the Eastern European phenomenon of nostalgia for its recent past.[48]

Nostalgia, once thought to be a curable ailment, is now understood to be part of the modern condition, a longing for something or someplace that never quite was.[49] In part, nostalgia is the stuff of dreams and imaginings, but it also takes concrete forms. In much of the region, nostalgia has meant votes for former communist parties, now generally restyled as "socialist," which have played a major role in regional politics since the 1990s. But it has also taken the form of memory-media that recall the recent past—both playfully and seriously—in books, museums, communist statue parks, newly opened stores selling goods with familiar communist-era packaging and tastes, "Titoland," a theme park in a suburb of Serbia, and—of course—Trabant-chauffeured communist tours through Krakow. In the Yugoslav case, nostalgia has different roots, a yearning for a country that no longer exists, devastated and divided by the violence of the 1990s.[50] The same might be said of East Germany, which was "Kohl-onized" after the fall of the Wall and disappeared off the map; and Czechoslovakia, whose politicians engineered its peaceable split largely for economic and political expediency. Elsewhere in the region, nostalgia is quite

FIGURE O.2.   A booth near the Checkpoint Charlie Museum in Berlin. This sort of communist memorabilia continues to be sold as popular souvenirs all over the former Eastern Bloc. None of the merchandise, of course, is original or authentic. Courtesy of Ian Withnall.

simply the wistful remembrance of a much simpler time (when potatoes arrived in stores on Mondays and books on Thursdays) and in many ways a more secure past (when, for the most part, only open political dissent could get you fired).[51]

Ultimately, however, *Ostalgie* is generational. Those who participate in it, never having experienced the "real version" but instead finding satisfaction in its simulacra, do so for their own campy, kitsch-laden entertainment. But behind those giant-sized statues of communism's masterminds and heroes that now stand in Budapest's statue park, on view for anyone eager to sample the artistic renditions of the twentieth century's most audacious experiment, were real people caught up in ideologies that touched every detail of their daily lives. Understanding the contours of consumption, the journeys that a socialist consumer traveled in search of necessary (as well as luxury) goods, the early plans and later machinations of Party technocrats set on creating the socialist "good life," we offer a tableau of everyday life that is far more complex than anything those statues now reveal.

NOTES

1. http://www.crazyguides.com/contact_us.html (accessed Aug. 26, 2011).

2. For this argument, see Susan Strasser, Charles McGovern, and Matthias Judt, "Introduction," in *Getting and Spending: European and American Consumer Societies in the Twentieth Century*, eds. Susan Strasser, Charles McGovern, and Matthias Judt. Publication of the German Historical Institute, Washington, DC (New York: Cambridge University Press, 1998), 6.

3. Even with the recent avalanche of literature on consumption in the Soviet Union, the bulk of it tends to focus on consumption in the prewar Stalinist period. See, for example, Jukka Gronow, *Caviar with Champagne: Common Luxury and the Ideals of the Good Life in Stalin's Russia* (Oxford: Berg, 2003); Elena Osokina, *Our Daily Bread: Socialist Distribution and the Art of Survival in Stalin's Russia, 1927–1941* (New York: Sharpe, 2001); and Julie Hessler, *A Social History of Soviet Trade: Trade Policy, Retail Practices, and Consumption, 1917–1953* (Princeton: Princeton University Press, 2004).

4. See, for example, Lizabeth Cohen, *A Consumers' Republic: The Politics of Mass Consumption in Postwar America* (New York: Vintage, 2003); and Gary Cross, *An All-Consuming Century: Why Commercialism Won in Modern America* (New York: Columbia University Press, 2002).

5. For a recent advocate of the category "consumption" over "consumerism," see Frank Trentmann, "Beyond Consumerism: New Historical Perspectives on Consumption," *Journal of Contemporary History* 3 (2004): 376.

6. The literature on the history of consumption in the West is too vast to enumerate here. For a few examples, see the work of John Brewer, including John Brewer and Roy Porter, eds. *Consumption and the World of Goods* (New York: Routledge, 1994); Woodruff Smith, *Consumption and the Making of Respectability, 1600–1800* (New York: Routledge, 2002); Daniel Roche, *A History of Everyday Things: The Birth of Consumption in France, 1600–1800*, trans. Brian Pearce (Cambridge: Cambridge University Press, 2000); Martin Daunton and Mathew Hilton, eds. *The Politics of Consumption: Material Culture and Citizenship in Europe and America* (New York, Oxford: Berg, 2001).

7. More recent studies have increasingly explored new "cores" of consumption, such as Asia, as well as colonial or postcolonial consumer "peripheries." See for example Sharon Garon and Patricia MacLachlan, eds. *The Ambivalent Consumer: Questioning Consumption in East Asia and the West* (Ithaca, NY: Cornell University Press, 2006); and Peter Sterns, *Consumerism in World History: The Global Transformation of Desire* (New York: Routledge, 2006).

8. See for example Ferenc Fehér, Ágnes Heller, and György Márkus, *Dictatorship over Needs* (New York: St. Martin's Press, 1983); and János Kornai, *Economics of Shortage* (Amsterdam: North Holland Press, 1980).

9. For a wider discussion of the citizen consumer, see for example Katherine Pence, "A World in Miniature: The Leipzig Trade Fairs in the 1950s and East German Consumer Citizenship," in David Crew, ed. *Consuming Germany in the Cold War* (Oxford: Berg, 2003). See also David Crowley and Susan E. Reid, eds., *Pleasures in*

Socialism: Leisure and Luxury in the Bloc (Evanston, IL: Northwestern University Press, 2010), 7. For broader discussions of socialism and modernity, see Katherine Pence and Paul Betts, eds. *Socialist Modern: East German Culture and Politics* (Ann Arbor: University of Michigan Press, 2008); and Johann Arnason, "Communism and Modernity," *Daedalus* 129 (2000): 61–90.

10. Slavenka Drakulić, *How We Survived Communism and Even Laughed* (New York: Harper Perennial, 1993), 26–27, 63.

11. See György Péteri, ed., *Imagining the West* (Pittsburgh University Press, 2010).

12. Alexei Yurchak, *Everything Was Forever, Until It Was No More* (Princeton NJ: Princeton University Press, 2006), 158–206.

13. Jonathan R. Zatlin, "Making and Unmaking Money: Economic Planning and the Collapse of East Germany," Institute of European Studies (University of California, Berkeley) 2007: 14.

14. A number of authors have explored consumption as a mode of agency under communism. See for example Susan Reid, "Cold War in the Kitchen: Gender and the De-Stalinization of Consumer Taste in the Soviet Union Under Khrushchev," *Slavic Review* 61 (2008): 211–52; David Crowley and Susan Reid, eds., *Style and Socialism: Modernity and Material Culture in Postwar Eastern Europe* (Oxford: Berg, 2000), 14–15; and Karin Taylor, *Let's Twist Again: Youth and Leisure in Socialist Bulgaria* (Berlin: Lit Verlag, 2008), 5.

15. The phrase *shortage economy*, much used to describe the Bloc, was coined by Hungarian economist János Kornai in Kornai, *Economics of Shortage* (1980).

16. Consumption practices in the West have drawn criticism throughout history. For more recent critiques, see for example Thomas Princen, Michael Maniates, and Ken Conca, eds. *Confronting Consumption* (Boston: MIT Press, 2002).

17. Although modernization theory was largely discredited in the late 1960s, globalization theory is its most recent incarnation, also subject to heated debate. For an overview and in-depth discussion of both in a global context, see J. Timmons Roberts and Amy Hite, eds., *From Modernization to Globalization: Perspectives on Development and Social Change* (Oxford: Blackwell, 2000).

18. See Ina Zweiniger-Bargielowska, *Austerity in Britain: Rationing, Controls, and Consumption 1939–1955* (New York: Oxford University Press, 2000).

19. Tony Judt, *Postwar: A History of Eastern Europe Since 1945* (New York: Penguin Press, 2005), 170.

20. Ibid.

21. Michael Haynes, "The Rhetoric of Economics: Cold War Representations of Development in the Balkans," in *The Balkans and The West: Constructing the European Other*, ed. Andrew Hammond (Burlington, VT: Ashgate, 2004), 118.

22. Judt, *Postwar*, 170.

23. For an early mention of "rational consumption under communism," see Phillip Hanson, *Advertising and Socialism: The Nature and Extent of Consumer Advertising in the Soviet Union, Poland, Hungary, and Yugoslavia* (White Plains, NY: International Arts and Sciences Press, 1974), 30. For a more recent one, see David Crowley and Susan E. Reid, "Style and Socialism: Modernity and Material Culture," in *Style and Socialism: Modernity and Material Culture in Postwar Eastern Europe*, eds. David Crowley and Susan E. Reid (Oxford: Berg, 2000), 10.

24. See, for example, Crowley and Reid, *Pleasures in Socialism*, 8. See also Fehér, Heller, and Márkus, *Dictatorship over Needs*, 98.

25. P. G. Hare, H. K. Radice, and N. Swain, eds. *Hungary: A Decade of Economic Reform* (London: Allen and Unwin, 1981), 3–22.

26. See, for example, Padraic Kenney, "The Gender of Resistance in Communist Poland," *American Historical Review*, 104(2) (1999): 399–425.

27. Albanian isolation and economic autarchy deepened further when Albania broke with China in 1970 after the warming in Sino-American relations. Timothy Less, "Seeing Red: America and Its Allies Through the Eyes of Enver Hoxha," in *The Balkans and the West: Constructing the European Other*, ed. Andrew Hammond (Burlington, VT: Ashgate, 2004), 58.

28. See Derek Hall, "Foreign Tourism Under Socialism the Albanian 'Stalinist' Model," *Annals of Tourism Research* 11 (1984): 547.

29. Kristen Ghodsee, "Red Nostalgia? Communism, Women's Emancipation, and Economic Transformation in Bulgaria," *L'Homme: Zeitschrift für Feministische Geschichtswissenschaft* 15 (2004): 31.

30. As quoted in Jiří Pernes, *Takoví nám vládli. Komunističtí prezidenti Československa a doba, v níž žili* (Prague, 2003), 292.

31. On Romania, for example, see Ghita Ionescu, *Communism in Rumania, 1944–1962* (New York: Oxford University Press, 1964), 59–60.

32. David Crowley and Susan E. Reid, "Introduction," in *Style and Socialism*, 10.

33. Judd Stitziel, "On the Seam Between Socialism and Capitalism: East German Fashion Shows," in *Consuming German in the Cold War*, ed. David. F. Crew (New York: Berg, 2003), 76.

34. In the Soviet Union, formation of what some historians have also called a new "middle class" emerged as the most important interest group within the Soviet Union in the 1930s. See Vera S. Dunham, *In Stalin's Time: Middle-Class Values in Soviet Fiction* (Durham, NC: Duke University Press, 1990), 4; and Sheila Fitzpatrick, *The Cultural Front: Power and Culture in Revolutionary Russia* (Ithaca, NY: Cornell University Press, 1992), 179.

35. For a personal account of a politically motivated eviction, see Heda Margolius Kovály, *Under a Cruel Star: A Life in Prague 1941–1968*, trans. Franci Epstein and Helen Epstein with the author (New York: Holmes and Meier, 1997), 167. Eventually, a segment of the prewar intelligentsia and professional classes were wooed by these regimes and integrated into the Party's political and professional elite.

36. See, for example, Ivailo Znepolski, *Bŭlgarskiiat Komunizŭm: Sotsiokulturni Cherti i Vlastova Traektoriia* (Sofia: Ciela Press, 2008), 220.

37. Reid, "Cold War in the Kitchen," 215.

38. Václav Havel et al., *The Power of the Powerless: Citizens Against the State in Central-Eastern Europe*, ed. John Keane (New York: Sharpe, 1985).

39. "Eastern Europe: The Third Communism," *Time* (Mar. 18, 1966), 44.

40. Ionescu, *Communism in Rumania*, 320.

41. For more on this, see Paulina Bren, "Mirror, Mirror, on the Wall . . . Is the West the Fairest of Them All?" *Kritika: Explorations in Russian and Eurasian History*, 9(4) (fall 2008): 831–54.

42. Liviu Chelcea, "The Culture of Shortage During State-Socialism: Consumption Practices in a Romanian Village in the 1980s," *Cultural Studies* 16 (2002): 22.

43. For more on how not just cash but also time was viewed and valued differently, see for example John Borneman, "Time–Space Compression and the Continental Divide in German Subjectivity," *Oral History Review*, 21(2) (winter 1993): 41–57, and Elizabeth A. Ten Dyke, "Tulips in December: Space, Time and Consumption Before and After the End of German Socialism," in *German History*, 19(2), 2001: 257–58.

44. Kathy Burrell, "Managing, Sending and Learning: The Material Lives and Journeys of Polish Women in Britain," *Journal of Material Culture*, 13(1) 2008: 69.

45. On the one hand, as in the case of Ceausescu's nationalist natalist policies, women were denied birth control. On the other hand, periodic shortages of birth control pills or condoms—as in the case of Czechoslovakia—had the same effect: early marriages as well as high abortion rates.

46. A film was made of this phenomenon, starring British actor Jeremy Irons as a Polish laborer in London: *Moonlighting* (1982).

47. Alenka Švab, "Consuming Western Image of Well-Being: Shopping Tourism in Socialist Slovenia," *Cultural Studies* 16 (2002): 74, 77.

48. Paul Betts, "The Twilight of the Idols: East German Memory and Material Culture," *Journal of Modern History*, 72(3) (Sep. 2000): 755.

49. Svetlana Boym admits to having "long held a prejudice against nostalgia," before writing about it: Boym, *The Future of Nostalgia* (Basic Books: New York, 2001), xiv.

50. Breda Luthar, "Remembering Socialism: On Desire, Consumption and Surveillance," *Journal of Consumer Culture* 6 (2006): 221.

51. See Ghodsee, "Red Nostalgia?" 3.

PART I

Living Large

In the aftermath of World War II and the onset of Communist Party rule regionwide, "bourgeois" modes of consumption became suspect, viewed as the primary characteristic of a class targeted to lose property, power, and status. More often than not, in these early postwar years "bourgeois" was made synonymous with "fascist": in Bulgaria, witch hunts for so-called Fascist sympathizers meant targeting women with leather coats and manicures.[1] Under such pressure, the former middle and upper classes were quick to hide signs of their previous wealth. In a recent documentary, Czech bourgeois women imprisoned for their political opposition to the new communist regime recalled their first view of the radically altered cityscape into which they reemerged in the late 1950s: former high society friends now hurried past them on Prague's streets, transformed into kerchief-clad working class women.[2]

At the same time a new elite—born of the communist parties' power hold over infrastructures—was emerging. Zdeněk Mlynář, a high-ranking Czechoslovak Communist Party member (later turned dissident), recalled the fat envelopes of cash regularly handed out to the Party elite.[3] Although still relatively little is known about the wealth accumulated by Party elite, it was always common knowledge that they were provided with special stores, schools, accommodations, and vacation spots. The historian György Péteri, himself the son of a high-ranking Hungarian Party official, recalls his family's privileges: "unlimited access to a state-owned car (from 1965 it was a black Mercedes 230 which, together with its chauffeur . . . stood at my father's disposal even after working hours, with no limits as to mileage, weekdays, or time); access to the country's best resort areas at Lake Balaton and elsewhere; access to a well-equipped health care infrastructure. . . ."[4] Considering the ideological conundrum of such privilege, the new wealth necessitated discretion and was routinely hidden behind compound walls and down unmarked paths.

The Yugoslav elite, cast early on as renegade after parting ways with Stalin, was less concerned with concealing its wealth and privilege. When Khrushchev traveled to Belgrade in 1955 to mark reestablished "thaw-era" ties, at a lavish dinner reception the Yugoslav officials and their wives did not hesitate to come in fancy dinner jackets and elaborate evening gowns while the Soviets showed up in "baggy summer suits."[5] Although privileged consumption for communist elites had become a central feature of the system across the Bloc, the blatant consumption of Tito and his retinue still shocked Soviet sensibilities. No wonder the Yugoslav elite became the subject of the most articulate and pointed social critique in the Bloc. Milovan Djilas, a uniquely well-placed observer of Yugoslav socialist class differentiation, was quietly shuffled out of power after the 1957 publication of his famous essay (and later book) in which he described himself and his fellow top-ranking apparatchiks as a "new class."[6]

A decade later, a yet newer "consuming class" had emerged, no longer merely the small coterie of party elite whom Djilas introduced to the world in 1957. As Djilas himself explained in his follow-up, *The Unperfect Society*, first published (abroad) in 1969, a "new, new class" had since taken root in Yugoslavia, a group he termed the "middle class," which had a much broader social base.[7] With this new, new class came new class antagonisms. In his chapter, Kacper Pobłocki explores these tensions through the urban transformation of Łódź, Poland's famous textile city. This new consuming class is usually traced to the 1970s and the consumerist turn that followed on the heels of failed reform and revolt, but Pobłocki looks to the lead-up to 1968. By putting urban collective consumption at the forefront of his analysis, he links public grievances over social mobility with contemporaneous displays of conspicuous consumption as well as the overconsumption of urban (and "public") amenities, particularly water. He shows how these new urban-based social stratifications were played out in the slum district of Bałuty, where socialist "gentrification" meant new apartment blocks for the cultural elite ("a veritable forerunner of gated communities") built among war ruins and dilapidated interwar tenements. Social envy, he suggests, was the engine behind the hostile anti-Semitic outcries of Poland's 1968. He goes on to challenge conventional interpretations of postwar urban development in Eastern Europe by arguing that even though it "may seem counter-intuitive to think of socialist-era apartment blocks as suburbia," "postwar cities, East and West, both being a product of urban Keynesianism, displaced working-class communities and, despite grassroots resistance in both cases, increased social exclusion and restructuring."

Kate Brown, in her chapter, makes this transcontinental comparison between the Eastern Bloc and the United States clearer still. She discusses two plutonium-producing cities: Richland, in eastern Washington State, and

Cheliabinsk-40, in the Russian Urals, where the consumer possibilities seemed boundless, and rights and freedoms were willingly forfeited for them. Residents of Cheliabinsk-40 were called "the chocolate eaters" because of the chocolate and sausages available in this "secret city," even in the bleakest postwar years, while Richland was referred to as the "gold coast." For many of those who came to these two cities from less-than-privileged backgrounds, Cheliabinsk-40 and Richland represented the utopian "dream"—be it of the capitalist or communist variety. No matter how damaging to one's health the dream eventually proved to be, few were willing to give it up. Brown argues that these "zones of privilege," where not only plutonium but desire was produced, allowed political leaders to insist "that their (Soviet or American) system did indeed produce affluence and prosperity," "glossing over the fact of their exclusivity." Brown's essay further points to the increasing parallels in the "dream" to which citizens, capitalist and communist, aspired, and to the ways in which postwar states enabled it.

Indeed, it was the concomitant mixed messages and resulting shifting values that eventually became overpowering in Eastern Europe. Already by the 1950s, the East German leadership had given up preaching delayed gratification and instead discussed "the importance of displaying winsome images of socialist consumer bounty" in East German store windows. By the 1960s, East Germans witnessed "state advertising agencies, snazzy product packaging, modern furniture, household decoration magazine and advice literature, self-service stores, mail-order clearinghouses, and even state travel bureaus."[8] The differences between the "socialist way of life" and the "capitalist way of life" were becoming fuzzy. Picking up on this, in 1976 a reader of the Czech daily newspaper, *Rudé právo*, observed: "You write about a socialist way-of-life as if it were somehow different from life in capitalist countries. I see no substantial difference in the two. There, just as here, people chase after things. . . . Is it that here it's called a 'socialist way-of-life' and in capitalist countries it's called a consumer society?"[9] The reply to the reader was fumbling at best.

This pivotal shift in values, particularly evident by the 1970s, also meant increased opportunities to acquire enormous wealth, even if one did not belong to the Party elite. The Czech sociologist Ivo Možný recalled the following personal encounter: "Some time already in the 1970s my day out was ruined by the complaints mouthed all evening to me by a south Moravian vintner, a millionaire who had rented out the Mikulovská Manor for his son's wedding, had a white tuxedo made for him, a new car to add to the three already in the garage of a new villa, where there was even a television in the bathroom. I tried to suggest to this wealthy man (["officially"] employed as a salesman of the State Tractor Enterprise) that under no other condition anywhere else would he ever be able to earn this much, with his prices as they were, based on a monopoly, and without being taxed."[10] Paulina Bren's chapter brings similar such socialist "entrepreneurs" into view: the hustlers, the money-changers, who took on a central role in everyday life during late communism as Czechoslovakia's hard currency stores expanded (as they also did elsewhere across the Bloc from the 1970s on).

Originally intended for visiting foreigners, these stores multiplied as the state thirsted for more hard currency; and as hard currency stores flourished, so too did ordinary citizens' desire to enter them. The middle-men who stepped in to make this happen were money-changers who illegally sold the special "currency" with which one could shop inside. Thus the hustlers came into their own, creating gangster-networks, often in cooperation with state officials. After 1989, some would go on to become legitimate businessmen, while others segued effortlessly into the new underworld. When asked what could possibly be missing in his life, Možný's Moravian vintner had answered "freedom." At the time, Možný did not understand but later came to realize that "what he meant was the legitimization of his status. He was tired of his ambivalent position, whereby, on the one hand, he was . . . a well-known country 'squire' and successful businessman, and, on the other hand, he had to cower and pay off everyone around him, everyone from less successful neighbors to the local police force . . . [even as] it was said that his wine was drunk up at the [Prague] Castle."[11] Možný in fact makes the provocative argument that "entrepreneurs" like the vintner, as well as the children of the Party elite accustomed to their privileges, helped bring about the Velvet Revolution because they wanted to see their family's non-mobile social capital converted into real wealth and thereby legitimized.

Dissident and later post-communist president Václav Havel called the late socialist period "post-totalitarian," describing it as the *historical coming together of a dictatorship and a consumer society.*"[12] The essays in this section take this point further still by exploring the social tensions that arose between socialist consumer haves and have-nots, and how the fantasies as well as realities of "living large" were manifested behind the Iron Curtain.

NOTES

1. Ivailo Znepolski, *Bŭlgarskiiat Komunizŭm: Sotsiokulturni Cherti i Vlastova Traektoriia* (Sofia: Ciela Press, 2008), 198, 210.

2. *The Sweet Century: Women Who Defied a Communist Dictatorship* (film), dir. Helena Třeštíková (1998).

3. Zdeněk Mlynář, *Nightfrost in Prague: The End of Humane Socialism*, trans. Paul Wilson (New York: Karz, 1980), 129–32.

4. György Péteri, "Nomenklatura with Smoking Guns: Hunting in Communist Hungary's Party-State Elite," in eds. David Crowley and Susan E. Reid, *Pleasures in Socialism: Leisure and Luxury in the Eastern Bloc* (Northwestern University Press, 2010), 311–12.

5. William Taubman, *Khrushchev: The Man and His Era* (New York: Norton, 2004), 343.

6. Milovan Djilas, *The New Class: An Analysis of the Communist System* (New York: Praeger, 1957).

7. Milovan Djilas, *The Unperfect Society: Beyond the New Class* (London: Harcourt, 1969), 146–47.

8. Paul Betts, "The Twilight of the Idols: East German Memory and Material Culture," *Journal of Modern History*, 72(3) (Sep. 2000): 749.

9. As quoted in Paulina Bren, *The Greengrocer and His TV: The Culture of Communism after the 1968 Prague Spring* (Cornell UP, 2010), 189.

10. Ivo Možný, *Proč tak snadno . . . Některé rodinné důvody sametové revoluce* (Prague: Sociologické nakladatelství, 1991), 41 (footnote #16).

11. Ibid.

12. Václav Havel, "Moc bezmocných," *O lidskou identitu: Úvahy, fejetony, protesty, polemiky, prohlášení a rozhovory z let 1969–1979*, Vilém Prečan and Alexander Tomský, eds. (London, 1984), 71. The italics are Havel's. For the English translation, see Václav Havel et al., *The Power of the Powerless: Citizens Against the State in Central-Eastern Europe*, John Keane (New York, 1990), 38. In this translation, however, Havel's italics were eliminated.

I

Tuzex and the Hustler

Living It Up in Czechoslovakia

Paulina Bren

In 1987, an astonishing film called *Bony a Klid* appeared in Czechoslovakia's cinemas.[1] With the political climate having changed little despite the rumble of perestroika elsewhere, *Bony a Klid* was starkly out of place in late communist Czechoslovakia. Its title combined word play with a nod to Western popular culture, consciously evoking the American film *Bonnie and Clyde*. Like the American original, criminality and its allure played a central role in the plot. But in this socialist version, *Bony* was a very different type of hero, indeed an inanimate one: *Bony* was the name of special vouchers used exclusively to purchase products at Czechoslovakia's chain of foreign currency shops, Tuzex. *Klid* was more complicated. It was a state of mind, but also gangster talk: a call to relax and go with the flow, for everything would be all right. Playing on this idea, Radek John, the film's creator and co-writer (along with the director, Vít Olmer), convinced the British rock band Frankie Goes to Hollywood to lend its hugely successful album, *Relax*, then being played on every radio station in the West, as the soundtrack for the socialist film.

The movie, filmed with a handheld camera in real time on the streets and in the bars of Prague, spared no punches. The look of it was gritty, grim; the socialist world it portrayed entirely contradicted the cheeriness of official propaganda. For example, the opening scene takes place outside one of Prague's most centrally located Tuzex storefronts. The male hustlers, known as *veksláks*,[2] who are the real (anti-)heroes, the genuine "Clydes" of the film, crowd the pavement in front. It is shortly before Christmas and cold. Dressed in the *vekslák* staple of leather or jeans jacket and a gold chain, the men stamp their feet to keep warm and toss out to passersby the phrase so closely associated with late socialism in Czechoslovakia: "*Bony, Bony!* Do you want some *bony?!*" A woman sidles up, looks anxiously over her shoulder, and makes a quick exchange with one of the hustlers: Czech crowns for Tuzex *bony*. With this quick transaction, she has bought herself access to the foreign currency store and the otherwise unattainable goods inside it. The camera next turns to a policeman standing nearby in his familiar army-green uniform, but he scarcely notices the transaction. The exchange between a *vekslák* and a socialist citizen is evidently nothing out of the ordinary; moreover, the policeman in all likelihood has been bribed by the hustlers who occupy this bit of Tuzex storefront turf—either with a more favorable exchange rate for himself or else with one of the new, highly sought-after Casio-brand watches.

The camera swings back to the storefront, lingering on the instantly recognizable white-and-blue Tuzex logo. Behind the store window, two objects vie for attention: stacks of boxed Sony video recorders and Party propaganda posters announcing the upcoming anniversaries of the 1917 Soviet Revolution and the 1948 Czechoslovak communist "victory." The Sony boxes, and all they represent, clearly win out. On a side street around the corner, another hustler is selling jeans out of the back of his car: a piece of cardboard laid out on the wet winter ground serves as an impromptu dressing room. Two women, their dresses hoisted up high, balance precariously as they try on the jeans. In a previous take of the same scene for the film, a policeman joined them to try on a pair of black-market jeans, but someone got hold of the director's cut and informed the authorities; Radek John was ordered to delete it. Even without such a blatantly incendiary scene, the film still highlighted the most central, yet taboo, topic of late socialism. The 1.5 million Czechoslovak citizens who went to see the film in its first two months understood this; they fully recognized this morally contradictory world projected large upon the screen.

But first: what was inside the Tuzex hard currency shops that had ordinary citizens breaking the law by buying Tuzex *bony* for Czechoslovak crowns off the hustlers standing out on the street corner? As the camera in *Bony a Klid* reveals, inside were not only Sony video recorders but also Marlboro cigarettes, French perfume, Levi's jeans, and more. These were shops with fully stocked shelves, and the stock included goods and foods largely unattainable elsewhere—be they foreign, such as West German deodorants, or domestic but mainly reserved for export, such as crystal ware. Altogether, the hard currency shopping chain had an expansive menu of items on offer. Through Tuzex, a customer could purchase Johnnie Walker whiskey, as well as the very house where he could serve it, and the car in which he transported it back home. In 1977, through Tuzex, one could purchase a 117 square meter house for $12,750 or a Chrysler

180 for $5,000.[3] The price was likely to be significantly lower than on the domestic market—if one could even get it there. It was, in fact, the immediate *availability* that was most significant. Thousands of people were on waiting lists for a Czech-made Škoda car, presumably with the money in hand, but they still had to wait months, and more often years. At Tuzex, one could find immediate gratification.

Hard currency shopping chains, although with significant variation, were a Bloc-wide phenomena tracing back to the Soviet Union and the establishment of the original Torgsin stores in the early 1930s (later renamed Beriozka). East Germany had Intershop, Bulgaria Corecom, Hungary Intertourist, Poland Pewex, and Romania Comturist. Of these, the Intershop and Corecom offered an experience that was somewhat analogous to Tuzex's. Corecom also sold apartments and houses, land on which to build them, and the materials with which to construct them. As Rossitza Guentcheva describes, "Mercedes and BMW cars, Elizabeth Arden cosmetics, AEG and Bosch refrigerators and washing machines, Grundig and Philips audio and TV sets, Doxa wrist watches and even jazz plates [records] found their way to the CORECOM shops."[4] This sensory overload had a distinct smell that lingered in the memory and whetted the appetite. For some, Corecom smelled "like aromatic soap (perfumery) and like candies. More commonly, Bulgarians described it in more abstract terms such as 'clean' and 'new'."[5] Entering these stores represented the closest possible approximation to crossing the Iron Curtain over into the West: the insides had the look, smell, and feel of the imagined West at its consumer best. In fact, so enthralling was the experience that the very scent of the Bloc's hard currency shops has also made it into the pantheon of postcommunist nostalgia. A mail order company located in the former East Germany even hoped to manufacture a new fragrance called Intershop, a "combination of sweet-smelling washing powder, tobacco, chewing gum and glossy magazines."[6] The irony is that although the longing for the contents of the hard currency stores during socialism was based on the wish to take possession of an imagined West, its post-1989 Ostalgie reinterpretation is based on reliving an imagined East.

Tuzex was established as early as 1957, in the wake of de-Stalinization. Its original intent was never to provide sought-after consumer goods to the domestic population.[7] Just as in the case of East Germany's Intershop (initially located at port cities as shopping outlets for Western sailors),[8] Tuzex stores were situated strategically, for the most part in the cities of Prague, Brno, and Bratislava, as well as the spa-resort towns at which tourists gathered. The thinking was that foreigners visiting from the West would have a place to purchase the items to which they were accustomed, such as Western cigarettes and alcohol, as well as the mandatory tourist souvenirs.

As in the GDR, yet another category of clientele was a rare kind of Czech or Slovak citizen with legal access to Western currency from inheritances, Social Security payments, honorariums, or temporary employment outside of Czechoslovakia. This small segment of the population was permitted to possess the acquired hard currency legally by converting much of it into Tuzex *bony*—"fake" paper bills, which, despite the grittiness of the film *Bony a Klid*, actually looked more like Monopoly money, printed in cheerful pastel colors with the Tuzex logo vividly displayed.

The final category of Tuzex clientele lived outside the country. For the émigrés (who were otherwise the bogeymen of anti-West propaganda), condemnation was temporarily displaced in favor of profit. Émigrés were wooed by Tuzex and its affiliated trading companies abroad, the largest being located in New York and West Germany. Extensive catalogues, decorated not with hammers and sickles and red stars but instead with nostalgic, folkloric illustrations of a bygone Czechoslovakia and pencil drawings of Prague's timeless castle, listed goods that could be bought with Western currency and "gifted" to relatives back home. The selection covered a wide spectrum of potential generosity: from butter, flour, canned fruit, coffee, beer, and cigarettes to clothes, washing machines, cars, and apartments. Consequently, in addition to tourist locales a disproportionate number of Tuzex stores were located in rural eastern Slovakia because so many of its inhabitants had emigrated to the United States in the first half of the twentieth century and were keen to either share or exhibit their dollar wealth with family left behind.[9]

A familiar scenario of Tuzex "gifting" was played out in an episode of a recent Czech television drama about everyday life after 1968. The protagonist father has mixed feelings about his brother, who emigrated to West Germany and now returns periodically with small gifts, driving a nice car, and sporting fashionable 1970s long sideburns. He is adored by all the members of the family, as much for the small treats he brings the children as for the whiff of the exotic about him. When the tension between the two brothers finally explodes and they are forced to talk, the émigré brother reveals how difficult life in West Germany is and how in fact he lives hand-to-mouth there. Even so, he leaves behind an enormous gift: money he has carefully saved up so that his brother can buy a car from Tuzex.[10]

The persona of the visiting Western relative, pronounced well off by virtue of his access to (if not possession of) Western currency, has also been read less generously. The late Czech-Canadian writer Josef Škvorecký described the Tuzex voucher and the black market that surrounded it as the building blocks for a new kind of "American uncle," poor in the West but able to take on exaggerated gestures of wealth "back home": "It is simple: for one U.S. dollar the foreigner gets five Tuzex crowns . . . which you can nowadays officially exchange for the regular plebeian crowns at the rate of one *Tuzex* crown for five poor man's crowns." In other words, the visiting uncle can change his dollar into Tuzex *bony* and then turn around and sell his *bony* for Czech crowns, ending up with 25 crowns per dollar, "the price of a beefsteak in a fairly good restaurant."[11] The "American uncle" became even more ubiquitous when, in the 1970s, precisely in a bid to enlarge the pool of visitors coming to Czechoslovakia with hard currency, the Czechoslovak government initiated measures that allowed its former (and otherwise stigmatized) ex-citizens, most of whom had fled in the aftermath of 1948 and 1968, to legalize their émigré status.

For a fee, to be paid to the Czechoslovak government in foreign currency, a former citizen of the country could in essence pay back the expenses incurred by the state for his or her education and training, the basis for skills that were now being put to use in capitalism. By doing so, the émigré earned the right to return for visits to Czechoslovakia free of the criminal charges (and consequent imprisonment) automatically levied on all those who had fled the country during the communist period. Škvorecký, unabashed in his contempt for those who took up this offer, wrote:

> I know a rather naïve man of limited resources in Toronto who, every other year, regularly boastfully makes his pilgrimage to Prague. Before the trip he stuffs his wallet with one-dollar bills. Once in Prague, he checks into one of the good hotels, and "then I tip everybody with my one-dollar bills, and you should see them jump around me as if I were a king. Later I invite my best friends to the hotel and treat them to dinner which costs me about fifty bucks but looks like a royal feast."[12]

Yet ultimately it was not so much the annual trip by the American uncle that made an impact as it was the trail of dollar bills that he left in his wake.

Those who got their hands on the dollar bills left behind by the American uncle, from grateful family and friends to hotel and restaurant employees, significantly increased their consumer access. Yet even for these lucky ones, the humiliating discrepancies that made the writer Škvorecký bristle when describing the American uncles' visits often continued inside the Tuzex store. A *New York Times* reporter observed from inside, "A few customers are tourists, paying in dollars and German marks, while most are Czechoslovaks clutching small bills in pastel colors."[13] The pathos was reinforced by the state's financially expedient decision to stamp the pretty pastel Tuzex vouchers with an expiration date of six months. Originally intended for the Western tourist passing through, an expiration date hardly mattered to them, but for a local having a mere six months to use his hard-to-come-by *bony* could be overwhelming.

In a January 1969 editorial, a woman compared the Tuzex process to "an absurdist play." A friend of hers from abroad, having heard that Czechoslovak citizens would no longer be permitted to travel West without hard currency bank accounts, sent her some dollars to open one. But not having specified that these dollars were intended for her friend's travel purposes, the money was automatically converted into Tuzex *bony* by the state bank—as was the practice since it was against the law for socialist citizens to hold larger sums of hard currency. The woman complained but was advised by the bank manager to reconcile herself with the policy and go spend her *bony*. When she entered the Tuzex store, however, she could not find anything that she wanted to purchase. At the same time, she overheard the pleas of a fellow customer whose *bony* were about to expire, and who had not known that the store was closing for the following two days for "inventory and restocking," an all-too-frequent and usually unannounced practice among sales staff in the Bloc's retail industry. As she listened to the customer being berated by the Tuzex store staff for not having realized that an inventory restocking was in the offing, she pondered: "So a person receives money as a gift. The state, without permission, takes it, gives out coupons instead, for which one cannot buy a tenth of what one can buy for hard currency (abroad), and it restricts their validity to half a year. . . ."[14] This did indeed read as an absurdist script, but a script that could be publicly critiqued for only a short window of time before a new wave of normalization-era censorship took hold.

Critiques continued to appear in the media in the years after, but calling attention to the state's victimization of its socialist consumers was now off-limits. Instead, the focus shifted to the tensions between capitalist-like business and consumer practices, centered around Tuzex, and socialism, which proclaimed a classless society devoid of the sort of commodity fetishism identified with the West. It was a tension that the Party itself was having trouble reconciling. Early on, recognizing the contradictions inherent in Tuzex, the state had sought solutions in the old dictum of "out of sight, out of mind," tucking the stores into side streets. Even as late as 1964, getting into a Tuzex store meant having to get past an official gatekeeper. Those who did not have Tuzex vouchers on them to show the gatekeeper could not go inside and browse, and the small or nonexistent window displays gave away few secrets.[15]

By the 1970s, Tuzex was no longer a hidden secret but a key part of the fabric of everyday life in late socialism. One reader's letter to the otherwise satirical magazine *Dikobraz* lamented:

> I remember how the establishment of Darex (a brief predecessor to Tuzex) angered my father. Only with great reservations did he come to terms with it, that in our postwar situation it was necessary, but he was only willing to tolerate its existence for up to five years. . . . If the poor man saw [what it has become] today![16]

Indeed, these sentiments were commonplace across the Bloc as hard currency stores expanded.[17] Even in present-day Cuba, the so-called dollar store is no less controversial. Stores that still take the local nonconvertible peso are routinely described as "dingy and depressing," whereas only the dollar stores are said to offer any worthwhile goods, and the English word *shopping* has been incorporated into the language to indicate that one is going to the dollar store specifically.[18]

Whereas the foreign currency stores were controversial from the start, in the 1970s the real issue, Bloc-wide, became who could enter them. The key for unlocking the stores' treasures was the Tuzex voucher, which could be bought using only foreign currency. Yet those who possessed foreign currency were, more likely than not, far from the socialist role model, whereas "good socialist citizens," who dutifully did not associate with the West, were placed at an unexpected disadvantage. Another reader of *Dikobraz* asserted: "As long as you're filling out information in your personnel file, you'd better not show off about your relatives in a capitalist country because you're probably a scoundrel as well. But if, however, they send you hard currency once in a while, then you're a beloved citizen of our state and we have special stores for you."[19] This was the crux of the problem: hard currency shops ensured that citizens in disfavor (politically) with the regime were often the same people rewarded by it. In a 1987 radio discussion program, the point was put forward that "in a state, where the law guarantees equality for everyone, we're . . . consciously creating social inequality."[20] The humiliation, as David Crew points out in the case of the GDR's Intershops, was in the now "new social divisions between those with and without access to foreign money. The 'place of residence of your aunt' (i.e., whether or not you had relatives in the West from whom you could get West Germany currency) was now as important as many other forms of social and economic difference."[21] In 1977, workers in East Germany—the group notoriously favored by the communist state—protested over their lack of access to the hard currency stores, even managing to shut down an Intershop in one district in East Berlin.[22]

There were thus two motivations to open up access to the hard currency shops. On the one hand, the state increasingly needed foreign currency for foreign trade. On the other, leveling this persistent sense of inequality among socialist citizens could help soothe tempers. Moreover, the two motivations were not in conflict; expanding the pool of Tuzex customers meant more foreign currency in the state's coffers as well as a more satisfied consuming public. But this did not mean that opposition to the very idea of the hard currency store ceased. Tuzex managers were often forced to defend the store to certain state authorities, pointing out that the chain had brought in more valuable Western currency than was generally known. For example, Tuzex was said to generate twice the hard currency earned through tourism[23] and yielded more hard currency than Czechoslovakia's number one export product, glass.[24] In 1987, Tuzex was able to report a foreign currency income of $230 million[25]—perhaps a drop in the bucket of Czechoslovakia's hard currency needs but nevertheless a loud splash.

Similarly, Bulgaria's Corecom managers "fought persistently to allow ordinary Bulgarians, holding hard currency illegally, to be able to spend it freely in CORECOM shops." One Corecom representative explained frankly: "We are fighting for every dollar!"[26] Corecom officials pointed to the examples of the GDR, Czechoslovakia, Hungary, Poland, and Yugoslavia, where increasingly citizens were not being asked where and how they had acquired their foreign currency as long as they relinquished it to the state by shopping at the state-run hard currency stores. To appease those with the nagging sense that this was not right in a communist state, Corecom sought to disassociate its shops from capitalism as such. Guentcheva argues that with the media frequently pairing the hard currency shops with social inequalities, the government "institute[d] . . . a specific regime of sale and purchase that would distance the CORECOM shop from its western models."[27] It meant that the Corecom socialist shopping experience was not to be analogous to a capitalist one: the chain's employees were extra vigilant about performing communist loyalty rituals, items ideologically frowned on ("such as nail polish, lipstick, perfumes, make-up, artificial eyelashes, anti-baby pills, condoms, or playing cards"[28]) were not sold, the stores were hidden from view in side and back streets, and "official authorities forbade the arrangement of window-shops in CORECOM."[29] Moreover, the sales personnel, in their familiarly gruff manner of dealing with customers, also ensured that the experience did not approximate a capitalist-driven one where, for the sake of profit, the customer is always right. Altogether, writes Guentcheva, the experience was intentionally "disassociate[ed] from the *flaneur* experience of western customers."[30]

Both with and without such preventive measures, by the 1970s the clientele base for the Bloc's hard currency shops was expanding. East Germany's Intershop had been founded soon after the construction of the Berlin Wall in 1961, and ordinary East Germans—just as in the case of Czechoslovakia—were initially barred. This changed in 1973 when First Secretary Erich Honecker permitted a flood of West German visitors into the GDR, who left behind piles of Western currency with relatives in the East. To transfer those deutschmarks from private hands to the state treasury, GDR citizens were given permission to legally possess them and then encouraged to spend them in the Intershops.[31] In Bulgaria, citizens were finally allowed in the 1980s to enter Corecom and

peruse the shelves without restriction.[32] Unsurprisingly, in Ceauşescu's Romania, its hard currency shop, Comturist, remained closed to most ordinary citizens, further restricting avenues for consumption there. Entry and purchase
here was limited to those holding a passport, and since "Romanians, by law,
had to surrender their passports 48 hours after entering the country,"[33] this did
not constitute any widespread access. But elsewhere, the trend was to fling
open the doors of the hard currency shops, which became a vital backdrop to
life in the Bloc and spawned a new creature of late socialism: the *vekslák*.

In the sparse scholarship on the hard currency stores in the Eastern Bloc,
there is little to no reference to the hustlers who were born of the shopping
chains. Yet it was the hustlers who profited extravagantly in what became an
officially sanctioned "two-currency economy."[34] This is made clear in the rather
odd example of political dissident Ladislav Lis, in 1982 serving as a spokesperson for the Czechoslovak Charter 77 opposition group, who received a threatening letter from members of an unknown entity calling itself "Kim of the
Revolutionary Action Group." The letter stated that the group would kill both of
Lis's children unless he handed over either 150,000 Czech crowns or 30,000
Tuzex *bony*.[35] In other words, by 1982 the use of Tuzex vouchers as a second
currency was so commonplace that these alleged terrorists (or else, more likely,
the secret police posing as terrorists with the intent to scare Lis) named their
price not only in Czechoslovak crowns, the official currency, but also in Tuzex
bony. Moreover, the terrorists' exchange rate was spot on: the steady black market rate of five crowns for one Tuzex voucher.

As the stores expanded, and access along with them, one no longer had to
possess hard currency to purchase the Tuzex currency; for that there was now
the middleman, the hustler, who purchased the vouchers and sold them to
ordinary citizens for domestic, nonconvertible currency. These money changers
came to be known as *veksláks* from the German verb, *wechseln*, meaning to
change or exchange. They most commonly hung out on the pavement right
outside the Tuzex shop windows and one could not pass by without being ver-
bally accosted by *veksláks* seeking to sell *bony*. Moreover, this being one of the
more equal-opportunity "employments" under socialism, many of the hustlers
were Roma.

If only because almost everyone of a certain age yearned for "real" (that is,
Western) denim jeans and parents sought to buy their children a special treat
once in a while—something small, like Donald Duck bubble gum or a chocolate Kinder egg—contact with a *vekslák* was practically inevitable for a whole
generation of Czechoslovak citizens. In addition to the densely packed, gang-
run turf outside the Tuzex stores, the *vekslák* was also a permanent fixture in
hotel lobbies and bank vestibules. Here, he was more likely to be offering to

FIGURE I.I.   Hustlers stand outside a Tuzex storefront. From *Bony a Klid*.

buy Western currency from tourists for a far more favorable rate than the official (and ludicrously low) one set by the state bank. Visiting foreigners, especially those more experienced with the ways of the Bloc, would often make the
more favorable illegal exchange after having exchanged their mandatory daily
sum through the state bank. The *vekslák* would then either sell the capitalist
currency to ordinary Czechs and Slovaks—who needed more hard currency
than the state would sell them if they received rare permission to travel
abroad—or else purchase Tuzex *bony* to resell for Czech crowns to ordinary
citizens. In a sense, then, the *vekslák* was the visible face of vital but veiled economic transactions between the state and its citizens, transactions that led to
the front door of Tuzex.

The ubiquitous *vekslák* was immortalized in *Bony a Klid*. The protagonist
of the film is Martin, a young man who travels to Prague from the provinces to
purchase some foreign currency for his friends with which they plan to buy
sound equipment for their band. He makes contact with one of the *veksláks*
standing in front of a Tuzex window display, who takes him to see a "friend"
with hard currency. The exchange is made and Martin returns home only to
find that the dollars are fakes. Fired up, he charges back to Prague, finds the
hustlers, and threatens to report them to the police. Even after they have him

FIGURE I.2.   Martin, the film's protagonist, in front of a Tuzex window display of Sony products. From *Bony a Klid*.

beaten up, Martin refuses to return home empty-handed, and so finally they incorporate him into their activities so that he can "earn back" the money they stole from him. He thereby enters the world of the *veksláks*.

One of the gang's small-scale but profitable ventures (indeed, a common practice by real hustlers) is to drive out onto the highway leading to Prague and meet up with West German tourist buses, which they board by prior agreement with the bus drivers. Once on the bus, they merrily make their way down the aisle, exchanging the tourists' deutschmarks for crowns.[36] The scene of this currency exchange is ebullient, a rollicking party of happy tourists excited to get a far better exchange rate than the official one. As Martin and his colleagues go down the aisles, working the crowd, they flaunt fistfuls of money. The West Germans laugh and blush, evidently thrilled by their safely illicit participation in getting one over on the communist system. The soundtrack, Frankie Goes to Hollywood's hit, *Relax, Don't Do it*, is revved up high. After this first night of easy profit, Martin goes to his newly acquired girlfriend, Eva, with his bundle of cash and loaded down with wine, cigarettes, and delicatessen foods. The night becomes an orgy of drink, smoke, food, and sex. The dizzying seduction of this hyperconsumption is what defines Martin's life from thereon.

The relationship between gangster life and these atypical levels of consumption is underscored more clearly still when the gang surprises Martin and his girlfriend with the gift of perhaps the most sought-after commodity in communist Czechoslovakia: the keys to a large apartment in the very center of Prague. Martin and Eva, awestruck, unlock the door to their new home and wander around like the two children they are, taking in the space of their new home, and the views onto a night-lit Prague. Hovering in the sky are the red neon Soviet stars then still scattered across the city's skyline. In this love nest perched high above the city, feeling invincible and impervious to what those red stars connote, Eva and Martin consummate their new life. For the last rite of passage, the gang sets up Martin with the mandatory fake employment so that he cannot be charged with "parasitism" if caught.[37] A visit to a local car repair shop takes care of it: the gang explains to the manager that Martin is to be the new night guard, but that the old retiree they brought with him—who hovers in the background—will actually be doing the job. The shop manager objects but stops his protests when they toss a bundle of money his way, as one might toss a dog a bone.

Bony a Klid oscillated between showing the *veksláks* as underworld rogues, born entrepreneurs trapped in a noncapitalist straitjacket, and the state's sanctioned middlemen. A bold article in the Slovak press, published on the eve of the Velvet Revolution in 1989, noted that the one thousand Prague *veksláks* in operation were "carefully monitored, their holdings and contacts are well known to the competent organs, there are strong interest groups which would be threatened by their temporary liquidation."[38] Recognizing this fact meant further acknowledging its implications: *veksláks* were "working people, facilitating exchange between potential buyers and Tuzex." They were "beneficial to the state," and "not private entrepreneurs but state employees of an institution that organized this form of exchange." "Those we see," noted the article, "and with whom ordinary citizens deal are merely executors, distributors."[39] In return for taking on this role, the *veksláks* profited handsomely.

While researching the film, Radek John, like his protagonist Martin, penetrated the real hustler world with the help of an old classmate who had been a *vekslák*. What John saw and the stories he heard there were incorporated into the script. He found that the hustlers' lives existed outside of the framework of socialist Bloc life: they were able to consume as no other, and with that consumption came almost limitless power.[40] Despite the notorious waiting lists for cars, *veksláks* routinely drove Ford Mustangs, Sierras, Escorts, Chryslers, and Mercedes. In *Bony a Klid*, when the police give chase following the tourist bus scam, Martin's gang outrun them long enough to pull off the highway, locate a beat-up Bloc car in an old man's driveway, throw their Mercedes keys and a wad

of cash at him, grab his car keys in return, and drive back onto tl
normal speed, blending in. But *veksláks* were not entirely opposed
made Škoda. Often they would buy an export model with extras at
forty thousand crowns, and after six months sell it off to someone
been on the domestic car wait list for years—and even charge them an ex
thousand crowns.[41]

Veksláks' conspicuous consumption was notorious. One well-known Prague
hustler, for example, having already earned enough to retire, decided to have
some fun with it: he had sand trucked in and poured out in front of the Tuzex
store on Palacký Street in Prague. Pretending it was his private beach, he put on
a pair of sunglasses and swimsuit, lit a cigar, cradled a whiskey, and sunbathed.[42]
Other similar acts of bravado were less comic. A typical bet among the *veksláks*
as they relaxed on the terrace of the Hotel Alcron on Wenceslas Square was to
see who could finish a large bottle of Scotch and drive to the spa town of Carls-
bad and back first; one well-known hustler, celebrating his eighth million, died
on the road. He was not the first or the last.[43] But ultimately, this lifestyle and
the excesses that came with it were possible only because of the state-run hard
currency store, Tuzex.

The giddiness of power, the sense of standing entirely outside the ordinary
and drab socialist world of scarce goods and muted colors and instead among
the privileged upper echelons of the Party elite and fortunate foreigners, was
perfectly played out in *Bony a Klid*. Martin and his gang, feeling invincible, spend
long boozy nights at Prague's nightclubs, including the infamous Admiral boat
restaurant docked on the river Vltava (the DJ punctuates their entrance by announcing: "And here comes the country's, perhaps the world's, richest man on
state disability") and the Hotel Jalta. The atmosphere is frenetic: loud music,
spinning disco balls, faces sweaty and wild from too much alcohol. One drunken
night ends at home with prostitutes who frequent these same spots. What follows is a virtually pornographic scene with the gang and the women naked,
leaning against the kitchen counter, on the bed, on the sofa, performing various
sexual acts, while the television plays a porn video—as rare and sought-after a
commodity for ordinary citizens as the *veksláks'* BMWs, Levi's jeans, and hard-
packs of Marlboro Reds. Of course, what the hustlers could acquire was little
different from what the Party elite had access to, but the difference was in exposure. The Party elite's equally "conspicuous" consumption was hidden from
view and, when occasionally exposed (such as the black chauffer-driven car sent
out on nongovernmental errands), justified on the grounds that it was earned.

In the crude blatancy of *vekslák* consumption, there was something socially
deviant. It was not only deviance in terms of consumption but deviance in the
acquisition of those commodities. Yet it belonged on an existing spectrum of

economic behavior embraced by almost everyone. The Slovak article from 1989 pointed to other forms of unorthodox economic behavior, recognizable to most citizens: "illicit operation (trading under the counter), hoarding (chain trading), gouging (demanding excessive price or interest), speculation (calculating on profit), preferential treatment, corruption, smuggling, and so on."[44] In practice it meant this: the hotel reception staff worked closely with *veksláks*, often doing their own trade with foreign currency as well; waiters and cooks made money off siphoning wine and diluting it with water and purposely serving smaller pieces of meat (restaurants listed the weight in grams of meat in dishes, since the quantity and not the taste or preparation of the dish was the indicator of value); café and hotel staff made extra money by buying beer or cigarettes in a shop and selling them to guests at hotel prices.[45] Others bought caviar off Russian country women selling it wrapped in newspaper on the streets of Prague for a mere three hundred crowns, and then sold it to grateful tourists for three thousand. Enterprising hotel receptionists prepared slices of dark bread with goose fat and crackling and sold it to their hungry guests as a Czech specialty for late night snacks. If a foreign visitor wanted a taxi, a metered one was not called but instead an illegal one, sometimes driven for extra spending money by "university students from better families with a solid car from their parents."[46] In the 1980s, what a factory worker made in a month, a *vekslák* made in half an hour.[47] But a wide spectrum of people within the *veksláks'* orbit similarly cashed in—as *Bony a Klid* makes abundantly clear. In fact, these practices themselves, this "socially deviant" economic behavior, stretched far beyond the *vekslák* and his orbit. Bartering, hoarding, speculating, and smuggling had become an everyday reality for almost everyone.

Tempted by the rewards, and with such practices increasingly seen as the norm, more than a few tried small-scale "hustling." One might, for example, sell *bony* received from a generous aunt abroad to friends of friends; or one might choose to buy goods in Tuzex with those same *bony* and then sell the goods for more on the black market. Along with organized hustlers on one end of the spectrum and ordinary citizens making one-off or occasional deals on the other, there was also another category of profiteers: those who worked independently but on a larger scale. It was these cases that appeared most often in the press; for example, the 1976 arrest and sentencing (to eight years in prison) of Milada Businová, who had bought Tuzex *bony* at the black market rate of 5 crowns apiece and sold them at 3.5 crowns, at a loss, in order to gain various people's confidence. Once established, she offered to sell them large sums of *bony* for the purchase of a car or a weekend cottage through Tuzex. Of course, she would disappear once a customer handed an enormous sum of Czech crowns over to her.[48]

FIGURE I.3.   Friendly relations between the underworld and the court judge. From *Bony a Klid*.

Bony a Klid also ended on a cautionary note. The alcohol-drenched, dollar-fueled life Martin and his gang lead comes to a screeching halt once they trespass into the territory of a far more powerful Prague hustler. With little effort, he shuts down their operation, tears apart their apartments, sends them all into hiding, and contacts his friends in the police. The gang is caught (one of them even falling to his death in the chase) and sentenced. Enjoying the wealth and power associated with the state, they forgot that they were still vulnerable to it—although only because they are low-level gangsters. The closing scene is of a convicted Martin sitting with his fellow gang members (who now seem less like friends than he thought) in the back of the police van, watching the prison gates shut behind him. It is a cautionary tale but with a twist. As the gang is bundled into the van, the scene switches back to inside the court house. There, the head of Prague's underworld, the one who set all of this in motion, is having a friendly chat with the very same judge who has just sentenced them. The point is clear: the higher-ups in both the Party-state and the *vekslák* world are in close cooperation.

After *Bony a Klid* was shown in cinemas, the media dutifully turned its attention to the role of the *vekslák* in Czechoslovak society, in turn prompting the

Prague government to create a special crime unit in May 1988 to crack down on the hustlers, who were now seen as the bane of socialism. The familiar joke about the municipal street cleaner possessing a top-notch villa and a collection of foreign cars was publicly acknowledged in the media.[49] Suddenly, Radio Prague was asking why someone such as Milan Vengl, who had stood around day in and day out in the vestibule of the Živnostenská bank, came to be viewed merely as part of the landscape; why did it interest "no one that Milan can stand in the bank's vestibule all day, and no one asked where he works"?[50] Of course the reason no one asked was because, one way or another, they were being taken care of by Milan. But now "honest citizens" were being called on to help in this public raid,[51] for example by "calling attention" to citizens with expensive cars.[52] The special crime unit set up in the aftermath of *Bony a Klid* swept the Tuzex pavements temporarily clean of *veksláks* and brought in "more than 70 owners of attractive cars for a check."[53] But all such efforts were merely cosmetic: during the airing of the popular television magazine show *Maják*, cameras pointed at a swank Bratislava villa while the news commentator explained that it had been built by Josef Zelík, the *vekslák* king of Bratislava. The state had caught up with him and sentenced him to fifteen years' imprisonment for speculation, but he "unfortunately managed to escape abroad into emigration." In all likelihood, he was alerted by the police and supplied by Party contacts with a passport to get him across the border, along with a back story that would guarantee him asylum (a scenario with the same implications as the closing scene in *Bony a Klid*). To compensate for the *vekslák* king's absence, the television program instead turned its cameras on an old woman, a retiree, whom the special crime unit had found with 5,000 Czech crowns and 700 Tuzex *bony*. As she unsuccessfully tried to shield her face from the camera, the interviewer made sure to announce her full name to television viewers while he interrogated her.[54]

Professional gangster *veksláks* were without exception men, occupying a violent underworld, but those caught for well-publicized smaller-scale speculation were just as frequently women. At the same time, the media was far less willing to acknowledge the existence of another type of woman closely associated with the hustler: the Tuzex girl. Somewhat different from a full-time prostitute, the Tuzex girl was said to be a housewife or student who occasionally sought to make a little hard currency on the side. A *Newsweek* article claimed that "there are growing numbers of ordinary Czechoslovakian housewives who are taking to part-time prostitution to help pay for a long-awaited car or a household appliance. According to a recent study by Prague's Research Institute of Criminology, quite a few sell themselves to strangers with the knowledge and consent of their husbands."[55] Even if exaggerated for *Newsweek*'s Cold War readership, the trend was also noted by others. On Friday nights, girls from all over Czechoslovakia would come to the city, often on the pretext of visiting a girl friend, but in fact to make extra money servicing hustlers and foreigners—in other words, those with hard currency and *bony*.[56]

One such T-girl, as the *Newsweek* article called them, was a "slim, mini-skirted blonde" with the (rather suspiciously un-Czech) name of "Masha." Masha explained that she used to go to the Hotel Alcron merely to sit among the Westerners; it had made her feel good to be there. But she eventually tired of slowly sipping her one cup of coffee while all around people were ordering foreign whiskeys. Now she does the rounds with the other T-girls, looking for customers from the Hotel Alcron to the Hotel Jalta to the basement bar of the Esplanade Hotel. When it's been a slow night, the last chance is the late night club and restaurant at the Lucerna.[57] One could, however, also be ostracized for dabbling with paid sex for the sake of Tuzex; according to one account, if a girl were to show up on the factory floor with a dress from Tuzex, she would immediately be called a whore by her fellow workers and would soon enough find herself summoned to the cadre office.[58]

Nor was it uncommon to hear the argument that prostitution continued to exist in communist Czechoslovakia only because Tuzex existed.[59] Certainly, except for the occasional gesture of condemnation, the state was content to see the T-girl sex trade continue; as in the case of the *veksláks*, they brought in foreign currency, most of which found its way into Tuzex stores and thus state coffers. In *Bony a Klid*, after Martin has been sentenced to prison, he is granted a few minutes with his girlfriend, Eva. She arrives with a child in tow (until then unseen), who lives in the countryside with her parents. Martin asks Eva to wait for him and promises to take on the child as his, but Eva merely scoffs. It is clear that Martin remains almost as naïve as when he first arrived in Prague. In the police van, as Martin grieves over Eva's reaction to his declaration of love and commitment, his fellow gang members break into laughter: "You still haven't figured it out, have you?!" they exclaim. Eva, a T-girl with whom they have all been intimate, was planted to keep an eye on Martin. In return, she was allowed to keep the money Martin showered on her in her role as his girlfriend.

With the onset of glasnost, the press tentatively took up the topic of prostitution. But in some cases there appeared a certain subtext to new media discussions about prostitution: guarded admiration for these young women who were managing not to overexert themselves and yet make large amounts of what everyone wanted—*bony* and foreign currency. In 1987, a commentator on Radio Prague's program "What Everyone's Talking About" pointed out that the profession was becoming glamorized because of the consumer possibilities it clearly represented: "Public opinion often does not condemn this prostitute, but admires how she has managed to arrange things for herself."[60] This is not to say that prostitution, or the *vekslák* trade, were being roundly applauded but instead that a tension had emerged, a tension as damaging as the Tuzex-initiated presence of first- and second-class consumers. The tension, also played out in *Bony a Klid*, was between glamorization, on the one hand, and condemnation, on the other, of capitalist modes of trade, exchange, and consumption.

As central as Tuzex, the *vekslák*, and the T-girl became to late socialism, it remains astonishing that *Bony a Klid*, which documented it all, and with such sexually explicit details, would be released in cinemas. In 1988, speaking to the Reuters News Agency, Radek John admitted that the censors were shocked by some of the scenes, such as those showing the police being paid off by the gang or the court judge cozying up to Prague's powerful hustler. Officials let the scenes remain, however, once John pointed to well-known, real-life instances of the same.[61] But what John felt compelled to tell Reuters at the time was in fact untrue; the real circumstances could come to light only after the Velvet Revolution. When Party authorities finally saw *Bony a Klid* in a closed prescreening, they were predictably horrified.[62] Even as the film's credits rolled, they forbade it to be shown to the public. Hearing of this, the *vekslák* community, eager to see the final product, intercepted the van that was carrying the film to the vault and had the driver take them to an empty Prague cinema. While the film was projected onto the screen, someone filmed it with a handheld video camera. The original film then continued on its way to the vault, but the pirated copy made its rounds among the *veksláks*, who, pleased with it, began to sell video copies on Prague's streets. Their sales pitch was: "Do you want to see what's forbidden?" The cassettes sold fast, far surpassing that year's favorite, the American film *Porkies*, and fetching as much as 500 crowns a cassette. It was the *veksláks'* ultimate coup: the state-financed Barrandov film studios had paid for the film, while they were making millions off it without having invested a crown. Weighing the political fallout from a banned film that was being seen illegally by thousands of citizens, along with the economic imperatives of lost revenue, Party officials finally removed the film from the vault and celebrated its official opening in 1988 with a film premiere and much fanfare. It was a moment when one might have wondered who were the rulers and who were the ruled.

Veksláks, hustlers, profiteers: they were the result of the enlargement of Tuzex during the 1970s and 1980s and became tightly interwoven with official economic structures. Tuzex not only manufactured socioeconomic difference, based on who had access to its shelves of goods, but further made of the hustlers a "new, new class"[63]—some of whom found a sure footing in the postcommunist world with the legitimization of relations between the black market and the state. By virtue of their centrality to late communism, and the access that their role afforded them, *veksláks* consumed like the Party elite (if not better) and exerted significant power on the basis of this unique level of consumption. Although the *vekslák* was frowned on by much of the public as criminal and extortionary, at the same time his consumption, for many, represented an attractive ideal. This contradiction had an impact on both the communist and the postcommunist era. On the one hand, excessive and ostentatious consumption was glamorized and aspired to (as shifting attitudes toward prostitution suggested); on the other, all business transactions were viewed a priori as unethical, inevitably conducted by criminals in partnership with the state. In other words, corruption and capitalist economic practices were closely linked in the public's mind long before the democracy revolutions of 1989 and the postcommunist economies. Nor was this view entirely inaccurate. The fact was that in the late communist period, the Czechoslovak economy as a whole could not be extricated from Tuzex, nor Tuzex from it. As a result, *veksláks* were indeed in partnership with the state, acting as its vital intermediaries. Moreover, the visibility of these middlemen and the simultaneous lack of transparency of the arrangement between them and the state led to the public's further distrust of the system. It did not help that the state-run media were forever warning citizens against buying Tuzex *bony* with Czechoslovak crowns—even by acting out potential swindles through dramatized television segments—while at the same time officials relied on the hustlers to in fact facilitate Tuzex trade.

At the same time, this "new, new class" of hustlers, and those who orbited their world, represented an extreme version of increasingly common practices. *Veksláks* partook of activities considered socially and economically deviant by official standards and values, yet this behavior had its less extreme counterparts throughout everyday life. Not only to thrive, but often to get by, ordinary citizens had to participate in some such activities, which included stealing materials from the workplace, bartering with others, participating in the black market, and buying reserved goods under the counter. Few "normal" economic transactions and business dealings existed. To succeed, some level of unofficial economic activity was demanded. Thus, even though the hustler stood outside of society—both of his own choosing and also by society's condemnation—his dealings represented merely the top end of a shared spectrum of economic behavior that came to define the times.

NOTES

1. *Bony a klid*; screenplay by Radek John and Vít Olmer; directed by Vít Olmer (Czechoslovakia; 1987).

2. *Vekslák* is singular for the male hustler; *veksláci* is the correct plural. Nevertheless, for the sake of narrative flow and an easier read for English speakers, I am using "veksláks" to denote plural.

3. RFE/RL Background Report: J. L. Kerr, "Hard-Currency Shops in Eastern Europe," Oct. 27, 1977.

4. Rossitza Guentcheva, "Mobile Objects: CORECOM and the Selling of Western Goods in Socialist Bulgaria," *Études Balkaniques*, 45(1) (2009): 14.

5. Yuson Jung, "Consumer Lament: An Ethnographic Study on Consumption, Needs, and Everyday Complaints in Postsocialist Bulgaria" (Ph.D. diss., Harvard University, 2006), 82.

6. Charles Hawley, "Sniff of the West: New Scent Recalls East German Intershops," *Spiegel Online*, Mar. 2, 2007.

7. "Interview with Tuzex General Director, Antonín Račanský," *Rudé právo*, Dec. 18, 1986.

8. Jonathan R. Zatlin, *The Currency of Socialism* (New York: Cambridge University Press, 2007), 245.

9. "Proč je Tuzex," *Rudé právo*, Oct. 6, 1965.

10. *Vyprávěj* (Czech Television 2009). They drive the car triumphantly from the Tuzex lot but run out of gas on the way home. The reason is that the Tuzex workers, who promise a full tank of gas with the car, siphon some off from each.

11. Josef Škvorecký, "Bohemia of the Soul," *Daedalus* 119 (1990): 126.

12. Ibid.

13. Paul Hoffman, "Luxury Business in Prague," *New York Times*, June 22, 1969.

14. "S čím se to vlastně smiřujeme," *Svobodné slovo*, Jan. 13, 1969.

15. "Observational Report," Sept. 29, 1964 (RFE/RL Internal Distribution: Item No. 1785/64).

16. "Souhlasíte s existencí Tuzexových prodejen?" *Dikobraz* 33, Aug. 23, 1988.

17. See chapter 6, "Consuming Ideology: The Intershops, Genex, and Retail Trade Under Honecker," in Jonathan R. Zatlin, *The Currency of Socialism* (New York: Cambridge University Press, 2007).

18. Amy L. Porter, "Fleeting Dreams and Flowing Goods: Citizenship and Consumption in Havana Cuba," *PoLAR: Political and Legal Anthropology Review* 31 (2008): 139.

19. Ibid.

20. "O čem se hovoří," *Radio Prague*, May 14, 1987: 16:25 hrs.

21. David R. Crew, "Consuming Germany in the Cold War: Consumption and National Identity in East and West Germany, 1949–1989, an Introduction," in *Consuming Germany in the Cold War*, ed. David F. Crew (New York: Berg, 2003), 4.

22. Pedro Ramet, "Disaffection and Dissent in East Germany," *World Politics* 37 (1984): 108.

23. Hoffman, "Luxury Business in Prague."

24. "Co s Tuzexem?" *Rudé právo*, June 20, 1968.

25. *Svobodné slovo*, Apr. 29, 1988.

26. Guentcheva, "Mobile Objects," 11.

27. Ibid., 18.

28. Ibid., 20.

29. Ibid., 22–23.

30. Ibid., 23.

31. Crew, "Consuming Germany in the Cold War, Introduction," 7.

32. Jung, "Consumer Lament," 88.

33. Dana-Nicoleta Lascu and Mircea Vatasescu, "Transition and Its Effects on Individuals: A Marketing Case Study in Romania." University of Central Arkansas, Small Business Advancement National Center, research archive, (http://sbaer.uca.edu/research/sma/1995/pdf/75.pdf): 2.

34. Jonathan R. Zatlin, "Making and Unmaking Money: Economic Planning and the Collapse of East Germany," Institute of European Studies (University of California, Berkeley) 2007: 15.

35. RFE/RL Background Report: Vladimir Kusin, "Political Terrorism: A New Phase in Combating Dissent in Czechoslovakia?" June 25, 1982.

36. In some cases, the hustlers simply handed the bus driver a bag of Czechoslovak crowns; the driver made the exchanges and the hustlers picked up the foreign currency from him the same evening at his hotel.

37. Moreover, most hustlers had their houses and cars registered in the name of their parents, wives, or children, which meant the items could not be confiscated or traced back to them.

38. FBIS Nov. 27, 1989 (JPRS-EER-89-130: p. 42): Josef Alan, "Vouchers—and What They Hide," *Slovenské pohl'ady* (Bratislava), No. 8 (1989): 123–28 [translated into English].

39. Ibid.

40. The following comes from interviews with Radek John in "The Film About the Film," on the DVD release of *Bony a klid*.

41. Jan Malinda, "Veksláci, taxikáři a pinglové," *Magazín Dnes*, Nov. 13, 2008: 28.

42. John, "The Film About the Film."

43. Malinda, "Veksláci, taxikáři a pinglové," 30.

44. Alan, "Vouchers—and What They Hide," 42.

45. Malinda, "Veksláci, taxikáři a pinglové," 26.

46. Ibid., 28.

47. Ibid.

48. *Czechoslovak Television*, Nov. 5, 1976: 22:05 hrs.

49. "Studio 7," *Radio Hvězda*, Aug. 9, 1988: 14:22 hrs.

50. "Frekvence 'B'," *Radio Prague*, Oct. 15, 1988: 16:20 hrs.

51. "Studio 7," *Radio Hvězda*, Aug. 9, 1988: 14:22 hrs.

52. Ordinary citizens, rightly suspicious, were particularly curious to know what happened to the money that the special crimes unit confiscated. A television broadcast explained that "it becomes income of the state budget and it then serves to finance the needs of the national economy" (*Czechoslovak Television*, Aug. 13, 1988). Thus even the crackdown was lucrative to the hard-currency-strapped state.

53. *Rudé právo*, Aug. 9, 1988.

54. "Maják," *Czechoslovak Television*, Nov. 4, 1988: 18:30 hrs.

55. "Sex and the Tuzex Girl," *Newsweek*, Aug. 10, 1970.

56. Malinda, "Veksláci, taxikáři a pinglové," 30.

57. "Sex and the Tuzex Girl."

58. "Observational Report," Apr. 3, 1962 (RFE/RL Internal Distribution: Item No. 641/62).

59. "Je Tuzex nemravný," *Hospodářské noviny*, Apr. 12, 1968.

60. "O čem se hovoří," *Radio Prague*, June 1, 1987: 16:25 hrs.

61. "Prague Black Marketeers Find Themselves in Unwelcome Spotlight," *Reuters*, June 8, 1988.

62. John, "The Film About the Film."

63. Milovan Djilas, *The Unperfect Society: Beyond the New Class* (London: Harcourt, 1969).

2

Utopia Gone Terribly Right

Plutonium's "Gated Communities" in the Soviet Union and United States

Kate Brown

In the United States in the 1950s, workers at nuclear weapons factories raced to produce yet more bombs to challenge Soviet rockets pointed at American cities. As they did so, American urbanites moved to suburbs located just outside the beltway, a radius that corresponded with the safe zone beyond the concentric circles of destruction of an imagined nuclear strike. Meanwhile, in the Soviet Union, writers asserted the mastery of the Russian nation in inventing everything from television to baseball, as Soviet scientists hurriedly copied the plans for the atomic bomb from stolen American blueprints. The nuclear conflict created the kind of unspoken anxieties that nurtured longings for a society sealed off, self-sufficient, well-stocked, and secure. I have found that these utopian desires matured notably in the cities dwelling directly in the shadow of the new bombs, cities created to produce plutonium for nuclear weapons. It was especially there, where the threat of nuclear annihilation was the most immediate, that the desire for utopia—a planned, affluent, risk-free society—mounted most critically.

Utopia is a much maligned and mistreated word, especially in the field of East European history. It is used as shorthand for the inevitably terminal mistake of applying technocratic knowledge to plan for society's needs in a way that disregards human behavior and normal (not "noble" or rational) human desire. Rational and pragmatic utopias are considered unworkable because they overlook exactly the quality of life that is considered unpredictable and unplannable, but essential: desire. At the heart of this analysis of the fatal flaw of utopia lie explanations as to why the Soviet Union, and socialist projects generally, have failed. The common wisdom is that the planned economy and hegemony of the Communist Party worked against human nature. But we have this characterization of utopia wrong, and before the concept expires, I would like to sound code blue and try to revive it one last time. For what is often overlooked in the critique of communism as a failed utopia is that utopias are all about desire, about creating a surfeit of it so that people need no longer worry about fulfilling their wishes and can move on to other aspirations. To illustrate this point, I want to bring into focus two planned communities that the residents considered very desirable. These communities were so attractive—such consumer utopias, in fact—that residents gave up important civil rights and freedoms in order to live in them. These cities were created, and the residents within controlled, by means of the production of desire. These planned communities were successful, though they leave a legacy of environmental and fiscal catastrophe.

Plutopia

I have in mind two special cities: Richland, on the windy plains of Eastern Washington State; and Cheliabinsk-40, buried in a thicket of forest, lake, and swamp in the Russian Urals. These cities emerged amid inspiration, patriotism, and secrecy to manufacture plutonium, the most volatile and lethal product in human history. Making plutonium is the most polluting aspect of nuclear weapons production. Richland's Hanford plant and Cheliabinsk-40's Maiak plant were each located in remote, sparsely populated continental interiors in order to secure nuclear secrets, but also to contain damage from possible large-scale radioactive contamination, accidental explosions, and enemy attacks. To produce a few grams of plutonium requires several hundred tons of uranium and a long production line stringing together over a dozen massive factories with tens of thousands of workers. In short, it takes a village (really a small city) to produce the kilograms of plutonium needed for a nuclear weapon.

Creating comfortable communities around plutonium plants was not the first impulse. Initially, American and Soviet leaders tried to produce plutonium with militarized labor in army, migrant, and prison camp settings. But soldiers, migrant workers, and prisoners brawled, boozed, and slept around. Reluctantly, Soviet and American leaders realized that those who would operate the plants could not be as volatile as the product they made. In order to secure trustworthy, reliable workers to run the plutonium plants, leaders in both countries built limited-access cities in the 1940s for plant workers, who, they decided, would live rooted in nuclear families within the atomic cities.

From the start, Manhattan Project security agents and KGB officers set up intricate security systems to guard the secrets of plutonium. First, they carefully selected applicants for political and ethnic reliability. In Richland, the DuPont Corporation and the FBI screened employees for political loyalty, social acceptability, and whiteness. Whiteness overrode other factors in determining a person's loyalty. For example, amid a dire wartime labor shortage of white laborers, Army Corps officers set up, at great expense, a prison camp and shipped in white prisoners, "peaceful, conscientious objectors," even though there was a glut of Mexican American and African American workers nearby.[1] Manhattan Project officials initially rejected African Americans and Mexican Americans because their status as minorities made them untrustworthy.[2] They further removed from the surrounding territory Japanese Americans and other "undesirables" "of a suspect nature."[3] Plant officials also rejected communists and those with leftward-leaning sympathies because of fears they would pass secrets to the Soviets.[4]

In the Soviet Union, enterprise leaders encircled Cheliabinsk-40 with a double row of barbed wire fence and gave entry passes only to employees and their immediate families. MVD General Lieutenant Ivan Tkachenko, young, handsome, and cruel, was in charge of security for the project. During the war, Tkachenko had orchestrated deportation of Chechens from the Caucuses, and in Cheliabinsk-40 he was no less concerned than Manhattan Security officials with political and ethnic reliability.[5] Soviet security agents combed the surrounding towns for undesirables—those with a prison record—and shipped about three thousand people out of the buffer zone around the plant. Local Bashkirs and Tatars were rarely hired at the plant. After 1948, Party and security agents suspected Jews of transnational loyalties; in the early fifties, they investigated Jews for cosmopolitanism and fired those who did not show contrition for believing in the international exchange of science.[6]

Tkachenko's security officials made employees sign security oaths and renew them regularly. In Richland, the Atomic Energy Commission, which took over in 1947, broadly published new laws meting out steep fines and harsh prison sentences for violations of nuclear security. GE managers also issued repetitive reminders to stay mum.[7] Corporate security officers, as well as the FBI, wiretapped phones, read mail, and cultivated ranks of secret informers to catch violators of the secrecy oaths.[8] The MVD and KGB took similar measures—selection, security oaths, surveillance—in Cheliabinsk-40. These measures were effective. Residents in Richland said they rarely knew what their friends did for work because no one talked about their jobs.[9] Residents in Cheliabinsk-40 were also careful about what they said; many feared even keeping a diary lest they give some secret away.[10]

Selection and surveillance, however, was only the first circle of security. Plant leaders in both countries set up a second, larger ring of security that ensured loyalty and fidelity by means of building zones of exclusive, mass contentment. And so, surprisingly, the powerful men charged with producing the world's first supplies of plutonium spent a great deal of time worrying about homes, schools, roads, sewers, and electrical lines in addition to reactors and chemical processing plants. For instance, more than half the diary of Colonel Frank Matthias, the wartime Army Corps officer charged with building Hanford, is devoted to town planning, recreational and sports programs, and community relations in Richland.[11] The initial sixty-thousand-person army camp set up to build Hanford was so unpleasant that in 1944 Matthias had hundreds of workers a day walking off the secret, barricaded construction site.[12] Matthias quickly learned how important consumer and job satisfaction was for keeping workers.

Since the thirties, Soviet leaders had been acutely aware of the production problems that consumer dissatisfaction caused. They had seen strikes, production disruptions, and riots because of shortages of consumer goods.[13] Stalin himself encouraged Igor Kurchatov, the director of the Soviet atomic bomb program, to spend liberally on the plutonium town. He told Kurchatov that although Russia was poor, "it is not so poor that a few can't live well" "with their own dachas," Stalin said, "and their own cars."[14] Kurchatov returned to Cheliabinsk-40 and set out to build not only bombs but a wonderful city. He told his workers: "And to spite them [enemies abroad, a town] will be founded. In time your town and mine will have everything—kindergartens, fine shops, a theater and, if you like, a symphony orchestra! . . . and if . . . not one uranium bomb explodes . . . you and I can be happy! And our town can then become a monument to peace."[15]

Kurchatov's prophesy came true. Residents of the secret city were supplied chocolate and sausage, unheard-of luxuries in the postwar years of famine. In the southern Urals, locals called the residents of Cheliabinsk-40 "the chocolate eaters." By the early fifties residents had more than chocolate. Kurchatov commissioned Leningrad architects to build, secretly, in the thick forest excellent modern apartment buildings with electricity and plumbing. They constructed theaters, swimming pools, preschools, sports stadium, dachas, restaurants, and cafes. Best of all, the shops in town had first-priority allocations, akin to the closed stores for the top leadership in Moscow.[16] In the city's shops, residents could buy German shoes, Finnish overcoats, and delicacies from Poland and

Romania. After 1953, when residents were allowed to leave the closed city, they were given passes to exclusive resorts reserved for atomic workers on the Black and Baltic Seas. In Cheliabinsk-40, the usual features of provincial Soviet life were nowhere to be found; there were no shortages, no long lines, no threadbare children, no gnawing hunger or damp basement dwellings. As L. V. Zhondetskaia remembered in 1988: "We had the feeling that we already lived under communism. There was everything in the stores, from crabs to black caviar."[17]

Nadezhda Petrushkina grew up in Cheliabinsk-40 in the fifties. Her parents worked at the plant. She showed me pictures of her apartment with a large balcony overlooking the lake, of her dacha and flower garden, and she described her childhood where the mostly young couples enjoyed a comfortable, social existence. "My father loved sports," she remembered. He used to swim in the lake in the mornings before work and play volleyball in the courtyard with his friends on the weekends." "My parents and their friends were always getting together for dinners and parties"; "I remember," she continued, "that smell of fresh bread each morning from the delivery trucks. They used to deliver bread and milk each morning." She spoke of her sunny and warm preschool, which had a swimming pool: "We swam every day."

Petrushkina gradually became aware they were richer than their neighbors outside the gates. But that didn't bother her. "We were proud of our wealth—proud that we never wore domestic shoes; that people could tell by looking at us that we were from 'there.'"[18] Other former residents concurred that they could tell a fellow resident of a Soviet nuclear city from fifty paces. How? I asked Vladimir Novoselov, a contemporary of Petrushkina: "Oh, sure, you could tell from the clothes and the shoes, but more from the posture, the air of self-assurance and confidence."[19]

Stocked stores and good housing were an unbelievable luxury in the fifties in the Soviet Union. Outside the closed city, in neighboring industrial settlements bearing utilitarian names such as Asbestos and Labor, workers finished their shifts and waited in line to buy gray macaroni and then disappeared, stooping and coughing, into hovels and dugouts. In the nearby city of Cheliabinsk, in 1948, two to three hundred people lined up daily for bread before dawn, and the line remained until 3:00 a.m. Seven years later, little had changed. In 1955, workers wrote on ballots: "I vote for you, but why are there still lines for bread?" or "Nothing to eat, give us meat, butter and sugar."[20] Sallow children walked miles to attend the second, third, or fourth shifts of their primary schools.[21] Gangs of disaffected youths and veterans attacked one another in spasms of senseless violence. Hunger, and with it illness and crime, haunted the towns and cities surrounding the peaceful, prosperous, orderly Cheliabinsk-40.

In Eastern Washington, people in neighboring towns called Richland the "gold coast."[22] The federal government owned all the land and property in Richland, and first DuPont and then General Electric managed the city. DuPont hired an architect who designed houses, shopping centers, and residential developments. The company built churches and rented them to congregations for a dollar a year. DuPont built and ran the town hospital, the best in the region, which admitted only residents and plant workers. DuPont and GE selected companies that were awarded monopolies to conduct business in Richland. GE set up, subsidized, and censored the town's newspaper and denied access and information to rival papers. In the absence of tax revenue, GE allocated federal funds for Richland's schools, parks, bus service, hospital, and recreational programs. Workers paid no local taxes and received wages that were 30 percent higher than those of workers in surrounding counties.[23] Richland residents were most pleased with the federally subsidized housing. White, male plant employees rented modern track houses with all utilities and maintenance included for a third or half as much as black and Mexican workers paid for dilapidated shacks across the Columbia River in neighboring Pasco.[24]

The contrasts between Richland and the surrounding "tiny, dusty" railroad towns were stark.[25] Denied access to Richland's hospital, locals had to drive eight hours over the mountains for a maternity ward. Neighboring schools were crowded and poorly staffed. Sewer systems, roads, and plumbing were spotty. Pasco had many problems with housing, sanitation, crime, prostitution, gambling, racial segregation, and corrupt law enforcement. Across the inland West at the time, little railroad and ranch towns, born of nineteenth-century dreams of agricultural prosperity, were going bankrupt and losing populations. Richland, meanwhile, boomed.

For many residents who came from hardscrabble, provincial towns in the United States or the USSR, residency in Richland or Cheliabinsk-40 was akin to winning the golden ticket; it meant a person had arrived in the kind of material comfort and prosperity that few expected in their lifetime. Ralph Myrick remembered his childhood in Gamerco,[26] a New Mexico company mining town of packed clay, slag heaps, and miserable company tenements. When DuPont moved his family into a plywood, prefabricated, two-bedroom house in Richland, his mother broke down in tears of happiness. She had never lived in a house with plumbing and appliances. She had never had a home so clean and new. Myrick's father had not finished high school. Myrick remembered that his father worried a lot: worried that the plant would close after the war, worried that the supply of plutonium would be satiated, worried that he or his children would do something wrong for which he would lose his job.[27] Nowhere else, he knew, could he provide for his family so well with his skills and education. Once as a teenager Myrick had a run-in with the town police. Terrified, he begged the officer not to write him up, for he was sure his father would get fired for his son's adolescent misbehavior. Myrick understood that when an employee was fired from the plant, he was given a week to move his family out of Richland.[28]

In fact, many residents of Richland repeated to me the same rumor of a neighboring family that had disappeared overnight when a wife asked a neighbor invasive questions, such as "what does your husband do for a living?"[29] The rumor reflects the fear of being evicted for saying too much, asking too many questions, or making the kind of trouble that would cost a person his spot in town. When Richland residents wrote letters to the editor, they frequently withheld their names.[30] Paul Nissen, the former editor of the GE-sponsored local newspaper in Richland, wrote about the town's exchange of comfort for conformity:

> Are you, John Doe likely to want to do anything, at least publicly,
> which will put you in a position where you will have to do any fast ex-
> plaining either to GE or the [Atomic Energy Commission] AEC. The
> question is . . . "do you like your present job?" "Don't you want to live
> in that nice house and this pretty little city any longer?"[31]

In Cheliabinsk-40, the contrast between life in the closed plutonium city and life outside was so great that residents referred to the territory beyond the gates as "the big world." It wasn't difficult to lose one's place in the socialist paradise. If a worker drank too much, brawled, missed work, or slept with other men's wives, these issues were taken up at Party meetings and the worker was threatened with eviction from town.[32] If a teenager misbehaved in school, dressed like Elvis Presley, or was caught listening to the Voice of America, he was evicted, barred from entering the city again, and sent to reform school.[33] Sometimes when husbands were evicted, wives stayed on at their jobs, alone in the closed city. After a major nuclear accident in 1957 at the plant, residents panicked and hundreds of people sent in resignation notices. But after living "in the big world" for a few months, many of the same people wrote letters asking to return. "I was stupid. Please take me back," they pleaded.[34] Cheliabinsk-40's charm was so arresting, so seductive that people chose to remain alone in their Eden even when their health was at risk and even after their loved ones were banished beyond the gates.

Not everyone was happy with the special status of these towns. Visiting congressmen in the fifties worried that Richland, government-owned and federally subsidized, was too "socialistic," even "communistic." They need not have worried. Richland epitomized what historian Lizabeth Cohen calls the consumers' republic, where activist-consumers give way to consumer-citizens, who were told that their civic duty and democratic freedoms lie in consuming. Cohen shows how in the postwar period government programs gave up on the New Deal promise of equitable redistribution in favor of prefatory federal subsidies for some over others.[35] White men won federal subsidies via the GI bill and FHA loans far more frequently than women and minorities. Increasingly segregated suburbs won massive federal aid for roads, schools, and infrastructures, while older inner cities populated with racial minorities were left to decay without funding.[36] Richland, which won the all-American city prize in 1961, epitomized these postwar inequities, exclusions, and hierarchies of suburbanizing America.

Security and the Production of Desire

In fact, the prosperity of Richland's consumers' republic lent credibility to the city's leaders. The orderly, universal well-being of Richland, which had no indigent, no elderly, and no unemployed, telegraphed to residents a heightened sense of superiority and safety. Residents enumerated their superiority in various ways—higher birth rate, longer life expectancy, higher average income, more expendable income, higher educational level—and this statistical superiority gave residents confidence that their community leaders were indeed knowledgeable, capable, and trustworthy.[37] For this reason, residents did not question plant managers' repeated claims that the plutonium plant was perfectly safe, despite the rumors of sheep dying on nearby farms and of unreported accidents at the plant.[38]

And in some ways, mass consumption did protect residents of Richland. Public health officials encouraged residents to consume milk and produce, closely monitored and shipped in from elsewhere. They also told them to rip up sage and thistle (which stored radiation) and instead plant and constantly water suburban lawns in their desert yards. Officials also told them to limit their consumption of (radiated) fish from the Columbia River—all without explaining why.[39] Meanwhile, outside Richland, ranchers and farmers continued to produce for their own consumption: they ate their own dairy products, game, sheep, vegetables, and fished from the river. The local Wanapum Indians fished, hunted, and gathered delicate (and radiation-absorbing) roots from the range.[40] And so the assertions that Richland residents were healthier were true—in part because they were younger, were more affluent, and had far better health care—but also because, as modern consumers, they did not live off the radioactive landscape.

Consumptive superiority also served as a surrogate for freedoms residents forfeited when they agreed to live in the plutonium city, dependent on one, classified product. Richland residents voted against incorporation and the end of government ownership in the early and late fifties.[41] Residents voted against private property because, quite reasonably, they feared that if they bought their houses and the plant closed, there would be no jobs and no market for their real estate investments. In so doing, residents also took a pass on the right to self-government, the right to free speech, free assembly, and an uncensored press.[42] Additionally, they gave up power over their bodies every week as they placed their urine and stool samples on the front porch, underwent compulsory medical exams, and rolled their school-age children through full-body radiation scanners. As consumers, however, residents of Richland won back some of their lost voice and power. For it was over issues of consumption where they could safely express their opinions—and indeed they did rise up vociferously against rent hikes in the midfifties, demanded parking for new cars at the new shopping center, and lobbied in favor of dog walking on carefully tended lawns.[43] These issues, though seemingly trivial, mattered a great deal because they simulated the motions of American democracy for which Richland residents were putting their lives on the line.

Party leaders in Cheliabinsk-40 also worried. They saw how residents bought up scarce goods, shoes, and cars in the closed city and sold them speculatively outside the gates. They feared their residents were becoming too "bourgeois," too materialistic.[44] They feared that young people, raised without the hardships known to their fathers and grandfathers, were losing their revolutionary, socialist consciousness.[45] In 1956, however, a young woman, Taishina, stood up at a Party cell meeting to note the capitalist-style inequities of her city: "We were chased out to hear a lecture on Marx. But I was out in the big world and there people don't live so well. There is poverty. Why don't you give us a lecture on that?"[46] Party leaders told Taishina that the residents of the closed city deserved the state's largesse because their work and sacrifice defended the nation and, in turn, the nation needed to support them, unconditionally. After her question, security officials opened a file on Taishina. They seemed to prefer the other residents' bourgeois materialism to Taishina's revolutionary vigilance. The local Communist Party council minutes show that Party members dwelt most on issues related to consumption: housing, supplies of sporting goods, film distribution, and service in the restaurants and grocery stores. As local leaders rushed to accommodate these complaints, consumer issues gave residents a voice and dramatized socialist democracy.[47]

As in Richland, Cheliabinsk-40 residents enumerated their superiority in material ways: they counted their larger living space, their greater volume of meat and dairy consumption, their larger number of appliances, their better access to health and child care, and their longer life expectancy.[48] They saw these indicators as a validation of their town and its leaders, and the community's safety. Indeed, the residents' superior consuming status did in part save them from contamination. Downstream from the plant, in poor and remote settlements, villagers who drank and bathed in the radioactive Techa River suffered much more significantly from radiation-related illnesses than residents of Cheliabinsk-40, where the water was tested regularly and drawn from monitored wells.[49]

Historian Elena Osokina shows how, in the wake of the egalitarian promises of the Revolution, Soviet leaders in the thirties created "hierarchies of poverty" by instituting a passport regimen that immobilized majorities on collective farms and cleared prized cities of political and economic undesirables.[50] Soviet planners then stocked limited-access cities and stores with scarce consumer goods where a higher class of citizen—passport holders—lived. In so doing, Soviet leaders created zones of prosperity amid greater zones of poverty. The zones of prosperity, such as Moscow and Leningrad, kept alive the myth of a thriving socialist utopia, a place to which one could aspire, while the countryside and provinces went hungry. Cheliabinsk-40 and its threadbare hinterland epitomized these inequities, written not in the equitable Soviet Constitution but across the Soviet landscape.

So long as one left Cheliabinsk-40 only for the special resorts reserved for atomic workers, then Khrushchev's promise that the Soviet Union would achieve communism and overtake the United States in consumption appeared to have been realized.[51] Residents had achieved communism, if secretly, and if only in one city. The consuming privileges of Cheliabinsk-40 spoke to the superiority of Soviet society, which residents continued to believe in long after the Soviet Union's collapse. In 1989 and 1999, the vast majority of residents polled voted to keep their Soviet-era fences, guards, gates, and pass system, which remain in place in 2011.[52]

In Richland, crowds gathered in the midfifties to see *General Electric Theater's* spokesperson and host Ronald Reagan demonstrate the "total new electric kitchen." Reagan transmitted the message that consumer freedom was the cornerstone to democratic freedom.[53] In Richland, where residents had given away most of their political freedoms, this message especially made sense. But residents of Richland were not alone. Across the postwar United States, white citizens turned their backs on espoused democratic values and New Deal promises of equal access and opportunity in order to protect their property values in segregated, federally subsidized, limited-access communities located just off limited-access "National Defense" highways.[54]

In other words, the lavish fiscal attention the American and Soviet governments paid the plutonium cities was not an accident. The well-heeled, carefully zoned, and policed utopias were necessary to maintain a stable labor force and create good workers, but the high-risk affluence also served to keep residents from questioning, talking, or blowing the whistle. Consumption became, in these cases, the seal on a new high-tech kind of social contract that multiplied spatially across the United States and the USSR in the fifties. In this case, the segregated suburb and the closed city stand in for Hobbes's commonwealth: "Outside the commonwealth is the empire of passions, war, fear, poverty, nastiness, solitude, barbarity, ignorance, savagery; within the commonwealth is the empire of reason, peace, security, wealth, splendor, society, good taste, the sciences and good-will."[55]

Crossing the Columbia River from the Jim Crow ghetto of dilapidated shacks and overrun outhouses in Pasco into the sunny living rooms of Richland might just have felt like passing into the state-protected commonwealth, or more so, leaving gray, dingy Asbestos and passing through the gates into Cheliabinsk-40 with its smell of fresh bread and the bright noise of children's nurseries. Or perhaps a person does not have to search so far to find Hobbes's commonwealth: drive from a muddy, shabby collective farm village and enter glistening Soviet Moscow; or leave the Robert Moses Cross Bronx Expressway, which roars right through the Bronx ghetto, and turn north into the peace and opulence of Scarsdale.[56] There were, in both the United States and the Soviet Union, many people willing to make the same kind of exchange of consumer goods for equal access and civil rights as the residents of the plutonium cities.

Much has been written about the controls and fears of the nuclear security regimes, but I am pointing to an interpretation that normalizes the nuclear security state, or perhaps universalizes it. At least as important to state security was the production of desire and the cultivation of thriving consumer cultures in step with the aspirations of the larger Soviet and American societies. These were, in effect, not failed but successful utopias that were realized in both countries and then exported internationally as "the American way" and "socialist democracy."[57] The blueprints of the utopian American suburb and the "socialist city" (sotsgorod) emerged in the postwar era fully radiant in nuclear cities because the exclusive, affluent, secure, and well-stocked qualities of the suburb/sotsgorod soothed anxious minds. The fact that we do not recognize the sotsgorod or the American suburb as utopias illustrates just how successful they were as models for postwar Soviet and American societies; they multiplied so quickly that we rarely acknowledge their original novelty or the inequities, social hierarchies, and (utopian) social engineering built into them.[58]

At the time, people did not recognize these utopias because they were too busy aspiring to join them, to have their American dream, or to achieve, finally, their corner of socialism, not just in the plutonium cities but outside of them as well. As residents of the plutonium cities sought to remain in their special towns and keep them exclusive, Soviet citizens schemed to obtain a residence permit to a well-supplied city, and once there to keep others out; American citizens saved for a down payment on a house in a suburb, and then once there supported restrictive covenants and zoning to keep tax dollars in and others out.[59] The suburb and the Soviet city were not for everyone. In the Soviet Union, millions of collective farmers and rural dwellers, blocked by passport restrictions, could not leave the village for the city, and so they could never achieved their private utopia. In the United States, racial minorities especially were blocked from achieving their suburban utopia. As racial minorities moved into suburbs, the suburbs (and their wealth) fled further afield.[60] Yet despite the glaring fact of these spatial inequities, most Americans and most Soviets believed they lived in just, equitable societies.[61] Why were they so easily fooled?

The utopian zones of privilege had an important utility. They enabled political leaders to point at them, glossing over the fact of their exclusivity, and argue that their (Soviet or American) system did indeed produce affluence and prosperity. And that was an essential argument to make during the Cold War: to argue that one's society produced universalized wealth, not just weapons of mass destruction. Certainly, for Soviet urbanites zoning territory into regions of privilege and poverty kept alive the myth of socialism, much as Lizabeth Cohen argues that "up-zoning" white, affluent suburbs to leave behind impoverished inner cities maintained for mainstream Americans the mirage of universal opportunity in an American democracy. The exclusivity of these utopian communities accomplished something else too: a certain docility and failure to question lest one be tossed from the Garden of Eden. For in these privatized and highly controlled zones of privilege, the space for political expression and questioning of authority narrowed greatly, while "civic activism" corroded into discontent over parking fees and sports facilities. In the pioneering plutonium cities, this exchange of political vigilance and social responsibility for consumer satisfaction bought a great deal of peace and prosperity and also purchased unannounced nuclear and social disasters played out on lethal landscapes.[62]

NOTES

1. "Federal Prison Industries Operating Contract," draft, 1947, Robert Taylor, private collection, Pasco, WA; Frank T. Matthias diary, June 10 and 11, 1943, July 5, 1943, Aug. 4, 1943, Public Reading Room (PPR), Richland, WA.

2. The plant finally accepted Mexican and black American labor following pressure from interest groups and with intense pressure to complete the project swiftly. Once they did so, Mexican Americans especially were subject to additional background checks. Both groups were segregated from the population of white workers in the vast residential construction camp built alongside the plutonium plant. Matthias diary, Sept. 23, 1943, Feb. 18, 1944, and Feb. 26, 1944; "Spanish-American Program," April 1944, Hegley Museum and Library (HML), Wilmington, DE, acc. 2086, folder 20.1. On discrimination against and segregation of African Americans, see Robert Bauman, "Jim Crow in the Tri-Cities, 1943–1950," *Pacific Northwest Quarterly* 29 (2005): 124–31; and James T. Wiley Jr., "Race Conflict as Exemplified in a Washington Town," M.A. thesis, State College of Washington, 1949. Matthias diary, Sept. 23, 1943.

3. Matthias diary, Apr. 11, 1943, and June 7, 1943. On clearing out "undesirables," see Matthias diary, Dec. 21, 1943. For the order to form "prohibited zones," see Stimson to De Witt, Feb. 1, 1943, Boris Pash Papers, Hoover Institution, box 2, folder 10.

4. In 1951, with pressure from the NAACP, a few token African American families were given access to Richland. The number of minority employees in Richland remained in the single digits for decades. See "Hanford Project Survey, 1950–1951," Seattle Urban League, in the Henry Jackson Collection, acc. 3560-2/55/12, University of Washington Special Collections. See Bauman, "Jim Crow in the Tri-Cities," 124–31.

5. V. N. Novoselov and V. S. Tolstikov, *Taina "Sorokovki"* (Ekaterinburg: Ural'skii rabochii, 1995), 107.

6. In the 1957 Cheliabinsk-40 Party roster, most candidates and members were Russians and Ukrainians. There were two Tatars and no Jews. "Spisok kandidatov v deputaty ozerskogo gorodskogo soveta deuptatov trudiashchiisia," Ob'edinennyi Gosudarstvennyi Arkhiv Cheliabinskoi Oblasti (OGAChO) 2469/1/120, 1957. For transcripts of the political working over of a Jewish administrator, see "Protokol #8, Biuro Ozerskogo Gorkom," Oct. 2, 1956, OGAChO 2469/1/4, 1–12.

7. General Electric took over as the main contractor of the Hanford site in 1946.

8. T. B. Farley, "Memorandum for the File: Protection Security Experience to July 1, 1945," dated Oct. 2, 1945, HAN 73214, folder 9, PPR.

9. Paul John Deutschmann, "Federal City: A Study of the Administration of Richland, Washington, Atomic Energy Commission Community," M.A. thesis, University of Oregon, 1952.

10. N. V. Mel'nikova, *Fenomen zakrytogo atomnogo goroda: Ocherki istorii Urala, vypusk 42* (Ekaterinburg: Bank kul'turnoi informatsii, 2006), 76.

11. Gordon Turnbull, Richland's master planner, stated that the purpose of town planning and investment in the city was to reduce employee turnover, which was not considered tenable for plutonium production. "Because of the technical skill and training required and clearance of all new personnel, such turnover can be less easily tolerated in the production of fissionable materials than in any other line of industry." Turnbull, *Master Plan for Richland, Washington* (Cleveland and Chicago, 1948), 48.

12. "Daily Employment During Construction Period" and "Total Daily Termina-tions," HML, acc. 2086, folder 20.13.

13. See, for example, Jeffrey J. Rossman, *Worker Resistance Under Stalin: Class and Revolution on the Shop Floor* (Cambridge, MA: Harvard University Press, 2005).

14. David Holloway, *Stalin and the Bomb* (New Haven, CT: Yale University Press, 1994), 148. Holloway quotes Stalin saying to Kurchatov: "Our scientists were very modest and they sometimes did not notice that they live poorly . . . our state has suffered very much, yet it is surely possible to ensure that several thousand people can live very well, and several thousand people better than very well, with their own dachas, so that they can relax, and with their own cars."

15. Gerard J. DeGroot, *The Bomb: A Life* (Cambridge, MA: Harvard University Press 2005), 144.

16. In Cheliabinsk-40 by 1958, 62 percent lived in one-room apartments with living space of 5.35 sq meters. The largest number were three-room apartments, with 11 percent of families in them. The better conditions were a cause for pride and envy. As one person mentioned at a Cheliabinsk-40 Party meeting, "Our city isn't on the map, but many can envy the conditions in which we live." OGAChO 2469/7/2, 67.

17. Zhondetskaia lived in Cheliabinsk-70, a small research settlement attached to the plutonium plant. B. Emel'ianov, *Raskryvaia pervye stranitsi* (Ekaterinburg: Ural'skii rabochii, 1997), 27.

18. Author interview with Nadezhda Petrushkina, June 25, 2007, Cheliabinsk.

19. Author interview with Vladimir Novoselov, June 27, 2007, Cheliabinsk.

20. In M. E. Glavatskii, ed., *Rossiia, kotoruiu my ne znali, 1939–1993* (Cheliabinsk: Iuzhnoe-ural'skoe knizhnoe izdatel'stvo, 1995), 266–67.

21. V. V. Alekseev, ed., *Obshchestvo i vlast': 1917–1985, Vol. 2, 1946–1985* (Cheliabinsk: UrO RAN, 2006), 93.

22. Deutschmann, "Federal City": 293.

23. For a description of the corporate management of Richland, see G. C. Houston, S. Badgett, and R. M. White, "Memorandum for the File, Village—Commercial Facilities Experiences to July 1, 1945," July 30, 1945, Han 73214, Bk 17; M. T. Binns, G. C. Houston, T. B. Mitchell, and H. B. Price, "Memorandum for the File: Village—Housing Experience to July 1, 1945," Aug. 3, 1945, in "Memoranda for the File; Village Operations, Part I," PRR. On subsidies to the newspaper and censorship, see Paul Nissen's expose on the *Richland Villager*, in the *Tri City Herald*, Oct. 23–25, 1950, A1.

24. According to DuPont guidelines, only "heads of households" of a "higher type" who were employed at the Hanford plant were entitled to housing in Richland. They interpreted that only men could be head of household, so women breadwinners or single mothers had to find housing elsewhere. See Binns, Houston, Mitchell, and Price, "Memorandum for the File: Village—Housing Experience to July 1, 1945." On complaints about the policy, see Richland Community Council Minutes, June 20, 1949, meeting no. 21, Richland Public Library. Pollsters in Pasco in 1949 found that 75 percent of blacks and 3 percent of whites lived in trailers; 78 percent of black families and 6 percent of white families lived in one room; 95 percent of blacks in Pasco lived east of the tracks in shacks and trailers in a region that had no city plumbing or electricity. Residents used outhouses and communal showers and hand pumps. The shacks rented for $15–20 a week, four times more than a modern, new one-bedroom in Richland with all utilities included. Pasco by this time had a full-blown Jim Crow establishment. Wiley, "Race Conflict," 53.

25. Deutschmann, "Federal City," 293.

26. Gamerco stood for the Gallop American Coal Company.

27. In 1946, the local journalist Paul Nissen called Richland a "nervous wondering community. . . ." Nervous not because it had been unknowingly producing the world's most volatile material but anxious about the survival of the local economy. Nissen: "Its purpose for being suddenly shot out from under it and worried about what, when, how and if the blow would fall that would make it another ghost town like Hanford." As quoted in Deutschmann, "Federal City," 20.

28. Author interview with Ralph Myrick, Kennewick, WA, Aug. 19, 2008. On the policies that evicted families from Richland housing once the male breadwinner was terminated for reasons of job performance, health, or retirement, see Richland Community Council Minutes, meeting no. 21, June 20, 1949, Richland Public Library.

29. Sanger, *Working on the Bomb: An Oral History* (Portland, OR: Portland State University, 1995), 170.

30. See for example the *Tri-City Herald*, Feb. 7, 1951, 4; and Deutschmann, "Federal City," 283.

31. Nissen, *Tri-City Herald*, Oct. 24, 1950: 1.

32. The subject of this meeting was young kids wearing wide-shouldered tops and wiping their noses on their sleeves. "Protokol sobrannia aktiva gorodskoi partiinoi organizastii," Nov. 3, 1957, OGAChO 2469/1/119, 159–70.

33. Author interview with Vladimir Novoselov, June 27, 2007, Cheliabinsk.

34. See "Doklad na 3-m Plenume gorkoma VLKSM 10 aprelia 1957 goda," Apr. 10, 1957, OGAChO 2469/5/118 and Mel'nikova, *Fenomen zakrytogo atomnogo goroda*, 99–100.

35. Lizabeth Cohen, *A Consumers' Republic: The Politics of Mass Consumption in Postwar America* (New York: Knopf, 2003).

36. See, among many examples, Robert Self, *American Babylon: Race and the Struggle for Postwar Oakland* (Princeton, NJ: Princeton University Press, 2003), Ira Katznelson, *When Affirmative Action Was White: An Untold History of Racial Inequality in Twentieth-Century America* (New York: Norton, 2005); Cohen, *A Consumers' Republic.*

37. "Managers' Data Book," June 1949, James Thomas Papers, acc 5433-001, Box 25, University of Washington Special Collections. For superior health indicators for Cheliabinsk-40, see "Protokol IX-i Ozerskoi gorodskoi partiinoi konferentsii ot 25 dekabria 1965 goda," OGAChO 2469/5/292, 53–54; Novoselov and Tolstikov, *Atomnyi sled,* 128; and Viktor Doshchenko, "Ekvivalent Rentgena," *Pravda,* Mar. 28, 2003.

38. One rumor in 1947 of a worker who had been frozen on the job led to a mass exit of workers from the Hanford Plant. "GE Security Bulletin #16," Nov. 19, 1947, HAN 22962, PRR. Rumors became such a problem for General Electric that in 1951 they instituted a new policy of investigating rumors. They announced that "those that are true will be confirmed." Deutschmann, "Federal City": 307.

39. Walter J. Williams, director of production, Washington, DC. "Certain Functions of the Hanford Operations Office—AEC," Oct. 8, 1948, James P. Thomas Papers, 5433-1, box 24, University of Washington Special Collections. Michele Stenehjem Gerber, *On the Home Front: The Cold War Legacy of the Hanford Nuclear Site,* 2nd ed. (Lincoln: University of Nebraska Press, 2002), 125.

40. Author interview with Rex Buck, Jr., Wanapum Dam, WA, May 18, 2008.

41. A 1952 U.S. Bureau of the Census poll conducted for the AEC found that most residents regarded home ownership as a risky proposition. In a 1955 poll, Richland residents also rejected plans for "disposal and incorporation" by three to one. Minutes of Richland Community Council, Feb. 7, 1955, Richland Public Library. See also Rex E. Owinn, Mark W. Fullerton, and Neil R. Goff, CHREST, 2006.001, 1, Folder 3.1, "Richland, Washington: A Study of Economic Impact" (1955), 49; and "Excerpts from Delbert Meyer, 'History of Tri-Cities'" (1959), CHREST Ass. 2006.1 Box 2, folder 6.1: 120.

42. For an exposé on censorship and lack of free market in Richland in the forties, see Paul Nissen, *Tri-City Herald*, Oct. 25–27, 1950: A1. For a broader (and brilliant) discussion of the "compartmentalization of information, populations and access to territory on American nuclear weapons territories," see Peter Bacon Hales, *Atomic Spaces: Living on the Manhattan Project* (Urbana and Chicago: University of Illinois Press, 1997), 115–62.

43. See "Minutes of the Richland Community Council," June 14, 1948, to June 28, 1953, located at the Richland Public Library.

44. "Protokol sobrannia aktiva gorodskoi partiinoi organizasii," Nov. 3, 1957, OGAChO 2469/1/119 ll. 159–70; Mel'nikova: *Fenomen zakrytogo atomnogo goroda*: 102–3.

45. Zasedanie partiinogo aktiva," Apr. 19, 1951, OGAChO, 1137/1/31, 1–75; "Protokol no 2, vtorovo plenuma Ozerskogo gorkoma KPSS," Feb. 15, 1966, OGAChO, 2469/6/1, 1–23.

46. "Stenogramma zasedaniia biuro gorkoma KPSS s uchastiem chlenov biuro pervichoi partorganizastii TsZL," Dec. 7, 1956, OGAChO 2469/1/5, 18–37.

47. "Protokol no. 1 zasedaniia plenuma Ozerskogo gorogdskogo Komiteta KPSS," Aug. 17, 1956, OGAChO 2469/1/2.

48. See, among many examples, "Itogi noviab'skogo plenuma TsK KSPSS i zadachi gorodskoi partiinoi organizastii," Dec. 2, 1958, OGAChO, 2469/2/4, 60–80.

49. Radiation levels along the Techa climbed so high that local officials had several villages removed from the banks of the river. They further set up a guard to prevent villagers from drawing water from the river. These measures failed; villagers evaded the guards, who were sparsely placed, and cut holes in the fences. And so the orders were renewed over the years to the same effect. "Reshenie Cheliabinskogo oblispolkoma o peredache zemel' i imushchestva kolkhoza "krasnyi luch" metlinskogo sel'soveta khimzavodu imeni D. I. Mendeleeva" Apr. 5, 1947, OGAChO 288/42/34, 59–60, and "Ob ustanovlenii strogogo sanitarnogo rezhima na reke Techa," Aug. 30, 1958, OGAChO R-274/20/48, 94–96.

50. E. A. Osokina, *Our Daily Bread: Socialist Distribution and the Art of Survival in Stalin's Russia, 1927–1941* (Armonk, NY: Sharpe, 2001). Collective farmers, most rural dwellers and former prisoners and deportees, were not issued domestic passports and thus had no legal right to travel within the Soviet Union. People who were found to be violating the passport regime were cleared in vast sweeps of the population in the 1930s. For work on the cleansing of Soviet cities after passportization, see David Shearer, "Elements Near and Alien: Passportization, Policing, and Identity in the Stalinist State, 1932–1952," *Journal of Modern History* 76 (December 2004), 835–81;

V. P. Popov, "Pasportnaia sistema v SSSR (1932–1976)," *Sotsiologicheskie issledovaniia* 8 (1995), 3–14; Gijs Kessler, "The Passport System and State Control over Population Flows in the Soviet Union, 1932–1940," *Cahiers Du Monde Russe* 42 (2001), 478–504; and Nathalie Moine, "Passeportisation, statistique des migrations et controle de l'identité sociale," *Cahiers du monde russe* 38 (1997), 587–600.

51. For a wonderful history of Khrushchev's promises and threats vis-à-vis the United States, see Peter Carlson, *K Blows Top: A Cold War Comic Interlude, Starring Nikita Khrushchev, America's Most Unlikely Tourist* (New York, Public Affairs, 2009).

52. In 1989, 97 percent of polled residents of the closed city voted to keep their gates and guards, mostly for fear of the riffraff lurking outside the gates. The poll was used by the city and plant administration to justify continuance of the security regime, the fence, and its guards. (The poll evidently was planned and taken for that reason, to fend off demands from Moscow to open the city.) A second poll, taken in 1999, found that 85 percent of the population wanted the gates. The somewhat lower later figure was attributed to the new migrants who had moved into the city, and who were not as fearful of the "big world." Viktor Riskin, "'Aborigeny' atomnogo anklava: V zhitelie Ozerska slozhilsia osobnyi mentalitet, oni protiv togo, chtoby ikh gorod stal otrkytym," *Cheliabinskii rabochii*, Apr. 15, 2004.

53. Thomas W. Evans, *The Education of Ronald Reagan: The General Electric Years and the Untold Story of His Conversion to Conservatism* (New York: Columbia University Press, 2006), 96–97.

54. Historians of American history have explored in convincing detail the major shift in demography from integrated cities to suburbs that banned, through covenants, zoning, and practice, large numbers of Americans from living there. These same suburbs were then greatly subsidized and serviced by federal coffers through discriminatory practices in granting federally subsidized FHA and VA loans. Poor and increasingly minority citizens were left to fend for themselves without government welfare in existing, aging, and "blighted" inner cities. For example, Robert Self points out that the older, working-class community of West Oakland, California, received *none* of the enormous government subsidized capital investment ($3.3 million in San Leandro alone) made in residential property in California between 1945 and the 1960s. Self, *American Babylon*, 104–5. Meanwhile, Beryl Satter argues that in Chicago blacks were paying $1 million a day in inflated rents and property values by the midfifties. Satter, *Family Properties: Race, Real Estate, and the Exploitation of Black Urban America* (New York: Metropolitan Books, 2009). In addition, there is a large body of literature that critiques the suburb as "privatopias," the physical manifestation of America's hidden classes. Among many, see David Harvey, *Spaces of Hope* (Berkeley: University of California Press, 2000); Cohen, *Consumer's Republic;* Kenneth T. Jackson, *Crabgrass Frontier: The Suburbanization of the United States* (New York: Oxford University Press, 1985); Elaine Tyler May, *Homeward Bound: American Families in the Cold War Era* (New York: Basic Books, 1999); Amanda I. Seligman, *Block by Block Neighborhoods and Public Policy on Chicago's West Side* (Chicago: University of Chicago Press, 2005). Among important correctives to the Lewis Mumford–inspired critique of the suburbs as solely elite and white, see

Matthew D. Lassiter, *The Silent Majority: Suburban Politics in the Sunbelt South* (Princeton, NJ: Princeton University Press, 2006); and Kevin Michael Kruse and Thomas J. Sugrue, eds., *The New Suburban History* (Chicago: University of Chicago, 2006).

55. Thomas Hobbes, ed. *On the Citizen* (New York, 1998), 115–16.

56. On Moses revisited, see Kenneth T. Jackson and Hilary Ballon, eds., *Robert Moses and the Modern City: The Transformation of New York* (New York: Norton, 2008).

57. Soviet propagandists characterized people in capitalist countries as "slaves" to corporate and political powers. The Soviet Union led the cause to free people around the world from capitalist enslavement and to help working classes fight for "new democracies." In a democratic socialist society, citizens were free from need, and also free, via the apparatus of Party and state representative bodies, to voice their opinions. A. V. Fateev, *Obraz vraga v Sovetskoi propagande: 1945–1954 gg* (Moskva: Maks Press, 1999), 71. On the postwar American mission to export high-production, high-consumption society to the world, so people everywhere could be "free from want" and enjoy what the American Chamber of Commerce described as "the abundance of American civilization," see Wendy L. Wall, *Inventing the "American Way": The Politics of Consensus from the New Deal to the Civil Rights Movement* (New York: Oxford University Press, 2008), 127, 167.

58. For a fuller exposition of the utopian aspirations of Soviet and American societies, see Susan Buck-Morss, *Dreamworld and Catastrophe: The Passing of Mass Utopia in East and West* (Cambridge, MA: Harvard University Press, 2000).

59. On utopian and exclusive aspirations to move into a private apartment in the Soviet Union in the postwar period, and how these plans dovetailed with American urban renewal projects, see Steven Harris, "Moving to the Separate Apartment: Building, Distributing, Furnishing, and Living in Urban Housing in Soviet Russia, 1950s–1960s," (Ph. D. diss., University of Chicago, 2003), 7, 198, and, on excluding others as "nonnatives" of one's city, 215.

60. For a more detailed exploration of this process, which I call "incarcerated space," of restricting the mobility of collective farmers in the USSR and minorities in the United States in order to contain their access to public welfare and opportunities for social mobility, see Brown, "Out of Solitary Confinement: The History of the Gulag," *Kritika: Explorations in Russian and Eurasian History* 8(1) (Winter 2007).

61. Scholars of the postwar Soviet Union have in the past few years found a surprising degree of affirmation among citizens for Soviet values of equity and justice among citizens. This is a main point of Alexei Yurchak's book. Sergei Zhuk finds that even young "resisters" who bought and sold black market rock music read into the Beatle's lyrics meanings about the justice and truth not of the West but of Soviet society. Serhy Yekelchyk finds Soviet citizens in Kyiv engaged in local elections as if the elections were not a sham. See Alexei Yurchak, *Everything Was Forever, Until It Was No More: The Last Soviet Generation* (Princeton, NJ: Princeton University Press: 2005); Sergei Zhuk, *Rock and Roll in the Rocket City: The West, Identity, and Ideology in Soviet Dniepropetrovsk, 1960–1985* (Washington, DC, Woodrow Wilson Institute Press, 2010); and Yekelchyk, "A Communal Model of Citizenship in Stalinist Politics: Agitators and Voters in Postwar Electoral Campaigns (Kyiv, 1946–53)," *Ab Imperio*, summer 2010, no. 2. On the

increasing affirmation of American society as the model for equity and opportunity, see Wall, *Inventing the American Way*, and Cohen, *A Consumers' Republic*. On the vigorous clandestine campaign to promote this image abroad, see Frances Stonor Saunders, *The Cultural Cold War: The CIA and the World of Arts and Letters* (New York: New Press, 1999). For evidence that white Americans continue to fail to see discrimination based on race in pursuit of education, jobs, and housing, see Susan Page and William Risser, "Poll: Racial Divide Narrowing But Persists," *USA Today*, July 23, 2008.

62. From more than 200 million curies of radioactive isotopes, the landscapes surrounding Hanford and Maiak qualify as two of the most irradiated territories on the planet. Stephen I. Schwartz, ed., *Atomic Audit: The Costs and Consequences of U.S. Nuclear Weapons Since 1940* (Washington, DC: Brookings Institution Press, 1998). On the more banal but just as costly price of suburban sprawl, see Andrés Duany, Elizabeth Plater-Zyberk, and Jeff Speck, *Suburban Nation: The Rise of Sprawl and the Decline of the American Dream* (New York: North Point Press, 2000); Dolores Hayden, *A Field Guide to Sprawl* (New York: Norton, 2004); Elizabeth A. Johnson and Michael W. Klemens, eds. *Nature in Fragments: The Legacy of Sprawl* (New York: Columbia University Press, 2005). On Soviet environmental degradation, see Jonathan D. Oldfield, *Russian Nature: Exploring the Environmental Consequences of Societal Change* (Burlington, VT: Ashgate, 2006).

3

"Knife in the Water"

*The Struggle over Collective Consumption in
Urbanizing Poland*

Kacper Pobłocki

Two commonplace assumptions about consumption in the Eastern
Bloc remain largely uncontested in our understanding of the processes that took place in the postwar period. The first is that, fueled by
a general dearth of consumer goods, individual consumption dominated consumption patterns in the region. The second is that socialist
societies remained largely underurbanized since resources and state
priorities favored industrialization.[1] Yet many socialist states did experience a success of sorts by rapidly turning societies that for centuries
had remained deeply rural into urbanized ones. Moving beyond these
assumptions thereby allows us to see what took place far more consistently: urbanization and its concomitant organization of collective consumption. Urban collective consumption might not always have been
of the "glittering" variety, but it lies at the very heart of an emergent
postwar Eastern Europe.

It was as true of the East as it was of the West: in response to the
underconsumption of the 1930s, postwar cities turned increasingly
Keynesian. This meant, as David Harvey has argued, that their "social,
economic and political life [was now] organized around the theme of
state-backed, debt-financed consumption." The result of this was a radical shift in group identities and alliances. No longer were class alliances
the principle organizing feature of urban politics. Instead, identities coalesced around "themes of consumption, distribution, and the production and control of space."[2] Indeed, the urban crises of the 1960s can be
seen as marking this shift toward a "new form of the class struggle."[3]

This global transformation was by no means restricted to the West and can best be understood as a move away from "supply-side" (production-driven) toward "demand-side" (consumption-based) urbanization. "The urban question," Manuel Castells famously argued, "refers to the organization of the means of collective consumption at the basis of the daily life of all social groups: housing, education, health, culture, commerce, transport."[4] This chapter discusses how the urban question was central to the social conflicts of the 1960s, how the struggles over urban space and collective consumption fed into the dramatic events of 1968, and how all this left an indelible mark on contemporary Polish society.

Despite the fact that, as it is often argued, the West in 1968 "turned a deaf ear to rumblings of discontent in Warsaw or Prague,"[5] there are reasons to see events on both sides of the Iron Curtain as related: in both cases, we can understand the urban crises of the 1960s as a clash between conflicting visions of what constituted meaningful urban life. Indeed, 1968 breathed political life into Henri Lefebvre's notion of the "right to the city," which claimed that urban dwellers have the right to shape the space around them.[6] Poland's 1968 was largely experienced as massive anti-Semitic rallies and a media campaign of anti-Zionist scaremongering that resulted in purges within the state apparatus (the Party, universities, administration, media, army, and the like) and the expulsion of more than twenty thousand people from the country. The Polish 1968 was a massive attempt at "state capture," performed by those who felt disenfranchised by what they saw as a metropolitan, cosmopolitan, "neobourgeois," and self-serving elite. The symbolic figure of the Jew tied all these attributes together and hence came in handy for propagandists who exploited social grievances that were aggravated throughout the 1960s. One cannot understand the peculiarity of the Polish 1968 without analyzing how such cleavages emerged in the course of struggles throughout the 1960s over the right to the city. This, in turn, is contingent on understanding the peculiar role the state played in urban expansion.

Capitalist suburbanization was achieved mainly thanks to the automobile and home ownership; in the socialist East, it was (largely, but not exclusively) based on public transit and cooperative housing developments. Yet this difference, East and West, was not necessarily parallel to an emphasis on the public versus the private. There would have been no automobile culture in the United States, for example, had there not been state subsidies of oil or a centrally financed interstate motorway system. By the same token, expansion of "public" housing in the socialist Bloc generated new strategies for appropriation of public space for private means. On the whole, in other words, the very same

FIGURE 3.1.   The old and the new, side-by-side in Łódź's inner city. Author's collection.

general development toward urban Keynesianism invited contrasting particular solutions on both sides of the Iron Curtain. Together, they constituted different facets of the urban crisis of the 1960s.

These developments were especially visible in the Polish city of Łódź, a major industrial hub, where the events of 1968 were particularly dramatic. Here, the roots of the conflict lay in the postwar spatial transformation, notably in the pattern of Łódź's suburbanization and consequent tensions over the means of collective consumption. Public grievances over social mobility were tied to concurrent displays of conspicuous consumption (particularly centered around private leisure) as well as to consumption of urban (and "public") amenities such as water.

Knife in the Water

Film director Roman Polański's 1962 feature debut, *Knife in the Water*, spoke directly to these very issues. In the same way as he would later portray the Los Angeles "water conspiracy" in *Chinatown* (1974), Polański brilliantly revealed how new social cleavages had arisen in postwar Poland from the struggles over collective consumption.[7] In the film, water—consumed not only for basic needs but also for leisure—becomes a powerful symbolic vehicle for articulating pent-up grievances. It played on the common yet difficult-to-translate Polish phrase, often evoked in public debates of the 1960s, *jesteśmy narodem na dorobku*: "we are still a nation of upstarts" or "as a nation we are still getting ourselves established materially."

The film describes how a successful journalist and his attractive wife, off for a sailing weekend, pick up a student hitchhiker in their posh automobile and later bring him onboard. A continuous rivalry between the two men is the film's main dynamic. The older man, who has already "established himself materially," seems to have a perpetual need to prove himself and his grit and comes up with countless dares. His ego is shattered when the younger man proves to be his superior in both audacity and cunning. The callow youngster, however, ultimately does not wish to denounce or ridicule the smug older man; quite the contrary, he is here to shamelessly take his place. The two male characters are, in effect, one—only in separate stages of life. "You want to be like him," the seduced wife tells her young lover. "And don't you worry—you will be, if you've got enough nerve."

Knife in the Water managed to capture two popular notions of the time. First, the rift between those who had already "established themselves materially" and those who had not was more a matter of cunning than of some "objective" criteria; and second, there might not be enough space for everybody on the ladder of upward mobility. As one of Poland's best film critics, Maria Kornatowska, pointed out in 1963, Polański "revealed with brutal honesty that we are becoming a nation of philistines," and that "the new social stratification is based upon the distribution of television sets and automobiles." Polański's film, she argued, was the very first serious "polemic with the cult of refrigerators and television sets."[8]

Yet as more and more Poles were getting established materially, critiquing these changes was an increasingly thankless task. The fruits of this national stampede to get established materially emerged in the 1970s during the decade of "socialist consumerism." It was in this period, a leading dissident recalled, when "I got scared of Poles for the first time, as they had been largely bought off by the system."[9] Usually this aspect of socialist consumerism is seen as having emerged in full force after two decades of isolation from the consumer-rich West, ignited by exposure to the wonders of the Western window display. The structure of socialist consumer "desire," however, cannot be merely reduced to this; it was also anchored in deep internal social tensions arising from a postwar social mobility that became clearly visible by the 1960s.

Using consumption to cajole Poles into "amicable cooperation" with the authorities had already begun in 1947. Soon after the war, the communists, whose grip over the Polish population was weak at best, developed a strategy of marginalizing the prewar working-class elite, who in industrial cities such as Łódź were relatively hostile toward the Party, by promoting a young and unskilled labor force fresh from the countryside. This conflict dominated the wave of strikes between 1945 and 1947 that shook the city. Although the authorities found they could exert control over the "unruly youth" in the workplace, outside of it they were virtually powerless. As "hooliganism" became the bane of Stalinism, the disciplining of youth had to move beyond the realm of production. Hence, social conflict gradually expanded from the area of production to that of consumption, and the "Battle over Trade," a countrywide campaign launched in May 1947 to nationalize both retail and wholesale commerce as well as to combat price gouging, profiteering, embezzlement, and high prices on staple commodities, gradually absorbed the bulk of working-class discontent.[10]

Yet Battle over Trade did not prove to be a surrogate for shop floor politics. Rather, it revealed that social conflict could spread to consumer items—a trend exacerbated in subsequent decades. During the 1960s, the Polish period codified in both historiography and popular consciousness as one of "crude socialism" (siermiężny socjalizm), when general consumption rates were still significantly lower than they would be in the 1970s, collective consumption was an increasingly significant topic of public debate. The "thaw" of 1956 opened up a Pandora's box of grassroots discontents with the housing situation and, more generally, initiated public debate over urban reform. Socialist cities, the argument ran, were growing dangerous and unpleasant to live in, and the task ahead was to facilitate urban consumption for the wider public. This is how an urban planner explained the ideal of a socialist city:

> A city adequate to our political system is one where everybody has
> equal access to public services. All districts ought to be equally
> saturated with services of mass use, and they should have an equal
> access to unique services located in the city center. In a socialist city
> it is unthinkable to make some districts better and others worse with
> regard to access to services.[11]

Although the post-1956 urban boom was in part a reaction to inequalities in access to urban amenities inherited from the prewar era and the Stalinist period, the objective of equal access was hardly ever met in practice.

Temporary liberalization of the press (curbed again in 1963) allowed journalists to disclose the previously hidden "dark sides" of Stalinist urbanization. The local weekly in Łódź, called *Odgłosy* (The Echo), founded in 1958, followed this national trend. Workers' hostels, for example, previously enshrined in propaganda, were described as "pockets of demoralization," populated by boys and girls "overwhelmed by the whirl of play, pleasures, and unrefined love affairs," who instead of attending evening schools "immersed themselves in the pleasures of metropolitan life."[12] Soon it became clear that the only way to contain the unruly youths was to turn workers into parents—which, given that the fresh migrants from the countryside had started establishing families themselves, could be seen as responding to popular needs. The post-1956 public debate made a clear link between juvenile delinquency and the housing problem. If people stopped living in "inhumane conditions," and children were given their own rooms, or at least could sleep separately from their parents, then juvenile crime would decrease. In old inner-city tenements, two generations often shared sleeping space, and this was believed by some to be a source of demoralization among young people.[13] In the new suburban apartments, youths would have the proper conditions to do their homework, which would mean fewer dropouts, and the school, together with official youth organizations, would be more effective in organizing youngsters' leisure time.[14]

This campaign was accompanied by the promotion of quasi-consumerist suburban lifestyles and the beginning of popular mass culture, both of which were intended to bolster the role of the family as the "elementary unit" of society. "Fridges, furniture, apartments are as difficult to divide as they are to get hold of," a journalist commented, further noting how suburbanization was bringing down the divorce rate: "Washing machines and the television set strengthen the solid character of the family-centered structure of the whole society. They create a new type of a cage, where people divided into families swarm with great enthusiasm. And objects such as the television set further solidify the family by closing it within the four walls."[15] In theory, getting established materially was a nationwide phenomenon, open to everybody. The fact that it was not accounts for the widespread view that the Polish 1960s were a period of "austere" or "crude" socialism, that is, one marked by deficiencies in consumption. Behind this belief lurks a more fundamental one: complaints about the low level of consumption during the 1960s were not about some universal absence of goods, but rather about some small, privileged groups having access to consumption items, while most of the rank and file did not.

This was as true of luxury items as of the more "ordinary" items of collective consumption, such as water.

Urban Waterscapes

The nationwide push to get established materially unfolded against the back-drop of often very local trajectories. Polański's film *Knife in the Water* mentions no city directly. But a close reading of local newspapers from 1960s Łódź reveals that Polański, a student of the Łódź Film School, perfectly captured the local "key symbol": water.[16] In the early nineteenth century, Łódź became "Poland's Manchester" precisely because of its springs, which made it the ideal location for water-powered manufacturing.[17] Later, when the steam engine took over, water continued to be consumed by the textile industry in enormous quantities. Eventually, depletion of water resources called for municipal action. Yet the industrial elite lobbied to prevent the city from partaking in the all-European "era of reconstruction" that elsewhere erected municipal water and sewage networks.[18] As a result, from the very outset the "urbanization of water" unfolded in Łódź against the backdrop of exclusionary politics;[19] the dearth of clean water available to its residents became the hallmark of Łódź well into the socialist period.

A much-quoted passage about the city described how the "lymphatic chil-dren" of Łódź's slum district of Bałuty had never seen clean water, only "rain-bow-hued gutter slime," and whose main amusement was sailing paper boats, afloat alongside rats, in open sewers.[20] A similar image of a bone-dry landscape was evoked in the most famous book on Łódź, Władysław Reymont's *Promised Land* (1898). Here, the city is dominated by clouds of dust that "hovered over the lanes, begrimed the dwellings, destroyed every speck of verdure on the crooked, sapless trees, whose gnarled, twisted boughs bent over the fences or stretched before the houses like dry skeletons."[21] These dry "skeletal" patches were "guarded," as a journalist recalled of his prewar childhood in Łódź, "with utmost care, because they were the only enclaves of greenery, and even the most mischievous kids in the neighborhood would not dare to pick a leaf from them." Since parks then charged entry fees, children were confined to play in the contaminated landscape.[22] After 1945, parks were opened up to everybody, and the new housing developments had running water. But the problem was hardly solved.

Usage of running water in postwar Łódź certainly increased at a brisk pace: from 2.4 cubic meters per inhabitant in 1946 to 34.5 in 1968. Yet access to water remained highly uneven. By 1966, 63 percent of apartments in Łódź were connected to the water network (in other major Polish cities this varied between 80 and 90 percent), and only 33 percent had their own separate bathroom.[23] Of course, all of the new suburban housing projects were connected to the system, whereas in the former industrial-cum-residential districts the struggle over water between workers and industry continued. In the district of Chojny, *Odgłosy* reported, many working-class families took "Saturday family baths" (i.e., washed themselves in the very same bathwater, usually in order of seniority) because water was still purchased.[24] In Widzew, another "old" district, more than 250 old-fashioned wells with wooden cranes were still the major source of water in the 1960s. Yet many (around 12 percent of Łódź's population) could not access water even in this way, and they were serviced by municipal water trucks.[25]

An inhabitant of a detached house in the district of Widzew recalled that around the year 1950 water from his private well disappeared. He drilled a deeper one, but it lasted only a few years. Then a public well was drilled in the vicinity of his house, but that too quickly dried up. In 1984, the year when he was interviewed, carrying plastic barrels every day to the place where water trucks arrived was the only way he could obtain water.[26] As water consumption in Łódź doubled every five years, by the late 1960s pundits spoke again of a dearth of water. Even people living on the highest floors of the new apartment blocks often had to walk to a downstairs neighbor to fill their water kettle.[27] Furthermore, the overall quality of water had in fact deteriorated. Tea brewed in Łódź, *Odgłosy* noted acerbically, "tasted of modernity—and more specifically of phenol," as water in the Pilica River (Łódź's primary water source since the 1950s) was contaminated by adjacent factories.[28] Only in 1974, when construction of a dam and an artificial lake in Sulejów was finally completed, did Łódź gain new access to fresh water. With this, the water crisis was somewhat mitigated,[29] only to return with a vengeance in the mid-1980s.[30]

Water was essential for more than satisfying the most elementary human needs. It was not only consumed for drinking or hygiene but also represented the most desirable recreation. Perhaps because of the special place of water in the industrial relations of the textile city, the favored form of leisure for the Łódź working class was a family picnic next to a water reservoir. The significance of water for textile workers is illustrated by a grassroots initiative during the peak of the urban boom to turn an old park into a recreational complex 170 hectares large and equipped with a waterpark to accommodate four thousand people.[31] Not incidentally, when the park was closed down in 1992, the surge of "nostalgia" for the socialist past focused on the old waterpark and the lost accessibility to on-water leisure in the urban milieu. During the post-2004 wave of reindustrialization and urban renewal in Łódź, a foreign investor erected

Poland's largest waterpark in place of the old socialist one. The symbolic significance of water was enormous; the happy ending to a popular 1970s television
series, *Daleko od Szosy* (Away from the Bustle), which unfolded in Łódź, was
played out in a poetic swimming pool scene. When the 2009 financial crisis set
in and the developer announced the waterpark might be closed, the Łódź Council decided to buy up all the shares. Today the recreational complex is again
entirely publicly owned.

In the 1960s, people traveled mainly by foot or public transport and so
could not go much beyond the vicinity of Łódź for their Sunday trips. Water
usage for recreational purposes in Łódź was therefore highly stratified. Open-
air swimming pools were mainly frequented by well-to-do youths, sportsmen,
actors, journalists, and lawyers—*Odgłosy* reported—and for the most part
workers swam in a pond in one of Łódź's main parks.[32] In fact, it was in one of
Łódź's swimming pools where Polański met the previously unknown actress
who would play the part of the beautiful wife in *Knife in the Water*.[33] While the
small car-owning elite could go out to the countryside, soon yachting became
the most fashionable form of leisure. *Odgłosy* wrote a year before Polański's
film was released that

> until yesterday, the automobile, scooter or motorcycle was the most
> attention-grabbing gimmick. Nowadays, urban life is tight and sti-
> fling. The ring around the city has become overcrowded with tourists
> too. Where is one to have real rest? The answer is: on the water!
> Solitude, the chance to get drawn away from the world's nuisances
> for a few days or even weeks guaranteed! This modern form of
> leisure is now being promoted all over the world.[34]

The yacht and the automobile were the instruments that allowed the protagonists in the *Knife in the Water* to appropriate water for leisure. On their
yacht, they alone seem to consume the vast lake and its beauty. As Lefebvre
argued, the nascent postwar technocratic elite embraced the consumption of
suburban leisure; turned away from the working classes and the "noise, fatigue,
and concentrationary universe of cities"; and made nature into "the separate
place of pleasure and the retreat of 'creativity.'"[35]

The Automobile and Suburbanization

Separation of the place of work from the place of residence became one of the
hallmarks of modern urban life. This seemingly banal detail had profound
consequences for contemporary political life.[36] Demand-side urban expansion

further exacerbated this trend; whereas earlier, mobility was largely a middle-class prerogative, and the working classes were essentially "fixed" in place, traveling to work by foot, the increased role of mass transit further divorced the place of work from the place of residence. This meant that the masses were increasingly "freed" from their local community and started inhabiting more than one place of the city. The erstwhile "urban villagers" gradually turned into full-fledged urbanites, whose allegiance to a single neighborhood (of their residence) grew increasingly loose. As a result, mobility became an important part of the urban experience. But access to it was ever more dependent on one's "pull" with the state authorities who decided how collective consumption was to be organized.

One pundit, who waxed enthusiastically about the emergent Polish "automobile fever," noted that Americans "claim that the twentieth century has discovered a new freedom that the human race should strive for (except for the freedom from hunger, fear, penury, war etc.)—the freedom of movement."[37] "It is hard not to realize," noted another journalist, "that the automobile has become one of the most important measures of one's social worth. If there is an automobile owner amongst the new inhabitants of a housing development (who do not otherwise know one another yet), then his neighbors will speculate and come up with wild conjectures about him being 'a somebody' [to musi być ktoś]."[38] The automobile expressed the possibility of escaping from the community and of finding a safe, isolated haven solely for private pleasures. The yacht represented even higher status than the automobile—but certainly one could never go for a weekend of sailing without a private automobile. By 1963, therefore, owning a car was no longer sufficient to place its owner at the very top of the hierarchy. The dynamic of escalating competitive consumption could be found elsewhere too: initially an apartment in a housing development was a status symbol, but at the point when it became widely available to the population, more and more voices could be heard (beginning as early as 1969) that described such dwellings as "noisy" and "crowded," and that argued a detached house in a "real" suburb was the ideal dwelling for the socialist middle classes.

Nevertheless, in the 1960s still, Łódź's nascent *crème de la crème* were content to reside in a housing development named Włada Bytomska. This is also where the unscripted prelude (in a sense) to Polański's film was played out. One of the main protagonists of this real-life drama was Leon Niemczyk, the actor who would later play the well-to-do journalist in the film, who was a resident of this "posh" housing development and an automobile owner. This elite housing estate was located in the former slum Jewish district of Bałuty. Unlike others in the city, the district had been destroyed during the war and thus was ripe for urban redevelopment. The suburbanization of Łódź started with renewal of Bałuty. Yet the change from old, dilapidated, inner-city tenements to new suburban housing projects, where all forms of collective consumption (water, electricity, gas, etc.) were available, was not experienced by everyone as a bonus or privilege.[39] In many cases, Łódź's working-class sociability was destroyed by this suburbanization. In fact, members of a single community were purposely given apartments in different parts of the new city so that old solidarities could not be brought to the new apartment complexes. Initially, the working-class community resisted the changes, but by the 1960s the grit and distinctiveness of the old urban community had been substantially diluted, and a spirit of envy eclipsed that of defiance—the attitude of Polański's hitchhiker being a case in point.

Although during the 1970s many of the housing developments were erected literally on empty fields, in Bałuty new apartment blocks were initially built among war ruins and dilapidated capitalist tenements. Włada Bytom-ska, dubbed the "symbol of great hope," was to be everything that the once-capitalist Łódź was not. It was peopled with Łódź's best: all of its thirty-seven hundred residents had been carefully selected as exemplary workers and citizens. No one had moved there from the ruined old tenements, notorious for their unedifying character, and no one was an alcoholic. Or, to be precise, one of the inhabitants had a drinking problem when working for a private company, but living in this new milieu served as the best therapy; "the ambience of the housing development cured him."[40] Forty percent of inhabitants were classified as working-class, and 60 percent as members of the intelligentsia. Here, *Odgłosy* claimed, prewar class divisions were becoming obsolete:

> The intelligentsia and the proletariat dwelling here are actually of
> the same ilk. Both are reliable employees, both plan their families
> responsibly, both are frugal and scrimp and save in order to get estab-
> lished materially. Even their tastes are increasingly alike, only that in
> one apartment there is a kitschy oleograph, and in the other there is
> a modern folk-styled plate, hanging on the wall above the ubiquitous
> television set. . . . Furniture is nearly identical in all the apartments:
> rather expensive, heavy, with no modern flamboyance. There is a
> dining room and a bedroom in each apartment. The only exceptions
> are the apartments of the artists and other members of the 'creative
> intelligentsia' [*inteligencja twórcza*], represented in droves here.[41]

This was not entirely true. As sociological surveys confirmed, working-class sociability was centered around the kitchen, and they preferred to share living space with other family members; the intelligentsia, on the other hand, had a preference for living in apartments where everybody had their "own" room. The houses built in the 1960s in Poland, where living space was divided into tiny rooms, were clearly fashioned after the intelligentsia's tastes.[42]

What distinguished Włada Bytomska from other places in Łódź and made it the ideal location for the new cultural elite was not only its new amenities but also its location. It was referred to as a "housing development where one can breathe," a place where "industrial odors do not reach, and the vivid colors of the plaster are not dampened by the dust from metropolitan thoroughfares."[43] It was a suburban paradise—especially desired by the creative intelligentsia, such as writers, journalists, or composers, who often worked at home and required peace and quiet for their labors. Although not in the midst of the over-crowded inner city and its noisy street life, Włada Bytomska was right next to a new highway leading to and from Warsaw. Hence it also became Łódź's most "representative district" precisely because it could change the stereotypes Var-sovians held about Łódź. Arriving by car from Warsaw, they would first see this "wide highway, an interesting panorama of the city and the colorful houses."[44] It was living proof that "Łódź was getting richer" and that it could now "cast off that fetid capitalist cloak of the past" in becoming a "colorful socialist city."[45] Although being located right next to a major highway is today considered a nuisance rather than a privilege, at the turn of the 1950s and 1960s, when there were only around thirty-eight hundred automobiles in the whole of Łódź (of which eight hundred were company-owned and a further nine hundred served as taxis), having direct access to Warsaw was especially attractive to the creative intelligentsia, who often traveled between Warsaw and Łódź.

Włada Bytomska was both suburban and very central; thus, while enjoying the peace of the suburbs and the amenities of the housing projects, the creative intelligentsia could also travel by foot to the cultural institutions located in the center of the city. This was not gentrification in the strict sense of the word (as in high-income residents moving into old neighborhoods, thereby triggering revitalization of old housing stock), but it was clearly linked to the remaking of the Old Town District (*Dzielnica Staromiejska*), a part of Bałuty that was now being revamped to resemble Krakow's and Warsaw's historic old centers, which Łódź, a city largely formed in the nineteenth century and marked by a grid structure, clearly lacked.[46] Bałuty used to be the district of lymphatic children, but now some of its streets, and especially the Old Town Market (*Rynek Staro-miejski*), "resemble[d] pictures from photography albums on Warsaw," *Odgłosy* wrote, promoting Łódź's new cultural spaces as the ideal site for a romantic stroll.[47] The suburbanization of Łódź implied that the inner city was losing its erstwhile industrial and residential role and was becoming an artifact of con-sumption. Young professionals living in the refashioned Bałuty were to become the bellwether of that cultural change. The widening social rift between the residents of Włada Bytomska (a veritable forerunner of gated communities) and the "regular" Łódź population soon became associated with the marginalization of Łódź as a whole within Poland's cultural, political, and economic space—which would be the very context for the social unrest of 1968.

Playgrounds for the Elite

Automobiles stirred highly contentious emotions precisely because they were both the mark and the instrument of social isolation, symbolizing appropriation of public spaces for private ends. In Łódź this was played out in conflicts over garage space. Already in 1959, when cars in Łódź were not yet a common sight, and when street space was still dominated by pedestrians, the twin problems of parking and garage space had emerged. There were officially only eight hundred garages in Łódź—and often car owners had to travel a long distance (by public transport) to get to a garage located far away from their place of residence. In 1960, the state authorities announced their support for the "healthy civic initiative" of building private garages. *Odgłosy* quickly picked up on this, even printing detailed sketches and cost estimates for those who desired to build them.

This was perhaps the reason a group of four "creative intellectuals" from Włada Bytomska (including the actor Leon Niemczyk, from Polański's film) wrote a letter to the Łódź authorities that was then reprinted in the press. They had been granted permission to build garages, but then the permission was revoked. "We feel we're being treated like criminals," they wrote. "Not only are we guilty of buying automobiles—now we are also guilty of demanding some garage space for them." They explained: "It is enough for a single neighbor to oppose such a construction for the permission to be withdrawn automatically." "The social climate," they continued,

> is unfortunately such that an automobile-owning citizen is a victim of
> local envy and his every step is carefully watched by the neighbors . . .
> the local, traditional and backward public opinion [*opinia magla i
> podwórka*] that usurps the mantles of the administration has a power-
> ful influence on what kind of decisions are made. Often authorities
> surrender to the demagogy that automobiles "ruin the air," "make
> noise," or "pose a threat to children."[48]

Odgłosy recognized their right to the garage space and wholeheartedly supported their plea.

Yet protests over the garages continued. "Early in the morning," those living in the tenements of Bałuty, the district's longtime residents, purportedly "pour[ed] dirty waste water under the windows of the apartment blocks."[49] The inhabitants of the new blocks responded in kind: in the morning they too "wait in ambush by their windows so they can chase away 'the rabble' coming with bucketsful of dishwater."[50] On the surface, it seemed to be a conflict between the old and new inhabitants of Bałuty, divided by their different "attitudes" toward modernity and change. Indeed, many journalists noted the strained relations between the two groups. Those living in the weather-beaten tenements "look[ed] up to the block residents [blokowi]: to their material standing, their lifestyle, their peaceful way of life," whereas the new inhabitants "did not really notice" what they called "the rabble" (hołota). "When I'm looking at these two distinct universes," the journalist Julian Brysz noted, "then maybe an ungrounded but certainly a lucid fear comes over me—the fear that the affluence of the new inhabitants may usher in some enduring forms of separation and egoism."[51]

It seemed for many that this was why the "rabble" opposed the building of garages. But the reasons were in fact more complex. The new inhabitants might well have wished to "prohibit their children from visiting friends who dwell in the dirty hovels," but the so-called rabble longed "for the times when everybody was equally poor, when nobody called anyone else rabble, when all children had parents living in similar houses, and when weddings were celebrated by the entire street."[52] Yet it soon turned out that some of the new inhabitants of Bałuty also opposed the building of garages, and they did so for reasons other than sheer envy. They argued the garages would take up space that should be designated for children's playgrounds. If Niemczyk and others built their garages, they argued in a letter to Odgłosy, some hundred or so children would be deprived of playing space. The four men, the letter read, "placed automobiles above human beings."[53]

A venerable institution also stood behind them and their claims: the Association for Children's Welfare (Towarzystwo Przyjaciół Dzieci, the TPD), a nongovernmental organization formed in 1949 with significant prewar roots and enduring moral clout. A journalistic investigation revealed the TPD had been very active in organizing extracurricular activities for the children of Bałuty because, in many ways, the children's circumstances had not changed much since the war. "The air smells of gasoline, rotten cabbage and steppe grass," Odgłosy reported. Children still had no playing space and spent most of their time on the dangerous streets, playing next to barrels with decomposing rubbish. Those who wanted to use the space between apartment blocks for their own garages favored privatization of space and championed the "splendid isolation" from the rest of the community. Others, however, still embraced a vision of urban life that was public and open and harked back to the old inner-city neighborhood-based sociability. Their vision for the urban future—based on the tacit assumption that the lot of the "lymphatic children" was a public and not a private (i.e., family) matter—was deeply anchored in the capitalist experience of Łódź. Throughout the 1960s, such working-class visions were increasingly on the wane; one might well say that today they have vanished altogether.

Conclusion

It may seem counter-intuitive to think of socialist-era apartment blocks as suburbia—and, indeed, at first glance, they have little resemblance to the American tract developments of detached houses surrounded by well-trimmed lawns. Yet there is a distinct correlation between the urban processes on both sides of the Iron Curtain, and it lies in the social linchpin of spatial processes. The American suburban expansion that unfolded between 1945 and the late 1970s produced a distinctive landscape (and a distinctive way of life attached to it) that represented a break from older European urban forms, as well as standing in stark contrast to "ways of life" promoted (at least officially) in the Soviet Bloc.[54] Yet postwar cities, East and West, both being a product of urban Keynesianism, displaced working-class communities and, despite grassroots resistance in both cases, increased social exclusion and restructuring. Still, the processes of social polarization unfolded in East and West according to differing spatial logic.

The shift from production-driven to consumption-driven urbanization did not necessarily entail building more equitable cities. Suburban expansion already bore the germs of what is known as "parasitic urbanization"—a model of urban expansion fueled on social exclusion and spatialization of social differences.[55] In the United States, this was manifest in the racialization of space and the increasingly sharp distinctions between white middle-class suburbs and black working-class inner cities. Race was not the central category in the shaping of socialist cities, where spatial pathways toward exclusion took a different turn. Instead, the new social cleavages coalesced around consumption items, especially around the issue of collective consumption.

The Polish 1968 was a rebellion against figures, such as the cocksure journalist in Polański's film, whose top positions in the (broadly conceived) state administration privileged their path toward getting materially established and gaining access to consumption items. Members of the creative intelligentsia—included in this category of the elite and residing in the new showcase apartment blocks of Bałuty—became objects of particularly virulent attacks (in Łódź, this centered on the Film School, the alleged "hotbed of arrogance"). Popular accusations of cosmopolitanism and "detachment" from the rank and file were the most important components of the anti-Zionist rhetoric of 1968, and they need to be embedded in the context of the 1960s. The centrality of water in the social conflict, so well captured in Polański's poignant film, stemmed from its links to the consumption of leisure, the automobile, and the use of urban space, but it was also a peculiarity of Łódź. Likewise, Włada Bytomska, the privileged apartment complex, as both a spatial and a social form was largely an outcome of many local forces at play, yet coupled with developments being experienced across Poland.

The web of forces that produced Włada Bytomska has vanished. Today, it no longer exists as a separate administrative unit in Łódź and has even disappeared from maps and vernacular spatial consciousness. Yet all of Poland's future urban processes can be found here in a microcosm. Although in the 1960s the "colorful" and modern Włada Bytomska was considered urban eye candy, today a passerby would be hard put to differentiate it from other dull and nondescript socialist housing developments. In the 1980s, the seat of the city's elite moved geographically, to the so-called Manhattan of Łódź, a high-rise housing development in the very center of the city, and more recently to scattered gated communities and suburban villas. Yet, as one Polish geographer noted, after the fall of state socialism "affluent areas became more affluent, whereas poor ones grew poorer"; that is, the *making* of these spaces occurred precisely during the socialist urban boom.[56] The social processes of spatial segregation and private appropriation of public space, already so visible in Włada Bytomska, were only aggravated in the decades that followed. From the urban point of view, in other words, 1989 did not constitute a major watershed. Looking at postwar Poland through the lens of urban studies, a different narrative emerges altogether, one in which postsocialist developments had already been "inscribed in space."[57]

NOTES

This chapter is based on a doctoral dissertation defended in June 2010 at the Central European University. I am very grateful to my dissertation committee, and especially to my external advisors Michał Buchowski and Neil Smith, for their continued support, guidance, and comments, which have helped to shape both my research and the argument that emerged from it.

1. Iván Szelényi, "Cities Under Socialism—and After," in *Cities After Socialism: Urban and Regional Change and Conflict in Post-Socialist Societies*, eds. Gregory D. Andrusz, Michael Harloe, and Iván Szelényi (Cambridge, MA: Blackwell, 1996), 294–97.

2. David Harvey, *The Urban Experience* (Oxford: Blackwell, 1989), 37–38.

3. Alain Touraine, as quoted in Charles Tilly, *The Rebellious Century, 1830–1930* (London: Dent, 1975), 23.

4. Manuel Castells, *City, Class, and Power* (New York: St. Martin's Press, 1982), 3. Manuel Castells, *The Castells Reader on Cities and Social Theory*, ed. Ida Susser (Malden, MA: Blackwell, 2002), 107–8.

5. Tony Judt, *Postwar: A History of Europe Since 1945* (New York: Penguin Press, 2005), 421–22.

6. Peter Marcuse, "From Critical Urban Theory to the Right to the City," *City* (June 2009): 185–97.

7. Mike Davis, *City of Quartz: Excavating the Future in Los Angeles* (New York: Vintage Books, 1990), 114.

8. Maria Kornatowska, "Antyfelieton" [An anti-column], *Odgłosy* 21 (1962): 3.

9. Jacek Kuroń and Jacek Żakowski, *PRL Dla Początkujących* [Socialist Poland for Beginners] (Wrocław: Wydawnictwo Dolnośląskie, 1995), 146–47.

10. Padraic Kenney, *Rebuilding Poland: Workers and Communists, 1945–1950* (Ithaca, NY: Cornell University Press, 1997).

11. Marian Benko, "Miasto przyszłości" [The city of the future], *Odgłosy* 4 (1966): 1, 3.

12. Czesław Garda and Władysław Rymkiewicz, "Tak zwany Pekin" [So-called *Pekin*], *Odgłosy* 37 (1958): 8; Tadeusz Szewera, "Kobiety z hotelu" [Women from the hostel], *Odgłosy* 20 (1958): 3.

13. 61 percent of all apartments in Łódź were single-room. See Adam Ginsbert, *Łódź: stadium monograficzne* [A monographic study of Łódź] (Łódź: Wydawnictwo Lodzkie, 1962), 138.

14. Wiesław Jażdżyński, "O luzakach . . ." [On the loose youth], *Odgłosy* 17 (1958): 2.

15. Zbigniew Chyliński, "Rodzina jak ją widzę" [Family as I see it], *Odgłosy* 41 (1960): 1, 4.

16. Sherry B. Ortner, "On Key Symbols," *American Anthropologist* (Oct. 1973): 1338–46.

17. Jan Fijałek and Ryszard Rosin, eds., *Łódź: Dzieje Miasta* [The History of Łódź] (Warsaw: PWN, 1980), 34–43.

18. Andrew Lees and Lynn Hollen Lees, *Cities and the Making of Modern Europe, 1750–1914* (Cambridge: Cambridge University Press, 2008).

19. Erik Swyngedouw, *Social Power and the Urbanization of Water: Flows of Power* (Oxford: Oxford University Press, 2004), 80–101.

20. Julian Tuwim, *Kwiaty Polskie* (Warsaw: Czytelnik, 1975), 36–37.

21. Wladyslaw Stanislaw Reymont, *The Promised Land* (New York: Knopf, 1927), 387.

22. Henryk Polak, "Gramy o zielone" [The greenery games], *Odgłosy* 20 (1973): 5.

23. Halina Mortimer-Szymczak, ed., *Łódź: Rozwój Miasta W Polsce Ludowej* [Łódź in Socialist Poland] (Warsaw: PWN, 1970), 104.

24. Roman Łoboda, "Na Lelewela łódki płyną" [Gutter boats], *Odgłosy* 46 (1961): 1, 6.

25. Andrzej Jarosławski, "Woda (to nie dotyczy treści)" [All about water], *Odgłosy* 35 (1959): 1, 5.

26. Danuta Halladin, *Łódzki życiorys* [A life in Łódź] (Warsaw: Wytwórnia Filmów Dokumentalnych, 1984).

27. Feliks Bąbol, "Bitwa o wielką wodę" [The battle for water], *Odgłosy* 31 (1971): 3.

28. Polak, "Gramy o zielone."

29. Teresa Wojciechowska, "Dlaczego jest potrzebny wodociąg Sulejów-Łódź" [Why the Sulejów-Łódź water system is essential], *Odgłosy* 33 (1968): 5; Feliks Bąbol, "Co zagraża miastu?" [What's the biggest danger?], *Odgłosy* 31 (1965): 1, 4; and Jan Bąbiński, "Batalia o zalew" [The battle for the reservoir], *Odgłosy* 31 (1974): 1, 11.

30. Eugeniusz Iwanicki, "Kiedy woda na kartki?" [Rationing water?] *Odgłosy* 41 (1986): 1, 5; Roman Kubiak, "Gwóźdź do trumny made in Łódź" [A nail to the coffin made in Łódź], *Odgłosy* 36 (1986): 1, 6; and Roman Kubiak, "Stan klęski" [A disaster], *Odgłosy* 32 (1985): 1, 6.

31. Andrzej Makowiecki, "Białe wygrywa, czarne przegrywa" [White wins, black loses], *Odgłosy* 25 (1975): 7; and Andrzej Makowiecki, "Zdrowie—wizja przyszłości" [Zdrowie park: a vision of the future], *Odgłosy* 32 (1972): 1, 3, 8.

32. Andrzej Makowiecki, "Żabką, crawlem i po piesku" [Breaststroke, backstroke, and crawl], *Odgłosy* 31 (1965): 3.

33. Jacek Szczerba, "Spieprzaj do Hollywood" [Get the f—out to Hollywood], *Gazeta Wyborcza* (Oct. 6, 2009): 12–13.

34. Wiesław Machejko, "Żeglarze z miasta Łodzi" [Sailors from Łódź], *Odgłosy* 18 (1960): 3.

35. Henri Lefebvre, *Writings on Cities*, trans. and ed. Eleonore Kofman and Elizabeth Lebas (Cambridge, MA: Blackwell, 1996), 157–58.

36. Ira Katznelson, *City Trenches: Urban Politics and the Patterning of Class in the United States* (New York: Pantheon Books, 1981).

37. Kazimierz Dziewanowski, "Głód nowej wolności" [Hunger for the new freedom], *Odgłosy* 49 (1959): 5.

38. Bogda Madej, "Komu samochód?" [Who wants a car?], *Odgłosy* 14 (1968): 5. This perception was in part due to widespread recognition that the only way for a "regular citizen" to obtain an automobile was through a state-run lottery.

39. To borrow E. P. Thompson's phrase; *The Making of the English Working Class* (London: Penguin Books, 1980), 231.

40. Julian Brysz, "Pod rajską jabłonią" [Living in clover], *Odgłosy* 28 (1961): 6, 7.

41. Ibid.

42. Andrzej Basista, *Betonowe dziedzictwo: Architektura w Polsce czasów komunizmu* (Warsaw: Wydaw. PWN, 2001), 70.

43. Brysz, "Pod rajską jabłonią."

44. Tadeusz Papier, "Miasto i ulica Liściasta" [The city and the Liściasta street], *Odgłosy* 11 (1960): 8.

45. Tadeusz Papier, Łodzianie 1960. Budowlani [The constructors of Łódź in 1960], *Odgłosy* 28 (1960): 4; and Jerzy Urbankiewicz, "Tak się zaczęło" [That's how it all began], *Odgłosy* 3 (1966): 3.

46. Especially the part of the Old Town rebuilt anew after the war, called Marien-sztat. See "Łódź i łodzianie" [Łódź and its residents], *Odgłosy* 4 (1958): 2; and Leszek Witczak, "Mała czarna" [A small coffee], *Odgłosy* 18 (1958): 3, 4.

47. Tadeusz Martyński, "Randka na Bałutach" [A date in Bałuty], *Odgłosy* 27 (1958): 5.

48. "List otwarty do Przewodniczącego Prezydium RN m. Łodzi" [An open letter], *Odgłosy* 17 (1961): 12.

49. Zbigniew Kwiatkowski, "Gdzie padają kule," in *Ucieczka Przedmieścia*, ed. Wiesław Jażdżyński (Łódź: Wydawnictwo Łódzkie, 1963), 47.

50. Ibid., 49.

51. Brysz, "Pod rajską jabłonią."

52. Kwiatkowski, "Gdzie padają kule," 49.

53. "Listy do redakcji" [Letters to the editors], *Odgłosy* 21 (1961): 12.

54. Robert A. Beauregard, *When America Became Suburban* (Minneapolis: University of Minnesota Press, 2006), 14.

55. Ibid., 97–100.

56. Grzegorz Węcławowicz, *Przestrzeń i społeczeństwo współczesnej Polski* [Polish contemporary society and space] (Warsaw: PWN, 2002), 76.

57. Węcławowicz, *Przestrzeń i społeczeństwo współczesnej Polski*, 76.

PART II

Quality Control

The question of the quality of consumer goods under communism has only recently attracted serious academic consideration. In spite of recent studies to the contrary, people continue to assume an overly bleak picture of communist goods and consumer opportunities—bad products, bad service, long lines.[1] Consumer desire was of the lowest priority, it is often assumed, in a system that dictated needs.[2] But as this volume and other new work in the field reveal, the selection and quality of goods in the region varied dramatically in time and space. Furthermore, as explored in depth in the following chapters, socialist regimes actively tracked and courted the consumer for much of the period. As Mary Neuburger's chapter demonstrates, some flagship industries such as Bulgaria's Bulgartabak were ultimately successful in responding to local tastes and preferences through market research, branding, and other techniques generally associated with capitalism. And, as Rossitza Guentcheva shows, it was not only in the privileged tobacco industry that quality was a concern for Bulgarian socialists. An entire infrastructure of quality control was in place in socialist Bulgaria as various institutes studied, mapped, and tried to improve the quality of socialist goods. There, as elsewhere in the Bloc, concerns with quality extended from design studios and research labs to production lines and retail venues.

Patrick Hyder Patterson's chapter on socialist department stores illustrates, for example, that "capitalist" technologies of display and distribution were deployed, with varying degrees of vigor, across the region. For Patterson, as for the other authors in this cluster, socialist engagement with the "West" looms large in issues of production and distribution of consumer goods. Competition with the West in the consumer realm was an overt aim of socialist regimes, as articulated in the notorious "kitchen debates" in 1959. In the famous American exhibition in Moscow that year, Nixon and

Khrushchev faced off in an imported and reconstructed "American kitchen," where they publicly quibbled over the merits of each system's ability to provide for its citizens.[3] It was in these years that Khrushchev openly expressed his intention for the communist East to "bury" the West by overtaking it in all fields (including standard of living) by 1980, when "ripe communism" would finally materialize. Socialist leaderships across the region—including nonaligned Yugoslavia—presented the consumer "good life" as a visible expression of socialist achievement, a quickening rather than an abandonment of revolutionary Marxist ideals. In practice, however, socialist utopian visions were pursued by whatever means possible, including open embrace of Western technologies.

In fact, even as socialist officials directed, enabled, encouraged, and discouraged particular cultures of consumption in the region, engagement with the West was a constant. New avenues of trade and exchange opened up under Khrushchev's policy of "peaceful coexistence," a departure from the intense postwar East-West divisions. As all three of these chapters explore, by the late 1950s socialist regimes were openly studying, tracking, and selectively incorporating Western technologies, methods, and designs for the purpose of building socialism.[4] Communists looking west, of course, was by no means new. Stalin also promoted "coexistence" with the capitalist world in the 1930s and openly appropriated "Western" means for socialist ends—such as Fordist methods of production and rationalization of distribution through the department store.[5] From early on, the Soviets were willing to separate form from content, importing Western technologies, methods, and designs for the purpose of building socialism.

But by the 1960s and 1970s the Iron Curtain was perforated by détente, and mutual discovery was facilitated by trade and technology transfer. Eastern European leadership and enterprise managers actively sought out Western technologies and consumer techniques and showcased their own progress abroad. Czechoslovakia made a splash at the 1958 World's Fair in Brussels with elaborate displays of innovative modernist designs.[6] Industrial and technical trade fairs, such as those held famously in the Czech city of Brno, and Plovdiv, Bulgaria, fostered this exchange on eastern turf. And by the 1960s and 1970s, trade with the West had grown substantially and companies such as Bulgaria's Bulgartabak even produced "Western" goods, like Marlboros and Winstons, in their own factories. Hence, not only were technologies appropriated but actual Western brands were produced, and local packaging—at least in part—emulated the style and polish of the West. At the same time, as Guentcheva and Neuburger illustrate, local research institutes went beyond mere "imitation" in pursuit of ever greater quality for local products. Indeed, contrary to history in hindsight, during the 1950s and 1960s especially, the superiority of the Western consumer model was by no means a foregone conclusion.[7]

As the following chapters reveal, by the 1960s and 1970s Western design, technologies, and retail methods were being employed to great advantage across the region. Neuburger explores how Bulgartabak used its own quality products and local expertise in conjunction with Western technologies to become a world-renowned enterprise, the toast of the tobacco world. And, as Patterson's chapter describes, the department store became a fixture in much of the communist world. As early as 1960, a British traveler claimed that one could live a month in Belgrade with its "bright and brisk" shops and lack of lines before "realizing that it is socialist."[8] Perhaps more surprisingly, the same traveler assessed the Bulgarian capital Sofia in 1961 in quite the same way: "but for the propaganda posters [also present in Yugoslavia] you would not know that you are in a socialist country." As he described it, the "shops are like shops anywhere," food and clothes are cheap and "adequate," ice cream and flowers are on offer in a city park full of Bulgarians relaxing in the sun.[9] Such relative parity may have prevailed in the early 1960s, but by the end of the 1960s Yugoslavia's more thorough embrace of Western aesthetics and goods would have been unmistakable. Travellers described Belgrade as swarming with "communist dandies" along with neon signs, advertisements, and Mercedes.[10]

Arguably, Western technologies and methods were employed to communist advantage, but they also opened up a Pandora's box. East Europeans were duly seduced by the Western goods they saw, held, and consumed firsthand or saw at trade fairs, on TV, and in packages sent by relatives or family members working abroad. Consumer desire was stirred, but not merely through glimpses of the West. These regimes had also created an expanded modern, urban consuming citizenry, in part with Western methods but also as a result of their own modernizing transformations. Furthermore, as these chapters show, socialist regimes actually stirred consumer longing through production and distribution of quality goods, newly spawned leisure venues, and institutions such as the department store. As Patterson argues, socialist business managers and planners believed that the retail store could be a vehicle of *socialist* distribution. In the end, however, department store tableaus of plenty revealed a new range of consumer possibilities. More pointedly, in leaner times—the 1980s in particular—their empty shelves put the bankruptcy of the system on display. In the final analysis, Western technologies and methods seem to have paradoxically prolonged and doomed the socialist system, both enabling the "good life" and whetting an appetite for ever-more-extensive consumer desires.

NOTES

1. See, for example, Adam Zwass, *From Failed Communism to Underdeveloped Capitalism: Transformation of Eastern Europe, the Post-Soviet Union, and China* (New York: Sharpe, 1995), 7.

2. Katherine Verdery, *What Was Socialism, and What Comes Next?* (Princeton, NJ: Princeton University Press, 1996), 25–28.

3. See Walter L. Hixson, *Parting the Curtain: Propaganda, Culture, and the Cold War, 1945–1961* (New York: Palgrave Macmillan, 1997).

4. Jukka Gronow, *Caviar with Champagne: Common Luxury and the Ideals of the Good Life in Stalin's Russia* (Oxford: Berg, 2003).

5. See, for example, Lewis Siegelbaum, *Cars for Comrades: The Life of the Soviet Automobile* (Ithaca, NY: Cornell University Press, 2008).

6. For a stunning visual presentation of these designs presented at a recent exhibition, see *Český sen: Československá účast na Světové Výstavě Expo 58 v Bruselu* (Prague: Arbor vitae, 2008).

7. See also David Crowley and Jane Pavitt, eds. *Cold War Modern: Design, 1945–1970* (London: Victoria and Albert, 2008).

8. Bernard Newman, *Unknown Yugoslavia* (London: Herbert Jenkins, 1960), 19.

9. Bernard Newman, *Bulgarian Background* (London: Robert Hale, 1961), 17–19.

10. David Tornquist, *Look East Look West: The Socialist Adventure in Yugoslavia* (New York: Macmillan, 1966), 7.

4

The Taste of Smoke

Bulgartabak and the Manufacturing of Cigarettes and Satisfaction

Mary Neuburger

In May 1981, a group of sixty serious Czech smokers, including the vice-minister for Czechoslovak trade, gathered in a spacious and comfortable hall in downtown Prague. Several major players from the Bulgarian tobacco monopoly, Bulgartabak, spoke to the crowd before the smoking began. They explained their objective: they "wanted their cigarettes to be the best . . . the preferred ones for this market." With this in mind, they asked for honest appraisals of "taste" as well as the overall "smoking experience." For almost two hours the Czechs smoked the various brands, old and new, offered for their smoking pleasure. According to Dimitŭr Iadkov, the director of Bulgartabak who presided over the event, a smaller group of "professionals" went off and smoked separately, offering evaluations in a way that was indicative of "a long established ritual." The rest of the Czech smokers, though, lit up more spontaneously, sharing their impressions and preferences with one another.[1] The event, as Iadkov describes it in his memoir, was more than just part of a pro forma trade ritual with a foregone conclusion. On the contrary, the event came after years of sincere efforts in market research, designed to determine and map Czech, Bulgarian, and wider Bloc *tastes* in cigarettes regarding flavor, smoking properties, and packaging appeal.

Bulgartabak was in the business of taste and had gone to great lengths to perfect and adjust the flavor of their cigarettes for domestic and Bloc smokers in the communist period. From the 1960s on, increasingly detailed consumer and laboratory research was conducted to perfect every aspect of cigarette consumption, from the flavor bouquet to burnability to packaging, design, and branding. This range of concerns and activities might seem out of place under state socialism, a system that was explicitly known for its "dictatorship of needs" and economy of scarcity.[2] Most scholarship on socialist production and consumption depicts a system focused on "provision" over response to demand, which certainly reflects an important dimension of socialist reality. Yet new scholarship has uncovered a range of consumer and producer experiences and experiments under Eastern European socialism.[3] A biography of Bulgartabak and Bloc smoking builds on this more complex picture of both the inner workings of the socialist economy and "lived socialism." Indeed, Bulgartabak's extreme success was expressly enabled by the conditions, alliances, and consumer cultures of Bloc socialism. A combination of factors, including centralized planning and state monopoly, the initiatives of Bulgartabak executives, and Bloc demand contributed to astounding accomplishments in the period. In fact, from the mid-1960s to the 1980s, Bulgaria was a cigarette manufacturing powerhouse, the number one exporter of cigarettes in the world, surpassing even the United States.[4] At the same time, smoking (for better or worse) became a widespread phenomenon with a central place in Eastern European consumer culture. Bulgartabak in many ways enabled cigarette quality and abundance, just as Bloc smoking enabled Bulgartabak's rise to fame as an industry giant.

The notion that Bulgartabak was a center of industry innovation that catered to consumers is particularly surprising given Bulgaria's reputation as the most loyal satellite in the Bloc. Scholars of East European consumption have generally looked to Hungary, East Germany, and especially Yugoslavia for presumably "exceptional" realms of consumer culture, based on more direct encounters or "imitations" of the West.[5] Though these states were exceptional, such characterizations are often overstated. The story of Bulgartabak elucidates the wide range of Western contacts and exchanges as well as approaches to production and consumption that were present in "Bloc loyal" Bulgaria in the same period. Not only does this complicate claims of exceptionalism elsewhere, it suggests that such consumerist experiments and Western contacts were exceedingly complex and also compatible with Soviet loyalty. Bulgaria was by no means disloyal in pursuing global success in tobacco by whatever "capitalist" means. Rather, Western engagement was central to Bloc productive and *consumer* experiences in this period. A range of appropriations of Western cultural and technological forms were both critiqued and promoted as constitutive elements of post-Stalinist Soviet culture. Western forms, then, were selectively amalgamated into a system that allowed a certain creativity and flexibility.[6]

With this in mind, the Bulgartabak phenomenon offers insights into the possibilities and nature of East-West commercial, technological, and aesthetic engagement. The persistently presumed teleology of "Western" innovation and "Eastern" imitation belies the true complexities of local and global flows of productive and consumer practices between the regions. In the Bulgartabak case, all of its initial successes in the industry, even the rise to global predominance in export, actually predated substantial technological exchanges with the "West." By the time these exchanges began, Western (and global) tobacco was as interested in Bulgartabak as Bulgartabak was interested in them. The 1960s–1980s were marked by mutual fascination and concrete encounters between the leaders of the industry, and Bulgartabak developed far-reaching contacts and exchanges with American tobacco firms R. J. Reynolds and Philip Morris, as well as a range of Western European tobacco companies. This resulted in a discerning and advantageous appropriation of Western technologies as well as packaging and flavor aesthetics in response to the changing desires of Bloc consumers. This encounter with global tobacco certainly shaped Bulgartabak's trajectory, but in the end the Bulgarian cigarette industry operated with clearly articulated and enacted socialist objectives. Their successes were predicated on the enabling structures of the Bulgarian socialist economy and Bloc trade and, most importantly, their ability to successfully cater to Bloc smokers. Until the end, the goal of *Bulgartabak* was to build socialism and serve the newly spawned, "modern" socialist consumer— emblematic of socialist progress.

Smoking in the Bloc

Bulgartabak successfully closed the Czech deal in 1981. The "Czechoslovaks" ordered an additional 300 tons of cigarettes to supplement their initial order of 4,174 tons for 1980.[7] Perhaps this seems predictable given that the Czechs, like others in the Bloc, generally purchased Bulgarian cigarettes without hard currency; it was a desirable arrangement all around. In 1981, in fact, a portion of Czechoslovakia's Bulgarian cigarettes order was in exchange for the latest Škoda cigarette machines, which the Bulgartabak representatives were shown in the renowned Škoda factory in Pilsen the following day. For Bulgartabak, Comecon trade certainly had great advantages; it was a kind of captive market that kept out significant volumes of Western and even Yugoslav cigarettes. But at the same time, it is quite clear from Bulgartabak documents that the Comecon market was by no means a given for cigarette sales. By 1981, there was considerable anxiety about securing this market, even while sales were still exceedingly high. Though Bulgartabak's research foresaw an increased consumption of 15–20,000 tons of cigarettes a year for the Bloc over the next few years, sagging or stable orders from Comecon partners did not seem to reflect this predicted trend. As a result Bulgartabak launched more proactive promotional campaigns in the early 1980s in a continuing effort to "supply cigarettes of the best quality, which were the most desirable for each locale."[8] But this was by no means the first Bulgartabak effort to satisfy and respond to the Bloc market. On the contrary, this pursuit characterized virtually the entire postwar period and was especially marked in the post-Stalinist years.

In Bulgaria, as elsewhere in the Bloc, the seeming shift toward approval and provision of consumer goods in the 1960s and early 1970s was not simply part and parcel of liberalization associated with de-Stalinization. Arguably, production of consumer goods was more of a return to high Stalinism, when a variety of goods—caviar, champagne, ice cream—were made available to the new upwardly mobile populations created under the conditions of 1930s early socialism.[9] By the beginning of the 1960s, postwar recovery was complete and social change wrought by socialist industrialization, urbanization, education, and expansion of working classes and professionals had created a new consuming class. The postwar rise in smoking was a global phenomenon, as soldiers who had been provisioned with cigarettes at the front brought home their tobacco addictions.[10] In addition, smoking was a natural accompaniment to postwar "emancipation" of women in the West and the Bloc, where new modes of urban leisure and sociability defied ideological (and gender) barriers. Smoking, it seems, was a modern consumer practice par excellence, one that accompanied postwar recovery and social change on both sides of the Iron Curtain. Within the Bloc, postwar scarcity and the ethos of consumer sacrifice for a socialist future was replaced, by the late 1950s, with the reality of relative abundance and the idea of the "good life" here and now. Beginning in this period, Bulgarian Communist Party sources repeatedly announced that a "new modern type of consumption" had emerged that was characterized by growing demand for quality consumer goods.[11] Far from bemoaning this development—though there certainly was criticism of some aspects of it—socialist leaders embraced and encouraged "modern" consumption patterns as indicative of socialist progress. Consumption within certain parameters was not only seen as ideologically sound, it was critical to socialist ideology.[12] It both reflected and created a *modern* citizenry and provided a necessary driving force to ever-greater production, as under capitalism.

Bulgaria, like the rest of the Communist world, became a veritable paradise for smokers in these decades. Smoking became ubiquitous, at work, at home, and at play, in a way that alcohol, food, or any other type of consumption of "nondurable" goods was not. Admittedly, this increasingly raised anxieties about worker productivity and proper "socialist" behavior, but state-sponsored antismoking programs never reached the fevered pitch of grassroots movements in the United States and parts of Europe in the same period. Behind the Iron Curtain, beginning in the 1960s and gaining momentum in the 1970s, the smoking phenomenon spawned antismoking writings and some limited measures to restrict smoking in the workplace, but such programs never had a decisive impact on ever-rising smoking rates in the region. Throughout the period, the number of smokers in Bulgaria, as elsewhere in the Bloc, skyrocketed. The more the regime railed against smoking, the more Bulgarians and other East Europeans smoked, with a growing percentage of their income devoted to the purchase of tobacco.[13] Though ultimately unsuccessful in curbing the phenomenon, the Bulgarian antismoking literature produced detailed descriptions of the world of smoking under communism that were undoubtedly evocative of the larger Bloc experience.

In Bulgaria, as elsewhere in communist Eastern Europe, the shop clerk or office worker with a cigarette in his or her mouth was a common feature of the workplace. Although smoking was gradually pushed out of public buildings in the United States and Western Europe beginning in the 1970s, efforts in the communist world were more limited. A 1976 article in the Bulgarian newspaper *Otechestven Front*, for example, complained:

> In our industrial section we have 7 workers, 2 of whom are passion-
> ate smokers. The director gave the order which banned smoking in
> the workplace. This was upheld for the most part. In June we got
> a new director. The smokers became active again and people from
> other areas of the workplace began to gather in our section to smoke
> all day. It became impossible to work.[14]

The article, ominously entitled "Evil Spirit in a Luxurious Box," was reflective of the fact that even limited strictures on smoking in public were largely ignored by the smoking populace, with few consequences. This state of affairs raised the ire of a number of antismoking theorists in Bulgaria who bemoaned the loss of productivity and the sullied work environment: "The smoker lights up for 80–100 minutes of his day while others around him are enveloped in the clouds of smoke he has created."[15] Even in cases where special smoking areas in the workplace were provided, the problem of "time lost" seemed to be compounded. As one anti-smoking theorist argued, "if one smoker smokes twenty cigarettes a day, and spends 10–12 minutes per cigarette, plus 14–16 minutes in getting to and from his smoking area, he will lose some 140–160 minutes a day!"[16] But concerns of time lost amid "clouds of smoke" were scarcely limited to the communist workplace.

When it came to leisure consumption, the contradictions between anti-smoking pronouncements and socialist practice were even more striking. In discussions of communist leisure, sources tended to portray smoking as contributing to the "waste" of socialist "free time," which ideally should be reserved for "productive" outdoor activities, sports, or cultural pursuits. As in the workplace, the minutes of free time "lost" by smokers were counted with palpable disgust:

> He who smokes tobacco, for example one pack a day, loses a minimum of 10 minutes per cigarette because it is smoked as a ritual— slowly, ceremoniously, as they say for "kef" [from the Turco-Arabic *keyf* for pleasure or bliss]. And so, unnoticeably, with the smoking of one or two packs of cigarettes a day, hours disappear from one's valuable free time."[17]

As the author, Geno Tsonkov, explains, it is not only work time but free time that is "squandered" by smoking (and also drinking), which "deflects one's thoughts" to "pleasure" and "bliss."[18] Here the notion of partaking in *kef* clearly invoked a sense of prolonged and shiftless laziness of a decidedly backward and "Oriental" character. But more often than not, antismoking sources linked smoking to "bourgeois" and "Western" decadence.[19] Accusations of the "Western" nature of smoking and sociability, however, were as vague and problematic as allusions to *kef*. The provision of "leisure" and the *modern* "good life" were not just Western or capitalist phenomena but also explicit promises of socialism. At what point did leisure become decadence, or *modern* consumption or sociability become Western?

More critically, did the population take these official jabs at their "Western" (or "eastern") behavior seriously? In discussions of youth smoking in particular, the "need to be fashionable" and "modern" was constantly cited as a contributor to the dangerous rise of the smoking phenomenon.[20] Although being "modern" was embraced throughout such discussions, fashion (*moda*) was seen as a destructive "Western" phenomenon.[21] "Fashionable" youth were often the targets of criticism, as in a "criminal photo story" in the magazine *Turist* that depicted a group of young hip Bulgarians smoking and drinking in a mountain cabin on Mt. Vitosha, within easy driving distance from Sofia. A picture of the aftermath of their debauchery was equated with a "crime scene," complete with cigarette butts, empty bottles, and muddy sheets defiling the cabin.[22] Yet on closer inspection, pictures of the stylish and attractive youths on Mt. Vitosha are less evocative of "crime" than of a normal and even fun weekend outing. The hyperbole of "crime" contributed to the tone of tongue-in-cheek sarcasm, and images of smoking and drinking youths in Black Sea restaurants appear elsewhere in the magazine and other tourist brochures, as acceptable and desirable weekend behavior. Such contradictory images reveal the true dilemma for communist theory and practice: was production, provision, and consumption of cigarettes critical to the making of a *modern* socialist Bulgaria?

The reality was that smoking had a range of social functions in modern society: a welcome escape, a source of pleasure, a social lubricant, a symbol of women's independence, and a rite of passage to manhood, to name a few. These were all readily recognized by the communist naysayers of smoking, and anti-smoking measures were hardly draconian. In fact, smoking remained cheap and associated with fun. Bulgartabak in fact purposely sold and marketed their goods at Bulgarian leisure venues, which began to proliferate in the 1960s and 1970s. In addition to their lively kiosk displays on the streets of Sofia and other Bulgarian cities, cigarettes were sold in cafes, bars, and restaurants, and at Black Sea resorts where "pretty girls" were hired to work at sleek kiosks that were open twice as late as the equivalent city stalls.[23] Legions of scantily clad (or topless) sunbathers smoked Bulgarian cigarettes on the white sand beaches and in the new gleaming discos and bars of the Black Sea coast, Bulgaria's "Red Riviera." Cigarettes were sold in kiosks for Bulgarian lev, but also—and more profitably—for hard currency in Bulgarian hotels and the Corecom (hard currency) stores that abounded in coastal resort cities. Brands such as "Varna" and "Stewardess" evoked tourist locales and travel; advertisements showing seductive images of airplanes, glasses of wine, candles, and card playing made an acceptable and desirable connection between cigarettes and leisure. Such abundance was not merely (or even primarily) for the benefit of Western tourists, who remained a minority in this period. In fact, most "foreign" visitors at the Black Sea coast and other tourist destinations were from other "brotherly" socialist states.[24] But Bulgaria's new leisure venues were also for Bulgaria's own citizens, not just Communist Party elite.[25] Although the latter certainly had the best access to such abundance, gardens of leisure blossomed everywhere and for everyone. The pages of *Bŭlgarski Tiutiun* were filled with articles and photographs showcasing "rest stations" that were built solely for Bulgaria's tobacco workers. One 1963 article, for example, described the "Palace Among the Dunes" at Sunny Beach:

> Of course on every table you will see various things according to the tastes of those staying in the room—books, fishing gear, needlework, cigarettes, toys, radios, letters, etc. . . . Is this not your house, workers with your golden hands, through which passes the gold of our homeland—tobacco!

Given their substantial contribution to the Bulgarian economy, tobacco workers were presented as naturally deserving of their time in the sun, lounging on the beach, fishing, playing cards, and of course smoking.

Indeed, the bulk of the public appeals against smoking were lighthearted and humorous jabs at Bulgaria's smokers. This "testimonial," for example, from a Bulgarian eighth grader in the health journal *Zdrave* illustrates how antismoking messages were often deployed and even received. A Bulgarian boy narrates the story of his teacher, "comrade Patlazhanov," lecturing the class on the evils of smoking:

> When he gave the example of how one drop of nicotine could kill a horse . . . everyone turned to Pesho Konia, the leader of the smokers in the class, and were giggling and whispering [because his name was derived from the word for horse]. Because the teacher thought the students were laughing at him, he called them hooligans and low-life. He ran out of the room and slammed the door, but the students opened it again to see that he did not even wait until he had gone into the teacher's lounge to light a cigarette with trembling hands in the hallway. The students were not so impatient. They lit up in the bathroom.

The mischievous boys were reportedly caught midpuff by another teacher and taken to the principal. As the story continues, that evening at home the student's father, who was informed of the incident, yelled at him, though meanwhile filling "a whole ashtray with [cigarette] butts." Finally, spent from the effort and out of smokes, the father sent the boy to buy him a pack of "Sluntse" (Bulgarian brand), and the impish boy used the change to buy himself some "Arda" (a cheaper brand), pointing out, "Shouldn't I follow my father's example?"[26] Although certainly a morality tale critical of teachers, fathers, and other bad role models, in many ways the smoking boy inadvertently emerges as the tale's hero. As much as the reader is supposed to be shocked by his insolence, one is also charmed by his sense of humor and independence. The boy's story, like the ubiquitous cigarette on TV, in novels, and in other media of that period in Bulgaria, was simply reflective of a life mired in smoke under communism. It was not likely to inspire fear, let alone provoke a fundamental change in consumer behavior.

An Iron Curtain of Taste?

Bulgartabak tracked, welcomed, and promoted the rapid growth in the Bloc (and global) smoking habit and was well positioned to turn its yellow leaf into "Bulgarian gold," as it was routinely called within the industry.[27] A rapid increase in exports was enabled by rising trade barriers to Western imports after 1947, as well as Bulgaria's designation as the major cigarette producer within Comecon.[28] As a result, cigarettes became what Iadkov called the "locomotive of the Bulgarian economy."[29] They brought in revenue for the state to purchase oil and machinery as well as other kinds of consumer goods from abroad to satisfy the newly urbanized population. Though some 80 percent of Bulgarian cigarettes went to the Soviet Union (the world's biggest importer by the mid-1960s), the other 20 percent went to Comecon clientele, propelling Bulgaria to number one in global cigarette exports by 1966, a position it held most years until 1989.[30]

Impressive numbers aside, Bulgartabak success was predicated not only on quantity but on quality, which was demanded by the growing market within the Bloc of educated, urban consumers having correspondingly new modes of leisure and taste. As far as raw tobacco was concerned, Bulgaria had produced renowned quality tobaccos in its ideal climate and soils since the seventeenth century. Bulgarian tobaccos of the "Oriental" variety (though also originally derived from an American plant) had a greater intensity of flavor and lower nicotine content than so-called American varieties, i.e., Virginia and Burley. Because of its unique flavor, Oriental tobaccos were also in high demand in the United States and Western Europe since the nineteenth century. In fact, since about 1913 the American cigarette market had been dominated by "American blends"—predominantly American tobaccos with a 10–15 percent Oriental mix. Camel, introduced by R. J. Reynolds in 1913, was the first such blend that became the model for the American mega brands that followed.[31] In the pre-1945 years, blends had also been popular in continental Europe, though in central Europe a far greater percentage of Oriental (35–40 percent) to American tobaccos predominated in the so-called European blends. Central Europeans had also adjusted to a more purely "Oriental" taste during both World Wars, when the continent was cut off from American supplies and greater Bulgaria became a primary supplier to the Central Powers and then Hitler's "New Europe."[32] In the same period, in Russia and the Balkans, cigarettes made of purely Oriental varieties, though also blended, were still the rule. With that in mind, Bulgaria was uniquely equipped to fulfill postwar tastes in Oriental tobaccos in both Russia and Central Europe when the United States was again shut out of Bloc trade in 1947–48 after a brief postwar hiatus. Ensuring a quality product, however, went well beyond procuring and processing raw tobacco.

By the late 1950s, Bulgartabak was also responding dynamically to perceived changes in consumer taste through aesthetic adjustments in packaging, branding, blending, and flavor variety. These Bulgartabak efforts both to exponentially increase quantity and to experiment with quality and flavor variety took place firmly within the context of Bloc technologies and tastes—including

Škoda cigarette machines—but primarily with Oriental tobaccos. Already in 1961, in a Bulgarian publication entitled *Tobacco and Cigarettes*, a wide variety of cigarette brands are presented, which reportedly "achieved the full satisfaction of desires of the most demanding smokers in the country and abroad." As the text continued, "Bulgarian cigarettes were greeted extraordinarily well by consumers [*konsumatori*] in the USSR, Czechoslovakia, the GDR, etc."[33] In lavish detail, some thirty-seven Bulgartabak brands (*marki*) are then featured, all with distinct names, labels, and flavor profiles. The names of the various Bulgarian "assortments" were, perhaps predictably, derived from "Bulgarian history and nature" (Shipka, Vitosha, Dunav) and tobacco regions and sorts (Rhodope, Dzebel), as well as based on Bulgaria's "friendship with other socialist countries" (Laika, Baikal). Bulgartabak also found no apparent contradiction in simultaneously describing brands with more Western-sounding names printed in Latin script (Derby, Sport, Travel, Virginia, Luks). Significantly, the distinguishing features of each brand—strength, flavor, in some cases filters, and even size and shape—were often described in direct reference to the Bloc "consumers" who preferred them. For example, the Soviets liked Vega and Rodopi, the Czechs liked Marica, the East Germans liked Yaka, and so on, not because of the names but because of the specific flavor profiles that seemed somehow suited to their "national" characters.[34] Courting a range of consumers, foreign and domestic, was indeed critical to Bulgartabak's success, a success that was forged out of purely local (or Bloc) materials, tobaccos, and technologies in these early years.

Admittedly, to produce a number of these brands Bulgartabak dabbled in a range of techniques, some of which were associated with interwar and postwar American industry practices, namely artificial (or natural) aromatization and blending of Oriental with non-Oriental tobaccos. But in 1961, these methods were still overshadowed by elaborate blending of Oriental varieties, a practice that had been common in the local tobacco industry since the nineteenth century. So-called American blends were not so different from purely Oriental blends; they were only a variation of the time-honored tradition of blending among global tobacconists. They were a "special recipe" that mixed American varieties with Oriental ones, though infusion of natural and artificial flavoring was certainly an American novelty. In 1961, Virginia was still the only Bulgarian cigarette brand produced that used (locally grown) "American" varieties of tobacco, with a smaller percentage of Oriental tobacco. But Bulgaria was growing more and more American varieties of tobacco in this period, a process begun during World War II with Nazi encouragement. Indeed, this range of technologies and techniques, tobacco types, and cigarette aesthetics was generally already in the Bulgartabak toolbox. They were employed, along with newly developed local and Bloc materials and technologies, in the broader project of "building socialism" via production, which assumed and indeed required a ready and willing socialist producer and consumer.

In recognition of the vast numbers and diversity of tastes of this consumer, Bulgartabak, with state and Soviet approval, was eventually given carte blanche in terms of the use of "global technologies." The warming of East-West trade in the mid-1960s made technology exchange in the cigarette world again possible, and American tobacco companies were some of the most aggressive in seeking trade relations with Bulgaria. Beginning in 1964, Philip Morris canvassed various officials in Bulgaria with "samples" of cigarettes including the American ambassador and embassy staff in Sofia, directors and vice-directors of Bulgartabak and Corecom (the institution in charge of hard currency stores), and other export officials.[35] Although both sides moved with caution, Bulgartabak slowly built a relationship with American tobacco, while also initiating wider "scientific" and technological exchanges across the tobacco world. In September 1965, Bulgaria hosted its first-ever International Tobacco Symposium, in conjunction with the city of Plovdiv's annual trade fair. Representatives from across the Bloc, as well as the United States, a number of Western European countries, Turkey, Greece, Yugoslavia, Egypt, and Israel, were in attendance.[36] In the same year, Bulgaria joined the international tobacco organization Coresta, which, like the Plovdiv symposium, amplified "scientific" exchange but also trade relations and aesthetic influence. Bulgartabak specialists were increasingly privy to American packaging, filtering, blending, and aromatization methods, which were presented through various channels and venues of exchange. At the Plovdiv symposium in 1965, for example, Fred Triest gave a paper titled the "Function of Tobacco Flavor," which described in lush detail the complex chemical process of creating a consistent and pleasing flavorful cigarette using a blend of tobaccos and aromatic additives—everything from vanilla, licorice, and cocoa to rose, jasmine, and wood resins. In positively alluring terms, Triest explained how the "taste and aroma of tobacco" was heightened by natural or synthetic mixtures that can achieve "honey and fruit notes," "jasmine top notes," "spicy effects," and "flowery sweetness."[37] Bloc tobacconists could not help but be seduced by the aesthetic possibilities of American "aromatization" technologies, which along with filter and packaging methods were already slowly penetrating local tobacco production practices.

At the same 1965 symposium, Bulgartabak was already impressing visiting delegates with its remarkable tobacco technologies. The lavish symposium program was filled with flashy advertisements of fashionable models smoking "new Bulgarian blends." Some of these new blends, such as the brand Luna, boasted "[a] new type of Bulgarian scented cigarette, combining the mild peasant flavor of Oriental tobacco with the peculiar flavor and strength of Virginia tobacco." Another brand, Ropotamo, was lauded as the "second blend which fully satisfies smokers used to this type of cigarette."[38] By 1965 Bulgartabak was clearly moving in a European (if not American) blend direction, as nicotine-rich Virginia tobaccos made their way into Bulgarian blends. Not surprisingly, this shift caused serious trepidation among Bulgartabak officials, given Bulgaria's more limited capacity to produce American-type tobaccos. As early as 1965 Bulgartabak documents also reveal that their trading partners from across the Bloc, including the all-important Soviet Union, were demanding filters, the American type "king size" (85mm), and European or American blend cigarettes.[39] With this in mind, Bulgartabak efforts to experiment in European and American blends gained considerable momentum, arguably less because of American overtures and more from perceived changes in local taste that were being continuously tracked. The Bulgartabak use of Western-sounding names, Latin script, and Western-looking packaging attests to their marketing with an attraction to "Western" products and aesthetics in mind. But taste tests were also "blind," confirming that there was something in the flavor or physiological effect itself that drew in Bloc consumers.

In the 1960s and 1970s, Bulgartabak quite aggressively canvassed its Eastern European market, showering the Bloc with samples and eliciting opinions. Cigarette displays and samples were a constant feature at Cold War trade fairs at home (Plovdiv) and around the Bloc (Leipzig, Riga, Kharkov, Poznan, Moscow, Warsaw, Berlin, and Bratislava).[40] In addition there were orchestrated events, such as the Czech taste test described above. "Promotional weeks" punctuated the period starting in the mid-1960s not just in the Bloc but also in potential "emerging" markets such as Afghanistan. Cigarettes were offered in taste test sessions that featured every conceivable ratio and blend of Oriental and American tobaccos, flavorings, and filters. Although a range of tastes in cigarettes were revealed, American and European blends were beginning to score higher on taste test results, especially in Poland, Czechoslovakia, and Hungary, as well as among a more select population in the Soviet Union and Bulgaria. As the Philip Morris director of research and development, Helmut Wakeham, reported after a trip to Bulgaria in 1967, there seems to be a market here "among the better classes" for American-type cigarettes.[41] Bulgarian studies, conducted primarily at the Tobacco Institute in Plovdiv throughout the 1960s and 1970s, also concluded that even Bulgarian smokers seemed to prefer the flavor and "smokability" of American-style blends.[42] As a result, the institute expended great effort conducting ever-more-local taste tests, experimenting with blends and aromatization to emulate American blends but also to create "Bulgarian compositions"—hybridized blends with a higher content of Oriental tobacco.[43]

ROPOTAMO, THE SECOND BLEND
VARIETY WHICH FULLY SATISFIES
SMOKERS USED TO THIS TYPE OF
CIGARETTES.

FIGURE 4.1.   Advertisement for new Bulgarian blend cigarettes Ropotamo, produced for the 1965 International Tobacco Symposium in Plovdiv. From the First Tobacco Symposium, Plovdiv Bulgaria (Plovdiv: Conference Publication, 1965).

Significantly, this "aesthetic" turn was not just about taste, as American blends were higher in nicotine and tar. To be fair, increased use of filters had some ameliorative effect, but regardless, switching to American blends meant a more addictive and carcinogenic cigarette as an accompaniment to "quality." At a time when the American antismoking movement and consumer awareness

KOM. ONE OF THE THREE NEW
BULGARIAN BLENDS WITH FILTER,
SCENTED, KING-SIZE AND IN MOLLINS
PACKING.

FIGURE 4.2.   Advertisement for new Bulgarian blend cigarettes Kom produced for
the 1965 International Tobacco Symposium in Plovdiv. From the First Tobacco
Symposium, Plovdiv Bulgaria (Plovdiv: Conference Publication, 1965).

were bringing about a rapid turn to "lights" and other low-tar and low-nicotine
varieties, Americans were exporting—or as some would accuse, "dumping"—
higher-tar cigarettes on world markets. In the Eastern Bloc, such dumping
was severely limited, but "technology transfer" favored "recipes" that were of
the American "classic" high-tar-and-nicotine varieties. It is impossible that

Bulgartabak was unaware of the implications of this change. They had been studying nicotine content and tar in tobaccos themselves in this period and produced numerous, widely read (in the West as well) studies on the low-nicotine properties of Oriental tobaccos. In fact, they had historically claimed that whereas "Western tobaccos" were highly carcinogen-laden, Bulgarian tobaccos actually contained anticarcinogens that countered the carcinogens in tobacco as well as those present in air pollution.[44]

Still Bulgartabak saw no apparent contradiction in reorienting the industry toward "modern aesthetics."[45] They were, after all, building on traditional tobacconist methods and developing new brands that conformed to "global taste," to complement but not supplant their still-popular older brands. Throughout the 1960s, Bulgartabak engaged in a veritable frenzy of consumer development, everything from "stabilizing quality" to improving packaging, gradually increasing the volume of filtered cigarettes, and introducing different aromatized tobaccos and tobacco blends.[46] Special labs applied many of the principles of perfuming to ensure that tobacco would have a pleasurable and consistent aroma and a taste—derived from cocoa, plum, vanilla, mint, and rose—that would be palpable from the moment the package was opened until the last drag on the cigarette. As the trade journal *Bŭlgarski Tiutiun* (Bulgarian Tobacco) boasted, "the taste and aesthetic demands of consumers have risen to a new level and from there demands for quality of product and a greater assortment." In response to such demands, Bulgartabak steadily refined and introduced new brands, expressing pride in their ability to "satisfy even the most capricious smoker."[47] Of course, this "satisfaction" was enabled at least in part by the appropriations of Western technologies that increased production quantity and delivered the perception of greater quality as well.

Smoking with the Enemy

The Bulgartabak engagement with the West, including the spread of Western cigarette aesthetics and "marketing" tactics, must be examined with considerable caution and nuance. Too often, assumptions about Eastern European "imitations" of the West in this period belie the complex nature of the East-West encounter and the selective appropriations of Western forms on the ground.[48] These suppositions obscure rather than elucidate the contours of local production and consumption success stories, as well as consumer dynamics that have their own local logic and are often part of much broader global dynamics. In the Bulgartabak case, exchanges with R. J. Reynolds and Philip Morris beginning in the mid-1960s and gaining momentum in the 1970s were integrated into a much larger engagement with global tobacco via Coresta. Bulgartabak sought and was sought out, initiating exchanges with parties in the tobacco industry initially inside and by the early 1960s outside the Bloc. Admittedly, in the course of such exchanges Bulgartabak officials ultimately integrated discrete strands of Western technologies and aesthetics into their production and sales, but this was always in the larger service of socialism.

Perhaps it goes without saying that Bulgarian-American trade initially developed in the shadow of serious trepidations on both sides about active commercial engagement with the "enemy." In fact, even when American tobacco companies first started doing business with the far less politically questionable Yugoslavia, there were massive boycotts and public outrage in the United States directed toward R. J. Reynolds and other American companies for using "Communist tobacco." It required a gargantuan public relations effort and political maneuvering from these companies and a series of presidential administrations to resume the tobacco trade unhindered.[49] Bulgartabak executives also worried at first about the ideological repercussions of working with American companies, as they feared the possibility of "capitalist exploitation" and loss of internal markets.[50] But others, such as Bulgartabak's director from 1970 to 1991, Dimitŭr Iadkov, viewed those fears as "superstitions" that prevented learning from "foreign experience." He, as well as other top Bulgarian officials, ultimately saw the great potential benefits in harnessing "Western" technologies for socialist aims.[51] As one Bulgartabak official advocated in a 1966 report, whereas "becoming partners with the devil" was a necessary measure, "the form is not important, it is the outcome."[52] This pretty much summed up the Bulgartabak engagement with "global" tobacco that followed, in which capitalist technologies as form were readily integrated into and enabled a system that was still socialist in content. Socialist claims to the "ideological neutrality" of such technologies and techniques deemed modern and global were not mere rationalizations of their need to "imitate capitalism."[53] Rather, they highlight the fact that most technology and even manufacturing and sales techniques *were* ideologically neutral. Socialism was a work in progress, after all, with no detailed blueprint for what was or was not socialist. With this in mind Bulgartabak, like other socialist enterprises and regimes, very selectively appropriated technologies and methods from the West that furthered or augmented already existing trajectories in the industry and used them to great effect.

Progress on actual trade and exchange was largely symbolic through the end of 1960s, but by the early 1970s Iadkov was moving Bulgartabak rapidly forward in this regard. In 1973, he and his Bulgarian tobacco cohort did a grand tour of American tobacco interests, complete with a ride on an R. J. Reynolds jet to Winston-Salem, North Carolina, and a meeting with Hugh Cullman, the CEO of Philip Morris, in New York. It was in Cullman's office that Iadkov was apprised of the real reason the Bulgarian tobacco delegation had been wined and dined across the American South:

> A few things were clarified in the office of Philip Morris during our last meeting in New York. . . . I looked at the map behind the president's desk and BULGARTABAK was written across it from East Germany, over the Czechs, to the huge area of the USSR all the way to Vladivostok. . . . The president stood and pointed at the map. "You see the spheres of interest. . . . I would say that we are almost everywhere with the exception of this huge territory that is held by Bulgartabak. I have to admit, Mr. Iadkov, that I really envy you. I always dream of those markets. I say this with sincere envy, because for our company the market rules."[54]

Iadkov's American tour exposed him to a great deal, from new tobacco harvesting and processing technologies to ways of business and the capitalist notions of "market." But the lessons of American tobacco, many of which influenced his future approach to the industry, did not inculcate the desire to emulate capitalism writ large. On the contrary, in Cullman's office, Iadkov began to fully appreciate the benefits of the Bulgarian position within Comecon and the fact that its "captive" market had propelled the enterprise to a place of prestige in the jet-setting, international circles of global tobacco. These circles included Cuba and Nicaragua, the next two stops on his tobacco tour, where Iadkov was genuinely energized by the "revolutionary atmosphere." Ironically, Bulgartabak would later reexport tobacco technologies to these anti-American strongholds (as well as a range of other postcolonial or anti-Western states) in Latin America, Africa, and the Middle East. Ultimately, American innovation filtered through Bulgartabak would be used to "build socialism" and bolster other anti-American systems on a global scale.

What did the Americans get in exchange? A toehold, however tenuous, in the Bloc market was their primary reward. A very limited supply of Philip Morris and R. J. Reynolds cigarettes were sold in hard currency stores, duty-free shops, and foreigner hotels in this period. In addition, by August 1975, Bulgartabak signed a licensing agreement with Philip Morris, and Marlboros began rolling off production lines in Bulgarian factories. In exchange for Bulgarian tobaccos and licensing royalties, Philip Morris and R. J. Reynolds provided training and new machines for sorting, curing, and fermenting tobacco and for production and packaging of cigarettes.[55] Quite advantageously, Bulgartabak also purchased the licenses and training to build such machines themselves for export within the Bloc and elsewhere in the "developing world."[56] At the same time, Bulgarta-bak continued to study and emulate Western cigarette aesthetics. By 1975, 82 percent of Bulgarian cigarettes were filters (as opposed to 20 percent in 1967), 62 percent were king-size (only 11 percent in 1967), and 30 percent were "American blend" types (a mere 8 percent in 1967). Much of the 30 percent of blends would have been headed for the "Western" Bloc countries (GDR, Hungary, Czechoslovakia, Poland), as Oriental cigarettes continued to dominate the market in the Soviet Union, by far Bulgaria's largest market, until the end of the period. As Soviet trade representatives categorically told a Philip Morris representative on a trade mission in 1967, Soviet "taste was mainly Oriental," and this remained the case despite aesthetic shifts.[57] Hence, even as Bulgarta-bak appropriated new methods and materials, they also continued to draw on their own (and Bloc-wide) tobacco research, technologies, methods, and time-honored tastes. Far from "imitation," the Bulgarian-Western engagement was more synthetic, a globalized interchange, from which a patently "socialist" amalgam emerged.

The growing exchange with the West seemed to have brought some changes in form but not substance to the work or rationale of Bulgartabak activities. Indeed, there was nothing particularly "capitalist" about responding to and fulfilling the needs and desires of Bloc smokers, which is how the notion of "market" seemed to be interpreted by Bulgartabak. Significantly, in the documents and press of the international tobacco world of the period, Bulgartabak was never accused of "imitation." On the contrary, the "Bulgarian phenomenon" was followed with interest and was characterized by a 1972 *Tobacco International* article as "what soon may become one of the most modern tobacco industries in the world." As the article details, Bulgaria's expansion of production from 500–1,100 tons annually to 45,000 tons in 1970 was seen as nothing short of miraculous. Bulgarian success, the article continued, was far from a result of Western technology transfer: "Bulgaria has been designated the cigarette producer of the Comecon nations and rightly so, for Bulgarian cigarettes, made predominantly from Oriental tobaccos, have been known for their excellent quality and appeal to East European smokers."[58] Notably, Bulgarian quality is defined as decidedly domestic and its success well deserved.

The parameters of Bulgartabak phenomenon can perhaps be more clearly visualized in relation to neighboring Yugoslavia, a country where the tobacco industry never enjoyed success on such a grand scale. Yugoslavia not only had similar climatic and soil conditions, its level of tobacco production was basically on par with the Bulgarians at the beginning of World War II. Macedonian soils, in particular, were ideal for Oriental tobaccos, with a range of other varieties grown in Bosnia, Montenegro, and Bosnia. In addition, Yugoslavia had established trade relationships with the United States and Western Europe prior to Bulgaria. As a result, the Yugoslavs signed licensing agreements with British American Tobacco to locally produce Kents in 1969, as well as with Philip Morris for Marlboros and R. J. Reynolds for Winstons in 1970. But their relationship with the United States, and its status as a Bloc outsider with only limited access to the Comecon market, severely stunted the local industry, which was described in a 1971 issue of *Tobacco International* as being "at a standstill."[59] In addition, the "self-management" and decentralized organization, fragmented by republic, was arguably a disadvantage in contrast to Bulgartabak's highly organized production structure. In addition, as American cigarettes flooded Yugoslav markets, local tobaccos were eclipsed by "American tastes," and American leaf was even imported to meet demand. At the same time, local research and development were stunted; in some ways "imitation" was the only order of the day, unlike the more creative development of Bulgartabak. In terms of pure numbers, though Yugoslavia exported a total of 523 million cigarettes in 1967, Bulgaria was exporting 10.5 *billion* cigarettes to the USSR alone in 1960 and 37.7 billion by 1970.[60] Perhaps in this case, as undoubtedly in others, Yugoslav exceptionalism did not deliver the goods; in fact it cost dearly in terms of creating overdependence on American tobacco and Western markets.

The Yugoslavs also did not have Iadkov, who by the 1970s was recognized internationally as a leader in the industry. He personally presided over Bulgartabak's increase in hard-currency profits by 158 percent from 1968 to 1971 alone.[61] By the 1970s, Bulgaria played a leading role in Coresta, hosting the first-ever annual conference behind the Iron Curtain in Varna in 1978. Iadkov was literally the toast of the tobacco world in the 1970s and 1980s, able to work openly with "Western" tobacco, supply the Bloc, and even export tobacco technology (and, in some cases, cigarettes) to the developing world, both capitalist and anticapitalist.[62]

By the early 1980s, Bulgaria was exporting cigarettes beyond the Bloc for the first time, namely to Iran, Iraq, and Tunisia.[63] In that same period, Bulgaria actually began to import (American-type) tobaccos, mostly from Southeast Asia but also from Zimbabwe and elsewhere, to keep up with cigarette export orders to countries that had acquired a taste for American cigarettes but ended trade relations for political reasons. In short, Bulgartabak was advantageously privy to the methods of the "Western" side of the Cold War, while retaining the benefits and markets of the "East."

With this in mind, it is ironic that the State Council of Bulgaria issued an antismoking decree in 1976 with the aim of "curbing and gradually doing away with this Western Imperialist evil."[64] Sources argued that smoking itself should "wither away" like other "vestiges of capitalism" that were incompatible with the approach of ripe communism. But such dictates did not require Bulgartabak to curb its productive capacity, which was so important in the larger goal of building socialism. In fact, before Zhivkov approved the building of a brand new cigarette factory in Blagoevgrad in 1982, he joked, "But won't they say that we are supporting smoking?"[65] While Zhivkov was privately flippant about countering the smoking habit, Bulgartabak sources sidestepped the issue by arguing (well into the 1970s) that "American-type" tobaccos were cancercausing while Bulgarian tobaccos had enough anticarcinogens to counter any possible cancer risk.[66] Bulgartabak, of course, continued to produce its cigarettes at home and abroad and display them in shops and kiosks with gusto.

By American standards, marketing efforts were very limited, consisting of store window displays or discreet advertisements in a number of Bulgarian publications. In fact, in Congressional hearings in the 1970s that sought to limit cigarette advertising in the United States, American tobacco used the "lack" of advertising in the Bloc as evidence that smokers smoked no matter what. The fact that "half of the world's smokers" (behind the Iron Curtain) had "never seen a tobacco advertisement" was offered as proof that there was no correlation between growth in the smoking rate and advertising.[67] In fact the rates of consumer growth, according to American industry documents by far outstripped those in the West. From 1970 to 1978, for example, cigarette sales increased by 40 percent in Poland, 25.3 percent in the USSR, 25 percent in Bulgaria, and were correspondingly high for the rest of the Bloc (and Yugoslavia). In the West, in contrast, smoking rates dropped 2.1 percent in the UK, 4.4 percent in West Germany, 14.8 percent in the United States, 18.4 percent in France, and 38 percent in Spain.[68] Though smoking still had some strongholds in the West, it was in the East that smoking continued to take off unabated. Bulgartabak, in fact, occasionally made offhand comments in documents and publications about the "authoritarian" nature of smoking restrictions and campaigns in the West that were robbing citizens of "freedom of choice." In contrast, Bulgartabak continued to "search for effective forms and methods for advancing our cigarettes in different socialist countries with the goal of popularizing these products in spite of the existing bans on the advertising of tobacco products."[69] Ironically, this echoed arguments and measures taken by the American tobacco industry in defense of, and after the curtailment of, cigarette advertising at home.[70] Issues of "freedom" aside, antismoking campaigns in the West were ultimately far more effective than in the Eastern Bloc in this period, perhaps because they were viewed as a result of grassroots concerns rather than as a result of state dictates. On the other hand, perhaps smoking was viewed as a form of consumer freedom and pure enjoyment that Eastern Bloc smokers were not willing to give up.

By the 1980s, the Eastern Bloc countries had some of the highest levels of smoking in the world and, unlike in the West, continued growth. By 1982, approximately 50 percent of Bulgarians smoked, a large percentage of them an average of twenty or more cigarettes a day.[71] In the 1980s, even when other goods were in ever shorter supply, Eastern Bloc consumers could count on cigarettes, which maintained an important place in socialist leisure consumption and sociability.[72] Although demonized in the "West" today, the development of a smoking culture under socialism was in its own peculiar way a story of resounding success.

In spite of ultimate failure as a political system, socialism also brought social mobility and spending power to large segments of the Bulgarian (and Bloc) population. As the Bulgartabak story amply reveals, the Bloc market and state monopoly of commodity exchange actually enabled productive and consumer success. Even before contact with "Western" technologies and methods, the Bulgarian cigarette industry was a recognized global success. Western engagement was direct and multifaceted, but it by no means determined or propelled Bulgartabak success. Indeed, to a certain extent these contacts were a *result* of that success, which attracted global tobacco attention and exchange. The result was a complex engagement that consisted neither of pure imitation nor mere socialist rationalization of capitalist forms. Détente gave Bulgarian tobacco the means to reach for technology and resources, to expand its reach outside the Bloc while maintaining its position within. Through taste tests at home and abroad, research on flavor and blend, and elaborate changes in packaging and branding, Bulgartabak attempted (and with a high degree of success) to meet the needs of a rapidly expanding and changing consumer base. Notably Iadkov, with his Russian-made Lada car and modest apartment in Sofia—unlike his R. J. Reynolds and Philip Morris counterparts with their mansions and private jets—remained a socialist to the end. He was able to travel the world in pursuit of tobacco trade partners, but like other tobacco "executives" in Bulgaria he was quite meagerly compensated for this exemplary building of the industry. For Iadkov, as for Bulgartabak more generally, responding to the tastes of the socialist consumer and the "building of socialism" remained paramount.

NOTES

1. Dimitŭr Iadkov, *Bulgartabak: Spomeni* (Sofia: Izdateslvo "Sibia," 2003), 169.

2. As Verdery argues, the regimes behind the Iron Curtain "dictated" taste to such markets through decisions on exactly what and how much to produce. Katherine Verdery, *What Was Socialism and What Comes Next* (Princeton, NJ: Princeton University Press, 1996), 28. See also Janos Kornai, *The Socialist System: The Political Economy of Communism* (Princeton, NJ: Princeton University Press, 1992).

3. See, for example, David Crowley and Susan Reid, eds., *Style and Socialism: Modernity and Material Culture in Postwar Eastern Europe* (Oxford: Berg, 2000). See also Krisztina Fehervary, "Goods and States: The Political Logic of State Socialist Material Culture," *Comparative Study of History of Society*, 2009.

4. *Bŭlgarski tiutiun* 2 (1966): 1.

5. See, for example, Patrick Patterson, "Making Markets Marxist? The East European Grocery Store from Rationing to Rationality and Rationalizations," in Warren Belasco and Roger Horowitz, eds. *Food Chains: From Farmyard to Shopping Cart* (Philadelphia: University of Pennsylvania Press, 2009). See also David Crew, ed., *Consuming Germany in the Cold War* (Oxford, Berg, 2003), Katherine Pence and Paul Betts, eds. *Socialist Modern: East German Everyday Culture and Politics* (Ann Arbor: University of Michigan Press, 2008); and Fehervary, "Goods and States."

6. Alexei Yurchak, *Everything Was Forever, Until It Was No More* (Princeton, NJ: Princeton University Press, 2006), 158–206.

7. Iadkov, *Bulgartabak*, 169.

8. Ibid., 168.

9. For a discussion of socialist consumption in the Stalinist period, see Sheila Fitzpatrick, *Everyday Stalinism: Ordinary Life in Extraordinary Times, Soviet Russia in the 1930s* (New York: Oxford University Press, 1999). See also Jukka Gronow, *Caviar with Champagne: Common Luxury and the Ideals of the Good Life in Stalin's Russia* (Oxford: Berg, 2003).

10. On the postwar rise in global smoking, see Allan Brandt, *The Cigarette Century: The Rise, Fall and Deadly Persistence of the Product That Defined America* (New York: Basic Books, 2007), 89, 100.

11. Todor Iordanov, *Materialnoto-tekhnicheska basa na razvitoto sotsialistichesko obshtestvo* (Sofia: Partizdat, 1973), 7. See also *Bŭlgarski tiutiun* 2 (1966): 3, and *Bŭlgarski Tiutiun* 12 (1967): 32.

12. On attempts by the Bulgarian regime to "modernize" Muslim women through consumption, see Mary Neuburger, "Veils, *Shalvari*, and Matters of Dress: Unraveling the Fabric of Women's Lives in Communist Bulgaria," in *Style and Socialism: Modernity and Material Culture in Postwar Eastern Europe*, eds. D. Crowley and S. Reid (Oxford: Berg, 2000), 169–87.

13. Atanas Liutov, Boris Atanasov, Violeta Samardzhieva, and Katia Stoianova, *Upravlenie na narodnoto potreblenie* (Sofia: Izdatelstvo na Bŭlgarskata akademiia na naukite—ikonomicheski institut, 1984), 116.

14. *Otechestven Front*, 1976, 3.

15. Dobrinka Atansova, *Tiutiun, sŭrdste, pol* (Izdatelstvo 'Khristo G. Danov," 1977), 132.

16. Nikolai Sikulnov, *Za da ne propushat nashite detsa* (Sofia: Meditsina i fizkultura, 1980), 3.

17. Geno Tsonkov, *Trezvenostta, svobodno vreme i vsestrannoto razvitiie na lichnostta* (Sofia: Meditsina i fizkultura, 1980), 14.

18. Ibid., 16.

19. See for example, Vasil Naidenov, *Borbata za trezvenost: Delo na tseliia narod* (Plovdiv: Okrŭzhen komitet za trezvenost, 1980), 38–39.

20. See for example, Mila Miladinova, *Esteticheska kultura i trezvenost* (Sofia: Meditsina i fizkultura, 1979), 17.

21. Ibid., 22–23.

22. *Turist*, June 1964, 29.

23. Central State Archive in Sofia, Bulgaria; or Tsentralen Dŭrzhaven Arkhiv (hereafter TsDA), TsDAf-347, O-18, E-147, 983.

24. Vicho Sŭbev, *90 Godini organizirano turistichesko dvizheniie v Bŭlgariia* (Sofia: Meditsina i kultura, 1986), 11.

25. On the Bulgarian system of subsidized holidays, see Kristen Ghodsee, *The Red Riviera: Gender, Tourism, and Postsocialism on the Black Sea* (Durham, NC: Duke University Press, 2005), 82–83.

26. *Zdrave*, July 1966, 11.

27. *Bŭlgarski tiutiun* 2 (1966): 1.

28. Prior to World War II, Bulgaria had produced cigarettes primarily for local consumption, exporting primarily raw tobaccos.

29. Iadkov, *Bulgartabak*, 8.

30. *Bŭlgarski tiutiun* 2 (1966): 1.

31. Brandt, *Cigarette Century*, 54–55.

32. See, for example, Ekaterina Ivanova, *Iz realni sviat na romana "Tiutiun": Neizvestni zapiski na Rusi Genev* (Sofia: Poligraficheski kombinat, 1994), 6–7.

33. P. Penchev, Ct. Banov, *Tiutiun i tsigari* (Sofia: 1961), 149.

34. Ibid., 151.

35. Philip Morris collection, Heymans, J. "Letter No. 9 Rumania and Bulgaria." July 28, 1964, Bates: 2012582864-2012582865, http://tobaccodocuments.org/pm/2012582864-2865.html, 3.

36. Twenty-seven countries were represented: the USSR, East and West Germany, UK, USA, France, Yugoslavia, Italy, Belgium, Holland, Poland, Czechoslovakia, Austria, Hungary, Rumania, Yugoslavia, Greece, Portugal, Switzerland, China, Vietnam, Cuba, Lebanon, Egypt, Korea, Turkey, Israel, and Somalia. *The First Tobacco Symposium, Plovdiv Bulgaria* (Plovdiv: Conference Publication, 1965), 10.

37. Ibid., 67–70.

38. Ibid., 4–5.

39. TsDA, F-347, O-14, E-2, L-213: 1965.

40. TsDA, F-347, O-16, E-6, L-1: 1968.

41. Philip Morris collection, Wakeham, H. [No title], 1967 (est.), Bates: 1000322484-1000322486, http://tobaccodocuments.org/pm/1000322484-2486.html, 1–2.

42. TsDA, F-347, O-14, E-148, L-7: 1969. In anonymous taste tests conducted in Bulgaria in 1969, 99 percent of participants reportedly selected an American blend as their number one choice.

43. TsDA, F-347, O-14, E-133, L-2: 1968.

44. Philip Morris collection, "Investigaciones del Humo del Tabaco; Tobacco Smoking Research," Beffinger, I. J. [No title], Sep. 21, 1967, Bates: 2025041470-2025041473. http://tobaccodocuments.org/pm/2025041470-1473.html, 3.

45. TsDA, F-347, O-14, E-131, L-103: 1968–69.

46. *Bŭlgarski tiutiun* 2 (1966): 3, and 12 (1967): 32.

47. *Bŭlgarski tiutiun* 9 (1971): 18.

48. See, for example, David Crew, "Consuming Germany in the Cold War: Consumption and National Identity in East and West Germany, 1945–1989, an Introduction," in David Crew, ed., *Consuming Germany in the Cold War* (Oxford, Berg, 2003), 7.

49. First and foremost, the American legion and other grassroots organizers had to be assured that "Yugoslavia was not supporting the Viet Cong."

50. From early on, Philip Morris was ready to move ahead with a full-blown joint venture based in Bulgaria, with Philip Morris owning a 51 percent controlling share. This proposal was deemed "unacceptable" by Bulgartabak managers, who were rightly fearful that "this is their effort to control the socialist market" (TsDA, F-347, O-14, E-3, L-3: 1966).

51. Iadkov, *Bulgartabak*, 34; TsDA, F-347, O-14, E-3, L-7: 1966.

52. TsDA, F-347, O-14, E-3, L-3: 1966.

53. See, for example, Patrick Patterson, "Making Markets Marxist? The East European Grocery Store from Rationing to Rationality and Rationalizations," in Warren Belasco and Roger Horowitz, eds. *Food Chains: From Farmyard to Shopping Cart* (Philadelphia: University of Pennsylvania Press, 2009).

54. Iadkov, *Bulgartabak*, 35.

55. Ibid., 36.

56. Philip Morris collection, Cullman, H. [No title], May 7, 1974, Bates: 1000272443-1000272445, http://tobaccodocuments.org/pm/1000272443-2445.html, 1–3.

57. Philip Morris collection, June 26, 1964, Bates: 2012582923-2012582927, http://tobaccodocuments.org/pm/2012582923-2927.html, 2.

58. *Tobacco International*, Feb. 18, 1972, 6.

59. Ibid., 6.

60. For the Yugoslav statistics cited here, see Kune D. Georgievski, *Macedonian Tobacco* (Skopje: Joint "Jugotutun" enterprise, 1972), 37. For the Bulgarian numbers, see *Tobacco*, July 21, 1972, 65.

61. See, for example, *Tobacco*, July 23, 1971, 23–25.

62. Like American corporations in this period, Bulgartabak begin to look to the developing world for markets. After conducting a prognosis on the growth of smoking rates for 1980–81, they concluded that in the West smoking was up only 1.3 percent and in the Bloc 2.3–2.5 percent, but in the Near East and Africa it was up 3.5–4.8 percent! As Iadkov put it, with these numbers in mind there is "no reason for pessimism"; Bulgartabak simply needs to find new markets. Iadkov, *Bulgartabak*, 143.

63. TsDA, F-347, O-14, E-158, L-10: 1986.

64. *Tobacco Reporter*, April 1976, 80.

65. Iadkov, *Bulgartabak*, 222.

66. *Bŭlgarski tiutiun*, 11 (1967): 31.

67. Philip Morris collection, "The Five Arguments Against Tobacco Advertising Censorship," 1982 (est.), Bates: 2028560389-2028560412, 1–3, http://tobaccodocuments.org/pm/2028560389-0412.html.

68. Philip Morris collection, "Comparison of Cigarette Increases Eastern Europe Vs. U.S. and Western Europe." 1979 (est.). Bates: 2015049012-2015049013, 3–4. http://tobaccodocuments.org/pm/2015049012-9013.html.

69. (TsDA, F-347, O-20, E-75, L-7: 1981).

70. Philip Morris collection, "The Five Arguments Against Tobacco Advertising Censorship," 1–3.

71. See Vlakhova-Nikolova, *Problemi na tiutiunopusheneto*, 59, 83.

72. (TsDA, F-347, O-16, E-6, L-89: 1977).

5

Risky Business

What Was Really Being Sold in the Department Stores of Socialist Eastern Europe?

Patrick Hyder Patterson

The aim of socialist commerce is not profit, but service to consumers.
—Štěpán Horník, on the duties of Czechoslovak retailing; "Na prahu páté pětiletky," *Propagace* 17 (1971): 2

What happened when the department store took root in socialist Eastern Europe? The overwhelming interpretive tendency in contemporary scholarship on consumption, retailing, and business is to treat the department store as both a *site* of capitalist practice and a *vehicle* for the creation and reinforcement of capitalist culture and values. Yet business managers and planners in the communist world believed that these stores could, in fact, be instruments of an unquestionably socialist system of distribution, fully consonant with communist norms and values.[1] This essay examines the nature and consequences of department store retailing in Eastern Europe, with particular attention to four of the most prosperous and consumer-oriented communist countries: Hungary, Yugoslavia, Czechoslovakia, and the German Democratic Republic.[2] In each place, the department store proliferated rapidly and took hold as a highly favored (if not numerically dominant) form of "modern," "progressive," "rational," and indeed even "scientific" retailing during the socialist period. It received such treatment precisely because socialist decision makers could—and did—judge it to be an essentially system-neutral commercial technique. But with the widespread adoption of the department store there arose dangers to the maintenance of reliably "socialist" cultural values that the authorities sought to promote, with real costs to the perceived legitimacy of the socialist system as well: the department store form itself engendered, reinforced, and communicated a distinctive set of cultural values that were, if not strictly speaking "capitalist" in their origins, content, and function, nevertheless potentially subversive.

Under discussion here is the nature of the transformations set in motion when officials and enterprise managers in socialist Eastern Europe adopted various methods, institutions, and techniques associated with the business practices of the capitalist West. These changes demand a rethinking of the relationship between socialism and "business," a term conceived broadly in this analysis to include not just the work of producers and distributors but retail interactions with consumers as well. But this rethinking should not assume that importing Western practices automatically meant importing capitalism. This more cautious interpretation requires a departure from the usual approaches to consumption that envision the various technologies of modern consumer outreach—including not just the department store but also the supermarket and similar large-scale self-service grocery stores as well as other "modern" retailing forms, along with complementary practices such as marketing, advertising, public relations, branding, packaging, display, and consumer credit—as characteristically, reliably, and definitively *capitalist* tools. These instruments of market culture are habitually theorized as forms inextricably connected with, and expressive of, the underlying logic of the economic system that has tended to produce them with such vigor and in such profusion.[3] But an examination of the state socialist experience—both the plans of socialist commercial specialists and the actual experience of socialist retailing "on the ground" and in the stores—calls into question this presumed linkage.

But why even pay attention to department stores? Does retailing really *matter?* In the "affluent societies" of the West, it certainly has. In those locales, the department store, with its distinctive merchandising, sales, and labor practices, has figured as one of the primary formative forces of modern consumption, and, as such, of modern capitalism itself.[4] These stores have, moreover, mattered for both those who shopped in them and those who earned a living there.[5] In each sphere, this new retailing format contributed to major cultural and social changes, not least among them a fundamental transformation of gender roles.[6] That women acted as primary *makers* of the department store experience is, it turns out, a fact with broad, cross-system relevance. As in the capitalist West, department stores in the communist East emerged as one of the most important venues for the feminization of retailing work.[7]

But as important as the department store proved to be for restructuring labor, it had effects just as profound, if indeed not more so, for the realm of consumption—that is, for the complex process of seeking, encountering, examining, selecting, purchasing, using, displaying, and, not least, conferring meaning on goods and services. For instance, the rise of the department store in Eastern Europe reinforced the tendency (one seen in other shopping settings as well) to mark out consumption as a domain in which women were understood to have distinctive talents and duties that merited, in turn, special opportunities.[8] Accordingly, women were continually and prominently featured in sources from the period as the principal market base for the department store's rich assortment of goods. Reaching the female shopper became a prime task of socialist commercial specialists. And in this respect, the very form of the department store—its layout and design, its traffic flow and display patterns— was understood to hold a unique potential for engaging and mobilizing feminine desire. Along these lines, the director of the Hungarian department store Skála observed in 1977 that the one of the secrets of his enterprise's remarkable success lay in recognizing precisely such implications of a pattern and flow of shopping that was characteristic of, and indeed unique to, the department store form:

> —At the innermost part lies the women's department, and then back behind that the children's and the menswear departments.
> —What's the trick in this?
> —If a woman comes into a department store, she begins by looking to see what kind of new items for women are there. If the merchandise is good and she likes it, in the great majority of cases she will buy it. When she comes back, she finds herself with a feeling of guilt about the purchase she made. This has to be gotten rid of. How? She buys something for her children in the children's section and something for her husband in menswear. The guilty-conscience complex is in this way resolved. And now she is already praising herself, since she is a caring mother and wife. This can keep going on over and over. . . . This store layout has increased the sales of the upper-floor departments to a significant degree.[9]

This Hungarian female shopper, it seems, was not only the arbiter of quality but also the intended audience for well thought out arrangements of goods that made it possible for her to shop for others, and so assuage her own guilt that would result from her purchases in the women's department. Through the deployment of a "trick" layout specifically designed to spur consumption, the department store operated, in a measured but nonetheless very significant way, as the producer of a new and distinctive market culture. The cultural message propagated through the form of the store itself was, in effect, that taking full advantage of the wide assortment of goods on offer was an affirmative moral good, that being mindful of opportunities to shop for one's family was a moral imperative that would, if ignored, burden the conscience. As a result, buying more meant buying better, and even *being* better. Abundance was not just there to be appreciated; it was also there to be *used*. And giving in to consumerist desires need not itself be a guilty pleasure if the indulgence was undertaken in the "right" way—which, in a department store, meant not limiting consumption in some ascetic manner but instead ratcheting up the level of spending. For these vital female consumers, as indeed for others, the store design itself was structured and calibrated to fuel a shared system of values, ideas, preferences, and behaviors connected with consumption—a culture of desire, in other words—that in practice often showed strong affinities with the corresponding values, ideas, preferences, and behaviors encountered in contemporaneous capitalist settings. Both systems, capitalist and communist, ended up positing the satisfaction of consumer wants and needs as an essential element of "the Good Life," thereby establishing this as a critical criterion by which the performance of "the system" would be judged. At the same time, the skillful and successful *pursuit* of those wants and needs by consumers also took on an increasing, and increasingly profound, social significance.

The construction of gender-linked consumption roles represents, to be sure, just one dimension in which department stores have given potent content to the culture of consumption. Historically, their effects have been even broader: these stores have figured not simply as prime locations in which essential consumer practices take place but, just as important, as sites that themselves shape and structure consumer practice, precisely as the chief of Hungary's Skála department store suggested was happening on his sales floor every day. That sales floor was, at least in some limited, nominal sense, a "socialist" space. Yet in the standard interpretations, these value-laden, culture-creating environments, these "cathedrals of consumption," have typically embodied (and taught) a specifically capitalist belief system.[10]

If the department store could exert so much apparent power under capitalism, and indeed so much apparent power *as* capitalism, the question of its consequences for a socialist order hostile to capitalism becomes, of course, all the more compelling. As retailing on this grand scale grew popular in socialist countries, the ability to build and manage large, well-stocked retail emporiums with an extensive range and selection of goods became especially meaningful, both to governments and to ordinary citizens. Indeed, the department store ultimately emerged as a highly visible measure of the socialist system's capacity to provide and "rationally distribute" goods, and hence consumer satisfaction, in ever greater quantity and variety. Modern department stores thereby came to represent the best that communism could offer: all of the abundance of the new consumer economy, all in one place. In the context of an intense international confrontation in which capitalist Western Europe was busily refashioning its storefronts and streetscapes not just to make money but also to announce and exhibit the successes of the private-enterprise system—an encounter that saw the stores in and around West Berlin's grand Kurfürstendamm shopping avenue self-consciously styled as the *Schaufenster des Westens*, the shop window of the West—these Eastern European counterparts became the clearest and most visible communist answer to the challenge of the West. They were, literally and figuratively, the shop windows of socialism.

Implicitly or explicitly, socialist retailers, like those who managed the manufacturing system that produced the goods they sold, found themselves in competition with the offerings of the capitalist way of life. They were indeed on the front lines of a much larger struggle, a rivalry that played out, not least of all, in the department store, with the contest between the two systems proclaimed and fought in the display windows and advertisements, and won or lost in the showrooms and the shoe departments, on the shelves and the dress racks. In the ensuing Cold War propaganda wars over the proper path to prosperity, retailing therefore played a critical, if still not fully appreciated, role. It was in this context of contestation and uncertainty that one Hungarian exposé of West Berlin "behind the shop windows," published in the tense period leading up to the construction of the Berlin Wall, reminded readers that the Allied enclave within East Germany was doing double duty not just as a "city on the front lines" (*front-város*) but as a "shop window city" (*kirakat-város*), one that the West used to "advertise" the "exploitative capitalist system."[11] This approach turned the idea of the celebrated *Schaufenster des Westens* on its head: the implication was that the superabundant retail displays of capitalism's shiny, flashy neon cities actually amounted to little more than either falsified assemblages of unavailable goods or seductive collections of luxury items that were accessible only to the wealthy elites of bourgeois society.

By the 1960s and 1970s, the effects of the post-Stalinist "consumer turn" had become especially noticeable in Hungary, Czechoslovakia, Yugoslavia, and the GDR, where the communist authorities proved most able to convert promises of prosperity into expanding consumer options in the stores and on the shelves. As elsewhere in the region, the leaders of these states steered their economies while acknowledging, if grudgingly, a growing imperative to reorient their systems toward the satisfaction of consumer desire. As part of this shift, department stores claimed an increasingly prominent place in both the planners' priorities and the public imagination.

As a venue of concentrated abundance and material success, the department store met with virtually universal approval, and often even outright enthusiasm, from people on both sides of the retail counter. The fervor was, of course, dampened by the more than occasional inability of the fragile socialist production and distribution systems to actually deliver the goods to the store shelves. But even when the big emporiums failed to stock all that was wanted, these lapses were typically interpreted not as a weakness of the department store form itself, but as a symptom of larger structural defects in the economic system. Its contents may have been flawed and inadequate, but the vessel itself still seemed faultless, and even worth acquiring in ever-greater measure.

Even in those places in socialist Eastern Europe in which department stores did not become widespread, they maintained a special cultural valence as displays of accomplishment in the consumer sphere. There they could, at the very least, function as celebratory demonstrations of communism's potential, if not of a dependable everyday experience of satisfaction. In other words, the big stores could exercise a powerful symbolic value in (and for) the socialist order in a way that was not strictly limited by their number, their scale, and their contents.[12] Moreover, unlike the supermarket and self-service grocery, which were not just new forms but alien forms as well, and difficult to navigate for shoppers accustomed to counter service, the department store required no introductory campaigns to explain its purpose and uses. It was already a well-known retailing method in many of the region's larger cities, where such enterprises had flourished in the interwar period. As such, historical continuities and widely shared popular expectations for the reestablishment of familiar shopping customs were clearly at work alongside the communists' big plans.

And those plans were big indeed. As early as 1966, the GDR had managed to build its way out of massive postwar privation and destruction to open a number of impressive department stores of varying sizes, including seven organized as part of the VVW (Vereinigung Volkseigener Warenhäuser) CENTRUM chain (with stores in Leipzig, Berlin, Karl-Marx-Stadt, Erfurt, Dresden, Rostock, and Halle), and sixteen incorporated in the cooperative Konsument organization (with three stores in Leipzig, two in Halle, and individual outlets in Berlin, Gera, Potsdam, Dessau, Zwickau, Plauen, Dresden, Stralsund, Gotha, and Frankfurt an der Oder, and a new store for Cottbus under construction).[13] These big, attention-grabbing stores served as important conduits for the various accomplishments of the GDR in the consumer sector as well as prime signifiers of those achievements. Indeed, they were explicitly acknowledged—and touted—in precisely such terms in the often heavy-handed pronouncements of the East German political and commercial establishment. One fairly gushing 1976 review of Berlin retail displays, for example, triumphantly labeled the storefronts "the shop windows of our successes" (*Schaufenster unserer Erfolge*). Of the many benefits to the system that the policymakers and commercial elites believed the department store would bring, these explicit propaganda functions were among the most noticeable and most enduring.

In Czechoslovakia, which like the GDR had a rigidly controlled economic system, state authorities pressed forward with development plans that emphasized the utility and productivity of the large-scale department store format. Among members of the country's retailing establishment, department stores were prized for what were taken to be their eminently forward-looking, "rational," technological qualities. As elsewhere in the Bloc, official Czechoslovak enthusiasm for the department store as a distinctive retailing form, whose presumed rationality and economies of scale were compatible with socialist distribution objectives, continued largely unabated throughout the socialist period. Along these lines, one retailing guide from 1971 stressed that the department store had become "the primary developmental form in the contemporary period" and played an especially important role in communicating the system's accomplishments to the public as "the representative of a good standard of merchandise and grocery items, and a rapid and rational system of sales."[14] As a centralized, concentrated, modern, and "scientific" form that lent itself readily to top-down planning, the department store made good sense in even the relatively orthodox socialist terms that the Czechoslovak authorities usually preferred. For this reason, it seemed destined to prosper in the newly "normalized" Czechoslovakia of the early 1970s, where a retrenched central planning apparatus sought to offer consumer pleasures as substitutes for the freedoms that had been lost with the suppression of the Prague Spring.

In communist Hungary, department stores had likewise gotten off to a quick and fairly promising start, becoming a standard feature of retail planning and development at least as early as the 1950s. With time, however, they faced decidedly fewer official constraints than their counterparts in the GDR and Czechoslovakia. After the market-sensitive economic reforms of 1965–1968, implemented under Party leader János Kádár, Hungary enjoyed a less strictly controlled economic (and cultural) climate as the regime attempted to buy back some popular support (or at least popular acquiescence) following the failed 1956 revolution. Kádárism famously sought to accomplish this with expanded consumer opportunities, and the new consumerist orientation required, in turn, an expanded emphasis on ever more attractive retailing innovations, which were often developed with conscious and essentially unapologetic reference to Western models and methods. Here was a chief difference between Hungarian practice and that of the regimes in neighboring Czechoslovakia and the GDR: Hungary opted for a much more freewheeling and tolerant style, with the result that both the business and the economic operations that fed consumption and consumer culture were more relaxed, free, and vibrant. Ultimately, that vitality showed up in the boutiques, shops, and department stores of Hungarian cities and the markets of the towns and countryside. In this atmosphere of relative openness and experimentation, reports and analyses of department store trends in Western countries became a standard feature of the Hungarian trade literature,[15] and department stores, popular with both planners and shoppers, spread rapidly beyond Budapest to many smaller cities and towns.

But in Hungary, as elsewhere in the more "successful" states of the region, prospects were not always entirely rosy. Even as Budapest became well known as a consumer paradise for shoppers from comparatively deprived parts of the Soviet Bloc, department store managers there and in other Hungarian cities faced recurring worries over the adequacy of stocks and consumer choice, with demand for the most modern appliances, furniture, and fashion sometimes proving hard to satisfy. Along these lines, one internal report from Budapest's Szivárvány Áruház (Rainbow Department Store) documented efforts made by the company's advertising and display department to assure customers that things were indeed getting better. To that end, one of the store's 1979 promotional campaigns tried to hammer home the message with the repeated proclamation that "The selection has grown broader" (*Bővült a választék*).[16] Yet all too often, the country's department stores remained at some distance from the pledge that the rather unimaginatively named State Department Store enterprise (Állami Áruház) had made many years earlier: "the choice is easy because the selection is big."[17] Despite the Hungarian commercial establishment's continuing advances in the techniques and styles of department store retailing, living up to that promise of abundance and a wide-ranging assortment of goods proved a constant challenge, especially in periods when global economic shocks hit the socialist countries especially hard and made shortages yet more common throughout the region, as happened on a number of occasions in the 1970s and 1980s.

When it came to practices of commercial promotion such as advertising and marketing, and other business innovations that were likewise potentially suspect as capitalist tools, Yugoslavia's enterprise managers were without a doubt the most unfettered and adventurous. This was to be expected, as Yugoslavia had been relieved of worries about Bloc conformity or Soviet oversight after the decisive break with Stalin in 1948. Ultimately this latitude translated into a system that was, of all the communist states, the most receptive to economic and cultural influences from America and Western Europe, which from the 1950s onward did their part to heighten the contrasts by plying the Yugoslavs with aid and eagerly engaging them as trading partners. The country's

FIGURE 5.1.   Promotion of abundance and security of satisfaction guaranteed:
outdoor advertising for Hungary's Rainbow Department Stores (Szivárvány Áruházak),
with the slogan "Rainbow Department Stores—small department store—big selection." From *Magyar Reklám* (1958), 34.

openness to the West led to a more experimental orientation and, with that, a wholehearted embrace of the department store and its associated sales techniques, often more or less directly "imported" from Western commercial practice. By the late 1970s, Yugoslavia had a total of 410 department stores;[18] of these 90 were in Croatia, which enjoyed a relatively sophisticated and well-developed retail infrastructure.[19]

Zagreb's well-known NAMA chain offers a revealing illustration of Yugoslavia's pattern of multiplication, expansion, and importation of foreign models. NAMA started as a traditional stand-alone store in the city center's busy Ilica shopping street. But after 1960 the company evolved rapidly into a major multistore concern, and by 1983 it had spread to sixteen sites, with new locations opened in the small regional centers of Vinkovci, Vukovar, and Sisak. Perhaps even more indicative of the Yugoslav commercial leaders' characteristic desire to keep the arts of retailing *au courant* and attuned to international standards, a big new NAMA location with an area of 8,700 square meters appeared on the edge of Zagreb, positioned "out in the fields" to serve the needs of "motorized" shoppers with ample parking.[20] Large-scale peripheral Opskrbni centri (provisioning centers or supply centers) of this type were, NAMA's planners believed, the wave of the future. As one assistant to the company's general director assessed the emerging trends of the time, the opening of the first big Zagreb Centar reflected "the desire to bring about, here in our country, the implementation of a form of retail commerce that, especially in the last decade, has begun to develop with great intensity in Western Europe."[21] Clearly, NAMA's leaders were keeping a close watch on what their capitalist counterparts were up to and hoping to follow suit. The same was true of many of their colleagues in the retailing field across Yugoslavia.

East European Department Store Culture, from Theory to Practice

Despite the many fundamental contrasts between capitalism and socialism in terms of the underlying economic structures of ownership and production, retailing presented something rather different: in practice there were substantial correspondences between the merchandising modalities developed in the West and those employed in Eastern Europe. In many instances, planners and retailing specialists borrowed explicitly from Western know-how, drawing on business expertise and store design models perfected in Western Europe and the United States. It is important not to overstate the case here: even in the most prosperous countries and cities, socialist department stores could still seem like poor imitations of their counterparts in the "countries of developed capitalism." The managers of a showcase among showcases, the large CEN-TRUM store on East Berlin's Alexanderplatz, found themselves having to report to communist Party officials regularly and earnestly, and in painful detail, on the wide range of items that were in short supply or completely missing.[22] While it was easily the most consumer-oriented of the socialist states, Yugoslavia too had occasional trouble keeping the stores stocked with everything that shoppers really wanted, although until the catastrophic down-turn of the late 1970s it was better positioned than most to weather the diffi-culties of changing demand and questionable supply.

How deeply indebted to Western practice were the retail establishments of these Eastern European countries? The inclination to borrow proved strongest in Yugoslavia and Hungary, where professional specialists in retailing paid con-tinuing, keen, and often admiring attention to developments in the West. In contrast, the business elites of more politically orthodox Czechoslovakia, and especially East Germany, showed comparatively greater interest in the effort to defend, at least rhetorically, what they held out to be a genuinely socialist mode of retailing. These new methods would, they claimed, help link the basic socialist system of production and distribution with an explicitly socialist form of urban planning and residential life.[23] Even in these more restricted settings, however, the workings of the socialist department store were by no means moving forward in a Cold War cultural vacuum. In all four cases under consid-eration here, the surprisingly rich professional literature of business and com-merce amply documents that the managers and planners were well aware that the big, full-range stores, with their concentration of shopping options and their intensification of consumer abundance, had become one of the corner-stones of the everyday economic order in the postwar West, a defining feature not only of commercial modernity but of economic success itself. The practical experience of the West offered what appeared to be reliable and unquestionable results, and those results proved, again and again, to be appealing to socialist business leaders.

Moving beyond the narrower professional circles of business and com-merce, one finds strong evidence that the new full-scale department stores were also deeply stamped in the consciousness of the shopping public. Even before the period of the most rapid retail change in the 1960s and 1970s, de-partment stores already enjoyed a favored place in customers' images of big-city shopping. For example, one of the most famous and fondly remembered Hungarian films of the early postwar period, Viktor Gertler's 1952 classic Áll-ami Áruház (State Department Store), tapped into widely shared public senti-ments with its themes of consumer desire, luxury, abundance versus scarcity, and wish fulfillment through material acquisition. With its wry look at what "regular" customers (as opposed to privileged apparatchiks and their associates) might or might not expect from their department stores, *Állami Áruház* evokes the early years of communist rule as a time when the consumer comforts that would come to characterize "goulash communism" and "refrigerator socialism" of the mature Kádár era were scarcely imaginable to most Hungarians. Yet the film leaves no doubt that, not only as a retail form but also as a cultural fixture, the department store mattered enormously in the everyday lives of ordinary city dwellers.

As the consumer resources of the socialist economies matured and new, "modern" stores became a more common feature of the commercial landscape, department store shopping became an ever more prominent element of public culture. Updates on the current status of retail selections as well as interviews that sought to establish just how the big stores were faring with ordinary consumers were frequent subjects of the "man on the street" reportage (or, perhaps, "woman in the aisles") that many popular magazines and other mass media outlets regularly served up to readers and viewers.[24]

The evidence suggests that socialist shoppers liked their department stores rather well. During the opening days of one large, much-anticipated Skála location in downtown Budapest, for example, store employees found themselves overwhelmed with eager shoppers. Planners had counted on approximately thirty thousand customers per day, but the actual daily average reached more than fifty thousand.[25] A dearth of Skála outlets was not the reason for the deluge; by this time the chain already had more than sixty department stores across the country. Public opinion research offered further support for the idea that department stores were a particularly well-liked feature of the retail landscape. One informal survey of 1,428 respondents in Slovakia found that, despite a noticeable public desire to see persistent shortages eliminated, 64.9 percent of those surveyed offered a positive evaluation of the services of the Partizanské department store (part of the PRIOR chain), with an additional 33.5 percent rating the store as average, and only 1.6 percent as merely satisfactory.[26]

Eastern Europe's department stores were popular because, like their counterparts in the capitalist West, they stoked (and, often but not always, managed to satisfy) a popular culture of consumerist desire. Indeed, their very design was plotted out to create and sustain key elements of that culture. Although sales-floor layouts were in some instances constrained by the architecture of inherited capitalist-era buildings, designers did their best to make the stores more modern, freshening the signage and façades with glass and neon where necessary, as in the case of Budapest's Úttörő és Ifjúsági Áruház (Pioneer and Youth Department Store), or, as happened with the landmark Corvin store in the Hungarian capital, simply wrapping the old-fashioned "bourgeois" storefront in hypermodernist sheet metal. Later on, when store designers had the luxury of building from scratch, interior spaces, display areas, and traffic patterns could be more easily configured to conform to the latest retailing theories about what made for an engaging shopping experience, and in turn a profitable department store.

In stores like these, the buyer's quest was supposed to transcend mere acquisition of provisions to become instead a matter of exploration and adventure. Shopping-as-excitement showed up regularly in department store advertising as well. A fanciful advertisement for a store in one of Hungary's regional centers, for example, depicted the multistory building being borne aloft by a huge, brightly colored, striped balloon, carried away to distant places over the hills and fields, with the message that "something is always happening in the Fehérvár Department Store!"[27] With their continuous attention to presenting new, exciting products and fashionable, in-season goods, the operational patterns of East European department stores reinforced the idea that shopping entailed not only the joys of spontaneity and discovery but also a satisfying encounter with novelty and innovation. Accordingly, retailing professionals monitored display trends in the West to ensure that the most important visual territory of the stores, both in the showcase windows and on the sales floor, was dedicated to the celebration of the fresh, the different, the previously unseen. The advertising and promotional work of the stores compounded this message, underscoring the idea that what was on the racks and shelves was new, and that newness was, by definition, good. Independently of any objective improvements in quality that might result from innovation and product development, novelty as such typically figured as a virtue in the culture built by socialist retailers. In this spirit, one media campaign for Budapest's popular Skála assured customers that they would, like their store, have access to the most innovative and most attractive apparel, because life was "One step ahead of fashion—in Skála."[28]

Eastern European commercial architects and store designers also took great care to make their sales locations physically attractive, using the favored modernist vocabulary of the times. Like their counterparts elsewhere in the region, the new Hungarian department stores of the 1960s, 1970s, and 1980s drew on international design trends to present visually arresting images of commercial progress: big, sleek, imposing, and technologically sophisticated boxes that announced a modern, forward-looking, and prosperous way of life. These boxes were not designed to be attractive merely in outward appearance. They were also meant to be beautiful for what they revealed, and for what they held. These boxes were supposed to be beautiful because they were supposed to be, in a word, full. They were to contain the complete range of consumer abundance, they were to contain it constantly and reliably, and they were to contain it in a fresh, modern way that made shopping easy, quick, uncomplicated, and advantageous to both sellers and buyers.

Through the design of the buildings and the layout of their interior and display areas, abundance was held up as an end in itself, and that message was picked up repeatedly in the stores' promotional campaigns. Hungary's Állami Áruház department stores, for example, trumpeted the virtues of this "modern," "efficient" form of shopping, using storefronts to announce to customers that "in our department stores you can buy everything in one place." This idea of the department store as a site of concentrated abundance had plenty of staying power. Budapest's famous Corvin offered up much the same appeal in its own advertising: "Buy everything in one place—The biggest department store!—The biggest selection!"

By virtue of their massive scale, department stores could put on display (producers permitting) a wide range of wares from rival manufacturers. The structure of the department store thus naturally brought choice and competition to the forefront. As also happened in the supermarket and other self-service stores in socialist countries, the very design of the department store constructed the shopping process as an individual journey of discovery, evaluation, and judgment. Although it took time, department stores in Eastern Europe gradually began to follow trends in the West and move away from traditional over-the-counter sales methods toward greater reliance on self-service. This shift not only heightened the experience of shopping as an individualistic pursuit and a leisurely, pleasurable end in itself but also had the effect of rendering labor as much far less visible. Here too, the design and operation of the department store worked to steer public attention away from work and from production processes and onto consumption. Increasingly, socialist-zone department stores began to respond, and sometimes even pay tribute, to the principle of consumer sovereignty, an idea that after the 1960s became ever more prominent in the thinking of business professionals in less orthodox Hungary and Yugoslavia (and even made some inroads in East Germany and Czechoslovakia). Along these lines, for example, the masthead of the employee newsletter of the Állami Áruház in the provincial city of Pécs blared out, "Let the customer be satisfied!" This stress on consumer desires was a recurring feature of the publication itself.[29]

The Department Store as a System-Neutral Form?

As these samplings from Eastern European department store practices suggest, the "modern" retailing regime encouraged under socialism came to bear many strong resemblances to the design and operation of department stores in

FIGURE 5.2.   Toward a universal model of modern, pleasurable, one-stop shopping: a reduced-scale department store in the city of Fonyód on Lake Balaton, with an adjacent self-service supermarket and parking for shoppers and tourists traveling in their own cars. Courtesy of the County and City Library (Megyei és Városi Könyvtár), Kaposvár.

the capitalist West. Although this retailing form was clearly recognizable to communist authorities as having a bourgeois provenance, the department store per se did not become a prime target of the anticonsumerist social critique that, especially in the 1960s and 1970s, marked many of these socialist societies. That the department store would emerge largely unscathed is a matter of considerable irony. Historically, department stores in other sociopolitical contexts have elicited withering critiques from scholars and cultural critics, not to mention the hostility of shopkeeping competitors who feared they could not match the stores' advantages and allure. Indeed, in the late nineteenth century, the new behemoths spawned nothing less than a "catastrophist literature," one that, as Geoffrey Crossick and Serge Jaumain put it, "underlined the bleakest consequences of the department store." A host of ills could, it seemed, be traced to the workings of this new retailing technique, including "moral depravity" and "the destruction of family life."[30] Communist Eastern Europe, however, largely ignored such criticisms, or at a minimum attributed the problems at hand to capitalism rather than to the department store itself. Instead, other features of commercial practice, especially advertising and marketing, drew fire as the subjects of long-lasting, heated, even rancorous debate. Large-scale retailing, in contrast, was cast as curiously innocuous.

There were, to be sure, occasional notes of concern about the possible negative implications of what seemed at times to be a flood of commercial innovations.[31] But in the main, the basic premises and practices of department store sales and operations did not generate much opposition. Department stores as such were not perceived as a threat to socialism, nor did they often provoke the sort of concerns about the spread of "consumer society" that many other elements of market culture did. Even the fairly rigid Czechoslovaks seemed to assume that, once the nationalization of their country's comparatively elaborate network of privately held department stores was accomplished, and the impermissible profit motive thereby stripped away, the stores themselves could operate in basic accordance with socialist principles and interests.[32]

The department store thus seemed, in a word, unproblematic—something that socialism could make its own. And so at the same time that East German contributors to Neue Werbung (New Advertising) were mounting a bitter and long-running campaign against the errors of the Western "marketing concept," the journal ran a puff piece on the opening of the GDR's new CENTRUM store in Magdeburg, at 13,300 square meters the country's second largest. The store's opening, Neue Werbung insisted, "should be interpreted as an important step toward the common realization of [our] primary tasks and, at the same time, through the abundance and orderly arrangement of the wares on offer, should make obvious the progress in provisioning."[33] In a similar vein, one Yugoslav specialist praised the enterprise that operated Croatia's NAMA stores as a "pioneer in the modernization of our commercial sales." NAMA had, according to this writer, taken the lead in efforts to improve Yugoslav retailing through technical and operational innovation toward "the most progressive form of commercial buildings, the so-called universal department store," that concentrated an enormous number of items in one location and was, as a result, "very convenient and rational for customers."[34] This celebratory tone was typical of the discourse on department stores in all of the countries examined here.

This view of the department store as a benign technology had a well-established prior history in the trade practices of the USSR. Even in the Stalinist era, Soviet policy embraced adoption of some Western methods (presumably ideologically neutral) and even at times emulation of "American efficiency" for the benefit of the Soviet socialist economic project. By 1935, the country had established eight "all-union" department stores, with orders issued to all of the republics to develop similar model stores for their capital cities as paradigmatic examples of what the communist leadership heralded as a distinctive new form of socialist "cultured trade."[35] In a break with the isolation of the past, Soviet commercial specialists of the mid-1930s were brought into close contact with Western methods and forms, with observers sent to Germany, Great Britain, and the

United States, where they studied techniques of store design, advertising, sales and service, placement of merchandise, staffing, infrastructure, and logistics.[36] As an exemplar of the kind of grand-scale, intensive, and therefore "rational" distribution that the Soviets thought most sensible and effective, the department store form was not merely innocuous. It was, instead, an affirmative good, a modern tool for rationalization, efficiency, scientific management, and cost control. This particular instrument of market culture could easily be, in other words, a socialist tool.

But were communist administrators and business planners correct in this assessment, or were they missing something fundamental here? Examining cases in the developing world and other poorer societies, critics and analysts have typically tended to conclude that the grand-scale shopping emporium and other related retail forms have served as reliable vehicles for "Westernization," or even more specifically for "Americanization."[37] Though there is plenty of evidence of the trickle-down of business styles and practices from developed Western countries into the socialist world (and this is true even of those states that engaged in less explicit borrowing), what developed in socialist-era Yugoslavia, Hungary, Czechoslovakia, and East Germany was not wholly and definitively "Americanization."

Clearly, department stores across these four communist countries ended up pursuing styles of display, advertising, sales, and product selection that did indeed evidence the transfer of elements of market culture from the West, if not necessarily the United States. There were occasional gestures toward providing ostensibly "socialist" content—especially through the messages used as part of in-store and display-window advertising—but it proved difficult if not impossible to create a genuinely "socialist department store," that is, one embodying the fundamental economic logic of socialism in the same way Western business has typically been said to embody the analogous logic of capitalism. Emblazoning the huge glass showcases of department stores with stilted proclamations of the values of Marxism-Leninism and its many accomplishments was a not-infrequent feature of communist practice. But merely using retail outlets as platforms for political propaganda does not make the underlying commercial and consumption processes that went forward in the department store—or the cultural dynamics that attended those basic retail relationships—distinctively socialist.

Department stores existing "under socialism" should not be assumed to constitute, by definition, a unique category of their own. The mere fact that many retail outlets were plagued by the recurring shortages typical of socialist economics, or that committed communists actively pursued their political programs among store workers or consumers, cannot suffice to somehow set those stores apart as "socialist" in their conception and operation. In a number of respects, department stores did function differently in socialist societies, but this does not necessarily mark these stores as conceptually and typologically distinct. Any effort to claim that socialist-zone practice ended up generating a truly system-specific form of the department store would require a long and wide-ranging comparative inquiry into the details of retailing practice under socialism, one that carefully seeks to determine what, if anything, was truly "socialist" about the department stores, supermarkets, and other retail outlets of Eastern Europe and the Soviet Union. That remains undone. But on the basis of the evidence brought to light thus far, it seems reasonable to suspect that even if they were to be found, any peculiarly socialist elements of retail engagement with consumers would likely be outweighed in the end by extensive carryovers from precommunist retailing and widespread new importations from beyond the communist sphere. Whether or not the department store form was system-neutral, as the members of socialist-zone commercial establishments tended to believe, there is little to suggest that any system-specific form ever emerged in these four prosperous, consumer-oriented East European countries.

Subverting Socialism?

Yet if it is indeed the case that socialist retail establishments ultimately borrowed heavily from the department store practices of their capitalist rivals, was what came to the communist world through the expansion of department store merchandising something alien and hostile? If there was no "socialist department store," does this mean that socialist business ended up importing and cultivating an inherently *capitalist* form, with capitalistic consequences, real yet unseen by contemporary observers?

In the growing literature on the more commonly studied American and Western European cases, the department store has typically been taken to be not just a classic manifestation but also a potent instrument of the system-specific needs and logics of capitalist practice. From this perspective, the department store in Paris during the late nineteenth century figures as nothing less than "the bourgeoisie's world," an institution crucial to class consolidation and the formation of a dominant culture, and "a bourgeois celebration" that ultimately both mirrored and reinforced a capitalist, middle-class identity.[38] A parallel approach finds department stores in the United States just as powerful, presenting them as "stewards of the middle class" that built a culture of mass consumption; gave structure and content to the values, hopes, and lifestyles of the expanding American bourgeoisie; and in the process "presided over much of the mundane life of the nation."[39]

The cultural and class implications of this style of selling, if almost universally acknowledged as rooted in capitalism, have nonetheless proven unpredictable and surprising at times. Examining the evolution of department stores and similar sales innovations in late-nineteenth- and early-twentieth-century America, William Leach goes so far as to assert that "without them, the new corporate economy could not have functioned and the Land of Desire would not have been born." Yet in the end they appear not as instruments of cultural narrowing and class restriction but rather as leading factors in a thoroughgoing democratization of tastes, hopes, wants, and expectations. In this view, the department store ranks among the country's most critical social and economic institutions: an essential fixture of the capitalist order, and one that for decades "brought the reality of capitalism— the dream life of capitalism, that is—directly, concretely home."[40]

The question of the department store's significance for socialist Eastern Europe is therefore one that arises in an interpretative environment already heavily freighted with assumptions about its power to advance the interests of capital and of capitalists. At this comparatively early stage of research into the workings of communist commerce and consumer culture under socialism, the evidence available does not warrant a conclusion that the department store functioned as a vessel more or less empty of cultural and political norms, into which "proper" socialist content could be poured. Quite the contrary, the department store form proved capable of creating and sustaining cultural practices rooted in consumer(ist) desire, with strong resemblances to those encountered in capitalist societies. But at the same time, it is far from clear that the department store was an inherently capitalist form. At least as they were put into service in Eastern Europe, these stores did not serve to any meaningful extent as instruments of capitalistic economic domination and alienation, nor was this at base a mode of retailing that dictated *embourgeoisement*.

That said, some aspects of modern department store practice may have had at least the potential to undermine socialist aims. The source of this risk lay in importing sales modes and store concepts that were, as it happened, packed with cultural significance: whether it was apparent or not, the retailing medium of the modern department store was, in its very design, imbued with the potential to communicate values and create culture. Though capitalist economics per se was not transplanted to Eastern Europe with the adoption of modern department store forms and techniques, these outlets nevertheless did appropriate, construct, express, and reinforce a powerful and decidedly transnational culture of modern retail shopping. This culture was characterized by a number of critical elements: emphasis on shopping as a pleasurable, satisfying activity; the promise of spontaneity and discovery; the celebration of the virtues of novelty; the security of satisfaction guaranteed; the restructuring of shopping sociability toward a more atomized individual experience; the demarcation of a feminine domain of consumption complementing new work roles; the promotion of abundance as an end in itself; the glorification of variety and choice; the affirmation of competition by marketing rival brands in the same store; the pursuit of "modern" distribution through cultivation of "modern" shopping; the ascent of leisure and diversion, and the simultaneous eclipse of labor; the elevation of consumption over production; and the acknowledgment of the sovereignty of the consumer.[41]

In its totality, of course, modern consumer culture is the creation of a very wide range of actors, institutions, and social forces. Its production is anything but monocausal. Yet it must be recognized that the characteristic values and preferences of the culture of modern retail shopping were, in important ways, generated and sustained by the form and operation of the department store itself. With its carefully programmed and sequenced presentation of consumer rewards and its profound visual and experiential emphasis on alternatives and variety, the department store insistently drove home the message that consumption was liberating, that abundance was essential, that choice was paramount. The medium was, as in Marshall McLuhan's famous formulation, the message.[42]

These values contributed to a culture of consumption that, though not essentially capitalist in character, was nevertheless difficult to square with the socialist project. Department store shopping reinforced a consumerist culture of desire among ordinary socialist citizens, training them to demand abundance, require choices, expect shopping to be enjoyable and rewarding, and above all think of themselves as "sovereign" and regard their perceived needs as consumers (rather than, per Marxist dictates, their interests as laborers) to be the critical beginning and end points of economic policy. As all this happened, the values carried by the culture of the market often could not be reconciled with the limits that socialist economic relations imposed. Ultimately, the authority of communist governments was also at stake, especially when troubling empty spaces appeared on so many department store shelves in the late 1970s and 1980s. In the end, the department store proved to be a cultural terrain on which state socialism, even at its most prosperous, was ill prepared to compete.

NOTES

1. The academic literature on socialist retailing remains somewhat thin, though the Soviet case—which is not always relevant to the questions presented by the more prosperous Eastern European societies—has attracted significant attention. See, for example, Julie Hessler, *A Social History of Soviet Trade: Trade Policy, Retail Practices, and Consumption, 1917–1953* (Princeton: Princeton University Press, 2004); Hessler,

"A Postwar Perestroika? Toward a History of Private Enterprise in the USSR," *Slavic Review* 57 (1998): 516–42; Amy Randall, "Legitimizing Soviet Trade: Gender and the Feminization of the Retail Workforce in the Soviet 1930s," *Journal of Social History* 37 (2004): 965–90; Marjorie L. Hilton, "Retailing the Revolution: The State Department Store (GUM) and Soviet Society in the 1920s," *Journal of Social History* 37 (2004): 939–64; Jukka Gronow, *Caviar with Champagne: Common Luxury and the Ideals of the Good Life in Stalin's Russia* (Oxford/New York: Berg, 2003), esp. chap. 6, "The Emergence of the Soviet System of Retail Trade."

2. For revealing examples of how socialist specificities shaped consumption practice in those communist countries that were less willing or able to reorient their economies toward satisfaction of consumer needs, see, for example, Sheila Fitzpatrick, *Everyday Stalinism: Ordinary Life in Extraordinary Times—Soviet Russia in the 1930s* (New York/Oxford: Oxford University Press, 1999), esp. chap. 2, "Hard Times," 40–66; Gronow, *Caviar with Champagne*; Liviu Chelcea, "The Culture of Shortage During State Socialism: Consumption Practices in a Romanian Village in the 1980s," *Cultural Studies* 16 (2002): 16–43; Mary Neuburger, "Veils, *Shalvari*, and Matters of Dress: Unraveling the Fabric of Women's Lives in Communist Bulgaria," in *Style and Socialism: Modernity and Material Culture in Postwar Eastern Europe*, eds. Susan E. Reid and David Crowley (Oxford and New York: Berg, 2000), 169–87.

3. See, e.g., George Ritzer, *The Globalization of Nothing 2* (Thousand Oaks, CA: Pine Forge Press, 2007), 169–70 (on capitalism, along with Americanization and McDonaldization, as one of the three "usual suspects" behind the globalization of consumer culture), and 174–80 (on branding as an instrument of capitalism); Celia Lury, *Consumer Culture* (New Brunswick, NJ: Rutgers University Press, 1996), 71 (explaining Jean Baudrillard's critique of the creation of consumer culture as a process in which "the logic of sign-value represents the final triumph of capitalism through the imposition of a cultural order compatible with the demands of large-scale commodity production"); and Michael Schudson, *Advertising, the Uneasy Persuasion: Its Dubious Impact on American Society* (New York: Basic Books, 1984), 215 (on advertising as "capitalist realism").

4. See, for example, Victoria de Grazia, *Irresistible Empire: America's Advance through 20th-Century Europe* (Cambridge, MA: Belknap Press of Harvard University Press, 2005), 155, 157, 158, 160, 405. Among the most important contributions to the historical and sociological study of the department store, and mass retailing more generally, are Rosalind H. Williams, *Dream Worlds: Mass Consumption in Late Nineteenth-Century France* (Berkeley: University of California Press, 1982); Michael B. Miller, *The Bon Marché: Bourgeois Culture and the Department Store, 1869–1920* (Princeton, NJ: Princeton University Press, 1981); Leach, *Land of Desire: Merchants, Power, and the Rise of a New American Culture* (New York: Pantheon, 1993); Susan Strasser, *Satisfaction Guaranteed: The Making of the American Mass Market* (New York: Pantheon Books, 1989); William Leach, "Transformations in a Culture of Consumption: Women and Department Stores, 1890–1925," *Journal of American History* 71 (1984): 319–42; Pasi Falk and Colin Campbell, eds., *The Shopping Experience* (London and Thousand Oaks, CA: Sage, 1997); Sharon Zukin, *Point of Purchase: How Shopping Changed American Culture* (New York: Routledge, 2005). For an early approach to

the subject, see John William Ferry, *A History of the Department Store* (New York: Macmillan, 1960). See also Daniel Miller, *A Theory of Shopping* (Ithaca, NY: Cornell University Press, 1998).

5. See, for example, Barry Bluestone et al., *The Retail Revolution: Market Transformation, Investment, and Labor in the Modern Department Store* (Boston: Auburn House, 1981).

6. See, for example, Mica Nava, "Modernity's Disavowal: Women, the City, and the Department Store," in *Modern Times: Reflections on a Century of English Modernity*, eds. Mica Nava and Alan O'Shea (London and New York: Routledge, 1996), 46. On the experience of women as consumers in East Germany, see Donna Harsch, *Revenge of the Domestic: Women, the Family, and Communism in the German Democratic Republic* (Princeton, NJ: Princeton University Press, 2007).

7. See, for example, William R. Leach, "Transformations in a Culture of Consumption: Women and Department Stores, 1890–1925," *Journal of American History* 71 (1984): 319–42.

8. See, for example, Katherine Pence, "'You as a Woman Will Understand': Consumption, Gender and the Relationship Between State and Citizenry in the GDR's Crisis of 17 June 1953," *German History* 19 (2001): 218–52. See also, Susan Reid, "Cold War in the Kitchen: Gender and the De-Stalinization of Consumer Taste in the Soviet Union Under Khrushchev," *Slavic Review* 61(2008): 211–52.

9. Sándor Demjan, "A reklám, mint a stratégia eszköze," in *Vállalati stratégia— termelési struktura: a Sopronban 1977. október 13.–15.-én tartott III. Tervezési konferencia előadásai, korreferátumai*, eds. János Polonkai et al. (n.p.: Szervezési és Tervezési Tudományos Társaság, n.d.), 313.

10. See, for example, Geoffrey Crossick and Serge Jaumain, eds., *Cathedrals of Consumption: The European Department Store, 1850–1939* (Aldershot, UK and Brookfield, VT: Ashgate, 1999).

11. Sándor Varga, *Nyugat-Berlin a kirakat mögött* (Budapest: Kossuth Könyvkiadó, 1960), 47.

12. On the power of even comparatively unattainable goods to command real cultural value through the experience of shopping, wishing, and window shopping, see David Crowley, "Warsaw's Shops, Stalinism, and the Thaw," in *Style and Socialism*, eds. Reid and Crowley, 25–47.

13. Gerd Baron et al., *Warenhäuser: Entwicklung, Leitung, Organisation* (Berlin: Die Wirtschaft, 1966), 24–25. At the time, CENTRUM had expansion plans that envisioned new large stores for Berlin, Halle-West, Hoyerswerda, Suhl, and Schwedt. Ibid.

14. Jiří Jindra et al., *Výstavba obchodní sítě* (Prague: Merkur, 1971), 20.

15. See, e.g., János Somogyi, "London egy propagandista szemével," *Magyar reklám* 3 (1962): 23. The article reports on retailing and advertising in London.

16. Az 1979. évre szóló kirakatpolitikai elképzeléseink (undated and unsigned report on the store's advertising and display practices). Budapest City Archives (Budapest Főváros Levéltara, BFL), Fővárosi Szivárvány Kereskedelmi Vállalat, BFL XXIX.1014.30.

17. Undated advertising placard for the Állami Áruház (circa 1964?), published at http://www.retronom.hu.

18. Nikola Knego, "Gdje su disproporcije?" *Supermarket* 8 (1983): 13, citing *Statistički godišnjak Jugoslavije 1979*, 534. The figures for the number of stores are based on then-prevailing local measures of store sales-floor area; there was (and is) no strict universal definition of the department store.

19. Ibid. The averages given in this chapter are from my own calculations; other figures cited in the same article give the average sales-floor area for Croatian department stores in 1978 as 2,046.2 square meters. Ibid.

20. Pavle Nikšić, "NAMA: iskustva, usmjerenja i neke dileme," *Supermarket* 8 (1983): 17. NAMA's name was derived from the words n̠arodni m̠agazin (national store). Following the nationalization of private stores in 1948, *NAMA* operated as an affiliate of the Belgrade-based state enterprise of the same name until 1952, when it became an autonomous enterprise. Josip Garvan, "NAMA: pionir modernizacije naše trgovine," *Supermarket* 5 (1980): 8–11.

21. Nikšić, "NAMA: iskustva, usmjerenja i neke dileme," 17. At least some Yugoslav observers were aware, however, that the classic urban-core department store was gradually falling out of fashion in the contemporary West. See, for example, one textbook's observation that, due to the competition inevitable in market-oriented retailing operations, the "era of the department store" had given way to, in turn, "the era of the branch stores" (*filiala*), "the era of the discounters," and finally, as of the late 1970s, "the era of the shopping center." Stipe Lovreta, *Savremena maloprodaja: planiranje razvoja i plasmana* (Belgrade: Savremena administracija, 1979), 23–24, citing Stanley C. Hollander, "The Wheel of Retailing," *Journal of Marketing* 25 (1960): 37–42.

22. See the numerous reports transmitted to Party leaders in the files of the *Sozialistische Einheitspartei Deutschlands* held in the German Federal Archive (Bundesarchiv), DY 30/8987.

23. For examples of the lingering self-referential tendency in Czechoslovak retailing, which took comparatively little note of models from the West and relied primarily on developments and conceptualizations from the socialist sphere, see Karel Pernica et al., *Organizace a technika vnitřního obchodu* (Prague: Státní nakladatelství technické literatury, 1962); Štefan Sloboda, *Rozvoj maloobchodu na vidieku* (Žilina: Vydavateľstvo politickej literatúry, 1964); Filip Hronský et al., *Ekonomika a organizácia obchodu* (Bratislava: Vydavateľstvo politickej literatúry, 1966); Josef Danihelka et al., *Řízení maloobchodních jednotek* (Prague: Merkur, 1980). On the legal framework of retailing in the Czech Socialist Republic, see Ladislav Šípek and Miroslav Škaloud, *Zákon o vnitřím obchodě: text a komentář* (Prague: Merkur, 1983). For the GDR, see, for example, Baron et al., *Warenhäuser*, and the coverage of retailing in the East German advertising trade journal *Neue Werbung*. See also Manfred Kirsch, *Die Marken Bitte! Konsumgeschichten* (Berlin: Eulenspiegel Verlag, 2004).

24. Such reports surfaced continually in high-circulation women's magazines such as Hungary's *Nők lapja* (Women's Pages), East Germany's *Für dich* (For You), Yugoslavia's *Svijet* (World), *Naša žena* (Our Woman), *Praktična žena* (Practical Woman), and *Jana* (Jane), where they regularly documented keen public interest in department store offerings.

25. Judit Reményi, "Metró a város felett," *Propaganda, Reklám* 27, nos. 4–5 (1984): 64–65.

26. S. Milarg, "Warenhäuser in internationalen Vergleich," *Neue Werbung* 20 (1973): 27.

27. Advertisement for the Fehérvár Áruház, undated, published at www.retronom.hu.

28. Advertisement for the Skála Áruház, undated, published www.retronom.hu.

29. See *Minaret: A Pécsi Állami Áruház üzemi lapja.* I have reviewed issues from 1962 to 1965, which appears to have been the entire publication run of the newsletter.

30. Geoffrey Crossick and Serge Jaumain, "The World of the Department Store: Distribution, Culture and Social Change," in *Cathedrals of Consumption*, eds. Crossick and Jaumain, 6.

31. As one Yugoslav analyst observed, "The fusion of new retailing forms with the old commercial networks" raised fears about "a closed local market structure that, in the main, behaves monopolistically," attracting all consumers and causing the closure of other retail outlets. Jovan Andrijašević, *Tržište i tržisne strukture u privredi Jugoslavije* (Belgrade: Institut društvenih nauka, 1975), 125, quoted in Stipe Lovreta, *Savremena maloprodaja: planiranje razvoja i plasmana* (Belgrade: Savremena administracija, 1979), 24.

32. See, for example, the continuing coverage of the nationalization of the country's major stores during the period 1947–1949 in the Czechoslovak retailing journal *Distribuce.*

33. M. August, S. Milard, and C. Triebenecker, "CENTRUM-Warenhaus Magdeburg: ein moderner Großbetrieb des sozialistischen Einzelhandels," *Neue Werbung* 21 (1974): 9.

34. Garvan, "NAMA," 10.

35. Hessler, *Social History of Soviet Trade*, 205.

36. Ibid. See also Julie Hessler, "Cultured Trade: The Stalinist Turn Towards Consumerism," in Sheila Fitzpatrick, ed., *Stalinism: New Directions* (London: Routledge, 2000), 182–209.

37. For an interpretation of the proliferation of modern retail innovations in postwar Western Europe as an example of a specifically American cultural dominance, see de Grazia, *Irresistible Empire.*

38. Miller, *Bon Marché*, 3.

39. Jan Whitaker, *Service and Style: How the American Department Store Fashioned the Middle Class* (New York: St. Martin's Press, 2006), 5.

40. Leach, *Land of Desire*, 5, 8.

41. Here I am extending to the department store context a conceptualization first developed in my prior study of large-scale, self-service grocery shopping and its impact on socialist culture, again with reference to the more prosperous, consumption-oriented communist countries. See Patrick Hyder Patterson, "Making Markets Marxist? The East European Grocery Store from Rationing to Rationality to Rationalizations," in Warren Belasco and Roger Horowitz, eds., *Food Chains: From Farmyard to Shopping Cart* (Philadelphia: University of Pennsylvania Press, 2009), 196–216, with notes at 285–88.

42. See McLuhan, *Understanding Media: The Extensions of Man* (Cambridge, MA: MIT Press, 1994 [1964]).

6

Material Harmony

The Quest for Quality in Socialist Bulgaria,
1960s–1980s

Rossitza Guentcheva

This is extremely motley furniture! OK, but then the problem arises: what type of carpet to put under this motley furniture, what sort of curtains to hang on the windows. If you think about these questions you will see that if we introduce this motley furniture into production, what kind of taste are we going to encourage? . . . Thus when approving a model, the Center's role is to think it over, and not just say the model is new, it's modern, let's produce it. Comrades! I am not against novelty; on the contrary, I praise it, I respect it, but I think when things are approved for production, they must be thought over from all sides, so that we avoid tastelessness. I think that the Center's task is exactly this: it must make every effort to take decisions about these objects not as separate products; it should look at them in total—where they should be placed, who will wear them, and when they will be worn.[1]
—Anna Bŭlgarova, at a meeting of the Center for New
Assortments of Goods and Fashion, Sofia, 1962.

On February 6, 1961, in the main hall of TSUM, the Central Department Store in Sofia, delegates gathered for the first annual meeting of the Center for New Assortments of Goods and Fashion (CNAGF), founded the previous year in Sofia.[2] Rusi Hristozov, minister of internal trade, presided over the summit, which was organized to discuss the achievements of the center's first year of activities and was attended by some of Bulgaria's highest-ranking officials, including representatives of the Ministry of Education and Culture, the Bulgarian Academy of Sciences, and trade and industrial activists, engineers, and artists from all over the country.[3] Established by a 1960 decision of the Central Committee of the Bulgarian Communist Party, the CNAGF was charged with organizing "enrichment of the assortment of food and other goods for people's consumption, management of the development of fashion, and improvement of the culture of dress and outer appearance and packaging of goods."[4] It was entrusted with the task of approving models and samples of all new products, whose prices and forms were centrally determined and hence identical throughout the country. The assembly, far from a predictable celebration of "socialist achievement," was marked by four hours of tense discussion as Bulgarian-produced consumer goods were harshly condemned for their poor quality. Remarkably, the various speakers often explicitly set aside their official positions, declaring that they spoke as "ordinary customers" who were exasperated by the lack of excellence in virtually all types of Bulgarian products. From women's underwear, forks, shoes, and leather products to souvenirs, children's toys, wrapping paper, and product labels—all of these goods were disparaged for insufficient quality and substandard production.

The issue of the quality of goods produced within socialist Bulgaria, and Eastern Europe in general, has been disregarded to a large extent by scholarship on the region. Research on socialist production and consumption routinely focuses on quantity, or the lack of thereof, in attempting to explain prevailing deficits and ubiquitous shortages of consumer goods of all sorts.[5] Generally, socialist commodities are presumed to have been inferior to Western ones, mediocre, and flawed, unable to satisfy the ever-more-demanding customer.[6] On the rare occasions when the quality of socialist objects is explicitly discussed, insufficient quantity is linked to a dearth of quality under state socialism. The consensus among scholars and the broader public alike is that the low quality of everyday objects was grounded in, and can be explained through, deficit: because commodities were scarce and their very procurement was a sophisticated, strategic endeavor, quality was subordinated by both consumers and state authorities. Some studies in fact focus on how socialist governments attempted to construct and foster particular tastes for or dislike of certain goods (from fashionable clothes to electric appliances) in an attempt to alleviate the burden of insufficient or imperfect production on central power.[7]

Quality was a principal concern of Bulgarian communist officials since the early 1960s, despite the fact that deficit was a ubiquitous condition of the Bulgarian economy. Indeed, during the last three decades of socialism the Bulgarian government not only cared about the quality of consumer goods but also had a vested interest in satisfying people's material needs since this was the basis of their very legitimacy.[8] State, party, and local officials were painfully aware of the rampant problems related to the quality of consumer products and were eager to take measures to remedy the situation, enlisting the help of experts on all levels of design, production, trade, and consumption. In fact, they regarded boosting quality as an instrument for fighting deficits, hoping that better, more beautiful, and more reliable products would reduce the public's insatiable desire for more goods. In the course of these developments, the CNAGF and a range of other institutions, such as the Center for Industrial Aesthetics, Artistic Construction and Design or the working groups on quality at the State Committee on Scientific and Technical Progress, became central arbiters of quality and taste. Here divergent classifications of "quality" emerged and sometimes collided head-on. Instead of adopting either a top-down or a bottom-up approach, this chapter uses the middle level of institutions and organizations as a prism reflecting concerns about material excellence, trying to uncover the constant interplay of state and society within them.[9] The complicated negotiations ensuing within these institutions reveal that their representatives were informed about state policies on consumption and also conscious of consumers' reactions to the quality of available products. Their efforts to balance these often divergent stances, coupled with specific engagements with the "West," produced an ever-evolving concept of quality, which provoked a variety of responses and strategies when ultimately put into practice.

To be sure, Bulgarian designers and experts on quality, as well as the other representatives of institutions and organizations, were state employees, as were virtually all other working Bulgarians. Yet the fact that they were employed by the state does not necessarily mean they were by default transmitters of state policies, especially within an economy where work outside of the state involved a negligible number of people. Research on state policies often adopts—too uncritically—the very discourse of state policies, which presents them as a solid, monolithic, and unambivalent body, elaborated by the regime's anonymous top leadership and in congruence with fundamental ideological postulates. By focusing on practices at the middle level, this chapter aims to reveal different mechanisms for policy elaboration, in which ideology is only one of a multitude of factors taken into consideration, and crude state society binaries are avoided.

Problems of Quality

At the February 1961 meeting of the CNAGF, both government officials and representatives of industry and trade were keenly aware of the unsatisfactory quality of Bulgarian goods. Combining their professional knowledge about how the numerous branches of the economy functioned with their personal experience as regular customers, the speakers dissected the "quality problem." They identified weaknesses everywhere: from creation of goods to actual production, from marketing to consumption. From CNAGF's own design process down to the consumer desires of the population, the Bulgarian socialist economy was in need of an overhaul to address a range of pressing problems.

Delegates complained of the bad quality that accompanied the very development of models and prototypes, the task with which CNAGF was charged. To be sure, the center actively researched foreign examples of modeling and design from French, English, German, and Italian magazines, sending its representatives on official visits to France, West Germany, and Switzerland (as well as to other socialist states).[10] Even so, the CNAGF was often criticized for distributing models of shoes, textiles, clothing, and other products that were not well designed, which meant they stayed on shelves in shops for months or filled up store warehouses.[11] Other samples were so complex and difficult to make that, in the context of mass production and the rush to fulfill production norms of enterprises, frequent mistakes yielded ugly and deformed products.[12] The center was compelled to design new styles in an extremely short time, and the patterns it sent out to enterprises were often incomplete or contained mistakes, causing grave losses when replicated in serial production. In addition, the center was constrained by the unavailability of fabrics and a preponderance of directives that forbade wasting materials, which in turn determined the length and width of clothes or the shape of shoes rather than creative inspiration or style.[13]

Thus, even when they were fashionable in design, the quality of the products offered by the center was often derailed during the production process. Coarse textiles, for example, could not produce a dress that was "elastic, soft, well designed, with a good edging . . . fitting like a glove to the body."[14] Government approval was needed for acquiring "luxurious" fabrics, which could not always be procured, and so factories instead used rough materials, which often had inappropriate color schemes or low-quality dyes that faded quickly, occasionally even before purchase. The issue of color in particular provoked complaints, such as this from Anna Bŭlgarova, from the Committee of Bulgarian Women in 1962:

> I think now women are dressed much more beautifully, but in many
> cases we can also see a lack of taste, thanks to the colors we have. The
> material may have perfect quality, but what about dye?—Pink, green,
> and so on! One cannot wear such colors the whole day, a woman cannot
> be in such high pink spirits the entire day! . . . The question of colors,
> comrades, and of their combination, stands very seriously in front of
> us, even more seriously than the problem of the quality of the fabric.[15]

Often such "inadequacies" were blamed on the personal taste of workers or the heads of production in enterprises making textiles, furniture, or children's toys, who decided on aesthetics without knowledge or skill in design.[16]

At the same time, Bulgarian officials had to contend with certain sectors of socialist industry being new and therefore plagued with inadequate expertise. Though the textile industry had a long history in Bulgaria, the ready-made garment industry was nascent. In the late 1950s, it still manufactured clothing in three sizes only, following ancient Greek principles for the proportions of the human body, rather than actual measurements of the Bulgarian population.[17] Old-fashioned construction theories for clothing and shoes as well as a lack of proper body measurements increased the number of goods that were visually appealing yet ill-fitting. In 1962, Neno Lalev, chairman of the Trade Union of Workers in the Foods and Light Industries, commented:

> Quite often, the fashion shows we organize offer many women's and men's clothes, which do not always correspond to the specificity of the body, to the structure of our people. For example, during the review organized in the fall, in September, a group of Czech women, who had been vacationing in our country, attended the exhibition and—I have to tell you—they all took notice of this: "Here we see only such slender, thin mannequins, but we saw as we toured your country around that your women are a bit heftier, more corpulent and none of them could choose a dress from what you are showing here." They asked: "Do you offer these for export, or for your people?" . . . It is the same, comrades, with the shoes.[18]

Such basic issues of composition aside, there were a range of reasons many of the center's new designs stopped short of being produced and ended up in the drawers of the center's experts, never making it to market and into the hands of willing consumers. In 1961, for example, only 2 percent of the textiles in Bulgaria were made according to the center's patterns.[19] In part this was because center staff were frequently accused of not taking into consideration the official requirements faced by industrial enterprises, namely to increase work productivity and save on materials. The new products, usually meant to be created from a combination of fabrics or yarn, were labor-intensive and increased the time necessary for the production process. Judging the center's prototypes to be too intricate and time-consuming, many industrial enterprises refused to buy the designs since they had no motivation to put them into production. In addition, technical staff at an enterprise—its workers, and above all amateur designers—often proposed their own patterns and saw in external designs a threat to their small surplus earnings.[20] Even when new products were accepted, industrial enterprises frequently intervened and transformed their shape and texture. They regularly substituted fabrics and colors in times of shortage or in order to save on expensive materials; in other cases, they added material into the design as a way to unload extra quantities of a particular cloth or substance. Product control staff in the industrial enterprises often sided with internal management—out of fear or loyalty—and closed their eyes to errors committed because of hastiness and oversight. Lack of subsequent control on the part of the center, which lost interest in the fate of the new product once the design was sold to industry, contributed to the potential disjuncture between goods circulating on the market and a well-designed prototype.[21]

Even when new, "fashionable" products were produced, they were often caught up in the next link in the chain, that is, the sphere of internal trade. Newly produced items had to receive CNAGF's formal approval before they were offered to trade organizations, and trade representatives often refused the new items, claiming there was no consumer demand for them. In response, the center sometimes accused trade organizations of being conservative, incompetent, and unreceptive to novelty and fashion. In 1962, Tsvetan Markov, from the Industry Department of Sofia City People's Council, which dealt with light industry in Bulgaria's capital, declared:

> We approve one model, and many representatives of trade and industry participate in this process; we conclude that the object is comfortable, appropriate, and complies with all requirements; but when the time comes for ordering, members of trade organizations order only 10 percent of it, so as to see how it will behave on the market![22]

Numerous trade organizations attempted to justify their hesitation in ordering particular new models by pointing to regional consumer demand. Protesting against the dominant practice of approving one design with a fixed price that was to be sold all around the country, trade representatives asked for more decentralization in planning consumption, which went against key policies of the central ruling bodies. As reactions from local trade officials reveal, there was a clear understanding that "quality" and sense of taste were not uniform and thus could not be simply imposed top-down; the urban-rural and regional dimension of taste required examination of and sensitivity to local choices.

Yet some officials from the center and other institutions were against allowing impulsive consumer demands to negatively influence their professionally determined parameters of quality and fashion. Indeed, at the 1961 CNAGF meeting in Sofia, Dinka Peeva, from the Ministry of Education and Culture, declared, "We think that people's taste must be cultivated. If we achieve this, we can be sure that people will like and look for those items that are now being rejected. Preferences and demand should not be a passive response. The Center, through active campaigns, must improve taste and demand."[23] Here as elsewhere the "blind duty of trade to follow the taste of all categories of customers" was found to be a problematic formulation. Giving in to customers' demands was seen as a sign of laziness, and such a stance was thought to be erroneous and even harmful: it held back development of customers' tastes and led to restoration of outdated "petty-bourgeois" concepts of beauty. Hence, members of trade organizations were encouraged to nourish within their clients a "healthy, aesthetically-developed taste and the pursuit of the beautiful."[24]

Despite its impulse to direct taste, the center—like other Bulgarian state agencies—continuously sought ever-more-sophisticated ways to both track and shape consumer desires. As a result, solutions were looked for and sometimes found in more systematic research on customer demand: the consumer became part of the design equation in the form of surveys on consumer taste. In 1961, Mr. Zayakov, from the District Trade Organization in Ruse, recounted how his organization had conducted such an assessment:

> We distributed written questionnaires with ten questions for the city and two questions for the villages. And I have to tell you, the citizens took this initiative very seriously and gave us very competent answers. The questions about the assortment of textiles, the color schemes and patterns were answered in detail. The citizens were exceptionally critical of ready-made clothing, of its quality, and above all of its sizes—a problem that is not yet solved. . . . And the citizens gave us a series of valuable recommendations on the quality of clothing and the appearance of furniture.[25]

But whether sketchy or statistical, consumer complaints and studies were chaotic, too messy to offer the center or other Bulgarian authorities a solid, comprehensive, and trustworthy vision of what to do. However, some consumer comments resonated with visions of quality developing among professionals in the center, who located quality not only in the aesthetical and "modern" outward appearance of goods but also in utility, financial prudence, and efficiency. In the decades that followed, state agencies responded in a variety of ways so as to "modernize" Bulgarian consumer tastes.

In Search of Solutions

Fully aware of the problems associated with the quality of consumer items and further alerted by sharp customer and institutional critiques, the Bulgarian government undertook a range of measures to improve the standards of state-produced goods. Steps varied from sanctions and punishments to material incentives and institutionalization of industrial design. This multitude of actions testified to the quality of goods having become a top state concern from the 1960s onward. Notwithstanding these initiatives, problems of quality persisted and continued to preoccupy the ruling bodies throughout the socialist period. Although questions of quality were never resolved, they became a central priority with a clear and critical place in socialist ideology.

The immediate and most drastic government measure taken to ensure quality products consisted of sanctions placed on the top management of enterprises that produced low-quality goods. As early as the late 1950s, such measures included fines and even dismissals. The latter was the fate, for example, of the director of the "Vitosha" tailoring enterprise in Sofia and the chief engineer of the "Marek" factory in Stanke Dimitrov for having allowed repeated production of low-quality clothing in 1958.[26] Subsequent checks at Vitosha factory in Sofia, however, disclosed ongoing problems with quality—clothes burnt during ironing, bad collars, incorrectly sewn sleeves—for which the director, chief engineer, workshop manager, and quality controller were fined between 600 and 1,000 leva (for each, about a month's salary).[27]

The flip side of sanctions and punishments were the material rewards offered to deserving enterprises for producing "new" high-quality items. Eager to fight the lack of motivation in industrial enterprises, the Committee on Work and Prices at the Council of Ministers approved new regulations for giving additional payment to artists and designers who introduced new designs into the textile industry. The regulations contained a definition of what state authorities considered a "new high quality product," which clearly demonstrated the necessity to blend good design with cheap production and cost-saving measures. In addition to being "a true novelty" and responding exactly to its purpose, the new high-quality item had to be made with low-priced materials, and be more labor- and material-efficient. It was also obligatorily approved by the CNAGF and contracted by trade organizations.[28] For the sake of implementation, the center provided explicit definitions of new models, assortments, drawings, and colorings. Specifically, a new model had to be "a type of clothing that was different from existing products in terms of its fashion line, use of materials, and the manner of construction of details; it must be more economically viable in combining the relative economy of materials and labor, and be adaptable to industrial production."[29] As of 1963, workers, engineers, and technical staff in industrial enterprises who participated in production of luxurious and fashionable items were allowed to receive up to 25 percent of the revenue from these goods, a serious stimulus to raising the quality of products and implementing quality control.[30]

Although the measures the Bulgarian regime had undertaken since the late 1950s in order to raise the quality of socialist goods were wide-ranging, by far the most ambitious of all such projects was the birth of Bulgarian design. Professionalization of design in Bulgaria represented a key step in the socialist government's attempt to improve the attractiveness of all produced goods. In the spring of 1963, the Council of Ministers' Decree No. 65 established a Council for Aesthetics of Industrial Goods within the State Committee on Science and Technical Progress, which was called on to improve the aesthetic level of industrial products in Bulgaria.[31] Splitting up CNAGF's original mission to direct development of all goods in the country, it created a new Center for Industrial Aesthetics, Artistic Construction and Design (CIAACD). Subordinated to the Ministry of Machine Construction, the CIAACD was responsible for designing electrical appliances, metal and plastic objects, machines, and transport vehicles, leaving textiles to the CNAGF. The decree ordered that the two centers send their staff to formally study design in socialist and capitalist countries and that the Academy of Fine Arts in Sofia quickly establish a new program in industrial aesthetics. In addition, the decree obliged the country's larger enterprises to fund the position of an "artist-designer" and urged them to be vigilant in constantly upgrading the quality of machines and objects of everyday life.

Over the next two decades, design was proclaimed to be among the state's highest priorities. Party programs espoused it as a guarantee for production of quality goods and further decrees attempted to introduce professional design standards more rapidly and fully into industrial production.[32] The directives of the Ninth Party Congress for the five-year economic plan for 1966–1970 set as a goal "the increase in production of consumables, the constant widening of their assortment, the improvement of quality and the aesthetic appearance of industrial products."[33] State and party leader Todor Zhivkov declared outward appearance to be a gauge for assessing quality. "No matter how technically perfect a radio might be . . . if it has no modern and beautiful outward appearance, it will stay in the shop forever," stated Zhivkov in his speech to the eighth plenum of the Central Committee of the Komsomol. He concluded: "It is more than evident that today the problems of industrial aesthetics are one of the paramount questions concerning the development of our economy."[34]

Although this turn toward design was by no means an original strategy of the Bulgarian regime, it found a rationale in the acute awareness in the early 1960s of the low quality of goods and the desperate search by state, trade, and industrial representatives for measures to correct it.[35] On the one hand, the Bulgarian authorities were clearly following in the steps of the USSR, where a similar decree was adopted in 1962, "concerning quality improvement of the production of machines and consumer goods through the inculcation of methods of artistic construction."[36] At the same time, however, Bulgarian artists and engineers-turned-designers, much like other Eastern Bloc designers in this period, studied and researched design in a range of capitalist countries. In 1964, the Bulgarian communist party's ideological journal, *Novo Vreme*, proclaimed that "the products of our labor in no way should be measured with quantitative indicators only; all we produce must be on the level of world production in its quality, in all indicators of its content and form," and it identified Switzerland, Denmark, Sweden, and Finland as explicit models to be emulated.[37] Two years later, Minko Hasumski, a long-term CIAACD director, declared that the best paradigm to learn from belonged to the Ulm School of Design in West Germany and its leader, Tomàs Maldonado. He appealed for Bulgarian designers to have increased possibilities for specialized study "in the Scandinavian countries, the UK, West Germany and elsewhere, in view of the valuable design experience these countries possess."[38]

Through a variety of means, Bulgarian designers and the wider public were exposed to the foreign designs of a significant array of goods. At the annual trade fair in Plovdiv, for example, West European exhibitors appeared beginning in 1958 (the United States in 1960), with ever-more-elaborate exhibits of goods.[39] The first specialized "design" exhibit—"Design in the German Federal Republic"—took place in Sofia in 1967 and was accompanied by a range of visits and lectures from Western designers.[40] Furthermore, the products and projects of capitalist designers proliferated in Bulgarian journals and books dedicated to design issues. Established in 1968 as a bulletin of the CIAACD, the journal *Dizain* published a multitude of articles by top designers from capitalist countries.[41] It chronicled the results of major design competitions such as the Italian Compasso d'Oro or the West German Gute Form, presenting the work of designers working for IBM, Braun, AEG, and Philips, and even larger projects such as the layout of a whole kindergarten from Dettingen, West Germany. In addition, Bulgarian experts continued to study design in Western Europe, and in some cases they even solicited designs for Bulgarian products from Western companies.[42]

Still, "Western" design was placed under close scrutiny by the Bulgarian design world. Bulgarian designers acknowledged the predicaments faced by their Western colleagues, who they believed were compelled to create objects that generated "artificial needs" among customers who would otherwise not buy them. In contrast, the socialist designer made products with the loftier goal of satisfying the consumer's "rational" needs.[43] Among the vices of capitalist design, "imitation" for the sake of prestige and "styling"—that is, extraneous pursuit of extravagant forms, decoupled from functional and technical considerations—were

FIGURE 6.1.   An example of U.S. design, from Arthur Pulos. From "Dizainerskoto obrazovanie v SAShT," *Dizain* 2–3 (1977): 50.

singled out. Finally, socialist designers critiqued the aspiration for novel products that nobody had yet seen, a goal that often generated uncomfortable and irrational objects.[44] Beyond any doubt, the planned economy, as one devoid of the quest for surplus and free of market constraints, was conceived as the best context for design to flourish. Yet by the 1980s, even these purported "faults" of capitalist design would be openly reconsidered.

Even before the 1980s, exchanges between Bulgarian designers and their counterparts from the capitalist West were deemed ideologically acceptable for a number of reasons. The influence of some Western designers on their Bulgarian colleagues was rationalized through their leftist leanings or links with the USSR.[45] Indeed, some of the articles of Western designers that were published in *Dizain* were first translated for Russian journals (mainly *Tehnicheskaia Estetika*) and only then into Bulgarian.[46] For decades Bulgarian designers had regarded their Western colleagues more as victims of capitalist greed than as active fighters in the brutal battle of capital. Capitalist designers were seen as entrapped by wealthy business owners' "insatiability" for profit rather than as actors enthusiastically involved in production of "fake utility."[47] As well-known designers Fiodorov and Somov explained, "Famous American designers convey with bitterness their helplessness to stop the irresistible outburst of formalism on the U.S. markets."[48] Other Bulgarian sources even went so far as to claim that the "majority" of designers in the capitalist countries were progressive thinkers and creators of expedient (*tselesŭobrazni*[49]), useful, comfortable, and beautiful objects. Capitalist designers were endowed with a vision, as it was assumed that "they continue to believe in the utopian idea of 'beauty that saves the world,' and the harmonious material environment, accessible to everybody."[50] Ideological differences between Bulgarian designers and their capitalist counterparts were glossed over, thereby opening a sufficiently wide niche for incorporation of global standards into Bulgarian design practice.

Designing Socialism

At the start of their work in the early 1960s, Bulgarian designers espoused a strictly functionalist vision of quality. Quoting profusely from the works of the modernist German Bauhaus and Soviet VhUTEMAS-VhUTEIN of the 1920s, they proclaimed utility, comfort, and beauty as the cornerstones of their design ideology. One of the first pioneers of Bulgarian design, architect Kiril Vŭzharov, explained that tastelessness often ensued from the inability to derive the form and beauty of an object from its primary function as well as from the material used. "The structural and plastic qualities of the material, its natural color, its inherent texture, its ability to take one or another form, the way it is processed— all this is an inexhaustible source of beauty," he insisted, adding that designers too often "violated" the material in processing it in an untypical manner or by resorting to imitation.[51] This rigorous functionalist stance allowed Bulgarian designers to locate quality outside of the form of a particular product. Thus, Vŭzharov was able to maintain that the most important indicators of the "quality" of a lamp were the "quantity, direction and color of the emitted light; only then comes the problem of its outward appearance." He appealed to consumers to purchase "not what they arbitrarily may have liked, but practical, comfortable and beautiful pieces of furniture, truly needed and suitable for their flat, only after they had thought over where they would be placed."[52]

Although functionalist positions permitted Bulgarian designers to take the focus of quality away from the form of individual objects, a theoretical move toward "composition" went even further in this direction. Function, though fetishized, was not to be privileged at the expense of composition, according to Ognian Shoshev, a leading Bulgarian designer and employee of

FIGURE 6.2.   Cartoon by T. Pindarev, ridiculing beds with head- and footboards depicting old-fashioned landscapes, with the text: "Do take it! You will have a bed and a picture gallery at the same time!" From Kiril Vŭzharov, *Promishlena estetika* (Sofia: Profizdat, 1969), 13.

the CIAACD. He understood composition as the "relations, which are created among forms in space, the influence one form has on another." Placing emphasis on volume and space, he propagated research in architectonics—the combinations among various bodies, between them and open space, and their effect on human senses. Shoshev positioned quality in "complexity, the unity of compositional elements, in total ensemble," understanding the material object as simply an element of the environment, which contributed to its appropriate organization.[53] Proportionality, commensurability, balance, ergonomics—the harmonious relationship of the product with man and the environment—became the new key words of Bulgarian design in the 1970s.[54]

Conceiving the object in a total environment unleashed a drive to educate both the customer and the shop assistant, who had no clue about tectonics or the interconnections of form, volume, and space. Popular books in the genre of animated short stories narrated the experience of the benefits of good design at a number of Bulgarian industrial enterprises, spreading the new message to workers and party activists.[55] Numerous sources advocated engaging customers in an active, creative relationship with the material world that would supplement their passive consumerism.[56] Trade organizations in Bulgaria embraced this rhetoric and introduced it into practice, urging shopkeepers to recommend products on the basis of how they would cohabit with other goods and suit them in color, size, and style. As instructional advice to future shop assistants maintained:

> There is no absolute beauty; this, what is beautiful under certain conditions, could be ugly under different conditions. For example, during the aesthetic evaluation of a chair that is to be bought, in addition to particular traits—common or specific only for this chair—it will be seen as part of a given milieu, the interior in which it will fit and which must be aesthetically arranged.[57]

Thus, by calling attention to the structural ties between products rather than to the intrinsic qualities of one particular object, Bulgarian designers appealed to both consumers and shopkeepers to recognize and appreciate "total design." In essence, they advocated critical reconsideration of the whole world of goods, in which "the totality of ensemble, the harmony of goods" was paramount.[58]

This, of course, required complex planning, taking the form of "scientific methods" and "intersectoral" design that would link goods produced in different branches of industry. Many of these notions were under the influence of Soviet designers, whose boldest visions required that design would be planned not only in a national context but within the whole socialist system.[59] Such ambitious schemes compelled Bulgarian designers to further shift responsibility for quality verification from the customer's individual taste to scientific and expert knowledge. It was the designer who was now asked to plan and coordinate the material world, shedding away the "enslaving and notorious market demand" and applying his creative imagination. Creativity had to rely on "scientific forecast of the natural, technical, and above all social phenomena" and on analysis of the economy, industrial possibilities, national income, welfare, and culture.[60] Thus planning the material world increasingly depended on project prognoses for whose smooth development a whole new science was to be born: the discipline of prognostics. The "geometry of the world of objects" was not simply a metaphor; the pages of books on design were filled with mathematical formulae, equations, and graphs. In addition, prognostics was coupled with qualimetry, a science developed in the USSR for quantitative measurement of quality. Subjective preferences for particular products now had to be based on evidence and "proof," while every single consumer good was scrutinized for its effects on ensembles of products. Quantitative analyses of efficiency led to elaboration of the notion of "optimal quality," which was to supersede "highest quality" as both index and ultimate goal. Optimization meant that it was not always economically justified to produce objects with the highest quality, regardless of price or the profit of the industrial enterprise. Optimal quality would theoretically save the customer from the chaos of oversupply and excessive variety. Thus "improvement of quality" was reconceived as the imminent curtailing of an unwarranted diversity of objects.[61]

Whereas in the 1960s disordered abundance was criticized as a main feature of the capitalist market, by the 1980s this critique had turned to socialist consumption as well. Bulgarian designers attacked the "sham bounty" of certain products on the socialist market and lamented the vice of "prestigious design" in Bulgarian furniture, TV sets, lamps, glass, porcelain, and clothing. The numerous varieties of these "superficially beautiful" products had alarmingly limited social and cultural functions, their production amounting to a "'socialist version' of wasting." Bulgarian designers openly rejected the notion that all consumer desires should be satisfied and now, instead of advocating introduction of new products, suggested diminishing the number of models that had "almost identical consumer qualities." This would save material and energy resources and untether the economy from the burden of redundancy.[62] The "scientific turn" increasingly pushed the consumer's individual taste into the background.

Consequently, Bulgarian design of the 1970s and 1980s was increasingly determined by and oriented toward visions of "progress" and idealized notions of a communist future, the designing and building of the material world of the future.[63] With this in mind, designers deemed customer demand as an extremely limited source of information, for it could not answer the question of what new goods were needed in the future. Indeed, Bulgarian designers were growing reluctant to closely copy the products of their Western colleagues who designed for clients of the present instead of planning the material world of their heirs. Looking for the "coefficient of the future" was the new catchphrase of the socialist design world.[64] As Soviet designer Georgii Minervin declared in 1972, "What is predicted today and realized afterwards should be positively received by the future consumer, answering to his (and not only to our!) needs, requirements, tastes and ideals."[65] As part of Minervin's image of the future, designers would craft only "multifunctional" products and ensembles of "product-organisms," which would adapt themselves to changes in human and social needs. Minervin concluded: "We imagine the design of future communist society not as the simple abundance of consumable products—products and pieces of 'mass art,' guaranteeing super-comfort and liberating the person from all intellectual and physical efforts—but as the foundation of a 'cosmos,' created and managed not by Gods, but by people."[66] According to Minervin's dream, it was the designer-specialist who would "create and manage" this cosmos.

In this way, well-articulated and neatly structured visions of quality gradually separated it from the individual product and even the consumer. With
the advent of architectonics and the subsequent weakening of functionalism,
as well as the rise of scientific methods such as prognostics and qualimetry,
quality was perceived to reside in the ties between objects and the complex
configurations of the environment. Concerns about texture, color, shape, and
size of a given commodity—so dear to ordinary customers—were destabi-
lized as evaluation depended now on how they fused with one another and the
surrounding milieu. Even though Bulgarian designers continued to selectively appropriate "global" standards, the real customer had once again vanished from view, eclipsed by pledges to create not for the present but for
future generations.

Quality in Practice

The principles that permeated discussions on design in Bulgaria from the
1960s to the 1980s did affect how state officials handled the thorny problem of
quality. Designer prototypes could not always make it into production, but
Bulgarian design ideologies still had a clear impact on the overall production
and distribution in the country. In particular, the practices of quality-control
bodies in socialist Bulgaria indicate that major design ideas were successfully
transferred to the authorities and institutions dealing with quality review. Starting from functional concerns about the utility of specific products, quality-control clerks soon began to apply complex "integral quality" criteria and talk about
multisectoral—or so-called multiplication—approaches in evaluating and controlling industrial production.

The evolution of quality control in socialist Bulgaria was quite dramatic.
Looking back to reports from the mid-1950s that evaluated garments for state
approval, few instances of rejection were noted.[67] Indeed, quality checks of
clothing from the period found almost all items to be "good," although many
had defects: bad stitching, curved stripes, sleeves too long, or too deep a collar.[68]
Yet by the 1960s, the Bulgarian state had introduced a stringent review of virtually all products before they appeared on the market. A permanent interinsti-
tutional commission of the State Committee on Scientific and Technical
Progress established working groups that surveyed goods during internal exhibitions of commodities, with the goal of "not permitting low-quality, old-fashioned
and functionally or aesthetically badly-developed goods to reach the market."[69]
In 1968, for example, eleven working groups examined the quality of an astonishing array of Bulgarian-produced objects at the annual Plovdiv trade fair—from

children's toys, textile, pottery, and porcelain to wooden items, souvenirs, household appliances, and packaging. Low-quality goods were described in lengthy reports, which included recommendations that certain goods be improved, or kept out of production.

Unlike their lenient and cursory predecessors, the 1968 state controllers provided abundant explanations and classifications of quality. They reflected on design, function, and aesthetics, and they pronounced their verdicts, convinced that good quality meant "functionality, beauty and comfort." Thus, in the 1968 review forty-four enterprises producing children's toys saw from one to a dozen of their goods rejected by the working group.[70] Four dolls from the "Children's Happiness" State Enterprise in Sofia were deemed to have old-fashioned clothing, while a bicycle made by the "Metal" State Enterprise in Sofia was rejected "until it is reworked with a better developed aesthetic and technical appearance." In another case, a dustbin and a barbecue were judged to be non-functional and nonaesthetic, while a chair with a reed-woven seat and back was found to "lack a harmonious connection between the lacquered wooden details and the weaving."[71] A cooperative in Suvorovo was blamed for producing lamps with a "bad combination of wood, colored plastics, golden bronze and celluloid paint," and the "Vasil Kolarov" plant in Sliven was taken to task for "delays in the introduction of new forms of glass and its surface treatment, which negatively affects the outward appearance of lamps produced in the whole country."[72] Decorative plates were declined because of old-fashioned or too complicated forms "unsuitable for contemporary settings" or for naïve and naturalistic drawing.[73] A carpet with poppies offended the reviewers because it lacked "stylization" and its composition was overburdened.[74] Other reasons for elimination included bad decoration and colors, insufficient thickness of the material, old models, heavy construction, impracticality, and "primitiveness." There often appeared vague descriptors such as "ugly" or "bad," or no reason at all was given, but other critiques were detailed and elaborate. Ending on a positive note, however, all reports finished with goods that were awarded with the prize of "Beautiful Object."

In later decades, however, quality reviews took a substantially different approach. Echoing designers' concerns for total and complex design, they steered away from the quality of particular products and focused instead on configurations of goods across various branches of the economy. In 1983, for example, Decree No. 40 of the Council of Ministers approved a taxonomy of 121 groups of products (expanded to 227 in 1984) with a "structurally decisive impact on the development of the national economy," whose quality had to be raised in the following year.[75] Each economic sector received a list of such products to be improved according to strictly determined indicators; in turn, these improvements would help raise the quality of a set of products from another economic sector. Function gave way to complex "multisectoral planning." By 1984, inspectors carried out "complex reviews," which showed that the "quality of particular sixty-seven products had been improved, and the planned 128 indicators reached." The Ministry of Machine Construction, for example, was allocated eight products with 24 indicators; it surpassed the plan by improving the quality of ten products with 32 indicators. There were, however, difficulties: the "Elprom" State Enterprise was not able to make adequate electrical motors, and so the state enterprise producing equipment for the tobacco industry was unable to guarantee their reliability. The Ministry of Chemistry experienced similar troubles: the toothpaste produced by "Farmahim" State Enterprise remained of a lower quality, since no plant in the country was ready to supply calcium carbonate with the appropriate granulometric content.[76] In 1985, the obstacles posed by the multisectoral approach persisted: the water resistance of windows for residential and office buildings, for example, could not be improved, as no plant in Bulgaria could offer appropriate softwood. Tap beer did not flourish on the market because shops and restaurants did not have needed equipment; moreover, packaging firms produced insufficient quantities of five-liter jugs to hold the beer.[77] Here assessments of quality were removed from the specificities of particular products and acquired meaning only within the intricate interconnection of webs of production and goods.

Discussions of the quality of toothpaste or tap beer might seem to have been entirely removed from previous debates on quality, but this complex approach on the part of the designers became the basis for the planning and functioning of the whole Bulgarian economy. In the late 1950s quality was understood mainly as technical perfection (well-sewn collars and no visible burns on clothes), and in the 1960s as a blend of beauty, comfort, and utility in a modern object. By the 1980s products were placed in a system of quality assurance, which put greater emphasis on coordination and interconnectedness than on the characteristics of the products themselves. Once toothpaste was selected as an object for improvement, it was a matter of elevating the quality in a range of other industrial branches such as chemical and machine production. The quality of the product itself dissolved within this complicated and colossal web of relations. Appropriating design ideas about architectonics and complexity, the quality of a good became the business of myriad related bodies and, most important, "scientific" management. Care for the product's concrete features waned, supplanted by an overriding interest in the smooth, coordinated operation of the entire economic system.

Conclusion

The prism of quality refracts a range of concerns and practices of the Bulgarian socialist regime, related to aesthetics, design, taste, style, and consumer demand. Since the early 1960s, urgent calls for improving quality were accompanied by innumerable proposals on how product excellence could be achieved and by initiatives bent on maintaining the quality of Bulgarian production. What followed was ardent debate among experts at various state institutions about the meaning of quality and how best to attain it. Some representatives of these institutions cared about efficient, modern, and functional design of goods; others embraced a new architectonic vision of design, propagating closer relationships between the object and its material environment. Still, various representatives of state institutions conceived of consumers in a variety of ways: some of them opted for respecting client demand and researched it thoroughly, whereas others, projecting quality onto the future, left present customers abandoned and unattended.

Even though in the 1960s advice on good taste proliferated, in the following decades Bulgarian designers concentrated their efforts not so much on direct reformulation and education of taste, but on creating objects of the future. In their utopian formulations about design, the intrinsic features of a consumer good became relative and ultimately contingent on interconnectedness, coordination, and harmony, while proper assessment could refer only to their total and complex blend. During the debate on quality, an innovative and highly original—"architectonic"—vision of quality emerged, which focused neither on the intrinsic features of the object nor on the customer's actual tastes. Despite being activated for just a short while, in the last decade of socialist rule in Bulgaria, it set in motion a new dream: of a perfectly manageable and controllable socialist economy.

The heated discussion within organizations dealing with design demonstrated the existence of social actors who conceptualized in distinct ways both the quality of an object and the needs of the customer. Thus the meso-level approach, by presenting the interplay of social actors and various publics, helps elaborate a more nuanced vision about the relationship between state and society under the socialist regimes. Approaching production and consumption from a meso level eliminates the sharp line between a leadership formulating the party line and the people who implemented it into practice. Yet this does not mean a return to the traditional totalitarian approach that envisioned an all-powerful state able to silence its citizens and procure either their critical agreement or their complete atomization and withdrawal into an "internal, spiritual exile." It was not possible to dictate all communist policies from the top level of state management; not all of them could be designed by merely reading Marx and Lenin. There existed other procedures for policy elaboration at the middle level of institutions and organizations. The party line was not simply communicated and imposed from above; it was shaped and fashioned on the meso level, where ideology, while always and imminently present, was removed from the forefront and rendered more discrete.

NOTES

1. Anna Bŭlgarova, at a meeting of the Center for New Assortments of Goods and Fashion, Sofia, 1962. Central State Archive in Sofia, Bulgaria; or Tsentralen Dŭrzhaven Arkhiv (hereafter TsDA), fond (hereafter f) 1482, opis (hereafter o) 4, arkhivna edinitsa (hereafter a. e.) 2, l. 32.

2. TsDA, f. 1482, o. 4, a. e. 1. The center was the heir of the State Model-making Center, founded in 1955 as a subdivision of the People's Store, with the task of producing and trading with clothing (models, sketches, patterns), testifying to the growing trend toward stimulating consumption. TsDA, f. 1482, o. 1, a. e. 1, l. 78. In 1963, the center was renamed Center for New Goods and Fashion (CNGF).

3. In attendance were Raiko Damianov, member of the Politburo of the Central Committee of the Bulgarian Communist Party and first vice-chairman of the Council of Ministers; Atanas Dimitrov, Vasil Balevski, and Ivan Nedev, chairman and vice-chairmen of the Committee on Industry; Peko Takov, chairman of the Central Cooperative Union; and Vasil Raidovski, chairman of the Central Union of Labor-productive Cooperatives.

4. TsDA, f. 1482, o. 4, a. e. 1, l. 4.

5. János Kornai, *Economics of Shortage* (Amsterdam: North-Holland, 1980); Katherine Verdery, "What Was Socialism and Why Did It Fall?" in Katherine Verdery, *What Was Socialism and What Comes Next?* (Princeton, NJ: Princeton University Press, 1996), 19–38; Liviu Chelcea, "The Culture of Shortage During State-Socialism: Consumption Practices in a Romanian Village in the 1980s," *Cultural Studies* 16, 1 (2002): 16–43. On consumption and deficit in Bulgaria, see Kristian Bankov, *Konsumativnoto obshtestvo* (Sofia: Lik, 2009), 217–37.

6. For comprehensive research on consumption in socialist Bulgaria, see Ivaylo Ditchev, *Grazhdani otvŭd mestata? Novi mobilnosti, novi granitsi, novi formi na obitavane* (Sofia: Prosveta, 2009), 132–219.

7. See for the USSR Victor Buchli, "Khrushchev, Modernism, and the Fight Against 'Petit-bourgeois' Consciousness in the Soviet Home," *Journal of Design History* 2 (1997): 161–76; Susan Reid, "Destalinization and Taste, 1953–1963," *Journal of Design History* 2 (1997): 177–201; Reid, "Cold War in the Kitchen: Gender and the De-Stalinization of Consumer Taste in the Soviet Union Under Khrushchev," *Slavic Review* 2 (2002): 211–52; and Natalya Chernyshova, "Consumption and Gender Under Late Socialism," (download www.ehs.org.uk/ehs/conference2008/Assets/Chernyshova FullPaper.doc); for Bulgaria, see Kristen Ghodsee, "Potions, Lotions and Lipstick: The

Gendered Consumption of Cosmetics and Perfumery in Socialist and Post-socialist Urban Bulgaria," *Women's Studies International Forum* 30 (2007): 26–39. A notable exception to this historiographic trend is Judd Stitziel's recent study on clothing, fashion, and consumer culture in the GDR; Stitziel, *Fashioning Socialism: Clothing, Politics and Consumer Culture in East Germany* (Oxford: Berg, 2005).

8. On the ideology of socialist regimes satisfying people's material needs, see Mila Mineva, "Razkazi za i obrazi na sotsialisticheskoto potreblenie (izsledvane na vizualnoto konstruirane na konsumativnata kultura prez 60-te godini v Bŭlgariia)," *Sotsiologicheski problemi* 1–2 (2003): 143–65.

9. Here I use Stitziel's meso-level approach, that is, "from the middle," which locates society, among other places, in the heart of the state—avoiding crude binary oppositions between society and state, both bottom-up and top-down analyses of state socialism. Stitziel, *Fashioning Socialism*, 6–7.

10. In 1960, the list of foreign journals imported for the center included more than sixty titles, among which *Vogue, International Textiles, Reflets de Paris, Donne eleganti*, etc. TsDA, f. 1482, o. 2, a. e. 12, ll. 86–86a.

11. TsDA, f. 1482, o. 4. a. e. 2, l. 5.

12. TsDA, f. 1482, o. 4, a. e. 1, l. 27.

13. TsDA, f. 1482, o. 1, a. e. 7, l. 101, 131.

14. TsDA, f. 1482, o. 4, a. e. 1, l. 19.

15. TsDA, f. 1482, o. 4, a. e. 2, l. 37.

16. TsDA, f. 1482, o. 4, a. e. 2, ll. 9–10.

17. TsDA, f. 1482, o. 4, a. e. 1, l. 29. When in 1962 Vladimir Miloikov, CNAGF's chief designer, returned from a month-long visit to the Institute of Clothing in Budapest, he wrote in his report how surprised he was to see that his Hungarian colleagues followed their own way in defining measures in length. "In all theories I have known so far, the proportion of the parts of the body is defined by 8 head heights, determined by the ancient Greek sculptor Polykleitos," he noted, and added that this method had already been found inappropriate for it referred only to ideal bodies.

18. TsDA, f. 1482, o. 4, a. e. 2, ll. 7–8.

19. TsDA, f. 1482, o. 4, a. e. 2, l. 7.

20. TsDA, f. 1482, o. 4, a. e. 1, l. 25. In contrast, directors of enterprises single-handedly decided on aesthetic issues in the USSR in the late 1950s. See Reid, "Destalinization," 194.

21. TsDA, f. 1482, o. 4, a. e. 1, l. 12; TsDA, f. 1482, o. 4, a. e. 2, l. 31.

22. TsDA, f. 1482, o. 4, a. e. 2, l. 22.

23. TsDA, f. 1482, o. 4, a. e. 1, l. 27.

24. Alexandŭr Dunchev, Venko Shishkov, *Izkustvo, estetika, tŭrgoviia* (Sofia: Tsentralen komitet na profsŭiuza na rabotnitsite v tŭrgoviiata i uslugite, 1972), 46–47. Yet customers' unwillingness to buy new products was only partly due to "old-fashioned" tastes. In fact, the chief reason "modern" goods could not find clients was their higher prices.

25. TsDA, f. 1482, o. 4, a. e. 1, l. 17.

26. TsDA, f. 1482, o. 2, a. e. 9, ll. 449–50a. Grounds for the punishments were 272 reclamations from foreign contractors for 1957, for twisted seams, misplaced pockets, loose buttons, badly sewed buttonholes, etc.

27. TsDA, f. 1482, o. 2, a. e. 9, l. 98–101a.

28. TsDA, f. 1482, o. 4, a. e. 23, l. 57.

29. TsDA, f. 1482, o. 4, a. e. 23, l. 60a.

30. TsDA, f. 1482, o. 4, a. e. 23, l. 55. The quest for quality on the part of the Bulgarian socialist state should be viewed hand in hand with similar developments within the broader Comecon environment. In the late 1950s, when the Comecon countries started debate on industrial specialization, Bulgaria was allocated the mining industry and export of grain to the whole socialist camp. Yet ever since, the Bulgarian government insisted on specializing in the machine industry and intensive agriculture that could secure bigger financial profits. Countering protests from other Comecon countries, Bulgaria managed to secure the machine industry as its specialization, after promising to buy Western licenses and raise its production to the level of "world quality" standards. Iliiana Marcheva, "Sotsialno-ikonomichesko razvitie," in *Istoriia na Bŭlgarite ot osvobozhdenieto (1878) do kraia na studenata voina (1989)*, vol. 3 (Sofia: Znanie, 2009), 516–49.

31. *Dŭrzhaven vestnik*, 44, June 7, 1963. For recent interest in Bulgarian design, see Pŭrvoleta Krŭsteva, "Razvitieto na dizaina v Bŭlgariia 1963–1973 godina," M.A. thesis, New Bulgarian University, 2008.

32. The Regulation of the Council of Ministers from May 6, 1978, on improvement of work in the sphere of industrial aesthetics was an additional contribution to the bureaucratization and centralization of design. It created a National Council of Industrial Aesthetics and reorganized the former CIAACD into a Central Institute of Industrial Aesthetics, thus bringing forward design's growing consolidation and integration. *Rabotnichesko delo*, 218, Aug. 5, 1972; Ivan Slavov and Iliiana Rizova, *Estetika na prostranstvenata i predmetnata sreda v promishlenite predpriiatiia* vol. II (Sofia: Profizdat, 1985), 52–53. By 1978, the center's staff had reached 146 people.

33. Kiril Vŭzharov, *Promishlena estetika* (Sofia: Profizdat, 1969), 1.

34. Nezabravka Ivanova, ed., *Khristomatiia po promishlena estetika. Podbrani materiali kŭm kursa lektsii po promishlena estetika za studentite ot VUZ kum AONSU* (Sofia: AONSU, 1975), 4.

35. Unlike the USSR, GDR, Czechoslovakia, Poland, and Hungary, which also turned toward state-sponsored design in the early 1960s, Bulgaria did not have its own tradition of design from before World War II.

36. G. Minervin, M. Fiodorov, E. Grigoriev, and L. Pereverzev, *Osnovi na promishlenata estetika. Razshireni tezisi* (Sofia: Tehnika,1972), 7.

37. Alexandŭr Obretenov, "Promishlenost i estetika," *Novo vreme* 2 (1964): 67–68.

38. Minko Hasŭmski, "Za promishlenata estetika," *Novo vreme* 9 (1966): 51, 57.

39. Mary Neuburger, "*Kebabche*, Caviar, or Hot Dogs? Consuming the Cold War at the Plovdiv Fair, 1955–1972," *Journal for Contemporary History* 47 (2012), 48–68.

40. Petko Mishev, *Promishlen dizain. Iz praktikata i teoriiata* (Russe: RU "Angel Kŭnchev," 2004), 20. Later, there followed exhibitions of British, Swiss, and Danish design. In 1968, Åke Huldt, director of the Swedish Council of Industrial Design, visited Sofia, while in 1982 such a visit was made by Herbert Ohl, leader of the German Design Council in Darmstadt. TsDA, f. 517, o. 7, a. e. 127, ll. 35–36.

41. Among them were Frederick Ashford, Yasuo Kuroki, George Nelson, and Peter Gorb.

42. In 1968–1971, for example, three Bulgarian designers were sent to specialize in Italy. Mishev, *Promishlen dizain*, 122; E. Vŭlchanova, "Dvadeset dni v Italiia," *Dizain* 1 (1971). In 1985, Bulgarian authorities solicited offers from Porsche Design in Austria and Pininfarina in Italy but ultimately chose Danish Je-Lau firm designers for a Bulgarian forklift project. Mishev, *Promishlen dizain*, 169–77.

43. Ivanova, *Khristomatiia*, 117. For more on the ideology of needs in socialist Bulgaria, see Iskra Velinova, "Za potrebnostite, potreblenieto i konsumatsiiata pri sotsializma," in *Antropologichni izsledvaniia*, ed. Tsvete Lazova (Sofia: New Bulgarian University, 2004), 71–81.

44. Ivanova, *Khristomatiia*, 92.

45. The Soviet All-Union Research Institute of Industrial Aesthetics (VNIITE), created in Moscow in 1962, was reputed to be "probably the most globally open Soviet institution behind the Iron Curtain, except for the Bolshoi Ballet." In the 1970s, the father of industrial design, Raymond Loewy, had a government contract with VNIITE to develop consumer products for the Soviet industry, such as a Moskvich passenger car, refrigerator, clock, etc. They were, however, not introduced into production. Dmitry Azrikan, "VNIITE, Dinosaur of Totalitarianism or Plato's Academy of Design?" *Design Issues* 15(3) (1999): 45–77.

46. Many more, though, were original translations from the journals *Form* (West Germany), *Design* (UK), *Design Engineering* (Canada), etc.

47. Minervin et al., *Osnovi*, 20.

48. M. Fiodorov and Y. Somov, "Otseniavane na esteticheskite svoistva na stokite," in *Problemi na formoobrazuvaneto v mashinostroeneto*, ed. S. Vulev (Sofia: TsPEHP, 1971), 151–72.

49. For discussion on the key 1920s Russian constructivist term of expediency (*tselesuobraznost*), see Christina Kiaer, *Imagine No Possessions: The Socialist Objects of Russian Constructivism* (Cambridge, MA: MIT Press, 2005).

50. Slavov and Rizova, *Estetika*, 40.

51. Vŭzharov, *Promishlena estetika*, 13–14. For a concept of form as a result of the purposeful materialization of function, see also Nezabravka Ivanova, *Promishlena estetika (kurs lektsii)* (Sofia: AONSU, 1976).

52. Vŭzharov, *Promishlena estetika*, 123, 100, 118.

53. Ognian Shoshev, *Razumŭt na krasotata* (Sofia: Narodna mladezh, 1972), 40–48, 79, 18, 53, 116.

54. As a textbook for the technical schools in the country demonstrates, these key words successfully crossed social layers to be incorporated even in specialized secondary education. G. Minervin, V. Munipov, *Za krasotata na mashinite i predmetite* (Sofia: Tehnika, 1977), 160.

55. Dimitŭr Lenkov, *Na dneven red—promishlenata estetika* (Sofia: Izdatelstvo na BKP, 1967).

56. Ivanova, *Promishlena estetika*, 37, 26.

57. Dunchev and Shishkov, *Izkustvo, estetika, tŭrgoviia*, 66.

58. Vidka Gencheva, Alexandŭr Trendafilov, and Ana Nikolova, *Promishlena estetika. Uchebnik za tehnikumite i SPTU* (Sofia: Tehnika, 1981), 27, 36, 211.

59. Minervin et al., *Osnovi*, 22, 128. For a slightly different vision of the "artistic ensemble of objects," but equally depriving the object of its self-sufficiency, independent image, and perfection, see Iurii Gerchuk, "The Aesthetics of Everyday Life in the Khrushchev Thaw in the USSR (1954–1964)," in *Style and Socialism in Post-War Eastern Europe*, eds. Susan Reid and David Crowley (Oxford: Berg, 2000), 92. For the practical impossibility of assembling all *ensemble* objects on the socialist market, see Susan Reid, "The Khrushchev Kitchen: Domesticating the Scientific-Technological Revolution," *Journal of Contemporary History* 2 (2005): 289–316.

60. Ivanova, *Hristomatiia*, 28. For socialist governments' scientific approach to consumption, see Ina Merkel, *Utopie und Bedürfnis: Die Geschichte der konsumkultur in der DDR* (Köln: Böhlau, 1999), quoted in Marga Goranova, "'Nishto izlishno': proektiraneto na sotsialisticheskoto vsekidnevie—ot utopichen dizain do konsumativnata kultura na sotsializma," *Sotsiologicheski problemi* 1–2 (2009), forthcoming.

61. Gencheva et al., *Promishlena estetika*, 219, 223–24, 211.

62. Slavov and Rizova, *Estetika*, 108–110, 112.

63. For the socialist state's near-monopoly over futurism and its effect on Eastern European designers, see David Crowley and Jane Pavitt, "Introduction," in *Cold War Modern: Design 1945–1970*, eds. David Crowley and Jane Pavitt (London: Victoria and Albert, 2008), 21.

64. A. Peremyslov, *Koeffitsient budushchego* (Novosibirsk, 1968).

65. Minervin et al., *Osnovi*, 139–40.

66. Minervin et al., *Osnovi*, 158–59.

67. TsDA, f. 1482, o. 1, a. e. 4, ll. 43–43a.

68. TsDA, f. 1482, o. 1, a. e. 4, l. 69.

69. TsDA, f. 517, o. 2, a. e. 198, l. 38.

70. TsDA, f. 517, o. 2, a. e. 198, ll. 39–45.

71. TsDA, f. 517, o. 2, a. e. 198, ll. 50, 70.

72. TsDA, f. 517, o. 2, a. e. 198, ll. 80–84.

73. TsDA, f. 517, o. 2, a. e. 198, l. 53.

74. TsDA, f. 517, o. 2, a. e. 198, l. 76.

75. TsDA, f. 517, o. 6, a. e. 63, l. 28.

76. TsDA, f. 517, o. 6, a. e. 63, ll. 30, 32, 34.

77. TsDA, f. 517, o. 6, a. e. 69, ll. 6, 7, 14–15, 17.

PART III

Kitchen Talk

There is nothing more critical to understanding consumption under communism than food and drink. Perhaps more than any other products, they provided a stark barometer of well-being from the lean postwar years to the decades of relative abundance to the last decade of sketchy supplies. Foods and beverages were, on the one hand, rationed in times of shortage and, on the other, also highly subsidized throughout the period. Communist states felt compelled to supply their populations with basic foodstuffs at almost give-away prices both on principle and as a legitimizing strategy. This took different forms in response to varied expectations across the region. As Katherine Pence notes in her chapter on East Germany, the regime's inability to supply real coffee of the quality and quantity available in postwar West Germany was a point of contention throughout the period. This, along with other shortages, fed into the mass protests in East Germany in 1953. The regime, in fact, took extraordinary measures in the aftermath to close the "coffee gap." But the politics of food and drink went well beyond East Germany, which was perennially forced to confront its doppelganger in the Western mirror. Across the region, food (and drink) intermingled with politics, and prices were continually intermittently lowered as a way of winning over disgruntled consumer-citizens.[1]

Indeed, consumers across the Bloc were notoriously incensed by price hikes, especially in Poland, where the price of meat and public protest seemed to follow the same rhythm.[2] But elsewhere in the region as well, people came to expect (and for the most part received) subsidized food as a basic right, though actual supply—its quality and assortment—varied widely. In general, dire postwar shortages were followed by the comparative abundance of the 1960s and 1970s. Note that Hungarian political and economic liberalization after 1956 was called "goulash communism," with the Hungarian stew becoming synonymous with political liberalization as well as relative abundance. But this period was followed again by comparative shortage in the 1980s, varying from bread rations in Romania to a diminished medley of foodstuffs in still-stocked Yugoslav grocery stores. All three of these chapters, by Wendy Bracewell, Pence, and Jill Massino, follow this rollercoaster of food and drink supply and the responses it engendered in three divergent contexts: socialist Yugoslavia, East Germany, and Romania.

In spite of the context-specific variations that they explore, there was one constant: the key role of women in procurement, preparation, mediation, and consumption of food and beverages, along with other household goods. It may be no revelation that, in spite of communist rhetoric promising "equality," communist states pushed women into the workplace without alleviating the "double burden" of work outside and inside the home.[3] But as these chapters reveal, official communist sources openly targeted women in advertisements for domestic products, cookbooks, etc., in direct contradiction to their own rhetoric about gender equality and a "revolution in consciousness."[4] This was as true in times of shortage as in the relatively abundant middle decades of the period. As Bracewell's chapter explores, cookbooks and recipes in Yugoslav women's magazines called on women to "make do" and become adept and resourceful cooks in the early postwar times of shortage. Similarly, Massino shows how women in Romania during the lean 1980s shouldered the bulk of the burden of trying to run a household and raise children under the extreme circumstances of mass shortages, lines, basic foodstuff rations, and frequent but unannounced electricity blackouts. Admittedly, as Massino notes, out of necessity men were required to play a heightened role as "hunter-gatherers" for foodstuffs. But in spite of these contributions, shortages placed particular burdens on already exhausted Eastern European women, who maintained households on shoestring budgets.

As the following three chapters also demonstrate, women's critical role as consumers of goods for household needs did not wane in times of abundance. Again women shouldered the primary burden of cooking and other household labor, even as it was eased by household technologies and more easily obtainable goods. To a large extent, women were the main audience for state promises, media pronouncements, and advertisements about consumer opportunities; they were the focus of state efforts to create happy citizen-consumers.[5] Hence, in many respects Eastern European women were expected to play the role of idealized housewives—Rosie the Riveter at work, but June Cleaver at home. To be sure, many state efforts to promote consumption among women were focused on educating—that is "civilizing" or even "disciplining"—"backward," formerly rural or minority, women.[6] But so too did communist regimes seek to produce, provide, and even import ever-more-specialized goods for their ever-more-sophisticated, *modern*, urban consuming women. This served the dual purpose of promoting modernity through the socialist citizen-consumer, and theoretically bolstering legitimacy via well-provided-for men, women, and children. As Massino's chapter shows, during Romania's consumer "golden age" women had a new range of available goods and services, "from caviar and cognac to vacuum cleaners and television sets," including "time saving devices" to alleviate their household burdens. Women's free time was directed toward Black Sea coast vacations and a range of new possibilities for individual "self-actualization." But, as Bracewell argues for Yugoslavia, time-saving appliances and self-actualizing rhetoric accompanied greater expectations for women to create ever-more-elaborate domestic utopias. The fanciful recipes in Yugoslav cookbooks, even though some were impossible to replicate outside the realm of pure fantasy, put pressure on women to produce Martha Stewart-type realms of Yugoslav living.

Although food and drink, along with a range of other products, were abundant, socialist legitimacy was on relatively firm footing in Romania and Yugoslavia. But by the lean 1980s, a scramble for state legitimacy ensued in the face of shortages of seemingly basic food and beverage products. As Massino argues, Ceauşescu's Romania turned decidedly away from consumer strategies to an autarkic and determinedly nationalist grounding, with dire consequences for provisioning of the Romanian population. Interestingly, Yugoslav cookbooks also reveal a turn to nationalism—as Croatian, Serbian, and other nationalisms were given space for identity reconstruction in the Yugoslav kitchen. Bracewell notes that Yugoslavia did not come equipped with a "melting pot," and the fragmented ethnic politics in the Yugoslav kitchen would be realized in Yugoslavia's collapse. In East Germany, by contrast, Pence explores how the looming presence of the West German "economic miracle" provided an onerous measuring stick against which the population and the regime itself judged East German economic achievements throughout the period. With this in mind, East Germany coupled its floundering efforts in the consumer arena in the 1980s with one of the most comprehensive police states in the Bloc.

But beyond state politics, food and drink were also inherently intimate and personal, their consumption generally outside the gaze of the Party-state. Pence's essay in particular offers a window onto the German institution of the *Kaffee-klatsch* (coffee gossip)—usually associated with women—that pervaded postwar East German culture. According to Pence, the *Kaffeeklatsch* represented a kind of public sphere as well as a form of *Eigensinn*, an exertion of personal will. Coffee was somehow special in this regard, but other foods and drinks in the period were also consumed among a collective—friends, family, co-workers—and so were embedded in collective experiences.[7] Across the region, this meant that sharing a treasured and rare find, or else the only available substitute, often translated into a collective experience of joy or disappointment. In short, in the Eastern European consumer experience, the meaning of food and drink seemed to loom larger than the sum of its parts.

NOTES

1. On Romania, for example, see Ghita Ionescu, *Communism in Rumania, 1944–1962* (New York: Oxford University Press, 1964), 59–60.

2. See, for example, Padraic Kenney, "The Gender of Resistance in Communist Poland," *American Historical Review*, 104(2) (1999): 399–425.

3. For a recent exploration of women under communism and the double burden, see Malgorzata Fidelis, *Women, Communism, and Industrialization in Postwar Poland* (Cambridge: Cambridge University Press), 212.

4. See, for example, Lalith deSilva, "Women's Emancipation Under Communism: A Re-Evaluation," *East European Quarterly* 17 (1993): 301–13.

5. For more on this, see Katherine Pence, "'A World in Miniature: The Leipzig Trade Fairs in the 1950s and East German Consumer Citizenship," in David Crew, ed., *Consuming Germany in the Cold War* (Oxford: Berg, 2003).

6. Mary Neuburger, "Veils, Shalvari, and Matters of Dress: Unraveling the Fabric of Women's Lives in Communist Bulgaria," 169–87, in David Crowley and Susan Reid, eds., *Style and Socialism: Modernity and Material Culture in Postwar Eastern Europe* (Oxford: Berg, 2000).

7. For an engaging discussion of coffee, food, and the social world of women under communism, see Slavenka Drakulic, *How We Survived Communism and Even Laughed* (New York: Harper Perennial, 1993), 1–10, 104–12.

7

Eating Up Yugoslavia

Cookbooks and Consumption in Socialist Yugoslavia

Wendy Bracewell

What can culinary texts—cookbooks, recipe columns in newspapers and magazines, television cooking programs—tell readers about the culture and politics of consumption in socialist Yugoslavia? Recipes represent perhaps the quintessential example of the prescriptive text for the potential consumer: buy that, fix it like this, eat it up! And what could be more straightforward? "Take two kilos of beef," begins a recipe for soup in *Žena u borbi* (Woman in the Struggle), a monthly magazine for women combining news about women's organizations and activities, propaganda exhortations, and household advice, including recipes. But consider the implications of that familiar culinary command "take" when this recipe was published, in the hungry year of 1950, two years into the economic blockade imposed by the neighboring Bloc countries and after a crippling drought that had affected conditions throughout the country. There was nothing much available for purchase in the marketplace: coupons and ration books were needed for flour, sugar, fat, and meat, and the United States was providing urgently needed food aid in the form of powdered milk and dried eggs. The effort required to "take two kilos" of virtually anything was considerable. "Woman in struggle," indeed. More telling is another menu from the following year, built around vegetables, with its repetition of the word "enough": enough on the market, enough nutritional value, enough for a meal. "If afterwards we offer a little fruit with some milk, then that will really be enough."[1]

Despite their lists of ingredients and their no-nonsense directions, cookbooks and recipe columns are not always the most straightforward guides to consumer realities. Nor is the relationship between prescription and practice always easy to identify. It is not just a question of the match between shopping list and market availability, nor even the distance between the demands of the recipe and the skills of the individual cook. A cookbook *might* be used as a shopping guide and a practical kitchen aid, but its real value to a consumer could reside in something else entirely. Cookbooks can be read as prompts to fantasy and desire, perhaps especially in the absence of the required ingredients. They can be treated primarily as material objects, rather than as texts: acquired as souvenirs, given as gifts, kept as reminders, handed down as mementos, displayed as emblems of national identity or educational qualifications or social distinction or something else. But even though this literature may not be a reliable guide to day-to-day consumer habits or desires, Yugoslav cookbooks and recipe columns were never entirely removed from political and economic realities. Their expanding shopping lists of ingredients and products bear witness to gradual improvement of living standards, and to democratization of Yugoslav socialism's version of the "good life"—not just "enough" but abundance, variety, and therefore choice, on the table as well as elsewhere. They also hint how one-time luxuries were taken for granted as necessities by the time they began to disappear from the shops in the straitened economic circumstances of the 1980s. And their contents tell other stories: about the ideological contexts within which food is acquired, prepared, and consumed; about gender regimes and national ideologies; perhaps most of all about the place where public and private fantasies meet and jostle. As supremely didactic texts, they taught the reader not just about cooking but also what it means to be a woman, a mother, and a worker; about how to behave in society; about belonging and difference.

Cookbooks published in socialist Yugoslavia thus provide an index to some of the intentions, aspirations, and contradictions of Yugoslav self-managing socialism. In showing the reader how socialism's promises were being turned into easy, healthy, varied, and happy meals—to use the vocabulary of the genre—cookbooks helped legitimate the system that put all this bounty on the table. At the same time such literature, in its small way, educated consumer desire to run ahead of what the system could guarantee when the economic underpinning of the Yugoslav "good life" came unstuck in the 1980s. Yugoslavia did not collapse because of shortages of cooking oil or coffee, let alone the disappearance from the shops of black pepper or cinnamon sticks. Still, when consumers could no longer take for granted the availability of one-time luxuries they had been taught to see as normal and even necessary aspects of daily life, their faith in the system eroded. This consumer "normality" had been a key marker of Yugoslav exceptionalism, the claim that the changes introduced in response to the confrontation with Stalin's Soviet Union in 1948 marked a separate Yugoslav way to communism. The Yugoslav model was distinguished by its political decentralization, nonalignment, freedom to travel, and market-oriented economic reforms. But for ordinary Yugoslavs, better living standards—measured in terms of the supply and quality of consumer goods, including food—represented one of the most obvious differences between their lives and those of their neighbors in the countries of the Bloc. Still, was Yugoslavia, in the end, all that different from its neighbors? Consumer realities may not have been the same in every case, but throughout the region they molded citizens who felt entitled to their rewards, and who blamed the political system for their frustrations when things went wrong.

Books in the Kitchen

The cookbook (and the recipe column published in newspapers and magazines) was already a well-established publishing genre in the Yugoslav lands well before the Second World War. The first nineteenth-century cookery manuals published in Croatian or Serbian were presented to their readers as translations and adaptations, drawing their authority largely from German or Austrian models. These were quickly followed by works presented as wholly indigenous productions. Some of these nineteenth-century cookery manuals enjoyed reprints and new editions even into the interwar period, though they were joined by more up-to-date authors such as Mira Vučetić, who combined culinary instruction with information on nutrition and manners, and whose first book, *Domaćica u kuhinji* (The Housewife in the Kitchen), was published in Zagreb in 1929, or Spasenija-Pata Marković, the publication of whose popular compendium *Moj kuvar* (My Cook, Belgrade, 1939) followed the success of a weekly column of recipes sent in by readers of the Belgrade newspaper *Politika*. As elsewhere in twentieth-century Europe, this steady proliferation of published cookbooks reflected a newly urbanizing society, where cooking skills were no longer solely transmitted orally, where changing lifestyles (especially for women) called for new domestic arrangements, and where social and economic change was leading to diversification of consumption patterns—and of consumer aspirations.[2] But these cookbooks also reflected specifically Yugoslav conditions and dilemmas, particularly in the new circumstances of the postwar years.

That is not to say that cookbook publishing paused with the war and occupation. Indeed, wartime circumstances offered opportunities to market recipes in different ways. Take, for example, a slender pamphlet put out in the fall of 1944 in Split by Dika Marjanović-Radica entitled *Praktična kuharica*, or "Practical Cook." It was based on her prewar volume *Dalmatinska kuhinja* (Dalmatian Kitchen, 1939) but revised to address wartime conditions of shortage and want, with recipes for "meatless stew" or "tripe without tripe" (crepes cut into ribbons and served in a light tomato sauce). In many ways, this sort of publication simply continued a program of popular education begun in the interwar period; like several of the other established cookbook authors, Marjanović-Radica had trained in domestic science and taught cookery in schools. Providing women, particularly peasant women and working-class girls, with skills and qualifications was a goal of interwar women's groups, political parties, and government agencies. Each had its own reasons but shared similar educational aims and methods: schools, courses, popular publications. These efforts would be taken over, in wartime, by the Yugoslav partisans. Organizations such as the Antifascist Front of Women (AFŽ) continued many of the programs of the "bourgeois" women's organizations and peasant-oriented parties as part of the wider set of goals summed up under the label of the national liberation struggle.[3] Raising the level of women's literacy and developing their knowledge and skills was both an end in itself and a means of improving social conditions, especially in the countryside. Household skills were part of this. It was the Antifascist Front of Women in Croatia that published *Žena u borbi*, for instance, with the first issue coming out in 1943, well before the liberation of the country and the end of the war.

Immediate postwar publications aimed at women were strongly marked by the same educational agenda. The recipe columns, pamphlets, and cookbooks published by bodies such as the AFŽ had titles such as "the significance of fruit and vegetables in the people's diet," "how to prepare powdered milk and egg," "100 ways with potatoes," or even, in an echo of the language of the party meeting, "the potato has the floor." The more comprehensive cookery manuals were intended to be used in the ubiquitous postwar courses intended to supply women with necessary skills or qualifications—or to act as a supplement or a substitute for them. One such book, published in successive editions from 1952 through the mid-1960s, was the *Knjiga za svaku ženu* (Book for Every Woman), which claimed with some justification to supply all the knowledge needed to be "a progressive housewife and mother," from women's bodies and women's rights to cooking and sewing, to the best way to construct a latrine and cesspit.[4] Other works combined roles and responsibilities slightly differently: cookery manuals aimed simultaneously at hotel, restaurant, and canteen managers and at housewives, for example. Here the justification was not just that the recipes and skills were the same, no matter how large or small the quantities, but rather that the housewife, the canteen cook, and the restaurant worker were all subject to the same duties and responsibilities: to understand the nutritional needs of both small collectives and large ones, and to supply them with the least possible waste of time, materials, and energy. The same imperatives ran through the culinary advice aimed solely at the housewife: these instructions would help her protect the health of her children and ensure the work capacity of grown-up family members, balance the family budget, and provide for future needs, both short- and long-term.

Through these texts we can identify the culinary discourse of postwar socialism: thrifty, collective-minded, "cultured" (an important term in the vocabulary of socialist consumption, avoiding the negative associations of practices formerly scorned as "bourgeois"), self-consciously modernizing, and above all "rational" and "scientific"—two keywords that recur throughout these culinary texts. This was not just a matter of standardized measures and precise amounts, but rather an insistence that purchase, preparation, and consumption of food should be underpinned by expert knowledge, planned according to available resources and desired outcomes, and treated as just one aspect of a wider social project. Hence the tables showing the vitamin content and calorific value of individual foodstuffs (and the exhortatory slogans: "get to know more types of vegetables—increase the variety of our menus!"). Hence the menu plans and the timetables of seasonal tasks ("what the housewife should do in September"). Hence the enthusiastic embrace of new industrial food products. And hence the concern for time management and labor-saving devices:

> Resourcefulness and the utilization of every possibility in the
> preparation of healthy and palatable food are particularly important
> for our housewives today, in this postwar period, when not only
> here at home but throughout the world, everyone is living in new
> circumstances and working far more intensively, and when a large
> proportion of women, employed in the economy, must count every
> minute of the time available and use it as well and as rationally as
> possible.

What was missing from this discourse was any recognition of the gustatory pleasures of the table.[5]

Although a few short cooking manuals were issued in the late 1940s, it was not until the early 1950s that cookbook publishing in the new Yugoslavia really took off, perhaps slightly ahead of the economic recovery that got under way from 1953. New editions of prewar classics were released, edited to fit the new circumstances. Sometimes this genealogy was suppressed. Spasenija-Pata Marković's classic prewar cookbook was reissued in Belgrade in 1951 with only minimal changes to the text, but with the author's name omitted (perhaps as the daughter of a prewar government minister?) and with a new foreword stressing the changed circumstances of the postwar period. Ironically, the epigraph to this foreword quoted the Norwegian playwright Henrik Ibsen identifying culinary literature as "the best books that exist" and noting that "it is just a pity that the cookbook authors are usually unknown." It was not until 1956 that the same publisher released an edition under Marković's name; presumably the bourgeois origins of her text had by then ceased to be a matter of concern.[6] Elsewhere the problems posed by such reissues were dealt with by other means: Mira Vučetić's prewar *Kuharstvo* (Cookery) was republished in Zagreb in 1952, again with the main text scarcely changed but with a new preface by Zora Ruklić, an educationalist and long-term political activist, stressing the social role of the cookbook: "It is in the interest of every progressive society for housework to be done correctly. The education of the broad national masses is contributing to the cultural and economic development of the whole nation and building a better life for every individual."[7]

The many revised editions of Vučetić's texts into the 1970s provide a running index of changing ideological expectations as well as culinary practices. As well as comprehensive cookery manuals, specialist titles started to appear in the 1950s, extending well beyond guides born of necessity—cookbooks devoted to appetizers, or game, or cakes, tortes, and sweets. Some of these clearly ran ahead of market realities. One writer of a 1954 cookbook meant for hunters (or more precisely for their wives) recognized that the ingredients her recipes called for might be expensive, or hard to come by. The reader shouldn't rebel, she says; "all it takes is a little resourcefulness on the part of the housewife, who can use something similar, which she does have on hand, in place of that which is lacking."[8]

But other publications arose directly from the new consumer possibilities that were emerging through industrial development. Cookbooks were becoming a means of advertising new products, and not just on brightly colored endpapers promoting well-stocked shops or high-quality goods to the housewife just as she was planning her menu. "The good housewife will always use this book" announced one such ad on the back of a 1953 cookbook published in Belgrade. "But is it all that is necessary for good food? No! You also need first-class high-quality goods and seasonings, which you will find in the RED STAR department store," with full details of address and telephone number, and a crude but bright illustration of a disembodied hand showering the most

FIGURE 7.1.   Advertisement on the back cover of *Moj kuvar i savetnik* (1953 ed.).

miscellaneous goods—a lemon, canned goods, cutlery, ashtrays, saucepans, a handbag, matches—into the kitchen of a woman trying to concentrate on frying some eggs.[9] Under these circumstances, the culinary verb *take* had quite a different connotation from what it evoked in 1950, at least for those living in Belgrade. For consumers outside Yugoslavia's big cities, the pleasures and temptations of department store shopping took much longer to arrive. But cookbooks themselves, often published in-house by a manufacturer, had also become a way of introducing the housewife to articles such as an electric oven, or a pressure cooker, or even new foodstuffs ("Klara, the ready-made pastry for every household: instructions and recipes"). Such promotional material could be issued in huge numbers; a thirty-two-page booklet of recipes published by the Zagreb cooking oil refinery, "55 Recipes for You Housewives, by Our Cook," was produced in fifty thousand copies.[10] This was advertising, of course, but with their information and practical instruction such booklets avoided the criticism being leveled at the advertising industry for artificially creating needs and inflating consumer expectations.[11]

The ever-proliferating cookbook titles pouring from the Yugoslav presses were beginning to do just this: cooking was becoming something more than providing "enough" and making sure it satisfied the family's basic nutritional needs. At the same time, these issues were becoming less and less of a preoccupation. The rise in living standards in the years after the war marked a tremendous change in Yugoslav conditions. In 1953, food accounted for 54 percent of the average family budget; in 1963 it fell to 45 percent, and by 1971, in Belgrade, below 40 percent.[12] For all its shortcomings, particularly in agriculture, the system succeeded in providing for the basic needs of the Yugoslav population on an unprecedented scale. In the cookbooks and around the kitchen tables of Yugoslavia, "enough" was definitely no longer as good as a feast.

Publishing statistics suggest that the demand for cookbooks grew steadily. By the 1960s and 1970s, cookbooks were a profitable branch of the self-managed publishing industry, one that helped to subsidize other categories of publication. Multiple editions of the established culinary classics were published, with impressive print runs: Andreja Grum, *Velika sodobna kuharica*, third edition 1961, ten thousand copies; Mira Vučetić, *Suvremena prehrana i kuhanje*, fourth edition, 1964, thirty thousand copies; Spasenija-Pata Marković, *Veliki narodni kuvar*, seventh edition, 1966, forty thousand copies; Marjanović-Radica, *Dalmatinska kuhinja*, sixth edition, 1967, ten thousand copies. A copy of a cookbook was an obligatory part of every bride's trousseau; a student going away to university might pack a new copy of the family favorite. These were texts that taught a standardized, fairly conservative, and, it must be said, often a somewhat monotonous cuisine. But consumers now had the money to experiment with something different, and their tastes were being shaped by greater exposure to other possibilities, particularly through travel. There was growing demand for new specialist titles, including translations of foreign cookbooks and introductions to exotic cuisines. Classic texts of the grand cuisines were translated and issued in multiple editions: Henri-Paul Pellaprat's *L'Art Culinaire Moderne* (1935), for instance, was published as *Veliki Pellaprat* in Rijeka in 1972 and reissued in 1979. The many more prosaic recipe translations from French and Italian sources, circulated in magazines as well as cookbooks, led Yugoslav cooks to feel part of a western European "normality" that shared a culinary culture and that could take the required ingredients for granted. But Yugoslavs could be more adventurous than that. The 1977 edition of Spasenija-Pata Marković's *Veliki narodni kuvar* had a new section encouraging readers to try Chinese dishes, in addition to older sections on dishes from French, Italian, English, and Russian cuisine and recipes from neighboring countries such as Bulgaria. The advice on ingredients noted blandly that soy sauce could be purchased in big self-service supermarkets, MSG was produced by Podravka under the name of Aji-Shio, and ginger was available in tins imported from China. If they wanted to explore further, that same year Slovenes could try out the recipes in Marinka Pečjak's *Kuharska umetnost Azije* (Culinary Art of Asia, Ljubljana, 1977). The popularity of books on slimming diets or on macrobiotic cookery reflected new concerns among a book-purchasing population that was clearly no longer primarily preoccupied with making do. New practical manuals also appeared, playing on the proliferation of more exotic titles. Thus Ivana Karačić's *Domaća kuhinja* (Domestic Kitchen, Zagreb, 1979) was introduced as an alternative to "the flood of all kinds of the most varied cookbooks," offering instead "tried and tested domestic recipes which can help to produce healthy, home-style, not too expensive cookery for the everyday diet of our people in town and village."[13] Individual recipes were credited to experienced housewives ("Slavica's redcurrant cake"), but Karačić's own credentials as culinary expert were established with reference to her American training and her contributions to the International Culinary Association.

Television introduced new authorities, and new means of promoting cooking products, most notably through a program hosted by Stevo Karapandža, the chef of an elite Zagreb hotel. The foreword to one of his books, *Moji najdraži recepti* (My Favourite Recipes, Zagreb, 1982), was written by the essayist and Francophile Saša Vereš, who placed this work in the same category as "Trimalchio's feast, Rabelais's hymn to life, Larousse's gastronomical lexicon and Bocuse's praise of the new cuisine."[14] But most Yugoslavs associated Karapandža with his TV catchphrase "and a spoonful of Vegeta!"—the Podravka-produced glutamate-laced seasoning powder that was one of the manufacturing successes of Yugoslav industry and a cult product both at home and throughout the Bloc. The cooking show ran for twenty-four years under the sponsorship of Vegeta, with a slot on Thursdays just before the evening news, and made Karapandža just as famous as the celebrity guests whose recipes he featured. Families watched together, made notes of the recipes, and bought the cookbooks as well as the Vegeta.

By the late 1970s, Yugoslav cookbook publishing reflected a highly segmented market, with titles offering instruction on all types of cuisine from the proudly regional to the international, from nostalgic to high-tech, for cooks ranging from harried housewives or recreational cooks to children and even men, who were targeted as hobby cooks or singletons fending for themselves before marriage. A fine example is a humorous but practical volume advertised as the first cookbook for men or women living alone, written by two male journalists who made much play of their "emancipation" in claiming cooking as an equal right and an equal pleasure for men as well as for women and who enlivened their text with recipes and anecdotes from male media stars.[15] Many of these books were not just guides to consumption but desirable consumer articles in themselves, expensive in comparison to the other products of the Yugoslav press, with high production values and glossy color illustrations. For readers who now had enough (though by the early 1980s many were finding it harder and harder to stretch the family budget far enough), these works offered not just food for the family but food for fantasy: ways to make everyday life that little bit more exciting or pleasurable or cosmopolitan, recipes for self-improvement or domestic contentment, shopping lists for social success or even for love. Modest domestic fantasies, it's true, but nonetheless seductive ones. The evolving culinary discourse had slowly made room for the individual, the impulsive, the hedonistic, and the variety-seeking; socialist culinary science and rationality retreated correspondingly. Writing about food was still marked strongly by claims to expertise, but this now tended toward connoisseurship and extended beyond nutrition or technique to the pleasures of the table (and, at least in the glossier women's magazines such as *Svijet* or *Bazar*, these were supposed to lead inevitably to the pleasures of the bedroom), the requirements of *bon ton*, the ways of the wider world, and the traditions of one's own regional or national community. But by the inflation-ridden late 1980s, some of these fantasies were becoming utterly impractical. How was one supposed to read a woman's magazine that first reported on alarming rises in the price of meat and the fact that buying food for a family could take up to 200 percent of an average salary, and then went on to offer a recipe for "a special pork dish," translated from the West German magazine *Neue Mode*, that called for 1.5 kilogram of pork, with a stuffing of ground beef?[16]

A Book for Every-Woman

This culinary literature was explicitly gendered. Women did the domestic cooking, at least as far as most of these publications were concerned. And not only the cooking. The cover of the every-woman's manual of household advice, *Knjiga za svaku ženu: uzorna domaćica* (The Book for Every Woman: The Exemplary Housewife, Zagreb, 1952 and subsequent editions), listed some of the roles women in postwar Yugoslavia were supposed to assume: "housewife, cook, seamstress, embroiderer, mother, teacher, preserver of health, nurse." And it might have added something that was taken for granted inside the covers as well: "worker." As elsewhere in the socialist Bloc, emancipation of women in Yugoslavia was to be achieved through equal status under the law, equal political rights, and most of all full participation in economic life. Women were encouraged into work, whether this was the unpaid "voluntary" labor of the first postwar years of reconstruction or, increasingly, paid employment. From the 1950s to the 1980s, with some variation across regions, an average of 39 percent of all Yugoslav women worked outside the home.[17] The political commitment to women's emancipation through work was not paralleled, however, by a shift in allocation of domestic tasks such as cooking, shopping, cleaning, or child care, which remained women's responsibilities, nor by provision of affordable social support (workplace canteens, child care facilities) that could reduce the burden of household labor.[18] The result was the notorious "double burden": women carried the main load of duties in the home even when working at full-time paid employment.

Housewives' tasks grew still more burdensome with the improvement of living standards from the 1960s, and the expectation that this would be converted directly into domestic comforts. It was women who were responsible for day-to-day consumer decisions, for cooking the more abundant and more varied meals, keeping the family's clothing and household furnishings up-to-date, preparing for holidays, and entertaining family, friends, and work colleagues. Even the new, prestigious household items that began to enter Yugoslav homes from the 1950s were not always the labor-saving devices they promised to be. Refrigerators, for example, cut down on the number of shopping trips but raised expectations about the variety and complexity of dishes that could be produced at home, and they increased the prestige of serving food that was homemade and fresh, not frozen. Washing machines, too, shifted the burden of washing into the home, where once it might have been sent out, and made it a more frequent task. In her memoir of postwar Zagreb, Sonia Bićanić describes how bundles of dirty clothes used to leave the city weekly for the villages of Šestine, to be washed by the village women, and she laments the way in which the arrival of washing machines meant the end of the cartloads of snowy laundry arriving back in the city on Sundays.[19] It was not only less picturesque; in the long run it also meant more work for the urban housewife and less independent employment for the rural women who had often worked as household help for urban housewives. But how could their services be justified when there were so many new home appliances to do this work?

It is tempting to celebrate the consumer abundance of Yugoslavia's 1960s and 1970s; after the long period of postwar austerity, life was becoming fuller, better, easier, more colorful. There were things to buy and enjoy, and Yugoslavs made the most of it.[20] Historians of Yugoslavia's trajectory of consumption generally locate the downside as appearing only in the 1980s, when economic crisis turned the Yugoslav Dream sour for consumers who had begun to take these pleasures for granted. But such opportunities for enjoyment were gendered. From the point of view of the housewife who bore the main responsibility of putting the "good life" into operation day-to-day, consumption could be an exhausting, repetitive grind, made more taxing by the periodic hiccups in supply and distribution of goods, especially foodstuffs, and by the pressure to keep up standards to the levels set by her social milieu—not just family and friends, but also the popular press.

Cookbooks and similar advice literature for women were there to help with these problems, at least ostensibly. Many of the earlier texts recognized the difficulties the housewife faced and were clear about the costs to women, though the consensus was that social revolution was worth the sacrifice. The first edition of *Knjiga za svaku ženu*, addressed primarily to rural women, was quite explicit about what the new system required: "Our woman participates in the great task of the rebirth of our village side-by-side and equally with the men, she works together with men in the village for the development of collective agriculture, but even today she also remains the mainstay of her house."[21] Other texts passed on much the same message for urban women, with employment outside the home seen as a modern norm. The working woman was addressed as someone whose time in the kitchen was limited and who would benefit from expert assistance in planning her tasks.

Some cookbooks retained a distinctly socialist slant in their approach to their readers well into the 1970s, offering ways to make their work faster, better, and easier, but also giving housework an explicitly ideological context. This was the case with the successive revised editions of Mira Vučetić's cooking manuals, which combined exhaustive information on nutrition "on a scientific basis" with lectures about the housewife's social role and responsibility. In 1961, for example, the reader was told that "today's social order demands that we live not only for home and family, but also that we take care for the interests of the collective"; though women have been made equal with men, "the new order cannot be achieved overnight" and "we are today in a transitional period in many things. This is also true of the way we eat." Women could not both work and care properly for their families, so "the state is investing immense effort in various services to help women with their domestic tasks, including opening as many public kitchens as possible." But this put the onus on their users not to be picky eaters: "these collectives can only pay partial attention to individual tastes, as they must first satisfy the principles of correct nutrition."[22] All this might seem to sit slightly oddly with Vučetić's detailed instructions in the same volume for entertaining, largely taken over from prewar editions of her book—how to throw cocktail parties, for example, or when to use finger-bowls, or the correct implements for serving asparagus. However, with Yugoslavia's rapid postwar urbanization, ideological attention was also being focused on manners or "culture," to use the period's key term. Vučetić's emphasis on what was appropriate in each context taught those Yugoslavs who had only recently moved from the countryside into the city how they were expected to behave in their new environment: manuals like this could be a means of democratizing society as well as stratifying it. The village was not forgotten either. Vučetić included notes on the right way to hold a pig-killing party: "a domestic ritual which cannot be kept secret in small places, and it would be very tactless if one did not remember one's neighbours or good friends during this event." The social rhetoric was toned down somewhat in the 1973 edition, though similar assumptions still permeated the text. In this edition, right after the section on hospitality and entertaining—and as a natural continuation of the same theme—there was a new section giving advice on catering for tourists in private houses, which needed to be done (naturally) in a "cultured manner." The housewife had to develop all the skills of those who worked in the various parts of the hotel industry; her task was equally responsible and important for society. The reward would be not just extra income but also "respect from those who understand how much help the housewife is offering the socialist sector in developing tourism."[23]

Other household manuals were more contradictory in their offers of help and advice, however. It was entirely conventional for cookbook authors to recognize the burdens shouldered by the housewife and to promise to make her tasks faster, easier, and cheaper (the very rationale for publication and purchase of their works), but they also multiplied her responsibilities with their suggestions for making life more varied, more comfortable, and more attractive. The keyword here was "nicer," "l(j)epše," a seductive term that appeared increasingly in Yugoslav household literature from the 1950s on. A paragraph introducing the first issue of the new woman's magazine *Praktična žena* (Practical Woman, Belgrade, 1956) sums up the contradictory offers that simultaneously simplified and complicated things for women: "In our country there is not a single journal, nor any sort of publication that can help the woman-wife, the woman-mother and the housewife to carry out her domestic tasks and bring up her children in a simpler manner, and to create in her home the pleasantest and most appropriate domestic atmosphere."[24]

In culinary manuals, squaring this circle meant rationalizing the organization of the housewife's time and suggesting shortcuts and labor-saving products—but at the same time promoting constant novelty, equating social success with the ability to entertain, and inflating the standards expected from the cook and on the table. New ingredients, new dishes, new skills, new responsibilities all took time, in shopping and preparing, time that was supposed to be saved by shortcuts elsewhere. What was all this labor-saving *for*, anyway? More work in the home, apparently. Sometimes this was staggeringly explicit:

> Since today you already have prepared the lunch you made on
> Sunday, and your flat is tidy (you probably cleaned it on Saturday),
> you have some free time, which you will spend on a special task. In
> the spring, summer and fall you made various sorts of preserves,
> jams and compotes; however, there are fruits for making preserves in
> winter too. Therefore we're giving you a recipe for lemon preserves,
> which are very tasty. Take 12 thick-skinned lemons. . . .[25]

The task of the cookbooks and the women's magazines was to make all this less tiring and repetitive and stressful by making it seem fun and fulfilling. Over the course of the 1960s and 1970s, housework as presented in household manuals became less and less a rational science or a heat-and-serve modernist utopia. Was it a coincidence that, over the same period, the capacity of workplace canteens was slowly contracting?[26] The more you read about it, the more shopping and cooking became an exciting adventure, an arena for social assertion, a labor of love, an outlet for creativity, a means of self-realization. It could be a struggle reaching this state of mind:

> Cooking is considered simple, even humiliating work. Yes, if done
> mechanically, without thought, without goodwill and without love.
> But if the housewife becomes absorbed in this task, she will see that
> it isn't so simple, and that it is not without charm. There is much
> here that is interesting. The housewife makes guesses, thinks up a
> new dish, decorates it today differently than yesterday, and how much
> joy it gives her, as well as the members of her family! Slowly, day by
> day, she gains experience, perfects herself, makes a whole art out of
> her labor, and then she does it with joy.[27]

Others simply took it for granted that this was what cooking was about, and what motivated women to spend time on it. Successive editions of Spasenija-Pata Marković's manual illustrate the sometimes awkward shift from educating the populace in socialist culture to helping the housewife express herself. In 1966 the *Veliki narodni kuvar* was still laying down the law about "what you should know about serving," with strict rules for setting the table only slightly modified by a comment that "the more original the table decoration, the nicer." By 1977, however, a new section had been added to the chapter on serving dealing with the "decoration of food," which "raises cookery to the level of a special art, not only with respect to the preparation of food, but also in creating an atmosphere and the experience of beauty." For this edition, the color photographs of food and table settings were taken from a French manual, *La cuisine de A à Z* (Paris, 1971); they managed these things better in Paris, or so this implied.[28]

The language that explained and promoted women's roles as cooks and housewives may sound very familiar to Western cookbook readers (or to second-wave Western feminists), but it is important to note that it had limits.[29] For the most part, Yugoslav cookbooks and cooking columns remained sturdy practical guides to putting food on the table. They did not hide the labor involved, making the food appear on the table as if by magic. They told readers what they needed for a particular recipe, and how to substitute ingredients if something was unobtainable or prohibitively expensive. The techniques they demanded were relatively basic, and their instructions worked: anyone was supposed to be able to make the food they described. There was very little of the culinary literature that was derided as "ornamental cookery" by Roland Barthes in his analysis of the recipe columns published in the 1950s in *Elle*, the French women's magazine. With their concern for surfaces, decoration, and elaborate luxury, *Elle's* recipes were not really meant to be followed in the kitchen. Instead they were food for the fantasies of the working-class women who were the magazine's main readership.[30] Nor did Yugoslav publishing produce any of the other genres of the decorative cookbook that proliferated in Western publishing in the 1950s to 1980s: the "beautiful" cookbook, for example, all glossy pictures but only sketchy instructions; or the chef's cookbook, relying on much demanding advance preparation; or the uncompromisingly, unattainably "authentic" foreign memoir-cum-recipe-book.[31] In all these cases the food described could not realistically be produced at home, though it might entice readers to plan a holiday, visit a restaurant, or just dream.

There were exceptions, of course. The Zagreb women's magazine, *Svijet*, reproduced much of its content from Western journals such as *Elle* or *Cosmopolitan*, including much socially ambitious cooking meant to impress, and occasionally cooking columns or restaurant recipes that could appear utterly fantastical in a Yugoslav context. The same could be said of some of the recipes published by Stevo Karapandža, not in his role as spokesman for Vegeta but instead as an exclusive restaurant chef sharing his favorite dishes. These included pricey items and elaborate dishes, but this selection of recipes was at least in part a work of imaginative literature. Saša Vereš acknowledged this in his preface to Karapandža's book, published and republished during the economic crisis of the early 1980s:

> We have such wonderful culinary manuals, irresistible reading material about the culinary arts, so that leafing through a book of recipes on some sorry evening, in the current climate we're in, is the same as making an excursion into the ideal sphere, the sort of gastronomic

festivity where no one is out of place or unwelcome, where there is at least a little piece of culinary paradise for everyone.

When Vereš wrote that it seemed as if Karapandža could "by some magic feed you with words, as if in some fantastic story confronting you with the most luxuriously laden table," it was almost as though the words were supposed to substitute for the food.[32] But even this volume of culinary porn included a practical inspirational message for the inflation-ridden cook: even the humblest dish of beans could aspire to gastronomic excellence if treated carefully, with respect and imagination—and here were the recipes to show how.

How did women (or indeed men) experience Yugoslavia's culture of consumer domesticity? One obvious point was that the opportunities to participate in the "Yugoslav dream" were not equally distributed across the whole population: spatial variation, social difference, and gender were all factors that shaped access to the pleasures on offer. Readers were more likely to be able to enjoy the "good life" if they lived in Slovenia than in Kosovo, in a city rather than the countryside, if they were managers or government officials, and if they were men, than if they were low-paid workers and married women. For women, the double burden of work and home posed particular problems in their embrace of the socialist "good life." The slow growth of the number of women in the work force and the concentration of women in lower-status, less-responsible positions, as well as their withdrawal from roles in workers' councils or assembly delegations, might suggest that a large proportion of women actively *chose* home over work, private domesticity over public responsibility. This was the argument made, for example, in at least one study of the women's press in Yugoslavia, which saw in these statistics a withdrawal of women to the home, seduced by mass media promises of consumerism and traditional femininity:

> An idealized picture of the housewife (largely American-derived) who waves her husband off to work from the threshold of her little house among the flowers, and a resurrected, home-grown, sugary Mir-Jam philosophy of the demure woman who embroiders or, in the Balkan version, puts up pickles.[33]

But employment was not always a matter of choice: access to work was limited by women's qualifications and skills, social prejudice, and legislation. Furthermore, women were consistently overrepresented among the Yugoslav unemployed, seeking work but not finding it, suggesting that other pressures and a different relation to home and work were shaping their lives.[34]

The humble literature of kitchen and table offered its own version of how to be a woman, a worker, and a housewife, visions that wavered between socialist virtue and consumer fantasy. It glorified women's difficulties as their contribution to socialism, it romanticized the consumer grind with the possibility of novelty, perhaps it even frustrated the housewife with unattainable promises of beauty, simplicity, or social mobility. But cookbook literature also offered the practical means to experiment with something new, develop culinary creativity, exercise one's ingenuity and skills. How people actually used their cookbooks is another question, but popular literature, memoirs, and personal reminiscences suggest a whole variety of attitudes to cooking and its literature, often cutting across the apparently fixed categories of gender or of social role implied by most of these manuals.[35] Women (and men) could be consumed by Yugoslavia's consumer society, but they could also eat it up and make it their own.

You Are What You Eat

Cookbooks attached regional and ethnic labels to specific dishes right from the beginning of the publication of cooking texts in the nineteenth century. For instance, Katarina Popović-Midžina's *Veliki srpski kuvar* (Great Serbian Cookbook) of 1878 identified a few dishes as being made "the Serbian way" or as "a dish from Serbia proper," along with many more given under a foreign name ("Wälscher Salat," "Mixed Pickles") or attributed to other peoples ("Bifstek the Greek way," "American haché"). Entire cookbooks devoted to regional cookery appeared somewhat later: Dika Marjanović-Radica's *Dalmatinska kuhinja* (Split, 1939) is a fine example of a text that surveyed and codified cooking practices and in so doing effectively invented the concept of a specifically Dalmatian cuisine. This book, like other such regional cookbooks, presented its subject as a distinctive repertoire of ingredients and techniques shared among the peoples of a specific territory, placing innumerable local variations within a single "Dalmatian" system. Publication of "national" cookbooks—which packaged and promoted particular culinary practices as uniquely characteristic of and appropriate to a particular place and people—was much slower in the Yugoslav lands. Books such as Popović-Midžina's *Veliki srpski kuvar* or Felicita Kalinšek's *Slovenska kuharica* (Slovene Cookbook, first edition Ljubljana, 1923) were in fact highly cosmopolitan compendiums, with their titles indicating only the language of publication, or at most appropriateness to the Serbian or Slovene kitchen. Other similarly cosmopolitan prewar manuals by Zagreb- or Belgrade-published authors such as Vučetić or Marković were simply presented as "cookbooks," though they closely reflected local tastes and ingredients and were often understood as national, in spite of their much wider reach. What they were *not*, however, was "Yugoslav" in any explicit way. Selected recipes attributed to other Southern Slav traditions appeared here without comment, mingled with those from farther afield.

When these prewar manuals were reissued from the early 1950s, there were few changes to their repertoire of recipes, though there was some lip service paid to culinary Yugoslavism. Marković's *Veliki narodni kuvar* (Belgrade, 1956) is a good example of the attempt to balance local tastes and identities with a wider political framework. The preface made the promise that "women will find in it the specialities of the various cuisines of our peoples,"[36] and it included recipes for a limited range of dishes identified as "Macedonian," say, or "Zagreb-style," again given without comment alongside other foreign dishes ("Russian piroshki," or "Paris torte"). It is the dishes listed as "Serbian" that are identified as really "ours." So, under "Serbian sauerkraut," the cook could read that "we all know that beans and sauerkraut are the basis of our national cuisine, and it is rare to find a man who doesn't happily consume these purely national dishes."[37] The title of this new, postwar edition, *Great National Cookbook*, was ambiguous: did this mean it was Serbian, Yugoslav, or just "popular" (another possible reading of *narodni*)? The recipes made it plain, in this case and others: these cookbooks made it possible to peer into one's compatriots' saucepans, so to speak, but home cooking was still defined locally and, increasingly, nationally. Apparently the Yugoslav kitchen was not equipped with a melting pot. Why should this have been?

Arjun Appadurai has shown how cookbook authors in postcolonial India constructed an overarching Indian "national" cuisine, one that did not preclude local specialization but rather prompted codification of distinct ethnic and regional traditions and in turn, dialectically, built a more encompassing national cuisine on this base. In his account, this process was both the creation and the reflection of a new, mobile urban middle class and its style of consumption.[38] In contrast, despite the existence of a Yugoslav state, a framework for Yugoslav communication, a mobile, urbanizing population, and a growing middle class, there was no such thing as a culinary literature framed explicitly as Yugoslav, for a Yugoslav audience—whether this was conceived as metonymic (with a specific cuisine standing for the whole) or integrative (built around pan-Yugoslav dishes) or representative (achieved by slotting dishes from separate national cuisines into a shared "Yugoslav" menu). If cookbooks are, as Appadurai concludes, "artifacts of culture in the making," does this then provide yet more proof of the failure of the making of Yugoslavism, this time in the kitchen? Not necessarily. Even apart from global foods such as pizza, the Yugoslav market in industrial food products, including such items as the prepared foods sold under Subotica's 29.Novembar label, or Gavrilović tinned meat paste, or Ledo frozen *štrukli* (cheese pastries identified with the Croatian Zagorje), for example, hints at a de facto Yugo-cuisine on the dinner table, often now the object of a post-Yugoslav nostalgia.[39] So do the handwritten notebooks of recipes swapped with friends and bundles of clippings from newspapers or magazines that still lurk on kitchen shelves across the post-Yugoslav space and beyond.

But as well as being artifacts of culture, cookbooks are also a product of politics—and of publishing houses. Both of these are relevant when considering culinary literature in Yugoslavia. The never completely resolved relations between (ethnic) nation and (socialist) state in Yugoslavia meant that any nation-defining or nation-building project, including cookbook publishing, was inherently political. The Yugoslav catchphrase of "brotherhood and unity" summed up ambiguities in these relations. "Brotherhood" meant the equal rights of Yugoslavia's nations: that was clear. But did "unity" imply their convergence within a single overarching national culture (with the inevitable echo of interwar Serb-dominated "integral" Yugoslavism)? Or was this unity nothing more than a shared socialist state?[40] These were issues that were debated throughout postwar Yugoslavia, in party debates, intellectual journals, and successive constitutions, and that reverberated even through the humble literature of the kitchen.

The big kitchen manuals solved the problem of a putative Yugoslav kitchen by giving a nod to other culinary traditions while retaining their own distinctive gastro-national basis. But a more explicit Yugoslavism in the kitchen was mainly an export commodity. Of the few examples of "Yugoslav" cookbooks, all were published in multilingual editions aimed primarily at a foreign market. The first, released initially in 1961 (and based on recipes drawn from Spasenija-Pata Marković's compendium), was published in English, French, German, Italian, and Russian as well as Serbo-Croatian by a publisher specializing in foreign editions and was clearly meant for the tourist trade, introducing the subject with a short history of Yugoslavia and a sketch of the cuisine that emphasizes its diversity.[41] The most notable feature of this book is its organization: recipes are arranged not according to the conventional structure of the menu (appetizers, soups, meat dishes, etc.) but by republic and autonomous province or region (Serbia, Vojvodina, Kosovo Metohija, Macedonia, etc.). The final, more general sections (desserts, preserves, wines, etc.) also follow a "national key," beginning with recipes for Belgrade cake, Zagreb cake, Ljubljana cake, and so on. The text scrupulously avoids any hint of a unified cuisine or culture, with its culinary "brotherhood and unity" summed up in a charming cover illustration by the famous Bosnian caricaturist Zuko Džumhur, showing a table laden with delicacies and surrounded by all the Yugoslav peoples, each

FIGURE 7.2.   Brotherhood and Unity at the dinner table. Illustration by Zuko Džumhur.

identified by national costume. Two later "Yugoslav" cookbooks, one from Ljubljana and the other from Zagreb, were also published in multilingual editions (English, German, Hungarian, Russian, Slovene, and Serbo-Croatian).[42] In these later books, the Yugoslav table is more integrated, defined in terms of regional specialities but also with many "traditional" dishes identified as shared throughout the whole country. The Ljubljana-published volume, by Olga Novak-Marković, described this as a deliberate response to the challenge of "how to produce a work blending our nations' dishes into a cuisine characteristic of Yugoslavia as a whole."[43] It is perhaps no coincidence that Novak-Marković had spent the previous decade as head chef for Tito, himself one of the symbols and mainstays of a cultural Yugoslavism. In the Zagreb volume *Yugoslav Specialities*, by Ljiljana Bisenić, "Yugoslav" cuisine was presented as a tradition that was rapidly disappearing, with homemade dishes crowded out by industrial food and therefore needing to be recorded and returned to the repertoire—the task of the Yugoslav-minded cook, native or foreign. The book was presented to Fulbright scholars going to or coming from the United States, as a part of the cultural agenda of the exchange program, so that what cultural ambassadors were being urged to cook and share was an idealized version of a shared Yugoslav past, vanishing before it even existed. What emerges from all of these texts is a recognizably politicized version of culinary Yugoslavism, from the carefully decentralized cuisines of the 1960s, in a period when Yugoslav unitarism was under attack, to the more integrated recipe books of the 1980s, when Yugoslavism on the political level seemed to be eroding. But it is telling that it was primarily foreign audiences who were imagined as having an appetite for an explicitly "Yugoslav" cuisine.

Cookbooks aimed at a domestic audience over the same period, however, were becoming increasingly national—or even nationalist. Partly this was the result of publishing profiles, with houses usually addressing publications to a local audience in one of Yugoslavia's six republics first, and only then a wider Yugoslav market. They were thus more likely to pitch works to local tastes and cooking cultures. But here too political ideology had a place at the table, especially since nationhood was both a part of the Yugoslav socialist system and, at the same time, available for opposition to it, and since it was difficult to distinguish completely between (protected) expressions of cultural nationhood and (prohibited) expressions of political nationalism. What this meant was that culture frequently became political. Even in cookbooks. Perhaps *especially* in cookbooks, given the role attributed to food and kitchen in creating and maintaining national identity.[44] This can be illustrated by reference to two cookbooks published in Croatia in 1976, from a period when Croatian political life was frozen following the 1971 suppression of the Croatian Spring, and when any expression of political nationalism was suspect. The first was a new edition of Mira Vučetić's standard cookery book, reissued after her recent death with a new afterword by the Zagreb critic and editor Branimir Donat (a noted gourmand, but also someone with public "form" with regard to Croatian nationalism). His text presented this familiar manual in a new light, entirely at odds with previous editions of her book, which had been framed as rational, socialist, and a-national. Vučetić's career had been distinguished, for Donat, by the tone she lent to Croatian social life, her nobility of soul, the way her recipes reminded the reader of a time "when cooking was still done with love, when the individuality of every pot, pan and dish was jealously guarded, when family recipes from tattered, grease-stained notebooks or 'kochbuchs' were handed down from grandma to grandchild." Donat set this in contrast to the contemporary alternative: "When, here among us, the chefs of famous international hotels shamelessly promote industrially prepared food, when in the name of publicity and profit they recommend recipes which attempt to replace the secrets of culinary inspiration and centuries-long tradition with artificial seasonings produced in industrial factories."[45] This was a scarcely veiled jab at Karapandža, then chef of Zagreb's Intercontinental

Hotel, and his association with Vegeta. Given that Donat emphasized Vučetić's national credentials through her family connections to a whole series of Croatian patriots and notables, he was perhaps also hinting at Karapandža's all-too-Serbian-sounding name and origins. In contrast, he writes, Vučetić's recipes

> have the effect of a voice of clear conscience, not only of a national but also of an international cuisine, a cuisine intended for a milieu of cultivated tastes and good manners at the table. Essentially populist, Mira Vučetić's concept of cooking both stands for and defends the individuality and variety of our everyday table . . . her recipes radiate the peace and charm of home-style sustenance which must be opposed to the hasty standards of "industrial feeding."[46]

Donat thus reclaimed Vučetić's work for a feminine, private, individualist, refined, middle-class Croatian kitchen, one that could serve as a bulwark against challenges that were not just cultural and culinary but also, ultimately, political.

A second volume published the same year, *Hrvatska kuharica* (Croatian Cookbook) took a different route to a similar conclusion. This was a hybrid work, a reissue of one of the first cookbooks published in Croatian, Gjuro Deželić's *Nova hrvatska kuharica* of 1868, expanded with two hundred contemporary recipes collected from all the regions of Croatia.[47] The dust jacket announced that it was for those "who want to offer national specialities which have over many years been squeezed out by dishes from foreign kitchens," while the publisher's preface continued the theme of national-culinary competition, noting that Deželić's book was one of the first truly indigenous Croatian cookbooks not assembled from other, foreign sources, and stressing that it was first published ten years before the Serbian equivalent, Katarina Popović-Midžina's *Veliki srpski kuvar* (Novi Sad, 1878). The publishers saw the book as their contribution not just to domestic households but to Croatian restaurants and hotels, "which have not yet shown enough wit to satisfy domestic and foreign guests with 'something special,' typical of this soil of ours." Other works followed in subsequent years, both further republications of early Croatian cookbooks and promotions of "authentic" rural tradition frequently tied to the notion of the family ("How Our Grandmothers Cooked," "Grandma's Cookbook").[48] The same patterns in cookbook publishing can be followed elsewhere in Yugoslavia, unfolding according to the rhythm and tempo of each national movement. Explicitly Serbian national cookbooks began to be published in large numbers only in the 1980s, for instance. Here too one variant was the reprint edition, for example the first "Serbian" cookbook by Jerotej Draganović (1855), which was expanded with recipes from a variety of manuscript sources and promoted as singularly appropriate for the contemporary patriotic kitchen (despite the fact that Jerotej had translated his recipes from a German *"koh-buh"*.[49] Other works revived culinary practices associated with religious or folk customs, which were seen as simultaneously being forgotten and crucial for national identity. These included special dishes for fasting periods, or for celebrating the *slava* (the family saint's day), thus instructing readers in Orthodox customs that, it was claimed, had been prohibited by Serbia's communist rulers.[50] There was an evident contradiction within these texts—such cookbooks made "authentic, traditional, national culture" something to be bought from a bookshop and learned from a printed manual— but they compensated with their claims that there was no alternative if the tradition was to continue: the "true" national cuisine was being crowded out by the pressures of modernity, if not by anything more sinister.

Books like these were selling the culinary nationalism typical of so many modern cookbooks: a reassuring return to "authentic, natural traditions" and home-cooked food at a time when local diets were becoming less and less distinctive and when industrially produced food was becoming a norm, when increasingly urban populations were losing their ties to the countryside, when women no longer spent most of their time in the kitchen. But they were also selling other commodities—anxiety and fear, even victimhood—as well as offering the reader a means of self-defense, all in one package. Cooking—and buying cookbooks—was marketed in these works as a patriotic act. It is easy to see why such books might be attractive and profitable as publishing ventures in an atmosphere in which the politics of nationhood was so contested. Not even the jumpiest of political ideologues was going to object to a cookbook promoting Serbian claims to beans and sauerkraut, or suggesting that restaurants in Croatia serve *štrukli* rather than *ćevapčići*. But even less overtly nationalist culinary texts played a political role. Whether these manuals of mundane everyday nationalism ultimately helped make the claims of nationalist politics easier to swallow is difficult to determine. But they played their part in inculcating and reproducing taken-for-granted solidarities and differences based around national cultures, in ways that were all the more powerful for being unexamined and unchallenged, as Michael Billig has shown in his study of banal nationalism in Western nations.[51] These identities, aversions, and fears were then available to be mobilized for other, less benign ends.

From Making Do to Having It All—and Back Again

Yugoslav cookbooks were never just guides to preparation of food. From the earliest postwar years, Yugoslav culinary texts struggled to reconcile the ideological expectations of socialism with very different messages. Cookbooks taught scientific nutrition and efficient strategies for organizing the household, but they also catered to social ambition and offered recipes for personal distinction. While proclaiming the equality of women under socialism, at the same time they naturalized cooking as women's work, reinforcing the double burden of work and domestic responsibility by celebrating cooking as a labor of love and a fulfilling leisure pastime, even promoting shopping and cooking as a means of self-definition. Though they operated within the framework of Yugoslav brotherhood and unity in the kitchen, they also acted as manuals of everyday nationalism, labeling and systematizing recipes on a national basis—constituting difference at the same time they made it familiar and accessible. They even brought nationalist politics into the kitchen, with recipes that made cooking dinner a matter of defending tradition and resisting assimilation.

Yugoslavia's culinary literature was far from unique in these tensions and contradictions; similar strains can be seen in the consumer literature of the countries of the socialist Bloc, where the task of inculcating socialist values often sat uncomfortably alongside efforts to shape a consumer culture.[52] The similarities should not be surprising: Yugoslavia may have prided itself on its self-managing socialism, but it was still socialism, however much internal critics may have despaired over its consumer orientation. The premises that governed "socialist consumerism" were the same as elsewhere in the Bloc: the socialist "good life" was the worker's well-deserved reward and the Party-State's gift. Not even Yugoslavia's vaunted self-management altered the nature of this relationship. After all, when the mandarins that were the fruit of one of Yugoslavia's successful agricultural industries were harvested, it was Tito himself who put them, very publicly, into the hands of the country's children. A sense of entitlement to the fruits of the "good life," promoted even by the cookbooks that took the ingredients for granted, accompanied by the absence of any meaningful popular political participation in the decisions that governed this life created a similar type of consumer-citizen in all these societies.

The difference between Yugoslavia and the countries of the Bloc was that Yugoslavia succeeded in satisfying consumer desires to a remarkable degree, at least for a while. The cookbooks described here did not just conjure up a mirage of plenty; the ingredients were there in the shops to be purchased and consumed. At the time of the Tito-Stalin split in 1948, Yugoslav party members criticized the Soviet political elite for their culinary excesses, and as long as times remained hard, Tito urged Yugoslavs not to succumb to "foreign" habits of conspicuous consumption.[53] But as things got better, all agreed that the pleasures of the table were here to be enjoyed now, not in some mythical future. And the Yugoslavs did enjoy themselves. They prided themselves on their ability to do so, and on the difference this marked between them and their neighbors to the east. But in the end the difference was, after all, based on a mirage, an illusion of plenty, one that could not be sustained when the money ran out. In both Yugoslavia and the countries of the Soviet Bloc, consumer frustrations helped undermine the political legitimacy of the regimes. Perhaps ultimately the difference lay in the fact that the Yugoslavs had become more accustomed to the consumer "good life," so that the frustration was all the greater when it slowly slipped out of reach and their country began to look more like the lands of really existing socialism than the Western capitalist societies they had learned to measure themselves against.

NOTES

This chapter had its beginnings in the 1980s, in Nada Šoljan's Zagreb kitchen. I extend grateful thanks to all the friends and colleagues who helped me track down cookbooks and who shared their culinary reminiscences, and especially to Bojan Aleksov, Jelena Bulić, Eric Gordy, Vesna Marić, Antonija Primorac, Ksenija Todorović, and Ivana Vukas.

1. *Žena u borbi* (November 1950): 19; (May 1950): 23. Predrag Marković, *Beograd između Istoka i zapada: 1948–1965* (Belgrade: Službeni list, 1996), 288, on American food aid.

2. On cookbooks and consumer culture elsewhere in the nineteenth and twentieth centuries, see especially Douglas Brownlie, Paul Hewer, and Suzanne Horne, "Culinary Tourism: An Exploratory Reading of Contemporary Representations of Cooking," *Consumption, Markets & Culture* 8(1) (2005): 7–26; for France, Amy Trubek, *Haute Cuisine: How the French Invented the Culinary Profession* (Philadelphia: University of Pennsylvania Press, 2000); for Mexico, Jeffrey Pilcher, "Voices in the Kitchen: Mexican Cookbooks as Cultural Capital," *Studies in Latin American Popular Culture* 14 (1995): 297–304.

3. See, on interwar women's organizations and the AFŽ, Lydia Sklevicky, "Karikteristike organiziranog djelovanja žena u Jugoslaviji u razdoblju do drugog svjetskog rata," *Polja*, 30/308 (1984): 415–17; 30/309 (1984): 454–56; Lydia Sklevicky, *Konji, žene, ratovi* (Zagreb: Ženska infoteka, 1996).

4. *Knjiga za svaku ženu* (Zagreb: Seljačka sloga, 1952).

5. *Knjiga za svaku ženu* (Zagreb: Seljačka sloga, 1952); *Žena u borbi* (September 1951): 21; *Moj kuvar i savetnik* (Belgrade: Narodna knjiga, 1952), ii. For American and German versions of "scientific" culinary modernity in twentieth-century cookbooks, see also Laura Shapiro, *Perfection Salad: Women and Cooking at the Turn of the Century* (New York: Farrar, Straus, and Giroux, 1986); Cecelia Novero, "Stories of Food: Recipes of Modernity, Recipes of Tradition in Weimar Germany," *Journal of Popular Culture* 34(3) (2000): 163–81.

6. M[iroslav] S[tefanović], ed., *Moj kuvar i savetnik* (Belgrade: Narodni univerzitet, 1951, foreword, i–ii; 2nd ed. Narodna knjiga 1952; 3rd ed. 1953); Spasenija-Pata Marković, *Veliki narodni kuvar* (Belgrade: Narodna knjiga, 1956).

7. Zora Ruklić, prefatory note to Mira Vučetić, *Kuharstvo* (Zagreb: Poljoprivredni nakladni zavod, 1952), 6.

8. Bosa Ivković, *Lovačka kuharica* (Zagreb: Lovačka knjiga, 1954), 5.

9. *Moj kuvar i savetnik* (Belgrade: Narodna knjiga, 1953), back cover.

10. L. Lastrić, *Klara—tjestenina za svaku kuću* (Zagreb: 8. maj, 1967); *Za vas domaćice 55 savjeta naše kuharice* (Zagreb: Tvornica ulja, 1967).

11. For this, see Patrick Patterson, "Truth Half Told: Finding the Perfect Pitch for Advertising and Marketing in Socialist Yugoslavia, 1950–1991," *Enterprise & Society* 4 (2003): 179–225.

12. Marković, *Beograd između Istoka i Zapada*, 317; M. Živković (ed.), *Beograd, sociološka studija* (Belgrade: Institut za kriminološka i sociološka istraživanja, 1977), 324.

13. Ivanka Karačić, *Domaća kuhinja* (Zagreb: Znanje, 1979), publisher's preface, n.p.

14. Saša Vereš, "O Karapandži i njegovu kulinarskim umijeću," in Stevo Karapandža, *Moji najdraži recepti* (Zagreb: Znanje, 1982), 15.

15. Alekandar Bubanović and Zlatko Glik, *Prva kuharica za samice i samce* (Zagreb: Alfa, 1985).

16. *Praktična žena* (Oct. 7, 1989): 12, 74.

17. Vera Gudac-Dodić, *Žena u socijalizmu* (Belgrade: Institut za noviju istoriju Srbije, 2006), 63.

18. Surveys in the 1970s indicated that workplace canteens were used largely by single men and catered to only about half their workers in any case; cooking at home was cheaper. Ibid, 107–8.

19. Sonia Wild Bićanić, *Two Lines of Life* (Zagreb: Durieux, 1999), 151–53.

20. On Yugoslav consumer culture of the 1950s and 1960s, Marković, *Beograd između Istoka i Zapada; Beograd šezdesetih godina xx veka* (Belgrade: Muzej grada Beograda, 2003); Igor Duda, *U potrazi za blagostanjem: o povijesti dokolice i potrošačkog društva u Hrvatskoj, 1950-ih i 1960-ih* (Zagreb: Srednja Europa, 2005); Patrick Patterson, *Bought and Sold: Living and Losing the Good Life in Socialist Yugoslavia* (Ithaca, NY: Cornell University Press, 2011).

21. *Knjiga za svaku ženu* (Zagreb: Seljačka sloga, 1952): 6.

22. Mira Vučetić, *Suvremena prehrana i kuhanje* (Zagreb: Nakladni zavod Matice hrvatske, 1961), 5–6.

23. Mira Vučetić, *Kuharstvo* (2 vols., Zagreb: Poljoprivredni nakladni zavod, 1952–53 and subsequent edns.), 656–61. Vučetić, *Suvremena prehrana i kuhanje* (1961 and subsequent editions); Mira Vučetić, *Zlatna knjiga kuharstva* (Zagreb: Nakladni zavod Matice hrvatske, 1973 and subsequent editions).

24. *Praktična žena* (1956): 1; cited by Neda Todorović-Uzelac, *Ženska štampa i kultura ženstvenosti* (Belgrade: Naučna knjiga, 1987), 79.

25. *Praktična žena* (Dec. 5, 1980): 26.

26. Gudac-Dodić, *Žena u socijalizmu*, 107–8.

27. B. Iveković, *Lovačka kuharica* (Zagreb: Lovačka knjiga, 1954), 6.

28. Marković, *Veliki narodni kuvar* (7th ed. 1966), 697, and 18th ed. 1977, 75–76). Earlier editions lifted illustrations from the *Larousse Gastronomique*, but without attribution (the full-color illustration of a New Year's Eve spread in the 1966 edition, for example, following p. 697 in the seventh edition).

29. On constructions of gender in American cookbooks, see Jessamyn Neuhaus, *Manly Meals and Mom's Home Cooking: Cookbooks and Gender in Modern America* (Baltimore: Johns Hopkins University Press, 2003).

30. Roland Barthes, "Ornamental Cookery," *Mythologies* (London: Cape, 1973), 78–80.

31. On exclusivity and unattainability as culinary tropes, with reference to the works of the American cookery writer Paula Wolfert, see John Thorne, "My Paula Wolfert Problem," in *Outlaw Cook* (New York: Farrar, Straus & Giroux, 1992).

32. Vereš, "O Karapandži i njegovu kulinarskim umijeću," in Karapandža, *Moji najdraži recepti* (Zagreb: Znanje, 1982; 6th ed. 1984), 15, 10.

33. Neda Todorović-Uzelac, *Ženska štampa i kultura ženstvenosti* (Belgrade: Naučna knjiga, 1987), 136–37. "Mir-Jam" was the pen-name of Milica Jakovljević, interwar author of popular love stories; the English equivalent here would be "Mills-and-Boon."

34. Neda Božinović, *Žensko pitanje u Srbiji u xix i xx veku* (Belgrade: Žene u crnom, 1996); Vera Gudac-Dodić, "Zapošljavanje žena u Srbiji i Jugoslaviji u drugoj polovini 20 veka," *Godišnjak za društvenu istoriju* 10 (2003): 1–3: 87–105.

35. Michel De Certeau's insights into everyday "making do" are particularly useful for thinking about what men and women actually get up to in the kitchen: de Certeau, *The Practice of Everyday Life*, trans. Steven Rendall (Berkeley: University of California Press, 1984); de Certeau, Luce Giard, and Pierre Mayol, *The Practice of Everyday Life*, vol. 2: *Living and Cooking*, trans. Timothy Tomasik (Minneapolis: University of Minnesota Press, 1998). Pierre Bourdieu has more to say about the way cooking for others might be used to create a public persona: *Distinction: A Social Critique of the Judgement of Taste*, trans. Richard Nice (Cambridge, MA: Harvard University Press, 1984).

36. Marković, *Veliki narodni kuvar*, 1956, 6.

37. Ibid., 210.

38. Arjun Appadurai, "How to Make a National Cuisine: Cookbooks in Contemporary India," *Comparative Studies in Society and History* 30(1) (1988): 3–24.

39. See for example I. Adrić, V. Arsenijević, and Đ. Matić (eds.), *Leksikon YU-mitologije* (Belgrade: Rende and Zagreb: Postscriptum, 2004).

40. For an overview of these debates, see most recently L. Cohen and J. Dragović-Soso (eds.), *State Collapse in South-Eastern Europe: New Perspectives on Yugoslavia's Disintegration* (West Lafayette, IN: Purdue University Press, 2008).

41. *Jugoslovenska kuhinja* (Belgrade: Jugoslavija, 1961 and subsequent editions; also editions in English, French, Russian, German, Italian).

42. Olga Novak-Markovič, *Jugoslovanska kuhinja* (Ljubljana: Cankarjeva založba, 1983 and subsequent editions; also English, German, Hungarian, Serbo-Croatian editions); Ljiljana Bisenić, *Jugoslavenski specijaliteti* (Zagreb: Znanje, 1984 and subsequent editions; also English, German, Russian editions).

43. Novak-Markovič, *Yugoslav Cookbook* (1984), 7.

44. On cookbooks and culinary nationalism, Sami Zubaida and Richard Tapper (eds.), *Culinary Cultures of the Middle East* (London: Tauris, 1994); Jeffrey Pilcher, *Que vivan los tamales! Food and the Making of Mexican Identity* (Albuquerque: University of New Mexico Press, 1998).

45. Branimir Donat, afterword to Mira Vučetić, *Zlatna knjiga kuharstva* (Zagreb: Nakladni zavod Matice hrvatske, 1976), 681–82.

46. Ibid., 682.

47. Gjuro Deželić, *Nova hrvatska kuharica* (Zagreb: Tiskom A. Jakića, 1868; rev. ed. 1876); *Hrvatska kuharica*, ed. M. Sagrak and T. Boško (Zagreb: Stvarnost, 1976).

48. E.g., *Tako su kuhale naše bake* [*How our grandmothers cooked*] (Zagreb: Znanje, 1982); *Bakina kuharica: izvorna jela regije Bjelovar* [*Grandma's cookbook: original dishes from the Bjelovar region*] (Bjelovar: Privredna komora regije, 1985)—with large doses of Vegeta!

49. Jerotej Draganović, *Srbskiî kuvar (po nemačkomu koh-buh)* (Novi Sad: Troškom Ignaca Fuhsa, 1855); *Srpski kuvar jeromonaha Jeroteja Draganovića*, ed. M. Radanović (Belgrade: J. Radovanović, 1989).

50. B. Grubačić & M. Tomić, *Srpske slave* (Belgrade: Litera, 1988); Z. Prodanović-Mladenov, *Mali srpski kuvar (400 savremenih recepata, 100 slavskih i posnih jela)* (Belgrade: BIZG, 1989).

51. Michael Billig, *Banal Nationalism* (London: Sage, 1995).

52. See especially Susan Reid, "Cold War in the Kitchen: Gender and the De-Stalinization of Consumer Taste in the Soviet Union Under Khrushchev," *Slavic Review* 61(2) (2002): 211–52; also Judd Stitziel, *Fashioning Socialism: Clothing, Politics and Consumer Culture in East Germany* (Oxford: Berg, 2005); and Krisztina Fehérváry, "Goods and States: The Political Logic of State-Socialist Material Culture," *Comparative Studies in Society and History* 51(2) (2009): 426–59.

53. For denunciations of the Soviet political elite for overindulgence in the pleasures of the flesh: Milovan Djilas, *Conversations with Stalin*, trans. Michael B. Petrovich (London: Hart-Davis, 1962), 50–51, 73, 137; see Marković, *Beograd izmedu Istoka i Zapada*, 288, for Tito's reference in 1950 to "irrational consumption" as a characteristic of "other socialist countries."

8

Grounds for Discontent?

Coffee from the Black Market to the Kaffeeklatsch in the GDR

Katherine Pence

"Every Berliner starts his day with coffee. Of all the hardships which the years of war and its sequel brought upon them, the lack of coffee was probably the hardest to bear. In those days the Berliner, in common with every other German, was prepared to give anything for coffee, and he is still prepared to do so."[1] This observation by a British journalist visiting Berlin in 1955 neatly points to how, for postwar Germans and especially East Germans, coffee was both central to everyday life and fraught with difficulties. Individual consumers struggled to get hold of real coffee beans and often resorted to the black market to do so.

The story of coffee in the German Democratic Republic (GDR) demonstrates how consumption in this German socialist state shared features with the rest of the Eastern Bloc but also was unique because of national division and competition with West Germany. Like its Eastern European neighbors, the GDR faced supply problems endemic to its planned economy. Coffee was an especially tough case for the planning apparatus since it had to be imported from tropical countries for hard-to-come-by "valuta," or hard currency, that could be exchanged on the world market. As East German consumers sought ways to circumvent this difficult marketplace, they resorted to the often illicit second economy of connections, barter, and speculation that thrived across Eastern Europe.[2]

The looming presence of its counterpart, the Federal Republic of Germany (FRG), added more complications to the GDR economy. The

West German "economic miracle" became a measuring stick against which the population and the regime judged East German economic achievements. For the coffee-drinking populace, the FRG became a Mecca for real beans, smuggled or sent as gifts across the border to the East. This fed into the socialist leadership's view of the West as a source of economic and political sabotage, especially when consumers who strayed westward to shop subsequently abandoned the GDR and became refugees in the West. Thus the regime, even at the highest state levels, struggled to maintain a steady supply of beans, while securing its borders to prevent smuggling or flight. The Berlin Wall, the consummate symbol of the Cold War, was erected in part to protect East Germany from this sort of economic "sabotage."

Coffee drinking in the GDR, therefore, was embedded in the international politics of the Cold War. But as with many consumer activities, coffee drinking was also a very personal and often private act, whether it was imbibed during a break at work or with friends gathered at a domestic *Kaffeeklatsch*. An examination of coffee drinking thus offers insight into the links between state and society in the GDR, because it was an everyday activity as well as a concern at the highest levels of the state and the Party. Avid East German coffee drinkers pressured the regime to provide a steady stream of the beverage and threatened to revolt when their supply was cut off. Coffee was associated with joy and sociability, as well as with frustration, grumbling, and even potential activism. Ultimately, coffee drinking in the GDR became an important component in the construction of social distinctions and discrete communities counter to the ideological commitment of the state to a unified mass society. These communities came to be defined not by class solidarity, as in the Marxist vision of the state, but through access to beans as symbols of privilege, connection to the West, and even illegality or foreignness. This chapter explores how these elements commingled in the complex everyday lives of East German citizens.

Coffee and Crisis

The "crisis" in provisioning postwar East Germany with coffee grew out of the fact that the substance was firmly entrenched in German consumption habits and social patterns. Coffee had been popular in Germany since the eighteenth century, as in much of Europe and the Near East.[3] Coffee became more widespread with the dawn of coffee houses, famous as arenas of debate characterizing the public sphere during the Enlightenment.[4] As a more informal institution complementing the primarily male coffee houses, the *Kaffeeklatsch* (literally "coffee gossip") was a peculiarly German form of mainly female sociability developing in the nineteenth century, contributing further to the prevalence of the beverage.[5] Though many derided these coffee-drinking gatherings as domains of idle, trivial gossip, they did furnish women with a context for sociability, for gossiping freely, and also for discussing ideas and politics.[6] By the twentieth century, afternoon coffee and cake (*Kaffee und Kuchen*), workplace coffee breaks, and the *Kaffeeklatsch* were integral to German everyday life. In thrall to a national coffee addiction, Germans came to demand coffee as an entitlement.

From World War I onward, international politics, hostilities, and economic crises led to shortages that prevented the flow of raw beans into the country. But given this pervasive level of consumption, when real coffee became unavailable Germans resorted to substitutes. During World War I, they drank beechnut, chicory, *Muckefuck* (made of acorns), and other infamous forms of ersatz coffee when the British naval blockade took its toll on their import trade. These beverages became symbols of the recurrent shortages plaguing the German economy in the twentieth century (even though these drinks do have their fans in Germany).[7] It became more difficult to ensure the coffee supply with the loss of German colonies through the Treaty of Versailles, such as the coffee-producing colonial territories including Tanganyika.[8] German coffee importers came to depend more on trading partners, such as the Netherlands, for the prized beans.[9] Coffee supplies during World War II were again a major concern of the government and the population. The Nazi regime established wartime economic regulations to combat the black market, through which much of the coffee supply flowed.[10]

This difficulty in gaining access to coffee in the early twentieth century set the stage for the ongoing struggle to supply coffee. The chronic scarcity of coffee beans is exemplified by the stereotype of the "Coffee Saxons" (*Kaffeesachsen*) living in the district of Saxony around Leipzig and Dresden. The celebrated German porcelain manufacturer, the Meissen Company from Leipzig, was renowned for its coffee services with flowers printed on the bottom of each cup. The *Kaffeesachsen* became famous for brewing weak coffee to preserve their scarce beans. Their drink became known as *Blümchenkaffee*, or "blossom coffee," because the drinker could see the trademark Meissen flower pattern through the thin brew. Saxony became part of the GDR, where this traditionally thin *Blümchenkaffee* aptly symbolized new problems in attaining real beans.

When the Third Reich fell, the victorious allies divided and occupied Germany in four separate zones, all of which faced challenges in provisioning the populations of the war-devastated region. In the Soviet Occupied Zone (*Sowjetische Besatzungszone* or SBZ) as well as in the American, British, and French occupied zones, military governments established new rationing systems controlling the limited distribution of coffee, along with other goods. According to these systems, most Germans were forced to drink rationed ersatz coffee made of acorns or chicory. Real bean coffee was a "restricted good," legally sold only with a permit and at a regulated maximum price in order to prevent speculation, which was in any event rampant.[11]

German and Allied officials recognized the value of coffee to the population. During the hunger winter of 1946, for example, dire material circumstances prompted one mayor in the British Occupation Zone to suggest that small quantities of coffee be distributed to the population as a "psychological restorative" to boost morale.[12] Similarly, American occupiers aimed to "lift the spirits" of Germans in their zone with CARE (Cooperative for Assistance and Relief Everywhere) packages. The lucky few who received these charity packages obtained a standard two-pound allotment of beans. The Soviet occupiers' equivalent was so-called *Pajok* packages (from the Russian word for "ration"), distributed primarily to Communist Party functionaries and privileged SBZ workers. The *Pajoks*, however, contained only basic groceries such as flour, sugar, and fat, and many Soviet Zone recipients traded these allotments with Westerners for their coffee.[13] This material discrepancy deepened when the British and American zones joined into one administrative unit (called the Bizone) in 1947, paving the way for establishment of separate East and West German states two years later.

Thanks to the inadequacies of the rationing systems across postwar Germany, in the Eastern and Western zones alike the black market was the primary place to get real coffee beans. The Bizone passed a currency reform in June 1948, freeing many consumer goods from rationing and largely eliminating the need for the black market in the West. Still, illicit trade in coffee continued to thrive there into the 1950s. A special case, of course, was the year-long Berlin Blockade immediately following the currency reform, in which the Soviets blocked land and water transport of supplies from the Bizone to West Berlin, which was located deep inside the Soviet Zone. The black market flourished in both halves of the city, even as the Berlin Airlift delivered coffee in its relief packages to West Berliners.[14] As the East Berlin worker newspaper *Vorwärtz* reported, in the British Sector bourgeois district of Wilmersdorf coffee was largely sold under the counter or on the thriving black market in the Tauentzienstrasse or Kurfürstendamm, where roasted coffee cost 28 Western marks.[15] In another example, reports emerged that the Dietrich Grocery in West Berlin's working-class district of Moabit had hoarded a hundred grams of coffee to sell at 18 Berlin marks (the currency in West Berlin during the Blockade before the Western marks were introduced there) per pound of unroasted coffee and 22 Berlin marks roasted. These rumors led to the owner's arrest and a search of his premises.[16] To combat such practices, West Berlin authorities set up a "price council" to monitor prices in stores and make sure shopkeepers were not dealing illegally in products such as coffee. In Berlin and beyond, the coffee trade became an object of strict policing in both the Bizone and the Soviet Zone.

Red vs. Black Markets

The black market for coffee in the Soviet Zone and the Soviet Sector of Berlin continued unabated in spite of the SBZ's own currency reform in 1948. Part of the reason for the persistence of the SBZ black market was that, unlike in the Western zones, the currency reform did not free goods, such as coffee, from the rationing system. Immediately SBZ trade functionaries sought to stem illegal trade while providing material incentives to workers to raise their productivity. The demand for coffee dovetailed with these issues.

In the autumn of 1948, members of the German Economic Commission and the trade administration started to plan a new state-owned retail chain that would offer goods at elevated but "free" prices, so called because the merchandise was sold outside the ration system. The result was establishment of the Handelsorganisation (HO) retail chain in November 1948, designed largely to counter black market trade.[17] The HO planning committee debated whether the stores should sell basic staples or "luxury goods," including coffee and chocolate. Early plans for these "free stores" designated 25 to 50 tons of coffee among the "luxury goods" to be sold outside of rations.[18] In part, this was a strategic decision, since the SBZ and its successor state after 1949, the GDR, lacked hard currency for imports such as coffee. One HO planner, Herr Uhlich, commented that if the supply of 25,000 tons of coffee available in the SBZ were rationed out to the whole population, each person would only receive a paltry two grams. Therefore, it made more sense to sell it at the HO, where select individuals would be able to buy it. HO planners aimed for these individuals to be the highly productive "activists," modeled on Soviet Stahkanovite ideal workers, who would be paid a so-called progressive piece wage for overfulfilling their work quotas.[19] The HO would give them a place to spend that extra money and be rewarded for their extraordinary role in "building socialism."[20]

The question of whether the HO would offer coffee as a luxury or a staple product available for all touched on one of the core issues of consumption in East Germany. Ostensibly, the GDR's ruling Socialist Unity Party (SED) aimed to offer all workers egalitarian access to goods that they needed. Over time the East German standard of living would presumably rise when higher productivity yielded a broader array of consumer goods. Thus, in the "worker-and-peasant state" consumer goods would ideally be available to improve the lives of workers and farmers, not a privileged few. SED planners worked with the stated goal of eliminating the exploitative nature of capitalist marketing and offering goods at fair prices set by economic functionaries.

Production problems, however, meant these goals could be approached only gradually. One ongoing problem was the high price of merchandise in HO stores. Planners deliberately set HO prices relatively high compared to subsidized, rationed goods by charging an excise tax. In part, prices were elevated at the outset because HO planners did not want black marketeers to be able to buy out their stock to resell at a profit. Compared to the price of coffee, which theoretically at least might be available from time to time through rationing, an excise tax in the HO elevated prices by as much as 966 percent, making this the highest rate of mark-up of any commodity sold at the HO in 1951. Thus, rather than winning over East German shoppers when it was launched, the HO was widely critiqued as the "state-run black market," because few were initially able to afford HO goods.[21]

Nevertheless, planners justified the HO as a site for offering rewards to deserving East German workers. The government successively lowered prices as supplies increased. In the 1950s, the Ministry for Trade and Supply triumphantly announced lower prices for a number of HO goods as rewards from the Party for an increasingly productive population. By ostensibly refusing to extract a huge profit from its customers, the HO, as a state-run institution, aimed to convince the population that the state and the SED were providing for their welfare.[22] In return for this benevolence and societal improvement, SED leaders hoped the population would offer the Party its loyalty. This concept was evident at an HO planning meeting where SED representative Frau Loessner claimed that East German workers were eager for establishment of the HO. Without it, she claimed, a certain "class"—not workers—would still purchase coffee on the black market. Loessner had faith that workers visiting the HO would shop responsibly and gratefully, strengthening their allegiance to the Party. Loessner suggested, for example, that for working women the purchase of coffee or chocolate at the HO would have real meaning and significance, perhaps denoting a transition away from wartime privation toward a brighter future within socialism. Furthermore, Loessner posited that though coffee was fervently desired, workers would not go overboard by wastefully purchasing a pound a month. Loessner may have been trying to deflect common postwar-era notions that consumers were irresponsible and either hoarded goods or bought too much at unreasonable prices. Given low supplies of coffee, such tendencies might have depleted HO stock quickly. But Loessner said working consumers would buy only "a quarter pound now and then, and would get pleasure from that."[23] Loessner, like other economic planners, was optimistic that the HO would help facilitate an ideal socialist society, in which shoppers would rationally aid the economy.

However, when the HO and other aspects of GDR consumer culture fell short of their promises, consumers also failed to conform to the ideals promoted by SED functionaries. The situation with coffee was a good example of this broken contract between the socialist consumer system and the consuming populace. The HO did indeed become a key location to buy real-bean coffee in the GDR, but even there supplies were often scarce. In December 1948, local trade unionists reported that although demand for coffee was high, the HO still did not have it in stock, even two months after the store's grand opening.[24] In 1951, the HO tried to introduce some sort of coffee mixture to stretch the bean supply; ersatz coffee was not just a thing of the past.[25] Thus East German coffee consumers sought coffee through illegal channels rather than at the HO.

The overall scarcity and restrictive prices in the HO meant that coffee speculation and smuggling continued into the 1950s and beyond. Coffee regularly flowed in both directions across the East-West border. West Berliners often bought HO goods with their more valuable currency exchanged at a favorable rate to smuggle back across the border.[26] A cartoon from around 1952 lampooned this common practice by showing a woman passing a GDR policeman with her baby carriage—her vehicle for smuggling East German coffee—while coffee beans trailed behind her on the ground. She says, "Darn it, the brat poked clean through the coffee bag with his legs again!"[27]

Along with these individual shoppers who smuggled coffee for personal use, professional black marketeers took advantage of Germany's economic division. A particularly notorious example was a "coffee smuggling ring" arrested in Leipzig in 1950. A "large group" of men in the "coffee ring" reportedly bought precious metals in the GDR and exchanged them for foreign currency. They then brought the foreign currency to West Berlin and bought large amounts of coffee, cigarettes, and cocoa—goods ironically originating in the Soviet Union and sold at establishments taken over by the Soviet Intourist travel agency in West Berlin.[28] These smugglers then distributed these untaxed goods to various stores and tradesmen in the GDR, who resold them, demanding up to 300 percent profit. In this way, 56,000 kilograms of coffee were sold in nine months in 1949. In November and December 1949, for example, it was determined that a certain Robinsohn was undertaking illegal coffee transport, and in connection with his lawsuit the prosecutors obtained 100,000 marks worth of cash and goods.

The "coffee ring" case demonstrates how the coexistence of an official economy and an illicit "second economy" afforded the state and Party a means of demarcating who would be considered insiders and outsiders to the socialist community. Targeting major black marketeers, such as the coffee ring as parasites on the "real" East German community became a way to reinvigorate xenophobic and anti-Semitic prejudices and imagery common during the Third Reich.[29] Significantly, the Central Commission for State Control, in its report on the coffee ring, identified the group as comprising primarily "Victims of Fascism"—the title given to Jewish Holocaust survivors as well as other political and ethnic groups persecuted by the Nazis—and "members of the Jewish community."[30] Certainly, a number of Jewish survivors did turn to the black market because they had no assets or opportunities for employment. But Germans labeled these black marketeers as "idle," a particularly problematic description in the SBZ and GDR owing to the socialist valorization of labor and the postwar campaign for higher productivity. In effect, associating Jews and career black marketeering served to demarcate the pardonable black-market activities of the average German petty trader from the "parasitical" crimes of the major profiteers, defined as outsiders from the reconstructing German community.[31] This attitude surfaces in the Central Commission for State Control report on the coffee ring, which recorded suspicion that the mostly younger employees in the new administration in charge of interrogating Jewish suspects exhibited "anti-Semitic behavior."[32]

Members of the remaining Jewish community in East Germany collaborated with a few corruptible judges to help the coffee ring members evade strict sentences. With the aid of the Saxony district attorney Hentschel, a number of the members of this criminal gang managed to shorten their sentences and subsequently flee from the GDR to West Berlin.[33] In addition, two lawyers from the Leipzig Jewish community—the head of the community, Helmuth Lohser, and the Republic-wide chair of the Association of Persecutees of the Nazi Regime (VVN), Julius Meyer—appeared before the criminal police to speak on behalf of one of the accused named Borenstein. Meyer expressed agreement with Borenstein's sentence, but the following day he got Hentschel to secure Borenstein's release from prison, after which Borenstein fled to the West. Meyer also intervened in the case of another Jewish black marketeer named Meinzer, who appeared before an investigating officer named Dümel. Meyer suggested that Meinzer should come to Berlin and pay a fine to the Jewish community to atone for his crime, which Dümel allowed. Meinzer went there, and then disappeared. Dümel was subsequently condemned as corrupt for accepting bribes.[34] A couple of years later, in 1953, while anti-Semitic purges were taking place across the Soviet Bloc, Meyer and Lohser were interrogated and, fearing persecution, fled to West Germany.[35] This case points to the complex relationship among the black market, members of the Jewish community, and the problems of the police and justice system in the GDR. It also suggests how coffee in the GDR was intertwined with this shadow economy and with the problems of reconstructing the East German polity. The fact that these participants in the case escaped to West Berlin mirrored the problematic movement of the coffee beans themselves between East and West. Images of convivial *Kaffeeklatsch* communities obfuscated the complicity of coffee drinkers in the continuation of the black market and of the anti-Semitic scapegoating of some of the major black market traders.

The Coffee Gap

Competition with the West and the presence of West Berlin as a transmission point for commodities such as coffee, as well as for persons wishing to escape the GDR, became a major liability to the regime, causing authorities to increase surveillance of the border between East and West. As the supply of coffee beans rose in West Germany in the 1950s and the price dropped after the lowering of a coffee tax in 1953,[36] GDR black market activity shifted even more heavily into smuggling beans from the West, especially from West Berlin. It became especially desirable to drink Western brands of coffee, such as Jakobs Krönung. The growing popularity of Western goods in part emerged from a worsening supply situation in the GDR. In 1952 and early 1953, the GDR was undergoing a major commodity crisis that contributed to the June 17, 1953, uprising that threatened to topple the SED regime.[37] Consumers demanded lower prices and more goods. The uprising shocked the GDR leadership, which sought out scapegoats for the rebellion among its own cadres and tightened surveillance of the general population. Smugglers and black marketeers became particular targets as so-called saboteurs of the GDR economy, particularly because of their ties to the West. When the GDR regime stepped up its efforts to arrest major career black marketers, it also extended surveillance to virtually all East German shoppers whether or not they were involved, at least on some level, with "illegal" purchasing or trade. For example, the Ministry of Trade and Supply sent observers to monitor East Germans who shopped for themselves and their families in coffee roasteries in West Berlin's borough of Neukölln.[38] This happened in the context of a stricter policing of the population at the border and around the GDR, especially following establishment of the Stasi secret police in 1950. The continuance of smuggling and illicit trade in general, exacerbated by the Cold War division of the country, made the simple everyday pleasure of coffee drinking into an act framed by surveillance and state repression. The search for real-bean coffee became imbued not only with the illicit trade of the shadow economy but also with the possibility of political betrayal.

The state reaction to the June 1953 crisis went beyond heightened surveillance of smugglers. Shortly before the June uprising, the regime followed the lead of the Soviet Union's March launch of a program called the New Course. In response to consumer complaints articulated during the crisis, the GDR's New Course prioritized investment in consumer industries to broaden the supply of consumer goods, partly so that GDR shoppers would not stray to the West. When the Council of Ministers declared the intention of rapidly and effectively improving provisioning for the population, it included "meaningfully raised availability of real bean coffee as merchandise for the second half of 1953" among its goals.[39] Following this imperative, the Minister for Trade and Supply, Curt Wach, planned to increase the availability of coffee to 1,180 tons in the third and fourth quarters of 1953. However, the Ministry of Foreign and Inter-German Trade informed Wach that there were no funds available to raise the supply of coffee to these levels, and that it could furnish only a maximum of 240 tons of roasted coffee from the beginning of June until the end of October. The State Planning Commission therefore lowered the allotment of coffee available for that year. Wach complained that the population would not tolerate this reduction for long—ominous words in the wake of the uprising.[40] The difficulty securing planned amounts of coffee in 1953 also indicated how the regime's promises to increase supplies often floundered in practice when the ministries implementing these plans faced lack of investment, distribution inefficiencies, inadequate communication and cooperation between state offices responsible for managing national consumer supplies, and other problems.

The discrepancy between the coffee supplies in the GDR and the FRG widened from the 1950s to the 1960s. By the 1950s, West Germany was the second-largest importer of coffee in the world behind the United States, and in 1955 it imported four times more coffee than the GDR.[41] It ensured this position through signing international trade agreements, such as the European Economic Community, GATT, and the UN International Coffee Agreement of 1963.[42] Significant amounts of West German coffee did make it to individual East German consumers, not only through smuggling but also in gift packages from FRG charities or from friends and family members. Coffee belonged to the standard ingredients of a typical gift package, as Western relatives knew it to be desirable and in short supply.[43] One account estimated that between 10 and 15 percent of coffee supplies came from gift packages sent from the West.[44] In response, the GDR regime tried to staunch the flow of Western coffee into the country via these gift packages, because these shipments fed the black market and were a humiliating reminder of the continuing deficits in the East's own supply. In 1954, GDR customs rules limited the amount of coffee sent in gift packages from West Germany to 250 grams, largely to "protect our people's economy from elements who exploit gift packages . . . for purposes of speculation."[45] In an attempt to control and profit from the traffic in gifts from West to East, the GDR regime also established a mail-order retailer, Genex, in 1957 through which West German purchasers could spend exclusively Western currency on gifts of coffee and other commodities for their East German friends and relatives.[46]

The coffee gap might have helped spur Walter Ulbricht's regime to declare in 1958 that its Primary Economic Task would be to "overtake West Germany in per capita consumption" in general by 1965, a goal that mirrored Khrushchev's own aspirations for the USSR. Since coffee could not be produced locally, the coffee gap could be closed only through increased trade ties abroad, particularly with newly independent decolonizing countries with left-leaning governments in Africa, Asia, and Latin America.[47] This would theoretically counteract similar international agreements cemented by the FRG. Following an end to domestic rationing in 1958, the GDR State Planning Commission worked to import more tropical products such as cocoa, fruit, and coffee. It called on the foreign trade office to ensure the import of three types of coffee blends at different prices for 1959.[48] In countries that were receptive to East German relations, such as Guinea and Ghana, the GDR aimed in the late fifties to help develop coffee production so that these countries could export coffee along with cocoa and bananas.[49] By the end of 1958, the year of Ghana's independence, that country's ambassador in Egypt suggested that the GDR could buy coffee in Ghana, provided that transportation of the commodity back to Europe was available.[50] Transport was only one of the GDR's problems in getting the beans, however. More problematic was access to hard currency that could be exchanged on the world market. The GDR tried, for example, to establish trade with Brazil, the world's main coffee exporter, but it was ultimately at a great disadvantage thanks to a lack of convertible cash; in lieu of valuta the GDR struggled to set up direct exchanges of coffee for GDR exports such as polygraph machines, Zeiss Jena camera equipment, or trucks.[51]

Despite these attempts to secure a better coffee supply in the late 1950s and early 1960s, the lack of hard currency meant that access to beans was seldom a sure thing. A plan to reorganize retailing in Berlin noted that coffee was one of the commodities still suffering from insufficient supply in 1959.[52] In an effort to deal with shortages after the end of rationing, state planners suggested, for example, that attempts at refining and improving (*Veredelung*) real-bean coffee were to cease, and instead production of a "Nes-type" coffee (instant coffee similar to Nescafe) should be produced.[53]

Chronic supply problems also meant that GDR consumers did not shop in the ideally restrained or grateful manner that Loessner had predicted in 1948. Until the end of the decade, the population complained bitterly about the high prices of bean coffee.[54] In the spring of 1961, the Economic Commission closely monitored shortages and popular reactions to them. A report from the district of Gera to State Planning Commission Chair Erich Apel's office noted that an older woman at a special coffee store bought a whole pound, which was considered to be an especially large amount. When the saleswoman asked why she wanted so much at once, the purchaser expressed anxiety about a false rumor: "Don't you know that coffee is going to be rationed again? I need to stock up, because I don't want to have to do without my coffee."[55]

The black market in coffee and other goods was one factor leading to the erection of the Berlin Wall in August 1961.[56] Shortages, misinformation about their causes, and hoarding continued thereafter. The supply of a number of food-stuffs at the end of 1961, including coffee, was much lower than in the previous year. Although in the 1950s the Soviet Union had helped supply the GDR with coffee in exchange for rubles, by the 1960s the East Germans were forced to buy coffee on the world market, spending 300 million hard-won dollars annually for the commodity.[57] These shortages struck a political blow against the regime as it tried to stabilize the country after sealing off the border. Western propaganda, particularly from the Radio in the American Sector (RIAS), exploited East German fears that Brazil and other countries would cut off their trade agreements with the GDR, thus ending its coffee imports. With rumors that they would be isolated from the nonsocialist world, the GDR population reacted with increased hoarding of goods, making coffee and cocoa unavailable for a short time.[58]

One response by trade administrators to discontented consumers was to establish new types of state-run stores in the GDR to exist alongside the HO and consumer cooperatives. These shops offered higher-grade coffee and other products to consumers who had better financial means. The Ministry of Trade and Supply founded a chain of Exquisit stores in 1961 to sell elegant home-grown and imported Western goods at elevated prices. In addition, a new chain of fancy delicatessen Delikat stores was established in 1976, offering West German goods, including the popular Jakobs Krönung coffee brand.[59] The offer of finer groceries at much higher prices for those who could afford them reflected continuing status distinctions among East German citizens even as the Party ostensibly aimed at social leveling.[60] The Intershops, introduced in the 1950s and expanded in 1962, made these distinctions even more visible as they sold merchandise only for West German marks, first to foreign visitors only and by 1974 to GDR citizens.[61]

Along with the stratification of stores, the GDR marketplace offered a variety of brands of coffee and other products at different price points. The segment of the population with elevated tastes and buying power could show off their higher status by purchasing more rarified brands of coffee. As each new elite store appeared, these elite brands migrated from chain to chain, where they grew more and more inaccessible to the general population. One example was the "First Class" brand coffee sold in an oval can. As Renate Z., a store manager, recalled in an interview, this coffee appeared first in normal HO, cooperative, or small private shops. Then suddenly First Class coffee was sold only in Delikat, then in Intershop, and finally only as an export product. The restrictive access to desired brands of goods, such as First Class coffee, made these stores generally reviled among the GDR population.[62] But despite the high prices and antipathy toward these shops, wherever coffee was offered customers still bought it. Renate Z. recalled that even though the prices "weren't cheap," "the money was there" for coffee.[63] Nevertheless, relegating the best beans to these fancy shops still pointed to the overall shortage of quality coffee nationwide, which fed the East German value of Western coffee over domestic products. Indeed, the Intershop particularly exacerbated the persistent black market in such goods, along with the social distinctions between East Germans with access to Western currency and those without.

As the system of trade and distribution evolved in the 1950s and 1960s, the GDR regime continued to grapple with the task of supplying coffee to its citizens. The top political elite, including Ulbricht and the Politburo, concerned themselves with securing the coffee supply along with myriad other commodities. Their inadequacy in doing so rendered them vulnerable to popular criticism, when promises of socialist equality and a higher standard of living did not pan out as projected.[64] In a political and economic system claiming to attend to the needs of the working population, lack of coffee was one symbol of the inadequacies of the system. Daily acts undermining the regime's system of provision, such as black marketeering, smuggling, and hoarding, constituted a kind of ongoing critique (or at least noncooperation) on the part of the citizenry. These practices and the regime's repressive responses to them, such as policing by the Stasi, linked coffee consumption with subversive and shadowy activities. But the regime also expended great effort in ensuring a supply of beans, along with other "necessities" and even luxuries. Indeed, the population came to accept the promise of fair and consistent prices for coffee and other goods, as their consumption became deeply embedded in everyday life under socialism.[65]

Coffee Breaks and the *Kaffeeklatsch*

Official records reveal much about the coffee supply, but they do not offer as much insight into the daily practices of coffee drinking by ordinary citizens. In the memoirs and nostalgic accounts of the GDR that proliferated after 1989 with the wave of *Ostalgie* or "nostalgia for the East," the quotidian struggle to prepare good coffee was a frequent theme.[66] These accounts often satirize the shortage conditions with which East Germans grappled daily. For example, one retrospective recounted a mock recipe for a Saxon cup of coffee, which recast the old stereotype of *Kaffeesachsen* enjoying very weak *Blümchenkaffee* for the context of the GDR. For this "recipe," one took a single coffee bean, preferably from the West, tied a string around it, hung it in a window, and allowed the shadow of the bean to fall on a pot of boiling water. The longer one let the bean cast its shadow over the water, the stronger the coffee would taste. In this manner, a family could stretch out a bag of coffee beans they received as a Christmas present from Western relatives from New Year's Eve until the following Christmas.[67] Another nostalgic account described the GDR method of brewing "Turkish coffee," apparently common since modern coffee makers touted in the design magazine *Kultur im Heim* (Culture in the Home) or on display at the semiannual Leipzig Trade Fair were not always available in stores.[68] "Throw a spoonful of coffee in a cup and fill it up with boiling water. Done. Tasted like shit and looked like dirty dish water."[69] Such anecdotes parodied both the inadequate GDR provisioning system and the occasionally extreme measures the population went to in order to cope with it.

Private snapshots offer another kind of evidence of everyday practices because they capture moments deemed significant by ordinary photographers. They are rare and elusive to the historian since family photos are collected neither in political archives nor in publications. This is partly why until recently historians have ignored amateur photographs, although there is growing recognition of their significance as a source of everyday history.[70] For one thing, amateur photographers were relatively free of official political agendas, artistic conventions, or censorship compared to professional photographers, although they certainly followed cultural conventions. In the 1950s, the GDR regime expected career photographers to conform to the Socialist Realist canon by depicting uplifting scenes of optimistic and happy workers building the socialist collective. Meant only for private consumption, snapshots by contrast seem to offer a more "authentic" window into what the ordinary person valued as memorable. In the search for authenticity, professional photographers in the 1970s even started to mimic the family snapshot by focusing on private scenes.[71]

In such private photos from the GDR, it is striking how frequently scenes feature coffee drinking. The penchant for photographing groups of friends or colleagues enjoying coffee together comes across in an unusual collection of GDR photos and family albums collected at the Wende Museum and Archive of the Cold War in Los Angeles. These photos, whether individual or collected in albums with descriptive captions, are a small sample, anonymous, and open to interpretation.[72] Nevertheless, this collection suggests that coffee drinking was central to many occasions in GDR social life that amateur photographers deemed worth remembering and recording.

In the GDR, coffee breaks were an important part of the workday, a respite from work and an avenue of sociability between co-workers. As one author put it, "The coffee break was holy."[73] Another GDR historian suggested that workplace gatherings over coffee became essential to GDR sociability (*Gemütlichkeit*) and a unifying source of identity formation for average people.[74] Workers demanded coffee as a staple in factory canteens. The regime tracked this desire for coffee. For example, a 1964 GDR Institute for Needs Research survey of 479 women working in three textile mills found that coffee was one of the main answers to the question, "Which foods would you definitely like to be provided with at work?"[75]

Unlike official images of the factory, which usually portrayed laborers during the work process,[76] coffee appears in photos of workers at rest. This association of coffee breaks with the work place is evident in several photographs from the Wende Museum collection, which show work colleagues in the late 1950s gathered around a table enjoying coffee in their factory kitchen or break room. One album even describes such a gathering as a *fidele Runde* or "jolly company." This label suggests that the bonding of colleagues or work brigades took place not necessarily through the work process itself or through formal organizations such as the Free German Trade Union (FDGB) but in the in-between times, when small pleasures such as coffee were enjoyed together. Another set of photos shows a group of nurses drinking coffee on a break. The images look slightly staged, as if to emphasize the solidarity of the group. However, it is significant that the photos, most likely taken for private rather than propaganda use, use the break room rather than the workplace as the setting in which to depict this unity of female workers.

Another set of photos suggests how the social networks and institutions structured by the FDGB trade union also solidified friendships over cups of coffee. The photographer labeled the setting for these snapshots as the dining hall at an FDGB Home, one of the leisure venues sponsored by the union's subsidized vacation service (*Feriendienst*), which gave families an opportunity to travel within the GDR under the auspices of this mass organization.[77] The *Feriendienst* contributed substantially to the high rate of membership in the FDGB (77 percent of eligible workers in 1949).[78] Here, as elsewhere in the Bloc, the regime offered subsidized leisure through the FDGB for the core of its citizenry—the workers—as compensation for demands for their high labor output and as an incentive to learn socialist political ideology. One photograph

FIGURE 8.1.   East German nurses enjoying coffee in their break room. Uncaptioned
photo, n.d. In the collection of the Wende Museum and Archive of the Cold War, 2010.

taken at the FDGB *Feriendienst* home, for example, shows, a gathering of four
women and a man enjoying coffee together with the caption describing, "In the
dining hall of our FDGB home 'Hitthim' [author's note: name barely legible]
—our happy table company [*fröhliche Tischrunde*]—Jutta, Annelies, Frau Pfan-
nenschmidt, and the two of us." The FDGB may have aimed to control the
conditions of both work and leisure by monopolizing recreational venues such
as this one, but these coffee drinkers made this space their own by calling attention to their happy private world within this mass organized environment.

The state's replacement of privately owned leisure venues with branches of
Party-controlled institutions, such as the FDGB Homes, is one aspect of what
has been seen as communism's suppression of civil society and the public
sphere in Soviet-type societies, such as the GDR.[79] Certainly, cafés in the GDR
did not serve the same function as the classic German coffee house, in which
open political or cultural debate took place.[80] Just as the borders between East
and West were heavily policed, so too the limits of public discourse were under
constant official scrutiny; in public cafés or FDGB vacation sites one could not
be sure that Stasi informants would not monitor critiques of the state and
Party.[81] Although the ever-present secret police apparatus circumscribed public
debate, frank discussions could take place among trusted friends. In fact, the
need to carve out a space for open discussion about living in the GDR gave the
Kaffeeklatsch in cafés or in homes greater significance. Conversation over coffee

may have been an important element of personal *Eigensinn,* or exertion of individual will, in a state that strove to control forms of community building and communication.[82] Taking and preserving photographs of these more personal events may have also constituted what Alf Lüdtke calls "stubborn photographing" or "eigen-sinniges Fotografieren," which willfully asserted these moments as significant in contrast to the regime's efforts to determine what were the "right images" to represent the GDR.[83]

The suggestion that coffee-drinking groups were a safe space for open discussion comes across in a group of photographs of a get-together of friends in the summer of 1956. The cheerful middle-aged company was labeled in one photograph as a "large *Kaffeeklatsch* with Mom, Rädels, and Klärchen Sötzold on our veranda." The compiler of the album added a telling label to a particularly delightful photo of the group laughing uproariously; it said *"Ja, Bohnenkaffee löst die Zungen"* or "Yes, bean coffee loosens the tongues." Here, the author draws attention to the fact that coffee made specifically from real beans, rather than ersatz materials, such as chicory, contained that magical quality—namely caffeine—that "loosened tongues" and lubricated social interaction, resulting in particularly humorous interchange. It is also worth noting that coffee was associated here with a sense of free expression at precisely the time in 1956 when authorities across the Soviet Bloc were cracking down on democratic exchange following the Hungarian uprising. The power of the Stasi was also broadening at home in the GDR. At a moment when Eastern Bloc citizens had to watch what they said in public for fear of repression, it is significant that this private gathering on the veranda established a relaxed atmosphere of fun, gossip, and jokes. This setting of free interchange in the *Kaffeeklatsch* was a potential alternative to the public sphere of the coffee house, because among trusted friends it might also have been possible to discuss political complaints or participate in the GDR's "grumble society."[84]

As the photo albums and other sources suggest, drinking coffee played a major role in leisure sociability at home as well as at work. This is corroborated by one interview-based study, which claimed that East Germans were more likely to invite friends or relatives over to their home for a cup of coffee than for a meal.[85] Domestic coffee drinking seemed to be a locus of pleasure and friendship. One pair of photos shows two female friends enjoying coffee in a kitchen inside an older house or apartment that is notably unrenovated, since it features none of mass-produced modular interiors or plastic commodities that would come to dominate socialist production in the 1960s.[86] In the foreground of the picture stand a large coffee pot and a transparent canister of coffee beans. Although in some snapshots drinkers might have been imbibing some sort of ersatz coffee, here the canister shows that these women were enjoying the real thing. This bit

FIGURE 8.2.   "Yes, bean coffee loosens the tongues." Caption for a photo in an album showing a group of friends drinking coffee and laughing on their veranda, labeled "large *Kaffeeklatsch* with Mom, Rädels, and Klärchen Sötzold on our veranda," from 1956. In the collection of the Wende Museum and Archive of the Cold War, 2010.

of luxury and pleasure inside a somewhat dilapidated kitchen becomes the focal point for a sweet and convivial scene of friends sharing a laugh.[87]

Coffee drinkers also enjoyed small moments of escape and social bonding by venturing out onto their verandas and balconies. Balconies, common to many German apartments, represent a liminal space between the home and the outside. They connote festive moments of togetherness in good weather, and it seems that the picture takers aimed to preserve memories of these miniget-aways as such. For a population that did not have great liberty to travel, lingering on the balcony, like beloved camping outings, might have played a special role in giving a sense of freedom to these coffee drinkers.[88] A series of photos in one album documents a group of friends congregated on the veranda in summer 1958 at the home of a family called the Guedemeiers. The album calls the group drinking coffee together on the veranda an "exemplary" or "perfect home community." The album's assembler emphasizes how coffee facilitated the unity of this friendship circle with the label "*Am Kaffeetisch sind alle einig*" or "At the

FIGURE 8.3.   Two female friends enjoying a laugh over real-bean coffee in an East German kitchen. Uncaptioned photo, n.d. In the collection of the Wende Museum and Archive of the Cold War, 2010.

coffee table all are one" or "all are agreed." This image of coffee fostering to-getherness poses an interesting counterpoint to the Party-promoted ideology of the "Einigkeit" or "unity" of the working class within the socialist state.

Everyday coffee drinking was not always an occasion for photographic commemoration. It took on another important function for those navigating the difficult circumstances of everyday life by circumventing official sources of goods and services. Not only was coffee drinking intimately linked to the black market as a source of Western beans, but being able to offer someone a cup of real coffee could help get other goods or services in the barter economy. In her retrospective, Jutta Voigt recounts, "A cup of coffee with colleagues, with com-rades, with a girlfriend, with the auto mechanic and the handyman who was supposed to install new Western fittings above the bathroom sink, constituted the fundamentals of all communication."[89] Jana Hensel's memoir adds that offering handymen or trading partners prized West German coffee could "open locked doors" to gain access to scarce commodities or services.[90]

Whether at home or work, with workmen or friends, coffee drinking was recorded on paper and film as a meaningful and memorable part of East German everyday lives. Though it was still often a means for exclusive female bonding, the *Kaffeeklatsch* was no longer just the domain of gossiping women, as it had been regarded in the nineteenth century.[91] In the GDR these coffee-centered gatherings were commemorated on film as spaces for independent social interaction; for joking about, critiquing, or otherwise grappling with life in the GDR; for exerting personal will or *Eigensinn*; and above all, as places for laughter.

Kaffee-Mix and the Coffee Dilemma

Because of the important role coffee played in East German social lives, it is significant that the process of attaining real-bean coffee continued to be complicated in the GDR. This dilemma became acute in the 1970s as the global coffee market faced its biggest crisis. The power of the GDR populace's demand for real beans became evident when a coffee crisis started brewing in 1977. A severe frost in Brazil in 1973 destroyed much of the country's coffee plants, sending the global supply into a tailspin. The weak status of the GDR on the world market was especially highlighted when global coffee prices rose by as much as 400 percent, and the yearly price the regime had to pay for coffee imports rose dramatically from 150 million marks to around 700 million.[92]

In response, the GDR regime banned coffee drinking in offices of the state and Party apparatus. In July, the Politburo decided on new "coffee guidelines" for distribution and sale, especially in restaurants, all of which were divided during this period into quality categories with corresponding price levels. According to the new guidelines, restaurants in the lower price levels II and III were forbidden to offer coffee at all.[93] In particular, this meant that coffee would not be sold in factory cafeterias. Shops also withdrew the relatively affordable Kosta and Melange brands and offered only the most expensive ones: Mona, Rondo, and Mokka-Fix Gold. In addition, the SED Central Committee raised the price of these remaining bean coffee brands; Rondo went up to 120 marks per kilogram.[94] The SED suggested that by doubling coffee prices, consumption of the drink would drop by some 30 percent.[95] Clearly such measures were bound to spark discontent among East Germans.

Even more provocatively, GDR functionaries promoted an alternative beverage, a new invention wrapped in a shiny gold bag costing six marks for 125 grams in HO stores: Kaffee-Mix, a brand containing 51 percent real coffee, combined with chicory, malt, dried sugar beets, peas, rye, and barley. Kaffee-Mix was meant, therefore, to satisfy the demand for coffee among lower-income East German workers. However, it was widely reviled, especially since state policies regulating the coffee supply ironically discriminated against workers. As a result, protests erupted in factories and through petitions to state functionaries. The Stasi monitored these protests and recorded statements that the state had betrayed its workers. Petitions flooded government offices bemoaning the disappearance of the Kosta and Melange brands of coffee, lamenting the poor quality and high price of Kaffee-Mix, and complaining about the lack of public information as to the supply situation.[96] In the second half of 1977, an unexpected fourteen thousand grievances about coffee appeared in central complaint departments.[97] Caffeine-addicted East Germans ridiculed this drink as "Honeckers Krönung," a spoof of the West German premium brand Jakobs Krönung. They even complained that the drink gave them stomachaches or impotence.[98] Consumers also revolted when their "Kaffeeboy" coffee machines stopped working after being filled with Kaffee-Mix. The protests peaked with worker strikes in places such as the Berlin district of Marzahn in October 1977.[99]

The strong consumer reaction forced the Politburo to react. First, on September 26, 1977, it lowered the price of a small bag of Kaffee-Mix from six to four marks, and efforts were made to improve the quality of the brew. In addition, the Ministry of Trade and Supply worked to disseminate more public information about the global coffee crisis.[100] Once it became clear that the population would not stand for this coffee substitute, as prices on the world market stabilized in 1978 Kaffee-Mix silently disappeared from store shelves. Party chair Erich Honecker then raised the status of coffee from a "luxury" to a "staple" foodstuff. The regime worked to invest more money in developing coffee roasting. The state-owned coffee company VEB Röstfein bought new machines for packaging beans. The Magdeburg Technical University developed an equivalent to patented Western mass steam roasting machines that cut the price, energy use, and roasting time considerably while improving the taste.

Acquisition of beans, however, still remained a problem. In 1978 the GDR spent 470 million marks on 500,000 tons of raw beans.[101] South American coffee may have tasted better, but these beans were more expensive. In fact, when foreign trade minister Horst Sölle tried to import South American coffee in 1978, the Politburo punished him by forcing him into a public "self-criticism."[102] Instead, the GDR leadership preferred to concentrate on trade with anti-Western or socialist-leaning countries in Africa and Asia, such as Ethiopia, Mozambique, Angola, and Vietnam. In 1978, the GDR secured a shipment of 8,000 tons of coffee from Ethiopia in exchange for heavy machinery and munitions.[103] The GDR also tried to broker a similar deal in Angola.[104] After the Vietnam War, with GDR encouragement, Vietnam planted an additional 500,000 tons of coffee. However, these plants did not bear fruit until ten years later, in 1990, when Vietnam became one of the world's leading coffee exporters.[105] Hence, even as the GDR traded munitions for beans on the global market, it was sometimes difficult to achieve the desired supplies. The long-term effect of the 1977 crisis, then, was increased efforts to secure supplies of coffee for the subsequent decade. The crisis demonstrated how the popular desire for coffee forced the regime to respond to significant popular criticism.

Conclusion

Despite the variety of barriers to bean access, GDR consumers continued to find a way to drink their coffee. Coffee remained one of the highest portions of GDR household budgets, even during the 1977 crisis; GDR citizens spent 3.3 billion marks per year on coffee, almost as much as their allotment for furniture and double their expenditure on shoes.[106] Despite the strictures on the GDR economy that came from an inadequate production and distribution system, lack of hard currency for foreign trade, competition with the West, and problems with illegal trade, GDR citizens still prioritized this imported drink. Their everyday lives were marked not only by efforts to circumvent this frustrating and restrictive system of supply but also by those special moments of enjoyment over a hard-won cup of steaming brew.

The photos of the *Kaffeeklatsch* offer telling examples of how the average GDR citizen negotiated the relationship of state, economy, and private life. The *Kaffeeklatsch* may often have taken place in private. However, these gatherings did not merely represent a retreat of society into niches.[107] Rather, coffee drinking bridged public and private, since the numerous individual strategies to acquire coffee beans represented the consumer's constant engagement with the difficult public system of provisioning.[108] Learning how to get real coffee (especially from the West), how to prepare it in a way that stretched the supply, and how to use it to get other desired goods and services represented a particular expertise cultivated by GDR consumers for coping with the socialist consumer economy. In addition, protests around consumer shortages in 1953 and following the introduction of Kaffee-Mix in 1977 reveal how consumer concerns led the population to confront the regime directly. Even though there was little opportunity for public debate as in the classic coffee house, coffee in this sense still spurred political action. In both crises, citizens pressured the state to respond to consumer demands by seeking out ever-more-expansive supplies of beans.

The GDR regime attempted to mold society into a community united by the ideology of socialism and enforced the boundaries of this community through intrusive policing by the Stasi and other repressive measures. However, as the case of coffee shows, communities in the GDR formed differently and sometimes in subversive ways. The scarcity of coffee led to status distinctions based on who had Western connections or other privileges that could garner them access to real beans in Intershops, in gift packages, or through the black market. Resentment of those who exploited this complex marketplace for profit fed tendencies in East Germany to demarcate national insiders and outsiders through, for example, anti-Semitic antipathy toward black marketeers seen in the case of the Leipzig coffee ring. The imperative of suppressing or covering over these potentially destructive social divisions added pressure to the regime to supply its citizens with coffee to restore a semblance of its purported national solidarity and equality. In the end, as GDR photo albums suggest, a perhaps more "authentic" solidarity among East Germans took place not through state-engineered mass organizations but in small social groups meeting over coffee at work or at home.

East German citizens' expertise in navigating the GDR marketplace for coffee may have brought a certain sense of pride at attaining precious beans. Popular memories of enjoyment in socialist-era commodities, hard won through individual consumer resourcefulness, might have contributed to the decision by private companies to re-launch some GDR brands following the fall of the GDR in 1989. Rondo and Mokka-Fix both reentered the German market as part of the wave of *Ostalgie* exhibited in the 1990s.[109] Or perhaps these GDR brands remind Germans from the former East of slices of life under socialism seen in their family photo albums: pleasurable times with friends sharing their beloved beverage. Even in a repressive system plagued by shortages and focused on work, GDR coffee drinkers chose to remember those happy leisurely moments when coffee was the center of sociability, laughter, and the good life.

NOTES

1. Ewan Butler, *City Divided: Berlin 1955* (London: Sidgwick and Jackson, 1955), 143.

2. Stephen L. Sampson, "The Second Economy of the Soviet Union and Eastern Europe," *Annals of the American Academy of Political and Social Science*, 493(1) (1987), 120–36; Alena V. Ledeneva, *Russia's Economy of Favours: Blat, Networking and Informal Exchange* (Cambridge: Cambridge University Press, 1998); Katherine Verdery, *What Was Socialism and What Comes Next?* (Princeton, NJ: Princeton University Press, 1996), 27.

3. Stadtgeschichtliches Museum Leipzig, *Süße muß der Coffee sein! Drei Jahrhunderte europäische Kaffeekultur und die Kaffeesachsen* (Leipzig: Stadtgeschichtliches Museum, 1994).

4. Jürgen Habermas, *The Structural Transformation of the Public Sphere: An Inquiry into a Category of Bourgeois Society* (Cambridge, MA: MIT Press, 1989), 31ff.

5. Brian William Cowan, *The Social Life of Coffee: The Emergence of the British Coffee House* (New Haven, CT: Yale University Press, 2005), chapter 8; Markman Ellis, "Coffee-women, *The Spectator*, and the Public Sphere in the Early Eighteenth Century," in *Women, Writing, and the Public Sphere: 1700–1830*, ed. Elizabeth Eger et al. (Cambridge: Cambridge University Press, 2001), 27–52; Joel Shapira, David Shapira, and Karl

Schapira, *The Book of Coffee & Tea (Second Revised Edition)* (New York: St. Martin's Press, 1982), 23.

6. Jörg R. Bergmann, *Klatsch: Zur Form der diskreten Indeskretion* (New York: de Gruyter, 1987), 101. An English visitor to Germany described the stereotypically gossipy *Kaffeeklatsch* as "that celebrated form of entertainment where at every sip a reputation dies." Mrs. Alfred Sidgwick, *Home Life in Germany* (New York: Macmillan, 1908), 200.

7. A Wartime Commission for Coffee, Tea and their Ersatz Products was set up especially to facilitate import of these goods from Holland because of the constraints from the British Naval Blockade in the First World War. Bundesarchiv Berlin (BAB) R8817/8 Kriegsausschuß für Kaffee, Tee und deren Ersatzmittel GmbH.

8. Coffee exports from Tanganyika were already increasing before Germany lost the colony (from 231 tons in 1905 to 681 tons in 1912), but this amount was far exceeded afterward (to 12,000 tons in 1939). Brad Weiss, "Coffee Breaks and Coffee Connections: The Lived Experience of a Commodity in Tanzanian and European Worlds," in *Cross-Cultural Consumption: Global Markets, Local Realities*, ed. David Howes (London: Routledge, 1996), 95.

9. Ursula Becker, *Kaffee-Konzentration: Zur Entwicklung und Organisation des hanseatischen Kaffeehandels* (Stuttgart: Franz Steiner Verlag, 2002).

10. Malte Zierenberg, *Stadt der Schieber: Der Berliner Schwarzmarkt, 1939–1950* (Göttingen: Vandenhoeck & Ruprecht, 2008), 82.

11. Paul Steege, *Black Market, Cold War: Everyday Life in Berlin, 1946–1949* (Cambridge: Cambridge University Press), 2007, 40; Karl Kromer, *Schwarzmarkt, Tausch- und Schleichhandel: In Frage und Antwort mit 500 praktischen Beispielen* (Schloß Bleckede an der Elbe: Otto Meißners, 1947), 20.

12. Michael Wildt, *Der Traum vom Sattwerden: Hunger und Protest, Schwarzmarkt und Selbsthilfe* (Hamburg: VSA, 1986).

13. Annette Kaminsky, "'Nieder mit den Alu-Chips': Die private Einfuhr von Westwaren in die DDR," in *Das Westpaket: Geschenksendung, Keine Handelsware*, ed. Christian Härtel and Petra Kabus (Berlin: Christoph Links Verlag, 2000), 269, fn3.

14. The American occupying army decided it was more efficient and lighter to deliver real coffee beans in the airlift planes than fuel for use in manufacturing ersatz coffee in West Berlin. Roger Gene Miller, *To Save a City: The Berlin Airlift, 1948–1949* (College Station, TX: Texas A&M University Press, 2000), 52.

15. Stiftung Archiv der Parteien und Massenorganisationen im Bundesarchiv (SAPMO-BA) DY30/IV2/6.02/99, ZK SED Abt. Wirtschaftspolitik, Redaktion Vorwärts Berlin, Chefredaktion, Informationen aus den Westsektoren 20. bis 30. Dezember 1948, Bezirk Wilmersdorf (brit. Sektor). Unit of measurement for the DM 28 coffee is unreported.

16. Landesarchiv Berlin (LAB) C Rep 303-09/81, Bl.268, Der Polizeipräsident in Berlin, Personalabteilung, Berlin, den 20.9.1948, Stimmungsbericht! Betr: Schwarzhandelsbekämpfung in Moabit.

17. BAB DA1/208, Deutscher Volksrat Sekretariat Abteilung III, V Fachausschüsse, Wirtschaftsausschuß, Unterausschuß Handel und Versorgung Landwirtschaft, 5. Sitzung 1949, Dienstag, dem 4. Januar 1949, comment by Erich Freund.

18. BAB DY34/20367, FDGB, Berlin, 4.10.1948, Bericht über die Verhandlungen bei der SMA-Finanz (Herr Kobrin) Betr. Einrichtung von staatl. Verkaufsgeschäften für freien Handel mit Luxuswaren, Rakow.

19. Lewis H. Siegelbaum, *Stakhanovism and the Politics of Productivity in the USSR, 1935–1941* (Cambridge: Cambridge University Press, 1990), 213.

20. Katherine Pence, "Building Socialist Worker-Consumers: The Paradoxical Construction of the Handelsorganisation-HO, 1948," in *Arbeiter in der SBZ-DDR*, ed. Peter Hübner and Klaus Tenfelde (Essen: Klartext Verlag, 1998), 497–526.

21. Jennifer Schevardo, *Vom Wert des Notwendigen: Preispolitik und Lebensstandard in der DDR der fünfziger Jahre* (München: Franz Steiner Verlag, 2005), 95.

22. This strategy contributed to a sense that the GDR was a "welfare dictatorship." See Konrad H. Jarausch, "Care and Coercion: The GDR as Welfare Dictatorship," in *Dictatorship as Experience: Towards a Socio-Cultural History of the GDR*, ed. Konrad H. Jarausch (Oxford: Oxford University Press, 1999), 47–72.

23. BAB DA1/186, Deutscher Volksrat Sekretariat Abteilung III, V Fachausschüsse, Wirtschaftsausschuß 6. Sitzung, 15. Oktober 1948, 65.

24. BAB DY34/20462, 14.12.1948, FDGB Landesvorstand Thüringen, HA Wirtschaft, Holl. to Bundesvorstand HA2, Zoellner.

25. BAB DC1/1 Zentrale Kommission für Staatliche Kontrolle, HO Hausmitteilung, HO Lebensmittel ZL, Berlin, From Meusel, July 5, 1951.

26. Katherine Pence, "'Herr Schimpf und Frau Schande': Grenzgänger des Konsums im geteilten Berlin und die Politik des Kalten Krieges," in *Sterben für Berlin? Die Berliner Krisen 1948: 1958*, ed. Burghard Ciesla, Michael Lemke, and Thomas Lindenberger (Berlin: Metropol, 1999), 185–202.

27. Patt Rehberg, *Schöne Grüße aus Berlin: Besinnliche Heiterkeit aus der 2-Welten-Stadt* (Berlin-Tempelhof: West-Ost-Verlag Werner Jöhren, n.d.), 39.

28. German restaurants and hotels were taken over by Intourist and supplied with goods sold at high prices. J. P. Nettl, *The Eastern Zone and Soviet Policy in Germany, 1945–1950* (Oxford: Oxford University Press, 1951), 229.

29. Zierenberg, *Stadt der Schieber*, 168–71; Michael Berkowitz, *The Crime of My Very Existence: Nazism and the Myth of Jewish Criminality* (Berkeley: University of California Press, 2007); Leonard Dinnerstein, "German Attitudes Toward the Jewish Displaced Persons (1945–50)," in *Germany and America: Essays on Problems of International Relations and Immigration*, ed. Hans L. Trefousse (New York: Brooklyn College Press, 1980), 242; See also Sven Korzilius, *"Asoziale" und "Parasiten" im Recht der SBZ/DDR: Randgruppen im Sozialismus zwischen Repression und Ausgrenzung* (Köln: Böhlau Verlag, 2005).

30. BAB DC1/74 Zentrale Kommission der Staatlichen Kontrolle, Berlin, 28. Okt. 1950, Aktenvermerk, Betr: Kaffee-Ring Leipzig. Signed Trotz and Masius.

31. Katherine Pence, "From Rations to Fashions: The Gendered Politics of East and West German Consumption, 1945–1961," Ph.D. dissertation, University of Michigan, 1999, chapter 2.

32. BAB DC1/74, Zentrale Kommission der Staatlichen Kontrolle, Berlin, 28. Okt. 1950, Aktenvermerk, Betr: Kaffee-Ring Leipzig. Signed Trotz and Masius, 3.

33. Ibid.

34. Ibid.

35. Jeffrey Herf, *Divided Memory: The Nazi Past in the Two Germanys* (Cambridge, MA: Harvard University Press, 1997), 132–33.

36. Jürgen Schmidt, "Goldmokka und Kaffeemix: Kaffee im geteilten Deutschland," in *Kaffee: Vom Schmuggelgut zum Lifestyle-Klassiker, Drei Jahrhunderte Berliner Kaffeekultur,* ed. Peter Lummel (Berlin: be.bra Verlag, 2002), 81.

37. Katherine Pence, "'You as a Woman Will Understand': Consumption, Gender, and the Relationship Between State and Citizenry in the GDR's June 17, 1953 Crisis," *German History* 19(2) (2001): 218–52.

38. See the files in BAB DL1/3906, DL1/3907, DL1/3908 Ministerium für Handel und Versorgung, Situationsbericht Westberlin 1958–1960.

39. BAB DC6/33, Berlin, 12.8.1953, Ministerium für Handel und Versorgung, Der Minister Wach, to Elli Schmidt, Staatliche Kommission für Handel und Versorgung, Betr.: Bohnenkaffee.

40. Ibid.

41. Mark Landsman, *Dictatorship and Demand: The Politics of Consumerism in East Germany* (Cambridge, MA: Harvard University Press, 2005), 147.

42. Richard B. Bilder, "The International Coffee Agreement: A Case History in Negotiation," *Law and Contemporary Problems* 28(2) (Spring 1963): 328–91.

43. Ina Dietzsch, "Deutsch-deutscher Gabentausch," in *Wunderwirtschaft: DDR-Konsumkultur in den 60er Jahren,* ed. Neue Gesellschaft für Bildende Kunst (Köln: Böhlau Verlag, 1996), 210.

44. Jutta Voigt, *Der Geschmack des Ostens: Vom Essen, Trinken und Leben in der DDR* (Berlin: Gustav Kiepenhauer Verlag, 2005), 159.

45. BAB DC20-I/3/233, Ministerrat, Anlage C zum Originalprotokoll der 167. Sitzung der Regierung vom 5.8.54, Verordnung über den Geschenkpaket- und Päckchenverkehr auf dem Postwege mit Westdeutschland, Westberlin und dem Ausland vom 5. August 1954, Berlin, Die Regierung DDR, Ministerpräsident, Min. für Handel und Versorgung.

46. Franka Schneider, "'Jedem nach dem Wohnsitz seiner Tante': Die GENEX Geschenkdienst GmbH," in *Wunderwirtschaft,* 223–31.

47. Rudolf Brauer, Ursel Mehlhahn, and Günter Schade, *Wir und der Aussenhandel: Was jeder davon wissen sollte! Ein kleines Lehr- und Lesebuch* (Berlin: Verlag die Wirtschaft, 1959), 22.

48. BAB DE1/07336, Staatliche Plankommission, 23.7.1958, Neue Fragen der Versorgung der Bevölkerung mit Konsumgütern, insbesondere mit Nahrungsmitteln nach der Abschaffung der Lebensmittelkarten.

49. BAB DY30/IV2/6.10/231, Kairo, den 12. Dez. 1958, Niederschrift über ein Gespräch mit dem Sekretär der Botschaft Ghanas in der VAR, Herrn Kuny, am 11.12.58, Kattner.; BAB DY30/IV2/6.10/232 Leipzig, 3. März 1959, Plans to help Guinea, Signed Bavogui.

50. BAB DY30/IV2/6.10/231, Bl.25, Kairo, den 12.12.1958, Niederschrift über ein Gespräch mit dem Sekretär der Botschaft Ghanas in der VAR, Herrn Kuny, am 11.12.58, Kattner.

51. André Steiner, "Vom Überholen eingeholt: Zur Wirtschaftskrise 1960/61 in der DDR," in *Sterben für Berlin*, 248.

52. BAB DY30/IV2/6.10/126, Entwurf, Berlin, den 11. Mai 1959 Sö/Schw., Programm zur Änderung der Lage im Berliner Handel.

53. BAB DE1/07336, Staatliche Plankommission, 23.7.1958, Neue Fragen der Versorgung der Bevölkerung mit Konsumgütern, insbesondere mit Nahrungsmitteln nach der Abschaffung der Lebensmittelkarten.

54. BAB DY30/IV2/6.10/10, Berlin, 15.2.1960, Analyse über die eingegangenen Bevölkerungsbeschwerden im 2. Halbjahr 1959, November 23.

55. BAB DY30/IV2/2.029/87, SED Hausmitteilung an den Leiter der Wirtschaftskomm. der Politbüro Gen. Dr. Apel, Von Abt. Handel, Versorgung und Außenhandel, Schr./Kb. 25.5.61.

56. Patrick Major, *Behind the Berlin Wall: East Germany and the Frontiers of Power* (Oxford: Oxford University Press, 2010), 106.

57. Dirk Diether Rohders, *Zöllner-Rapport Ost-West* (Norderstedt: Books on Demand, 2005), 96.

58. BAB DY30/IV2/6.10/34, Bl.148, SED ZK Bereich Wirtschaftspolitik, Über die Lage in der Versorgung, 27.10.61.

59. Jonathan R. Zatlin, *The Currency of Socialism: Money and Political Culture in East Germany* (Cambridge: Cambridge University Press, 2007), 268.

60. Ina Merkel, *Utopie und Bedürfnis: Die Geschichte der Konsumkultur in der DDR* (Köln: Böhlau Verlag, 1999), 243ff.

61. Katrin Böske, "Abwesend anwesend: Eine kleine Geschichte des Intershops," in *Wunderwirtschaft*, 214–22.

62. Zatlin, *The Currency of Socialism*, 243–85.

63. Evelin Grohnert, "'Es gab nichts, aber jeder hatte alles': Renate Z., Verkaufsstellenleiterin, erzählt," in *Fortschritt, Norm und Eigensinn: Erkundungen im Alltag der DDR*, ed. Dokumentationszentrum Alltagskultur der DDR e.V. (Berlin: Christoph Links Verlag, 1999), 117–18.

64. Mary Fulbrook, *The People's State: East German Society from Hitler to Honecker* (New Haven: Yale University Press, 2005), 184.

65. Rainer Gries, *Produktkommunikation: Geschichte und Theorie* (Vienna: Facultas Verlag, 2008), 187.

66. For example, Stephan Dettmeyer, *Sack Haun: Von einem, der ausstieg, das Laufen zu lernen* (Norderstedt: Books on Demand, 2008), 43. On *Ostalgie*, see Paul Betts, "The Twilight of the Idols: East German Memory and Material Culture," *Journal of Modern History* 72(3) (September 2000): 731–65.

67. Georg Naundorfer, *Sächsischer Kaffee: Satirische Nostalgien* (Norderstedt: Books on Demand, 2009), 10.

68. M.P., "Technik im Haushalt," *Kultur im Heim* 2 (1958), 27.

69. Naundorfer, *Sächsischer Kaffee*, 12.

70. Marita Krauss, "Kleine Welten: Alltagsfotografie—die Anschaulichkeit einer 'privaten Praxis,'" in *Visual History: Ein Studienbuch*, ed. Gerhard Paul (Göttingen: Vandenhoeck & Ruprecht, 2006), 71.

71. Paul Betts, *Within Walls: Private Life in the German Democratic Republic* (Oxford: Oxford University Press, 2010), 196–200.

72. For a discussion of issues addressed in recent historiography on German photography, see David Crew, "Visual Power? The Politics of Images in Twentieth Century Germany and Austria-Hungary," *German History* 27(2) (April 2009): 271–85, here 278.

73. Voigt, *Der Geschmack des Ostens*, 160.

74. Stefan Wolle, *Die heile Welt der Diktatur: Alltag und Herrschaft in der DDR 1971–1989* (Berlin: Christoph Links Verlag, 1998), 201.

75. Workers were surveyed in the Leipzig Cotton Spinning Mill, the Middle German Worsted Spinning Mill, and the Kirow Factory. Bundesarchiv Aussenstelle Coswig, DL102/131, Ministerium für Handel und Versorgung, Institut für Bedarfsforschung, Bericht zur Meinungsumfrage unter werktätigen Frauen aus drei Großbetreiben über die Versorgung mit Waren und Dienstleistungen, Leipzig, 18.01.1964.

76. Dietrich Mühlberg, "Rekonstruktionsversuch einer ergebnislosen Betriebsreportage von 1956," in *Die DDR im Bild: Zum Gebrauch der Fotografie im anderen deutschen Staat*, ed. Karin Hartewig and Alf Lüdtke (Göttingen: Wallstein Verlag, 2004), 147–68.

77. Wolle, *Die heile Welt der Diktatur*, 113.

78. Werner Müller, "German Democratic Republic," in *European Labor Unions*, ed. Joan Campbell (Westport, CT: Greenwood, 1992), 190.

79. Verdery, *What Was Socialism*, 104.

80. Elizabeth Mittmann, "Locating a Public Sphere: Some Reflections on Writers and *Öffentlichkeit* in the GDR," in *Women in German Yearbook 10*, ed. Jeanette Clausen and Sara Friedrichsmeyer (Lincoln, NE: University of Nebraska Press, 1995), 22.

81. Fulbrook, *The People's State*, 250.

82. Alf Lüdtke, ed., *The History of Everyday Life: Reconstructing Historical Experiences and Ways of Life* (Princeton, NJ: Princeton University Press, 1995).; Thomas Lindenberger, ed., *Herrschaft und Eigen-Sinn in der Diktatur: Studien zur Gesellschaftsgeschichte der DDR* (Köln: Böhlau Verlag, 1999).

83. Alf Lüdtke, "Kein Entkommen? Bilder-Codes und eigen-sinniges Fotografieren; eine Nachlese," in *Die DDR im Bild*, 227–36; on the idea of constructing the "right images" in photography, see Crew, "Visual Power?"

84. On the "grumble society," see Andrew I. Port, *Conflict and Stability in the German Democratic Republic* (Cambridge: Cambridge University Press, 2008), 115ff.

85. Charlotte Brinkmann, "Bananen mit Ketchup: Eßkultur: Beobachtungen in einer markt- und einer planwirtschaftlich orientierten Gesellschaft," in *Blick-Wechsel Ost-West: Beobachtungen zur Alltagskultur in Ost- und Westdeutschland*, ed. Wolfgang Kaschuba et al. (Tübingen: Vereinigung für Volkskunde, 1992), 95.

86. Eli Rubin, *Synthetic Socialism: Plastics and Dictatorship in the German Democratic Republic* (Chapel Hill: University of North Carolina Press, 2008); on GDR interiors see Paul Betts, "Building Socialism at Home: The Case of East German Interiors," in *Socialist Modern: East German Everyday Culture and Politics*, ed. Katherine Pence and Paul Betts (Ann Arbor, MI: University of Michigan Press, 2008), 96–132.

87. Thomas Heubner recounts many of these jokes in *So schmeckte es in der DDR: Ein Lach- und Sachbuch vom Essen und Trinken* (Berlin: Eulenspiegel Verlag, 2004).

88. Rubin, *Synthetic Socialism*, 144ff; Scott Moranda, "East German Nature Tourism, 1945–1961: In Search of a Common Destination," in *Turizm: The Russian and East European Tourist Under Capitalism and Socialism*, ed. Anne E. Gorsuch (Ithaca, NY: Cornell University Press, 2006), 266–80.

89. Voigt, *Der Geschmack des Ostens*, 160.

90. Jana Hensel, *After the Wall: Confessions from an East German Childhood and the Life That Came Next* (New York: PublicAffairs, 2004), 48.

91. Katja Mutschelknaus, *Kaffeeklatsch: Die Stunde der Frauen* (München: Sandmann, 2008).

92. Hans-Joachim Döring, *"Es geht um unsere Existenz": Die Politik der DDR gegenüber der Dritten Welt am Beispiel vom Mosambik und Äthiopien* (Berlin: Christoph Links Verlag, 1999), 115; see also Annette Kaminsky, *Wohlstand, Schönheit, Glück: Kleine Konsumgeschichte der DDR* (München: Becksche Reihe, 2001), 131.

93. Voigt, *Der Geschmack des Ostens*, 159.

94. Wolle, *Die heile Welt der Diktatur*, 200.

95. Döring, *"Es geht um unsere Existenz,"* 116.

96. Gries, *Produktkommunikation*, 182.

97. Döring, *"Es geht um unsere Existenz,"* 121.

98. Voigt, *Der Geschmack des Ostens*, 160.

99. Axel Bust-Bartels, *Herrschaft und Widerstand in den DDR-Betrieben: Leistungsentlohnung, Arbeitsbedingungen, innerbetriebliche Konflikte und technologische Entwicklung* (Frankfurt/Main: Campus Verlag, 1980), 134.

100. Gries, *Produktkommunikation*, 182–83.

101. Wolle, *Die heile Welt der Diktatur*, 201.

102. Döring, *"Es geht um unsere Existenz,"* 122.

103. Rohders, *Zöllner-Rapport*, 96.

104. Döring, *"Es geht um unsere Existenz."*

105. Heubner, *So schmeckte es in der DDR*, 124.

106. Kaminsky, *Wohlstand*, 132.

107. Günter Gaus, *Wo Deutschland liegt: Eine Ortsbestimmung* (Hamburg: Hoffmann und Campe, 1983).

108. On the role of privacy in relationship to the public and to politics in the GDR, see Betts, *Within Walls*, especially 13–16.

109. Katja Neller, *DDR-Nostalgie: Dimensionen der Orientierungen der Ostdeutschen gegenüber der ehemaligen DDR, ihre Ursachen und politische Konnotationen* (Wiesbaden: VS Verlag, 2006), 51.

9

From Black Caviar to Blackouts

Gender, Consumption, and Lifestyle in Ceauşescu's Romania

Jill Massino

In 1963, or whenever Ceauşescu came to power, until 1970–72, it was a time of blossoming. One began to find everything. One even found black caviar in the grocery stores. You found it by the kilogram. You found everything that you had: whiskey, gin, bitters, everything that was over there [the West] was over here. And at affordable prices. But I didn't ask myself—people didn't ask themselves—what the use of this was, why did this happen?[1]

—G. N., interview with author

Postwar Romania is rarely imagined to be a place of abundance, let alone affordable black caviar. Instead, it is most often remembered for the latter years of the period, when unlit streets, empty shelves, cold apartments, and the Securitate were common features of everyday life. As communist rule in the region entered its final decade and most countries began to embrace liberalization—especially after the advent of Gorbachev—Romania became increasingly nationalist, repressive, and isolated, and daily life more difficult and desperate. Because of the shortages of these later years, and the role this played in the ultimate downfall of the regime and the brutal end of the Ceauşescus, analyses of consumption in the region tend to bypass Romania. Yet in the years after Stalin's death, the Romanian party-state employed strategies similar to its Bloc neighbors to legitimate communist rule, among other things an opening up to the West, the broadening of consumer culture, and the promotion of a modern lifestyle, particularly in the 1960s and early 1970s.

As the quote illustrates, this period of relative consumer abundance still lingers in Romanian personal memories. An exploration of Romania during the 1960s and early 1970s permits a fuller picture of consumption in the region, challenging the notion that consumer liberalization existed only in more liberal countries of the Bloc such as Hungary and East Germany. At the same time, it opens a window onto Romania under communism, when consumption played a prominent role in state strategies, as well as the lived experiences of ordinary people.

Over the past decade, scholars of Eastern Europe and the Soviet Union have argued that socialist states sustained power by redirecting people's interests toward consumer goods. This was indicative of a new kind of negotiation of power that replaced simple coercion.[2] Supplying the population with consumer goods and "the good life" therefore became important elements in bolstering the legitimacy and supposed systemic superiority of post-Stalinist states in the region.[3] But provision and promotion of new modes of consumption were also potential tools for eradicating backwardness and building a modern socialist citizenry.[4] Consumption thus played an important role in reformulating and articulating gender identities, including fashioning a modern socialist woman.[5] Yet although socialist states attempted to transform women into modern socialist consumer citizens, women in turn exercised agency and even resistance through consumer practices and demands.[6]

Drawing on a combination of official sources and oral histories, this chapter explores consumer polices and experiences in socialist Romania through the lens of gender. It begins with a brief sketch of consumer policies under Romania's first communist leader, Gheorghe Gheorghiu-Dej (1947–1965), exploring how his promotion of nationalism and consumerism in the late 1950s and early 1960s set the stage for the further expansion of these policies under Nicolae Ceauşescu (1965–1989). Through the official women's monthly, *Femeia* (Woman), and the official fashion quarterly, *Moda* (Fashion), the state used advertisements, fashion spreads, articles, and advice columns to advance modern notions of socialist womanhood, manhood, and lifestyle.[7] To be sure, the imagery, goods, and to some extent the type of lifestyle being advanced in *Femeia* and *Moda* had much in common with Western magazines. But in Ceauşescu's Romania, the "marketing" of modern fashions and furnishings accompanied policies, in particular reproductive and family policies, that were highly repressive and conflicted with the seemingly progressive lifestyles being promoted in the magazines. Considered from this perspective, the promotion of consumerism and modern lifestyles in the 1960s served in part to counterbalance or mask the more repressive family and reproductive policies that were instituted during this period.

In an effort to understand how these policies played out on the ground, I interviewed women about their everyday experiences as consumers during the periods of liberalization (early 1960s to mid-1970s) and austerity (1980s), focusing on the generation that came of age in the 1960s and early 1970s.[8] In many cases, my respondents' positive memories of communism were related to the consumer possibilities made available to them during this period of liberalization. This included the consumption of films, fashions, chocolate, and caviar, as well as household durables such as washing machines and home furnishings. To be sure, Romanians did not experience de-Stalinization on a par with most Eastern European countries; nevertheless, the 1960s and early 1970s were a period of relative consumer abundance. Because access to consumer goods meant an improved standard of living for many, consumerism was the basis on which some people constituted their identity, as well as their memories of life under communism. These memories reveal that, in Romania, the communist past evokes more than just vivid recollections of blackouts during the harsh conditions of the 1980s but also nostalgia for black caviar and the Black Sea coast.

Rather than a long-term strategy for maintaining power and redirecting people's lives toward the nonpolitical, the state's nod to consumer goods and improved lifestyle was short-lived as Ceauşescu embraced nationalism as a basis for legitimating communist rule. Faced with fiscal crisis in the 1980s, Ceauşescu attempted to nourish the population with nationalist rhetoric and policy, rather than healthy diets and material goods. The results for ordinary people were devastating, as Ceauşescu's drive for political and economic autonomy led to rationing of basic foodstuffs, as well as gasoline, heat, and electricity. For women, Ceauşescu's nationalism meant the criminalization of abortion (beginning in the mid-1960s) and draconian attempts to raise the fertility rate. As my collected oral narratives show, Romanian women found it ever more difficult to fulfill their multiple roles under the shortage economy of the 1980s. At the same time, these shortages could lead to more equal sharing of domestic duties, as men often assumed responsibility for food procurement. Most significantly, although individuals positively identified with the consumerism of the 1960s and early 1970s, the lean 1980s lent stark evidence of the ideological bankruptcy of the regime.

Consumption Under Dej

During his first decade in power, Gheorghe Gheorghiu-Dej followed Stalin's principles of mass industrialization and repression—albeit on a much smaller and less horrific scale. During the late 1940s, Romania was still reeling from the aftereffects of war and famine, the latter of which was brought on by a drought in 1946 and the Soviet policy of confiscating food surpluses to feed the Soviet Army. Although many experienced privation, according to Mircea (a retired pharmacist who was in his midtwenties at the time) some suffered more than others since "manual workers were allocated 700 grams of meat a week, while stay-at-home wives were allowed only 500."[9] As the new privileged class, industrial laborers were given priority in terms of not only food rations but also state-subsidized housing. By prioritizing workers over other segments of the population, the new socialist state was making a powerful statement about what constituted productive work, and indeed human value. Thus the state veered away from the Marxist principle of "from each according to his ability, to each according to his needs" to a Stalinist system in which productive output, as well as political position, became the basis for preferential treatment.[10] Unequal distribution of food, along with the program of collectivization introduced in 1949, would leave innumerable individuals hungry, if not on the verge of starvation, in the early years of communist rule.

By the late 1950s, the period of austerity, uncertainty, and repression was ending and Romania entered an era of relative political, economic, and cultural liberalization. Under Dej, liberalization was accompanied by rising nationalism. Although he mimicked some of the de-Stalinization efforts of the USSR—relaxation of censorship, amnesty for political prisoners, and promotion of consumerism—he also pursued a distinctly Romanian road to socialism. In 1958, Dej secured the withdrawal of Soviet troops from Romania. In the early 1960s, Russian language requirements were abolished in schools and universities, street and city names were Romanianized, and Romanian cultural figures, most notably the dramatist Eugene Ionescu and the historian Nicolae Iorga, were rehabilitated.[11] Finally, in 1964 Dej moved further away from the Soviet orbit by refusing to participate in Comecon's Valev plan and by declaring Romania's right to follow its own path to communism.[12] In less than ten years, then, Romania went from being one of the USSR's staunchest allies to being the Soviet satellite most actively engaged in trade with the West.[13] This, however, did not signify a departure from state socialism but instead an effort to relegitimate it according to nationalist principles.

In Romania, as elsewhere in the Bloc, these political and economic changes were accompanied by changes in consumer and cultural policies. Fashionable clothing and household durables appeared more frequently in the windows of state-owned shops and on the pages of magazines. In addition, Western films, publications, and exhibitions—along with Western tourists—began to trickle into the country in 1963. Changes in family and reproductive policies were instituted as well. In 1956 a new family code equalized spousal relations, and in 1957 Romania decriminalized abortion.[14] A shift in how women were represented in official media also occurred. Rotund farm workers and plain-Jane factory hands were still featured in *Femeia*, but they appeared alongside images of glamorous, fashionably clad, and feminine-looking women. For example, the cover of the August 1959 issue (in commemoration of the fifteenth anniversary of Romania's "liberation" by the Soviet Army) featured a sensuous, heavily made-up woman in a pinup-like pose holding the Romanian flag and gazing enticingly at the camera. The message was clear: women no longer had to sacrifice beauty or femininity for socialism; instead these attributes were reflective of socialism's success in building a modern socialist citizen. This shift was by no means unique to Romania, as the Soviet leadership also promoted fashion and femininity as aspects of the thaw. Perfumes, cosmetics, and fashionable clothing and footwear were available to ordinary consumers in the USSR, East Germany, Poland, Yugoslavia, and Hungary.[15] No longer bourgeois frivolities, fashion and beauty now served as signs of socialist modernity, with consumerism becoming a palpable medium through which socialist leaders legitimated their rule.

At that same time, socialist propagandists were quick to remind women that consumerism should not be embraced with reckless abandon. Instead, practicality and "rational consumption" were promoted. A short piece titled "Hello, 'Father New Year' on the Phone," which appeared in the December 1959 issue of *Femeia*, is illustrative: ordinary women (whose photos appeared alongside their occupational titles) shared their New Year's wishes with *Moş Gherla* (the communist substitute for Santa Claus). Rather than a new dress or a pair of earrings, the women asked for "PEACE," the desire to "work better than I have up until now, for our dear country, The Socialist Republic of Romania," and "fewer divorce suits and criminal cases."[16] Outside of toys for children, none of the women requested material goods of any sort; instead they wished for things that would increase production, promote family harmony, and foster peace. In contrast to its consumer-oriented Western counterpart (Christmas), in socialist Romania the New Year's holiday was a time for encouraging national and moral growth. By reconfiguring the New Year's wish into something nonmaterial and by mobilizing it for ideological purposes, the state sought to reappropriate terms such as "wish" and "want," and to privilege the collective over the individual. At the same time, by containing individuals' desires, the state sought to garner popular support without overburdening the economy's productive capacity.

Ceauşescu and the Gender of Consumption

On the death of Dej in March 1965, Ceauşescu assumed the position of general secretary of the Romanian Communist Party. While denouncing the repressions under Dej, Ceauşescu built on the nationalist and anti-Soviet tendencies of his predecessor, expanding diplomatic and economic relations with a number of Western countries. Most significantly, in 1968 he brazenly denounced the Soviet invasion of Czechoslovakia. In addition, Ceauşescu further liberalized the consumer sphere, offering up heretofore scarce or unavailable luxury items and household durables from caviar and cognac to vacuum cleaners and television sets. Finally, in 1967 he allowed a limited number of privately owned stores, restaurants, and inns to open.[17]

The various goods on offer served as important icons of Ceauşescu's liberalization and were presented by party propagandists as visual symbols of the success of Romanian-style socialism. As in the West, consumer durables were meant to liberate women from domestic drudgery. In this respect, an advertisement for the Record vacuum cleaner invites interesting readings of consumer policy, the gendering of housework, and private life: a woman lounges in a chair reading a book while her new cherry-red Record is prominently displayed in the foreground. The caption reads: "Do you want to complete your housework in record time? Use the Record vacuum cleaner."[18] Described as utilitarian, practical, and economical, the Record, in reducing the amount of time women need to devote to housework, provides them with "timpul liber" (free time)—which, according to this image, involved cerebral activities such as reading. Seemingly delivering on the Leninist promise to liberate women from domestic servitude, it also represents a shift in how the state conceived of the individual in that leisure was now acknowledged as an important aspect of the socialist woman's life. What is not acknowledged, however, is that even by this period of "mature socialism," only 40 individuals per 1,000 owned a vacuum cleaner.[19]

Moreover, by featuring a woman rather than a man or a couple, the advertisers were sending the message that, even though modern technology could make housework easier, it did not necessarily lead to a radical restructuring of gender roles. Indeed, as in the West, nearly all of *Femeia*'s advertisements for household durables featured a woman using or displaying these goods, indicating that the state still regarded women as primarily responsible for household consumption and housework.

In addition to such advertisements, in the 1960s *Femeia* also focused on personal and everyday issues, from tips on health and beauty to recipes and suggestions on home décor. Along with *Moda*, it featured the latest fashions—often accompanied by patterns. Fashion, in particular, served as visual evidence

FIGURE 9.1.   Advertisement for the Record vacuum cleaner. From *Femeia*, February 1967.

that Romania was progressing toward mature socialism. As an article in *Moda* asserted, "fashion is no longer considered to be a frivolous matter" but instead has "become a mandatory preoccupation for every woman."[20] Most fashions presented in the magazine aped Western designs, but some featured Romanian versions of these styles. For example, the photo essay "Fashions of Voroneţ," which appeared in the spring 1970 issue of *Moda*, showed modern interpretations of traditional Romanian styles with images of Voroneţ (a medieval monastery in Moldavia) as the backdrop. In one of the pictures, a woman is wearing a peasant-style minidress and heels, while smoking a cigarette. This blending of the traditional and the modern could be read as a sartorial expression of Ceauşescu's national communism. At the same time, because peasant styles were also in vogue in the West, these fashions were considered trendy and stylish rather than simply provincial or traditional.

The proper clothing (along with makeup and a good hairstyle), *Femeia* claimed, could make any woman look beautiful, as the before and after photos of N. M., a woman featured in the article "There Is No Ugly Girl," illustrate. Yet, even though stylish women were visual symbols of a modern socialist lifestyle,

FIGURE 9.2.   Fashions of Voroneț. From *Moda*, Spring 1970.

the author stressed that beauty was not just skin-deep: "I think that we have reached the age when one ounce of intelligence weighs more than a ton of beauty, because today even a small amount of brains can play the role of the magic wand which transforms . . . whatever is ugly into its opposite."[21] Makeup and clothing could do a lot to compensate for Mother Nature's failings, but in the end physical beauty could not compensate for inner beauty.

Ideas about the modern woman were also promoted in *Femeia's* surveys, one of which asked its readers to answer the question, "Are you a Modern Woman?" According to numerous respondents, the ability to successfully combine the role of worker, wife, and mother was the most important quality of a modern woman. As Ana Florescu commented: "I am trying to be a modern woman. As an engineer I work in the most modern technical domain—nuclear energy. As any modern woman (and one must admit that it is not easy to be one) I carefully divide my time between work obligations, family obligations, and any other duties that the word modern implies."[22]

By presenting the modern woman as someone who could "do it all," the state sought to transform women's multiple burdens (or roles) into something validating and ennobling; indeed, some of my respondents took pride in their ability to successfully combine these roles. Meanwhile others, such as Steluta Marcu, stressed the importance of a cultured lifestyle: "Being modern means listening to music (Verdi, Beethoven, Tchaikovsky) and also performing in the theater productions at the House of Culture."[23] Thus, although still devoted to work, family, world peace, and the party, the new, modern socialist woman engaged in a variety of recreational activities, traveled, and even competed in "Miss Femeia" contests, for which she could receive not some useless medal but a transistor radio, a twelve-day vacation on the Black Sea, or, if she won first prize, a trip abroad.[24]

Alongside the modern woman, *Femeia* began to focus on the modern man, or more specifically the modern husband. Images of modish husbands with briefcase, baby, and duster in hand, or a column of men pushing baby buggies, served as visual symbols that the modern lifestyle also entailed, at least officially, a more progressive understanding of gender roles. Moreover, articles (ostensibly written by men) chided men for their lack of attention to the domestic sphere and their wives' well-being, presenting patriarchal behavior as bourgeois, even barbaric.[25] Just as the modern socialist woman was able to balance work, home, and family—and look good while doing it—so too, the magazine reasoned, the modern socialist husband could change diapers, vacuum, and cook (as well as bring home) the bacon.[26]

The new socialist man's concern for domestic life, however, was supposed to extend beyond the kitchen and into the bedroom. Articles in *Femeia*, as well as sex manuals, took up the issue of women's sexual satisfaction. Arguing that frigidity and women's lack of sexual desire were, in part, related to men's insensitivity to women's emotional needs, sexologists encouraged men to engage in foreplay and display more tenderness toward their wives in bed.[27] Considering Romanians' conservative attitudes toward sex, such frank discussion of women's sexuality probably appeared scandalous to some, though others may have found it enlightening.[28] However, far from mimicking the racy articles found on the pages of *Cosmopolitan*, these pieces were designed to demystify the sexual act and help women regain their sexual desire so that they could procreate. Thus the magazine's presentation of marital and sexual satisfaction must be considered with respect to Ceauşescu's pronatalist policies.

Articles on family, parenting, and maternal and infant health proliferated in the magazine after the passage of Decree 770 in 1966, which recriminalized abortion.[29] In particular, motherhood was both medicalized and glamorized. Images of haggard though happy heroine mothers surrounded by their flocks of children and grandchildren were eclipsed by images of young, attractive, and seemingly carefree mothers cradling their newborn babies or frolicking with their two toddlers.[30] Donning stylish haircuts and fashionable maternity mini-dresses, these young women made motherhood and pregnancy appear not just effortless but glamorous. Although the glorification of motherhood publicly validated women's maternal roles, which was perhaps welcomed by some, it also masked the inhumanity of Ceaușescu's pronatalist policies and their effects on women's health. As Party poets wrote paeans to motherhood, the maternal death rate was rising dramatically in Romania and by 1989 was the highest in Europe.[31]

By focusing on everyday and even intimate issues, Femeia sent the message that the state viewed women as complex individuals with a multiplicity of concerns, needs, interests, and desires. Moreover, by focusing on fashion, home décor, and leisure the magazine seemed to be promoting the pursuit of interests and pleasures that were heretofore peripheral or antithetical to the building of socialism. At the same time, by presenting marital and sexual happiness as important elements of a modern socialist society, the state was using the modern for more regressive policies. In spite of these inherent contradictions, Romanian officials were attempting to make attractive and hence legitimize the socialist project to a new generation that was coming of age in the 1960s and 1970s. The message was clear: socialist countries could not only emancipate their women but also provide them with modern, even Western goods and lifestyles. Yet in contrast to the West, where youth, beauty, and sex were mobilized to sell products, in socialist Romania they were strategies for selling socialism.

Although these visual and written messages were, at least in part, ideologically driven, this does not mean that women were manipulated by them—or that they found them useless. For example, Elena, a librarian in her late forties, recalled about Femeia: "Of course there were articles that were propaganda, but you could skip over them. I read about how to take care of my skin and my complexion, and how to decorate a corner of my house and things like that . . . travel, exhibitions, and history, the culture of other countries."[32] A number of respondents echoed these sentiments. The fact that respondents stressed the utility of the magazines' more practical pieces (patterns, recipes, fashion spreads, and articles on infant and family health), while dismissing the ideological articles and pictures of "him and her" (Nicolae and Elena Ceaușescu), indicates that people did not wholly embrace or reject socialist media but engaged with it critically and selectively. It is impossible to know the degree to which media representations of consumer culture and the modern lifestyle influenced people's attitudes; what is clear is that by the close of the 1960s people were enjoying an improved standard of living.

From Black Caviar to "Chicken Silverware"

The consumer thaw was inextricably connected to politics, and both appeared liberating for men as well as women—especially those who came of age in the 1960s and early 1970s. As Vladimir Tismăneanu writes, "during the sixties and early seventies, large social segments found themselves stirred and exhilarated by what they saw as Romania's prospects for grandeur, the *conducător's* [leader's] defiance of the Soviet controls, and the rapprochement with Yugoslavia and the West."[33] This grandeur included not only changes in policy and proclamations of Romanian sovereignty but also, as one woman noted, "the means to go out for dinner every two weeks and to stay at the bar all night, maybe until three in the morning."[34] Increased opportunities for socializing were facilitated by opening more bars and restaurants and by the fact that more individuals had disposable incomes.[35] Liberalization also meant increased freedom of movement, at least for a short period, as passport regulations were relaxed between 1968 and 1970.[36] For some, Ceauşescu's assumption of power signified a new era. As Valeria, who was in her teens during the early Dej years and experienced a "life of hunger," recalled: "When Ceauşescu came to power, all the aristocrats were freed from prison. In addition to stockings there was chocolate and coffee. We also had foreign films. Through culture they began to promote new ideals and import certain things."[37] According to Valeria, political, cultural, and consumer liberalization were the definitive aspects of Ceauşescu's early years in power. The ability to consume such delicacies as chocolate and view films from the West on cinema screens was, for Valeria, a symbol of progress and a brighter future. The majority of my respondents, who were in their twenties and thirties during this period, recalled it with great fondness, invoking cognac, the Beatles, blue jeans, and other cultural icons and goods from the West, as well as the best of the East. Şerban, an anthropologist, recalled that Bucharest looked and felt vibrant: "There was nightlife in Bucharest, the city was lit up; there were bright advertisements . . . restaurants, bars open until the early morning . . . people [were] on the street . . . it was liberal in comparison to the years of my childhood and adolescence."[38]

Praise for this period was also related to the fact that these goods, along with cultural pursuits, were affordable and available to all. As Vali, a retired postal clerk who was in her early twenties at the time, noted: "It was a good period in that you could find everything . . . there were no restrictions . . . [you could go] to restaurants . . . for a beer . . . to the pastry shop . . . or the theater . . . films. . . . The salaries were enough for buying a home and a car—though there were only Dacias [the Romanian-brand car]—televisions and radios."[39] Moreover, Alexandra, a retired manager who was in her midtwenties when Ceauşescu came to power, recalled: "From a cultural perspective things were good; theaters with excellent actors [and plays], Ibsen, Shakespeare, Beckett, Steinbeck. Once a week we saw a film. Hollywood films. Between 1965 and 1975, people lived normally."[40] In addition to Hollywood films, the works of Godard, Truffaut, Fellini, and Antonioni appeared on cinema screens. Although such activities may seem commonplace, for Romanians who had been fed a hearty diet of Soviet film and theater and who, according to Rodica, "didn't have great expectations," viewing a Western film was indeed remarkable.[41] So too was purchasing French perfume and Italian blouses and lingerie in Romanian shops. In retrospect, this was clearly a strategy designed to legitimate the socialist project, for in offering up silk underwear, cars, and Hollywood films the state was seemingly going beyond ideological rhetoric and actually making good on its promises of a radiant future.

By the mid-1970s, however, the political and consumer honeymoon was over. In 1971, after visiting North Korea and China, Ceauşescu initiated his *mica revolutie culturala* (small cultural revolution), which involved the increased use of nationalism and Ceauşescu's personality cult to legitimate socialist rule. Politically, Ceauşescu further centralized power through rotation of party cadres and by packing his cabinet with relatives and other sycophants.[42] Economically, Romania continued to distance itself from the Soviet sphere, entering into trade agreements with a number of Western countries and institutions, which allowed Romania to keep its debt relatively low.[43] This, however, also made Romania vulnerable to changes in the global economy, and the global recession and oil crisis of the late 1970s were devastating.[44] Moreover, in 1980 the European Economic Community chose not to renew its trade partnership with Romania, mainly due to the inferiority of Romanian goods. Most countries in the Bloc dealt with these crises by assuming more debt in order to appease consumer appetites; Ceauşescu took a highly autarkic, nationalist approach. Although Bulgaria and Poland also embraced nationalism as a source of political legitimacy, in these countries nationalism served as a companion to consumerism.[45] By contrast, in Romania nationalism became the sole basis on which policies were made. Asserting the need to be independent from the USSR and the West, in 1981 Ceauşescu decided to pay off the foreign debt, which at the time stood at $10.2 billion (up from $3.6 billion in 1977).[46] This was done by exporting gasoline, clothing, and some foodstuffs—with dire results for average Romanians.

Although the curtailment of goods had already begun in the mid-1970s, this was indeed a rude awakening for Romanians whose hopes for a better life had been raised by the political and consumer liberalization of the 1960s. As one woman recounted: "After '70 the good things began to disappear, the luxury items, and after '77 much more . . . and by '81 or '83 things were already un-available."[47] By the early 1980s, rationing of meat, oil, and sugar had been in-stituted, and by the mid-1980s queues appeared outside of stores for such basic items as cheese, milk, and, in provincial towns and villages, bread.[48] Ceauşescu justified these measures on the basis of Romanian sovereignty and in the name of good health, promoting his program of "scientific nourishment," which reduced daily caloric intake by upwards of 15 percent.[49] In lieu of food, Ceauşescu attempted to sustain his people through a megalomaniacal form of nationalism. This was most visible in the growth of Nicolae's and Elena's cults of personality and in the Casa Poporului (People's House), an enormous eleven-hundred-room wedding-cake structure, designed to house the Parliament, that Ceauşescu began building in 1983. In a sharp departure from socialist leaders in Hungary, Czechoslovakia, and East Germany, who placated their popula-tions with consumer goods and other trappings of the "good life," Ceauşescu offered his people neither material goods nor privacy. Instead, intensified na-tionalism, which he presented as the culminating stage of socialism, was the preferred instrument of regime legitimation and social control in Romania. As a result, Romanians never experienced the consumer-centered "post-totalitar-ian era" so derided by Václav Havel in Czechoslovakia.[50]

Because of the repressiveness of socialist rule and Romania's isolation during the 1980s, people were far less able to negotiate with their state for improved living standards than were their counterparts in neighboring Bloc countries. They were especially dependent on the black market, informal net-works, and the barter system for acquiring basic as well as luxury goods. Status was the surest route to acquiring both types of goods, and party higher-ups, the Securitate, and others with respected positions were more or less ensured a good, if not luxurious, standard of living through the use of magazinele inchise (closed stores) or foreign currency stores. The "luxury" items sold at these stores included French cognac, American whisky, blue jeans, and Kent ciga-rettes—which were so coveted that they constituted a form of currency in the second economy.[51]

Although status might stem from holding a position in the party hierarchy, it was also related to one's occupation. Those who worked in restaurants, food processing plants, bakeries, butcher shops, and grocery stores were also in a privileged position for securing food, which they used for personal consumption or bartered for other goods. In addition, employees of state institutes had access to canteens that offered up a variety of food at subsidized prices. Moreover, resorts were a good place for buying food, as well as foreign goods, since Western tourists frequented them. As Elena recalled: "In the women's solarium on the Black Sea they would sell things: chewing gum, sweets, condoms, whatever."[52]

Having a chronic illness—such as diabetes—was also a form of status in that such individuals had access to meat and other high-protein foods. Finally, doctors, dentists, teachers, and those who provided important services were often remunerated with food. As Domnica, a retired dentist, recalled:

> For me food was not a problem; on the contrary, it was abundant. I had patients who were in commerce and so whatever I wanted they would bring to me. In addition, I had relatives in the countryside where I could go and buy beef and pork. Then we ate a lot of pork. There was an abundance [of food] on the table, all types of food, with sweets and so on. We never went without anything.[53]

Effectively, a type of barter system was reinvented under socialism; at once traditional and modern, the socialist barter economy involved peasants and city dwellers, and exchanges occurred in a variety of places, from the shop floor to the apartment block.

For most individuals, acquiring goods required connections, money, and a great deal of fortitude and patience. In the 1970s, *Case de comenzi* (home delivery food services) emerged, from which food could be ordered for home delivery. However, because it often took two or more hours just to reach them by phone, this was not a useful resource for most working families. Therefore, most people relied on co-workers, acquaintances, kinship networks, and friends and family abroad to secure essential goods. The continued importance of these networks underscored the state's inability to provide materially for its citizens, illustrating the crucial role played not by socialism but by personal relationships in material survival.

Finally, the queue was the most common means of procuring food and other goods in the 1980s. Queuing in Romania was a strategic practice, requiring alertness, assertiveness, and at times craftiness. The character of the queue could vary according to the neighborhood and the product being sold. In some cases, the experience of everyday shortage facilitated the creation of an organized system of queuing—monitored typically by an elderly man—in which people followed a particular code of conduct. Indeed, according to one respondent, this code of conduct was so ingrained that, in the milk queue in her neighborhood, people would line up their empty bottles the night before delivery, go home, sleep, and return the next morning, bottles untouched.[54] The fact that such communality existed reveals that society was not as atomized as scholars have claimed.

By the same token, since there were often not enough goods for everyone, the survival instinct, rather than sentiments of communality, could guide people's behavior. For example, Adrian, a policy analyst in his midforties, recalled one episode during which his father went to queue up for eggs and was engulfed by the crowd and ended up fainting.[55] In addition, according to novelist and sociologist Dan Lungu, queues for meat, because it was so scarce, could be especially disorderly and even aggressive.[56] Finally, since food was distributed according to the number of family members, people frequently "borrowed" children in order to increase their rations. As Stela humorously recounted:

> And then you'd hear a voice: they've got *telemea*! [feta cheese] You'd rush down the stairs to be at the front of the line . . . and if you had a kid next to you, they'd give you 2 times [the regular] quantity. . . . And kids, you'd borrow them. For example I had a neighbor [who would ask], won't you lend me Nae so I can wait in line.[57]

According to many women, "borrowing" a child to secure additional rations was not an uncommon practice, even though this meant reduced rations for those at the rear of the queue.

By the 1980s, procuring food had become a daily activity requiring considerable time and effort. According to some respondents, this was a responsibility for which their husbands assumed primary or even full responsibility. As Marcela recalled:

> No, he didn't help me in the sense that he did housework. But he had other attributes; he could get a hold of food that you couldn't find, we never went without meat, coffee, or anything, he succeeded in finding it. He was the type who managed to make circles of friends, and one of them was a guy at a restaurant. He had many acquaintances in the area and he bought [food] at cost from a restaurant.[58]

The efforts of Marcela's husband were much more significant than simply picking up a few things at the corner store. Instead, food procurement in the 1980s was a labor-intensive process that required a great deal of time, energy, and fortitude. Compared with certain countries in socialist Eastern Europe, where queuing was less prevalent, the widespread participation of Romanian men in procuring food was exceptional.[59] At the same time, because food procurement did not assume a negative stigma in Romania, as did other feminized chores such as cleaning and ironing, men's participation in this activity does not necessarily reveal increased sensitivity to women's multiple responsibilities.[60] Indeed, the experience of braving subzero temperatures in the dark of winter for a kilo of pork may have been construed by some men as a reflection of their physical endurance, masculinity, and status as breadwinners. Considering the control the regime exerted over most aspects of life, food procurement thus might have allowed men to articulate a paternalist identity in the face of an emasculating system.[61] As Mircea H. put it, "Naturally men waited in line; I would go and my wife would stay at home with the children."[62] Regardless of how men perceived their contributions to the family's well-being, they were welcomed by their overworked wives.

Rationing affected men's roles as breadwinners, and it compromised women's roles as nurturers. For numerous women, the perceived inability to adequately fulfill this role took a heavy emotional toll, fundamentally affecting their experience of motherhood. C., an interpreter who gave birth to her son in 1985, had bittersweet memories of raising an infant during this period:

> It was like everything else, a mixed blessing. On the one hand, I was
> happy because I had him, he was a very cute baby, and it was a joy
> for me, but from a material standpoint, it was terrible. It was during
> the winter, there wasn't any heat, there wasn't any electricity, every-
> thing was rationed, there was no clothing for children . . . everything
> I needed was brought in somehow from contacts abroad, the same
> with food, through acquaintances of my father-in-law or through
> acquaintances of my father. I remember they cut off the electricity
> and I had to carry the child and buggy up seven flights of stairs to our
> apartment. In order to give him a bath, I had to heat the water on the
> stove in a pot. I had a ten liter pot and the flame was so small that it
> took two hours for the pot of ten liters to heat up. After that I put him
> in a plastic basin on the table in the kitchen, I would light a candle,
> because there was no electricity, and I would give the baby a bath. It
> was horrible.[63]

C.'s memories of early motherhood are inextricably connected to the hardships she faced as a result of Ceauşescu's rationing schemes. Although women who raised their children in the 1960s and 1970s were able to care for them with relative ease, this became especially challenging in the 1980s when food—and later heat and electricity—were rationed. Of particular concern for many mothers was securing infant formula, a luxury item by the 1980s.[64] The anxiety produced by this shortage was evident in Maria's recollection of this period more than twenty years later:

> You know why it was difficult? Because you couldn't find powdered
> milk, you couldn't find special food for kids. I had many problems
> with my son. [Because] my milk had run out after three weeks . . . I
> needed to supplement it. I wandered around like crazy to all the phar-
> macies, to all the groceries.[65]

Fortunately, Maria, an electrician, managed to secure formula through connections with co-workers; meanwhile, others relied on the black market, trips to Hungary, and friends and family abroad. As C.'s and Maria's recollections illustrate, the introduction of food and heat rationing in the 1980s crucially hampered women's ability to fulfill their maternal role. Moreover, this took place against the backdrop of Ceauşescu's draconian pronatalist policies and incessant glorification of motherhood in the press. Although no respondents claimed that their children suffered significant health problems as a result of such scarcity, many expressed frustration and anger over the difficulties they had faced in nourishing their children.

Just as the difficulties in securing infant formula imposed a heavy psychological burden on women, so too did the daily experience of preparing family meals. Women thus relied on ingenuity and resourcefulness in crafting meals, as Maria stoically recalled:

> I'd come home, sit down on the chair in the kitchen, and begin to
> invent meals . . . because I couldn't follow a cookbook . . . hmmm . . .
> I don't have parsley . . . I can't make this because I need cheese . . . so
> then I prepared food that you would not find in any recipe . . . I would
> make the first and second course and I only had potatoes. . . . I would
> make potato soup and mashed potatoes. . . . I'd add a vegetable . . .
> some eggs with flour . . . and also make a goulash soup.[66]

This is illustrative of what philosopher Michel de Certeau has referred to as "the art of making do with what the system provides."[67] Although coined in reference to capitalist systems, de Certeau's notion of making do, of devising everyday strategies within set parameters, made sense to these women in late-socialist Romania. Making do did become an art form as women concocted meals out of an odd array of seasonings, inferior meat trimmings, and ersatz and imported foods. Some of these included sardines and canned shrimp from Vietnam, "chicken silverware" (the wings, heads, and claws of chickens), "adidas" (pork hooves), and "the Petreuş brothers" (two scrawny chickens named after the Maramureş folk musicians who performed drunk on TV).[68] Other items on offer included bread made from stale or infested flour, coffee made from chickpeas, and salami made from soy.[69] In addition, the ersatz butter, alongside the meager egg ration, meant that preparing a tasty torte was nothing short of miraculous.

Despite (or because of) these challenges, some women spoke with great pride about how families, beyond being able to simply "make do," offered up veritable feasts to friends and family. As Elvira remarked:

> Romanians are very curious. When foreigners would visit during the
> Ceauşescu period and everything was rationed . . . the freezer was

full of chicken, meat, everything. It's incredible, the inventiveness of Romanians. . . . How did one get a hold of it [food] . . . I can't say. . . . If you went to anyone's house, they'd put it on the table like you wouldn't believe. Everyone managed, everyone had relations.[70]

Since food is an expression of friendship, love, and hospitality, the well-stocked dinner table assumes both cultural and national significance in Romania and is a great source of pride for many women.[71] Consequently, offering up such meals was a sacrifice Romanians happily made in order to demonstrate affection for friends and impress guests from the West. Yet in the latter case this act was perhaps less one-sided than it appears. Instead, it might be considered more of an exchange than a sacrifice since Romanian families received needed goods—as well as gifts—in return for offering their Western hosts such feasts.

As if shortages of such basic provisions as eggs, oil, and milk were not bad enough, by the mid-1980s the definition of deficit consumption was broadened to include heat, electricity, and gasoline. In an effort to conserve energy and cut costs, the state reduced the temperature in factories, offices, schools, and even hospitals to 57 degrees Fahrenheit. At certain points of the day, gas for cooking was simply turned off, forcing women to cook the family meal at midnight or one o'clock in the morning. In the midst of such shortages, propagandists still attempted to convince the public that things were better in Romania, as C.'s recollection of the TV show, "Roundtrip Journey on the Road to Capitalism," illustrates:

> I remember—I will never forget—they were showing an image from France, how bad the lives of the French were and how they had to wait in line for bread. Why? Because they opened a new pastry shop in Paris—an extraordinary one—and the French were fighting to buy the first croissant from this pastry shop. But they [state television] presented it to us as if there was great penury over there and they [the French] didn't have anything to eat and had to fight in line to get bread . . . but they didn't look at our lines . . . people waiting in line for meat at 12 o'clock at night.[72]

One of the few shows to air during the 1980s, when television was limited to two hours a day, this particular "exposé" was remembered by C. as underscoring the absurdity and meaninglessness of state propaganda, revealing the enormous gulf between Ceauşescu's rhetoric and everyday Romanians' reality. Eventually, protracted shortages and continued state repression, most evident in the bloody crackdown of the peaceful protests in Timişoara in December 1989, would lead to the collapse of the regime. In the end, Ceauşescu's version of national communism proved wholly unpalatable to the vast majority of the populace.

Conclusion

Far from being superfluous, consumption was a constitutive aspect of socialist politics, identity formation, and everyday life in socialist Romania. Yet even though the state promoted consumerism in the 1960s and early 1970s to attract popular support, by the 1980s this policy had been replaced by extreme rationing as a result of Ceauşescu's quest for political and economic autonomy. Although most countries in the Bloc also experienced periods of shortage, over the course of communist rule these regimes increasingly used consumption as a form of state legitimation. Moreover, although nationalism was also used to varying degrees across the Bloc, in Romania it found its strongest expression precisely when shortages were also almost unparalleled.

As consumer policies varied over time, so too did people's experiences as consumers and their attitude toward the state. For those who came of age in the 1960s and 1970s, Ceauşescu's assumption of power signified a momentous change as a range of consumer goods became available—a harbinger of a new socialist approach to lifestyle. Significantly, many Romanians still retain fond memories of this period, viewing it as a time when their country stood up to Soviet aggression and when eating out and purchasing durable goods—along with enjoying Westerns and Elvis—were pleasures that could be enjoyed regularly.

But once these hopeful years passed, people's experiences as consumers began to change. The introduction of rationing in the 1980s, in particular, took a heavy toll on women. From bathing their infants by candlelight to desperately seeking powdered milk, the psychological and temporal burdens produced by rationing often made the experience of parenthood bittersweet. At the same time, successful negotiation of the system could also be validating: men took pride in their ability to procure scarce goods while women proudly concocted veritable feasts from scraps of food. And, in some cases, rationing led to a more equal division of domestic labor as men assumed greater responsibility for food procurement. Still, in the final analysis Ceauşescu was hard pressed to convince a population that had tasted caviar in the 1960s that national communism could provide the utopia he promised.

Despite this, the socialist period is still remembered fondly by some people. This is especially the case for those who have struggled financially since the collapse of communism. As Tatiana, a former textile worker in her late forties, remarked:

> I hoped that it [the transition] would be better, but, sincerely, I am not satisfied. I have the impression that they destroyed everything that was good. It wasn't better then? It's been six years since I've had a

vacation. Everything I have I received under Ceauşescu: my car, my house, my furniture. I just want to be healthy and live a decent life.[73]

Though it is easy to simply write off this comment as nostalgia for communism, it must be remembered that Tatiana experienced, and vividly remembers, the material difficulties her family faced during the 1980s. Thus her memories of the period, though perhaps selective, are not totally rosy. Because the goods that she acquired in the early 1970s positively shaped her lifestyle, her consumer experiences affected how she framed not only the past but also the present, revealing that, for some, communist rule brought an improved standard of living (at least for a time) unmatched since 1989. Just as the promises of national communism offered up by Ceauşescu failed to sustain his people, for Tatiana so too have the freedoms offered up by the market economy and democratic system.

NOTES

1. G. N., interview with author, Braşov, June 2003.

2. See Susan E. Reid and David Crowley, eds., *Style and Socialism: Modernity and Material Culture in Postwar Eastern Europe* (Oxford: Berg, 2000); David Crowley and Susan E. Reid, eds., *Socialist Spaces: Sites of Everyday Life in the Eastern Bloc* (Oxford: Berg, 2002); Julie Hessler, *A Social History of Soviet Trade: Trade Policy, Retail Practices, and Consumption, 1917–1953* (Princeton, NJ: Princeton University Press, 2004); Sheila Fitzpatrick, *Everyday Stalinism: Ordinary Life in Extraordinary Times: Soviet Russia in the 1930s* (New York: Oxford, 1999); Patrick Patterson, "The New Class: Consumer Culture Under Socialism and the Unmaking of the Yugoslav Dream, 1945–1991" (Ph.D. diss., University of Michigan, 2001); Paulina Bren, *The Greengrocer and His TV: The Culture of Communism After the 1968 Prague Spring* (Ithaca, NY: Cornell University Press, 2010); and Patterson, "Just Rewards? Communism's Hard Bargain with the Citizen Consumer," NCEEER research report, 2008.

3. Paulina Bren, "Mirror, Mirror, on the Wall . . . Is the West the Fairest of Them All? Czechoslovak Normalization and Its (Dis)Contents," *Kritika: Explorations in Russian and Eurasian History* 9(4) (Fall 2008): 831–54.

4. See Katherine Pence and Paul Betts, eds., *Socialist Modern: East German Everyday Culture and Politics* (Ann Arbor: University of Michigan Press, 2008), 8–9.

5. See Susan E. Reid, "Cold War in the Kitchen: Gender and the De-Stalinization of Consumer Taste in the Soviet Union Under Khrushchev," *Slavic Review* 61(2) (2002): 211–52; Katherine Pence, "'You as a Woman Will Understand': Consumption, Gender, and the Relationship Between State and Citizenry in the GDR's Crisis of 17 June 1953," *German History* 19(2) (2001): 218–52; and Malgorzata Fidelis, "Are You a Modern Girl? Consumerism and Young Women in 1960s Poland," in *Gender Politics and Everyday Life in State Socialist Eastern and Central Europe*, ed. Shana Penn and Jill Massino (New York: Palgrave, 2009), 171–84.

6. See Padraic Kenney, "The Gender of Resistance in Communist Poland," *American Historical Review* 104(2) (April 1999): 399–425; and Mary Neuburger, "Veils, *Shalvari,* and Matters of Dress: Unravelling the Fabric of Women's Lives in Communist Bulgaria," in *Style and Socialism,* 169–88.

7. *Femeia* was published by the official communist women's organizations, the Democratic Union of Women in Romania (1947–1957) and the National Women's Council (1958–1989). *Moda* was published by the Handicraft Cooperative of the Popular Republic of Romania from 1957 to 1989.

8. For this project 110 women and men of varying educational, socioeconomic, occupational, and ethnic backgrounds were interviewed. All were born between 1924 and 1972. The interviews followed the life-history approach and consisted of approximately seventy open-ended questions dealing with a range of issues including schooling, work, marriage, family relations, sexuality, consumer culture, and leisure, as well as major political events such as the communist takeover, the rise of Ceauşescu, the collapse of communism, and the postcommunist transition. Ages given reflect the age of the respondent at the time of the interview unless otherwise indicated.

9. Mircea J., interview with author, July 2003.

10. On the movement to reward privileged workers in the USSR in the 1930s, see Lewis Siegelbaum, *Stakhanovism and the Politics of Productivity in the USSR, 1935–1941* (Cambridge: Cambridge University Press, 1990).

11. Vlad Georgescu, *The Romanians: A History,* ed. Matei Calinescu, trans. Alexandra Bley-Vroman (Columbus: Ohio State Press, 1991), 246–47.

12. The Valev plan divided Eastern Europe into industrial (northern tier) and agricultural (southern tier) sectors. Unwilling to let Romania languish as an agricultural backwater, Dej refused to participate in this plan, distancing Romania from Comecon altogether. Georgescu, *The Romanians,* 242–44.

13. Ibid., 244–45. Imports from the West increased to 40 percent in 1965 (up from 21.5 percent in 1958) and exports to the West increased from 24 to 33 percent during the same period.

14. Ministerul Justitiei, "Codul Familiei al Republicii Populare Române din aprilie," in *Coleţie de Legi, Decrete, Hotâriri si Dispoziţi 1956* (Bucharest: Editura de Stat pentru Literatura Economica si Juridica, 1956), 63–64.

15. Judd Stitziel, *Fashioning Socialism: Clothing, Politics, and Consumer Culture in East Germany* (Oxford: Berg, 2005); Reid, "Cold War in the Kitchen"; Malgorzata Fidelis, *Women, Communism, and Industrialization in Postwar Poland* (Cambridge: Cambridge University Press, 2010); and conversation with Eszter Zsofia Toth, February 2010.

16. *Femeia,* December 1959, 7.

17. Georgescu, *The Romanians,* 251.

18. *Femeia,* February 1967, 34.

19. This, however, represented a dramatic increase from 1955 when only 0.7 inhabitants per 1,000 owned a vacuum cleaner. See "Bunastarea Familiei," *Femeia,* July 1978, 6.

20. "Din Paris," *Moda,* Spring 1969, 35.

21. Sanda Faur, "Nu Exista Fata Urita!" *Femeia,* January 1969, 12–13.

22. Elizabeta Moraru, "Sunteti o Femeie Moderna? De Ce?" *Femeia,* January 1970, 3–5.

23. Ibid.

24. This contest was advertised in the May 1969 issue of *Femeia.* The magazine did not specify what it meant by "abroad."

25. "'Sa depașim patriarhatul!' spune un barbat," *Femeia,* February 1974, 24.

26. On marriage and spousal relations in socialist Romania, see Jill Massino, "Something Old, Something New: Marital Roles and Relations in State Socialist Romania," *Journal of Women's History* 22(1) (2010): 34–60.

27. See "Adevarul despre Frigiditate," *Femeia,* October 1968, 25–26. According to the article, frigidity was also the result of glandular problems, trauma, drug and alcohol abuse, and in some cases use of contraception.

28. Culturally, Romania tends to be highly conservative and traditional with respect to sexual matters. See Adriana Baban, "Women's Sexuality and Reproductive Behavior in Post-Ceausescu Romania: A Psychological Approach," in *Reproducing Gender: Politics, Publics, and Everyday Life After Socialism,* Susan Gal and Gail Kligman, eds. (Princeton, NJ: Princeton University Press, 2000), 225.

29. In 1966, abortion became a criminal offense in socialist Romania. Women who sought abortions—along with the individuals who performed them—faced fines, job loss, revocation of licenses (doctors), and in some cases imprisonment. Ministerul Justitiei, "Decretul nr. 770 din 1 octombrie 1966 pentru reglementarea întreruperii cursului sarcinii," in *Coleție de Legi, Decrete, Hotâriri si Alte Acte Normative 1966* (Bucuresti: Editura Stiintifica, 1967): 30–31.

30. Of note here is that these younger mothers typically appeared with one or two children, not the four or more desired by the state.

31. Kligman, *The Politics of Duplicity: Controlling Reproduction in Ceausescu's Romania* (Berkeley: University of California Press, 1998), 208.

32. Elena, interview with author, Bucharest, May 2009.

33. Vladimir Tismăneanu, "Understanding National Stalinism: Reflections on Ceaușescu's Socialism," *Communist and Post-Communist Studies* 32(2) (1999): 155–73.

34. D. M., interview with author, Brașov, June 2003.

35. David A Kideckel, "Drinking Up: Alcohol, Class and Social Change in Rural Romania," *East European Quarterly* 18(4) (1985): 431–46.

36. Georgescu, *The Romanians,* 251.

37. Valeria, interview with author, Brașov, June 2003.

38. Șerban, interview with author, Bucharest, July 2009.

39. Vali, interview with author, Bucharest, July 2009. The Dacia was, essentially, the Romanian equivalent of the East German Trabi, and was named for the ancient region that constitutes some of present-day Romania.

40. Alexandra, interview with author, Bucharest, June 2009.

41. Rodica, interview with author, Bucharest, July 2009.

42. Georgescu, *The Romanians,* 254–57.

43. In 1971 Romania joined GATT (the General Agreement on Tariffs and Trade); in 1972 it was admitted to the IMF and the World Bank; and in 1973, it was granted preferential status by the European Common Market.

44. Romania also lost Iran as an oil supplier as a result of the Iranian Revolution, which began in 1979.

45. See Mary Neuburger, *The Orient Within: Muslim Minorities and the Negotiation of Nationhood in Modern Bulgaria* (Ithaca, NY: Cornell University Press, 2004); and Jan Kubik, *The Power of Symbols Against the Symbols of Power: The Rise of Solidarity and the Fall of State Socialism in Poland* (University Park: Pennsylvania State Press, 1994).

46. Dennis, Deletant, "New Evidence on Romania and the Warsaw Pact, 1955–1989," Cold War International History Project, e-Dossier No. 6. http://www.wilsoncenter.org/publication/e-dossier-no-6-new-evidence-romania-and-the-warsaw-pact-1955-1989. Accessed Jan. 25, 2012.

47. G. N., interview with author, Braşov, June 2003.

48. As the country's capital and Ceauşescu's showpiece, Bucharest was spared the extreme rationing of other towns and cities.

49. Georgescu, *The Romanians*, 260. On the disparity between state-promoted diets (particularly for pregnant women) and the actual availability of food during the 1980s, see Kligman, *Politics of Duplicity*, 140–41.

50. Post-totalitarianism refers to the period of communism characterized by a complete lack of faith in the socialist project, on the part of both the masses and the party leadership. During this phase, the state attempts to stave off dissent by promoting consumerism. Meanwhile the population retreats into the private and consumer spheres in exchange for official obedience to socialism. Vaclav Havel, *The Power of the Powerless: Citizens Against the State in Central-Eastern Europe* (London: Sharpe, 1978), 37–40.

51. See Chapter 10 in this volume.

52. Elena, interview with author, Bucharest, May 2009.

53. Domnica, interview with author, Braşov, May 2003.

54. T., interview with author, Braşov, May 2003.

55. Adrian, interview with author, Bucharest, July 2009.

56. Dan Lungu, "Avatarurile cozii in socialismul de tip sovietic" in *Viaţa Cotidiana in Comunism*, ed. Adrian Neculau (Iasi: Polirom, 2004), 179.

57. Stela, interview with author, Braşov, May 2003.

58. Marcela, interview with Anca Coman, Braşov, June 2003.

59. Although men also queued up during martial law in Poland, it was usually for alcohol and not food. Conversation with Jean Robinson, April 2007.

60. See Gail Kligman, *The Wedding of the Dead: Ritual, Poetics, and Popular Culture in Transylvania* (Berkeley: University of California Press, 1988), 50–51.

61. Katherine Verdery, *What Was Socialism, and What Comes Next?* (Princeton, NJ: Princeton University Press, 1996), 65–66.

62. Mircea H., interview with Ionut Iuria, Braşov, July 2003.

63. C., interview with author, Braşov, July 2003.

64. Most of my respondents were highly dependent on formula for nourishing their infants, primarily because they had to return to work shortly after giving birth and thus could no longer breastfeed.

65. Maria, interview with author, Braşov, March 2003.

66. Ibid.

67. Michel de Certeau, *The Practice of Everyday Life* (Berkeley: University of California Press, 2002), 15.

68. Paul Cernat, "Cozi şi Oameni de Rand in Anii '80," in *Viaţa Cotidiana*, 193.

69. By the mid-1980s the state was providing food production plants with recipes for ersatz bread and coffee.

70. Elvira, interview with author, Braşov, March 2003.

71. See Ofelia Vaduva, *Steps Toward the Sacred: From the Ethnology of Romanian Food Habits* (Bucharest: Romanian Cultural Foundation, 1999).

72. C., interview with author, Braşov, July 2003.

73. Tatiana, interview with author, Braşov, May 2003.

PART IV

To Market, to Market . . .

One of the more fascinating aspects of consumption in postwar Eastern Europe was the complex phenomenon of informal exchange. Though the black market in local goods is hardly a new subject, the following chapters offer nuance and detail to a story whose complete picture has yet to emerge. In many respects the myriad forms of exchange under Eastern European communisms were far more complex than patterns of exchange familiar to their Western neighbors. For example, in the East one found highly elaborated patterns of "trader tourism," that is, traveling for the purpose of shopping. Yugoslavs, in fact, organized monthly trips to Italy and Austria—with pooled resources, shared cars, and "lists" of goods—from which they "soft-smuggled" not just for themselves but for friends, family, or sale on the black market.[1] The mostly women shoppers, who were at the center of various well-organized social networks, hid things in the nooks and crannies of cars, dressed carefully in multiple layers of newly purchased clothes, and thereby brought in luxury items not found in Yugoslav stores. But as Mark Keck-Szajbel shows in the Polish-East German case elsewhere in this volume, in contrast to Yugoslavia the relatively closed borders of the Bloc meant that trader tourism happened most often *between* Eastern Bloc countries. Likewise, well-documented trade routes crossed the Hungarian-Romanian, Yugoslav-Romanian, and Bulgarian-Romanian borders.[2] Since the availability of goods was so uneven across the Bloc, citizens became adept at tracking who had what where and for what price, and "packing" for their trips accordingly. Indeed, savvy Bloc shoppers were known to keep lists of which goods from their home country were desirable outside and what was available at their point of destination.[3]

Perhaps even more prevalent, however, was the informal exchange of locally produced goods *within* various domestic contexts. As these three chapters show, for people of the region acquiring goods was often less about going "to market" and more about participating in extensive black or gray market networks, the so-called second or unofficial economy. Such networks, of course, are much harder for scholars to track than official production and distribution venues, whose shortcomings have been well documented. But new work in the field has begun to explore how empty shelves were just one part of the story of Eastern European consumption, obscuring as much as they reveal. Many travelers' accounts from this period note tables piled high with all sorts of delicacies in bleak post-Solidarity Poland and Ceaușescu's poverty-stricken Romania. In part this is because of strong traditions of hospitality, but the contrast of groaning tables versus empty store shelves was also due to the accelerated second economy of the 1980s.[4] From bacon to lipstick, producers and retailers swapped goods and services through vast networks of connections and exchange.

The black market, in fact, became deeply ingrained in the immediate postwar period as a result of both shortages and postwar criminalization of "bourgeois" modes of distribution. In cities, as in villages, communist efforts to stigmatize and criminalize wartime and prewar practices of capitalist exchange not only were unsuccessful but in many cases backfired. As Karl Brown shows in the case of immediate postwar rural Hungary, there was an active black market in meat and wood in this period, and state actors were complicit in networks of newly illegalized exchange. Brown points out that the communist state actually created the conditions for illegal entrepreneurship to flourish, as new laws and rations were not viable or sustainable. This indeed was one of the greater ironies of the period, namely, that a "free market"—far more unfettered than Western capitalism—was tolerated in the interstices of the official market. In the end, perhaps, it was the forms of entrepreneurship it engendered, more than the persistent shortages, that created the conditions for the black market to blossom and grow in the course of the period. Many have argued, in fact, that this mounting second economy played a role in undermining the "official" socialist economy by denuding it of any visible goods.[5]

It is not clear, however, that the black (or gray) market undermined the system, though the sporadically empty shelves may have undermined state control of the distribution of resources. Rather, these modes of exchange became part of the "normalized" functioning of the system that so many learned to aptly negotiate. As Małgorzata Mazurek shows in the case of Poland, for example, both men and women under communism developed particular forms of consumer "resourcefulness" and "creativity," skills carefully honed during the communist period. According to Mazurek, elaborate and efficient kinship and friendship-based ties were integral to the everyday movement of goods and hence the workings of the system. As Narcis Tulbure explores in his chapter, such networks had very local specificities, as in rural Romania where home brew (moonshine) played a unique role, acting as both a substitute currency and a lubricant for male sociability and exchange. Throughout the period, the black market did seem to cohere along gendered lines, and as Tulbure notes for rural Romania men and women played particular roles within local networks of exchange. Karl Brown further shows that ethnic groups, such as Roma, also played particular roles within newly forged unofficial networks of exchange.

In the final analysis, it is almost meaningless to explore "official" production, consumption, or exchange under communism without simultaneously looking at its "unofficial" underbelly. Worn-out binaries should be used with extreme caution, if not abandoned, since the "official" and "unofficial" were so deeply entangled. Across the region, the collusion of state actors and the prevalence of such practices made the black or gray market an everyday, commonplace experience. Indeed, for many of those who mastered this system, the end of communism meant more loss than gain when suddenly the rules of the game, in which they had been so proficient, radically changed. As Mazurek's interviews amply show, the new game was much more impersonal, global, and corporate, while networks of family and friends were no longer paramount to the functioning of the system.

NOTES

1. Alenka Švab, "Consuming Western Image of Well-Being: Shopping Tourism in Socialist Slovenia," *Cultural Studies* 16 (2002): 68. Breda Luthar, "Remembering Socialism: On Desire, Consumption and Surveillance," *Journal of Consumer Culture* 6 (2006): 240.

2. See Liviu Chelcea, "The Culture of Shortage During State-Socialism: Consumption Practices in a Romanian Village in the 1980s," *Cultural Studies* 16 (2002): 16–43; Gerald Creed, "(Consumer) Paradise Lost: Capitalist Dynamics and Disenchantment in Rural Bulgaria," *Anthropology of East Europe Review* 20 (2002): 120.

3. See, for example, Radka Yakimov, *Dreams and Shadows* (Bloomington, IN: iUniverse, 2006), 179.

4. Even popular culture poked fun at this. In Czechoslovakia, the common practice was expertly and comically presented in a series of films directed by Petr Schulhoff in the 1980s.

5. See, for example, Ferenc Fehér, Ágnes Heller, and György Márkus, *Dictatorship over Needs* (New York: St. Martin's Press, 1983), 99–101; and Lewis Siegelbaum, *Cars for Comrades: The Life of the Soviet Automobile* (Ithaca, NY: Cornell University Press, 2008), 251.

IO

The Socialist Clearinghouse

*Alcohol, Reputation, and Gender in Romania's
Second Economy*

Narcis Tulbure

In early August 1978, the headlines in the Romanian daily *Scînteia*
were dominated by reports on the arrest of Gheorghe Ştefănescu
and the dismantling of his extensive network of cohorts with whom
he had carried out the greatest moonshine fraud in Romanian history. The descendant of a family running alcohol depots since the
nineteenth century, Bacchus—as Ştefănescu was nicknamed by his
accomplices and clients—was able to turn the state alcohol ware-
house he managed into a profitable venture, earning for himself
more than $5 million in less than a decade by putting into circula-
tion better than 400,000 tons of adulterated wine and spirits. The
search following his arrest led Romanian militia[1] to more than 19
kilograms of gold, the equivalent of some $500,000 in cash, nu-
merous bank accounts, two foreign-made cars, a luxurious apartment, and a villa in Prahova Valley.[2] All of his possessions were
confiscated, and three years later Bacchus received the death
sentence.

But his immense wealth was not the most interesting aspect of the
case; rather, it was how he had been able to accumulate such a vast
collection of valuables and monies under one of the most restrictive
regimes in Eastern Europe. The investigation identified a group of 284
collaborators working with Bacchus: among them agronomic engineers on state and collective farms growing vineyards; directors of state
factories where pure alcohol could be stolen; managers of restaurants

and bars; militiamen; prosecutors; judges; Party secretaries; and Securitate (Romanian secret police) officers. Altogether, they represented a vast network of people and resources created for the distribution of adulterated (or watered-down) alcohol in Ceauşescu's Romania. The demand for booze was so great, the circulation so rapid, and the consumption so intense that the scheme was exceedingly successful, as long as everything stayed on track and everyone involved was complicit. But it all began to fall apart when Bacchus sold adulterated wine to a Securitate officer who was organizing his daughter's wedding. Unfortunately for Bacchus, the wedding was postponed and the purchased wine began to separate from its water additive. It was enough to start the investigation that would lead to the dismantling of this immense network.

Yet for all its publicity and fame, the successful investigation of Bacchus did not put an end to, or even significantly diminish, Romania's second economy, which was premised largely on circulation of alcohol. Even after the Bacchus affair, alcohol continued to be a key component of the socialist underground sector in Romania, facilitated by contradictory state measures and popular demand for alcoholic beverages. Indeed, the changing relationship among social drinking, state policy toward alcohol, and the expanding socialist second economy during the 1970s and the 1980s in Romania offers important insights into the workings of the socialist regime at the time. Throughout the period of late socialism, drinking in taverns situated in villages and in working-class neighborhoods was constitutive of a key sphere of material and symbolic exchange. Consumption of alcoholic beverages was associated with the exchange of goods and services, appropriated from state enterprises and circulated in the sphere of the second economy. Social drinking became a critical arena for display of reciprocity as well as construction of masculinity.

Reproducing the social life of alcohol under late socialism, as this chapter sets out to do, illuminates a zone of ambiguity in which commodities were in continuous movement, facilitating manipulation of resources and social relations for creation of value. In late socialist Romania, the second economy was premised on concentrated circulation of alcohol, which undergirded exchanges of a diverse range of commodities, favors, information, and valuables. Furthermore, the performative aspect of drinking staged in ritualized social settings was central to these networks of exchange, where reputation and trust had heightened importance. Although Romania under Ceauşescu was known for its harsh political repression, the regime, like others in the region, tolerated the second economy on some level because it provided a necessary corrective for the scarcity induced by extreme austerity measures. But the rampant black market that resulted became deeply embedded in the Romanian economy, producing intricate webs of complicit officials and ordinary citizens.

Drinking in Oltenia

A commodity with a dense social biography, alcohol also has a history of in-volvement in the deep play of politics.[3] In Romania, as elsewhere, groups within the state, civil society, or the religious sphere have intermittently attempted to circumscribe and contain its consumption and social acceptability. At the same time, individuals and groups have historically subverted legal or social con-straints, thereby underscoring the potentially subversive nature of desire and consumption. In recent decades, diverse streams of social and cultural history have highlighted the ubiquity of alcohol in the rituals of daily life, its constitu-tive role in social life and sociability, and its powerful symbolic dimensions.[4] Preserving a certain historical outlook but shifting attention from alcohol to social drinking and commensality, the "anthropological turn" in alcohol studies reveals how relations and practices involving convivial consumption of alcohol are critical to the constitution of societies and the processes of social change.[5] Particularly significant for this chapter is the body of work focused on the role of drinking establishments and social consumption of alcohol in forming alter-native channels of distribution and exchange.[6] Such approaches have a marked significance for understanding the second economy, and particularly alcohol consumption in socialist Eastern Europe.[7]

Romanian socialism is often seen as one of the most densely regulated and restrictive regimes in Eastern Europe. This was true in many respects, but there were always areas of social life where locally created meanings and social negotiation of policies adopted centrally convey a different image of the socialist regime. A good illustration of such negotiations, social drinking was both con-stitutive of and specific to social life under "actually existing socialism." Roma-nian state regulations and disciplinary practices pertaining to alcohol were mediated by networks of the second economy. Most scholars writing about the socialist second economy treat it as a functional substitute of the "inefficient" official sector, a source of necessary goods.[8] With few exceptions, anthropolo-gists tend to emphasize the parasitic nature of an informal sector that drew on the resources of the official economy, or else they call attention to the social networks and cultural conceptions that make possible the second sector, with-out necessarily exploring its creative dimensions.[9]

This chapter, based on documentation of the social life of alcohol during the 1980s in the region of Oltenia, analyzes the category of the socialist second economy from another perspective, revealing some of the creativity involved in informal exchanges at the time. It aims to afford insight into a domain of prac-tice where consumption and the second economy were both omnipresent and problematic. Alcohol was a key element for the second economy that increased in importance in Romania during the 1980s, a period of heightened shortage. Consumption of alcohol was ensconced in a deeply political give-and-take in this period, both as an object of state economic regulation and disciplinary measures and as a commodity with intensely local significance. A cash-poor agricultural region until the Second World War, Oltenia was an experiment in accelerated industrialization and forced urban development, especially in the last decades of socialism. The native region of Nicolae Ceauşescu, Oltenia is an excellent illustration not only of the social problems generated by the socialist model of development but also of the role alcohol consumption—a favorite pastime and form of sociality—came to play in the constitution of the second economy.

Since the beginning of the communist period, the state had attempted to control alcohol production and distribution, including drinking venues and commercial outlets, through imposition of a state monopoly.[10] This is by no means just a communist strategy; large-scale production of alcohol as well as commercial distribution of spirits was monopolized by the Romanian state as early as 1932.[11] During the postwar period, this control was increasingly political, a clear attempt to weaken the economic base of *chiaburi* (the Romanian equivalent of *kulaks* or rich peasants), who were seen as the ultimate class enemy of Romanian communists. With the post-Stalinist thaw during the late 1950s, the monopoly on production of alcoholic beverages was relaxed as small-sized stills for distillation of brandy became legal practice by 1957.[12] Creating room for small-scale "entrepreneurship" in an economy controlled by central planning, the law of 1957 proved quite important, a base for the growth of a second economy for which alcohol was central. But in spite of liberalized production, wholesale distribution and retail of alcohol were kept in state hands. This meant that villagers could buy alcohol only from two establishments: the village tavern, licensed by the Alcohol and Tobacco Monopoly (M.A.T.), and Cooperativa (Centrocoop), the village store operated by the main cooperative organization under socialism.[13] In reality, however, parallel to these retail outlets, sales of home brew became one of the most fertile niches for the second economy that would grow continuously after the 1960s.

In Oltenia, drinking played an important part in social life even before socialism. In a region that was characterized primarily by small-scale farming, drinking in the local tavern was an opportunity for institutionalization of local hierarchies and celebration of kinship relations. Frequently, one of the more affluent peasants offered a drink to all those present in the tavern, reinforcing social hierarchies and village reciprocity. Older informants remember such ritualized drinking sessions as a way for affluent villagers to thank people for previous favors or to secure future ones. More significantly, they regarded this

practice as an idealized form of social drinking that persisted throughout socialism but was no longer practiced by the younger generations. For many poor
peasants, in contrast, even moderate drinking in the tavern was condemned by
the village community, especially if land was sold off or if it was at the expense
of subsistence. During a period when the plots of land to be inherited by
descendants were being fragmented, this undermining of the subsistence base
for families—known as "drinking children's land"—was socially condemned.
For peasants, consumption of wine and *tuică* (traditional, home-distilled plum
brandy) was calculated and planned in advance to cover needs for the holidays
and general consumption for the entire year. Work on the land and around the
household was realized with the help of relatives and neighbors as part of a
system of reciprocity that was celebrated in the presence of alcohol. Everyone
who could afford it drank in such situations, as a sign of health and social
inclusion.

The advent of socialism in the region led to profound changes in organization of the local economy, social life, and patterns of consumption. A small
market town before the Second World War, Caracal was part of an intense industrialization program implemented by the communist government.[14] This
process was facilitated by simultaneous implementation of urban development
projects leading to construction of several residential districts for the workers
in the local industry.[15] The inhabitants of surrounding villages, among them
Dobrosloveni, were subjected to forced collectivization, which was completed
at the beginning of the 1960s. Left without land, peasants were offered the
possibility of being trained to work in industry newly created through communist central planning. Many young villagers moved to nearby towns and worked
in the factories built there after 1965.

These deep socioeconomic changes considerably affected the regime of
alcohol circulation and consumption. New categories of individuals—members
of the collective farms, commuting workers, and those employed in the growing
administrative and educational apparatuses—now had increased access to economic resources, more regular work schedules, and numerous opportunities
to drink. An activity structurally integrated into the system of social relations
before collectivization, drinking became important for creating new social relations, meaning, identity, and prestige under socialism. Alcohol was transformed
into a symbol of socioeconomic success, often subject to conspicuous and even
competitive consumption; it was a matter of consumption not merely during
leisure time but during work time as well.

The rigors of industrial production—which required discipline, routine,
and isolation—were not easily integrated by the masses of people coming
from the countryside, used to a system of production where work and ritual

consumption of alcohol were often integrated. Although prohibited by strict laws, drinking at work was prevalent throughout the socialist period. As T. I., an engineer at a tire factory from Caracal, remembers: "People used to drink at work during those times . . . and that was it. You could not stop it no matter how 'Tartar'[16] you were because it was in their blood."[17] T. I. was born in a village in the eastern part of Romania and was trained as an engineer at the Polytechnic University in Bucharest. Knowledgeable about village life and working arrangements, he was inclined to be flexible with the teams of workers he coordinated in his two decades of work at the tire factory. But his was not a unique example of tolerance toward drinking-related delinquency. Especially at large factories, with a substantial labor force spread out over a wide area, strict control was not always possible. In what the Romanian writer I. D. Sîrbu calls "fieldwork" (evadarea pe teren),[18] workers would jump over the factory fence to quickly drink a glass of brandy in one of the nearby taverns or buy some alcohol from a nearby food store. Others managed to bring in bottles hidden under their clothes and drink during their shift.

Though such behavior was often tolerated, the inebriated and especially those on record as alcoholics also faced some of the harshest disciplinary measures of the communist period.[19] Such measures were not limited to the postwar Stalinist period; they were a central feature of the post-Stalinist thaw.[20] During the 1960s and 1970s, perpetrators of hooliganism or public drunkenness were sentenced to two weeks to several months of forced labor at construction sites, collective farms (CAP), or agricultural state farms (IAS). According to journalists of the time, the regime was responding to the fact that, in spite of disciplinary measures and state regulations, alcohol consumption in socialist Romania grew continuously (as elsewhere in the region).[21] Well aware of such trends, after 1963 under Ceaușescu the Communist Party was particularly vigilant about restricting circulation, sale, and consumption of alcohol by limiting the opening hours of taverns, restaurants, and cafeterias and by imposing stricter conditions on the sale of alcohol in other commercial establishments. Prompted by Ceaușescu's concern over the increase in alcohol consumption,[22] new measures forbade sale of alcoholic beverages on the premises of state factories or within their proximity,[23] sale of alcohol before 10:00 a.m. or after 1:00 a.m., sale to minors or inebriated persons, and finally any form of advertising for alcoholic beverages.[24] The strictest disciplinary measures were implemented by the Communist Party in the mid-1970s and were designed to "strengthen order and discipline at every workplace"[25] and to criminalize "lax behaviors."[26] Associated with Ceaușescu's turn to a neo-Stalinist model after 1975, the notorious decree no. 400 of 1981[27] and the subsequent law no. 5 of 1985 were meant to curb the adverse effects of drink on labor productivity and work safety.[28]

In spite of comprehensive regulation of alcohol distribution and consumption, social drinking continued to be a key social practice overlapping the spheres of work, leisure, and domestic life throughout the entire socialist period. Although state regulations forbid sale of alcohol in stores and taverns near industrial complexes, informants describe that period as one in which the interdiction stimulated temptation rather than decreasing it. For many, the fact that alcoholic beverages were sold only after 10:00 a.m. was almost a stimulus to buy something to drink immediately following opening hours. Other people were constantly inventing excuses that would allow them to purchase alcohol even prior to that hour. Some of the most frequently deployed excuses were the visit of a close relative, having to work in the fields and not being able to come back just to buy alcohol, and the need to treat (să cinstească) those helping one to collect firewood in the forest. The new time schedules did not fit people's traditional rhythms of work and leisure or social obligations. Because sales personnel in local shops understood this, such excuses and strategies were often successful, depending ultimately on the buyer's skill and powers of persuasion. Amusing stories about the side-effects of such practices describe daily collection by Roma driving horse-drawn carts of literally hundreds of empty bottles that were dropped outside the fence of the wagon factory. They would recycle the empty bottles for money at some of the same grocery stores that had sold the alcohol to the workers in the first place.

Implementation of strict time schedules and enforcement of discipline during work hours were further stymied by workers' social solidarity. Those who drank during their shift often went to sleep on a lawn at the back of the factory or in the locker room, returning at the end of the day or not at all. Many such "undisciplined" acts were covered up by workmates and even by lower-level supervisors, who were more interested in building informal authority over their teams than strictly obeying the rules. Those who lived through the period remember that work discipline regulations became stricter over time, culminating in tough penal treatment of alcohol consumption at work prescribed by Decree no. 400 (1981). Yet, they also remember the fictive "Decree no. 402," invented by the workers themselves to mock state Decree no. 400. The real decree stated clearly that drink at work was prohibited; Decree no. 402 was meant to create an imaginary, ironic system of justice for delinquent workers—"Decree 402: The boss drinks, and we do too" (Decretul 402: Bea şi şeful, bem şi noi). Drinking regulations were thus only loosely enforced at the factories in Caracal. As F. D., a Dobrosloveni commuter to the furniture factory, remembers, "If somebody just smelled like alcohol, it was not such a big deal . . . it wasn't a problem. Problems appeared if he was drunk. They immediately sent him home [i.e., they fired him]."

A permissive attitude toward drink at work was confirmed also by those meant to oversee the workers. In exercising their leadership over work teams, engineers and foremen acted rather "like shepherds" and had little interest in strict enforcement of the law. As T. I. again explained, "Those [engineers] who treated their workers more kindly [*moale*] usually had workers who did a better job." And as he further noted, that "every skilled craftsman is also a drunkard" was "common knowledge." Engineers and foremen were also generally attentive to the personal reasons that could prompt drinking since they knew their subordinates quite well. They tended to take into consideration the social situation of the delinquent (number of children, domestic situation, relations with a spouse) before adopting a drastic measure such as salary reduction or dismissal.

Alcohol and the Second Economy

The ambivalent, multifaceted relations between workers and their supervisors that made drinking possible in spite of disciplinary regulation on the part of the socialist state was complicated by the logic of the second economy at the time. For most of the workers, being employed in the new and growing industries of the region meant regular access not only to cash resources (hardly accessible to most peasants in the presocialist economy) but also to diverse materials, tools, and skills that could easily be converted into the goods or spare parts scarce in the official sector. The desire of peasants or other workers for various goods and services made them valuable in the growing informal sector. Valuable objects, stolen from state factories or produced clandestinely using its facilities, were traded for other scarce commodities in a system of reciprocal exchange, sometimes traded for money, and very often used to procure alcohol.

Most of the workers employed by the new socialist factories in essence became suppliers of goods for the second economy. Informants remember having access to things and processes that could be purposefully transformed or diverted for unofficial exchange. Those in the wagon factory would take out anything, from paint to nails or welding rods, and could easily manufacture iron spare parts for household appliances. Those at the furniture factory would create various items and ornaments that were carried out of the workshop premises in pieces during successive nights and then assembled at home. Those at the pig-fattening complex not only received a daily allocation of meat products, husk, and fodder (shared with their friends and neighbors rather than kept only for their own use) but would find ways to steal "sausages wrapped around one's waist" or a "salami hidden under one's sleeve." Women working for the garment

factory would wrap themselves up in pieces of various articles to be sewed together at home, or just wear the stolen items through the factory gates.[29]

Such details of practical ways of smuggling clothing items out the gates of
the garment factory or resources from other state factories were related by
M. O., a woman from Dobrosloveni who used to commute to Caracal during
the 1980s. Having accomplished ten years of education in the village (the minimum level for vocational schools under socialism), she was later employed at
the garment factory where she also attended evening classes at a vocational
school toward a diploma that would help her get a promotion. Although proud
of her work at the factory, she had no moral dilemmas when it came to stealing
things from the state. She was well aware that times were hard and that she had
to make a living for her family.

Stealing and informal production—key resources for the socialist second
economy—have long been analyzed by scholars of Eastern European societies.[30] However, most scholars rather neglect the forms of exchange that me-
diate circulation of informal goods. Almost none of the scholars of Eastern
European socialism have analyzed the pivotal role of alcohol in informal
exchange. Under the weakly monetized economy of socialism, alcohol went
from an object of ritual and limited consumption to a commodity consumed
daily by people with increased access to economic resources. As alcohol became
more expensive and harder to procure, in spite of increased production, the
popular desire for alcohol drove up its value and stimulated proliferation of a
web of informal transactions constitutive of the second economy. Very often,
alcohol played the role of a local money substitute, changing its status from
terminal commodity to a mediator of exchange. It created numerous opportunities for relations between workers and supervisors to be negotiated and
reconfigured, making the structures of the second economy in fact very fluid.

The mild and understanding attitude of many managers and supervisors
was facilitated by the sharing of alcohol and other benefits of unreported exchanges with those they oversaw. G. F. was head of personnel at the Caracal
wagon factory and in charge of enforcing work safety regulations, which included measures against drinking during work. He remembers that "supervisors used to realize when somebody was drunk. They knew those for whom
drinking was a weakness [slăbiciune], pardoned them once, then pardoned
them twice, and later ended up drinking on their open tab [au ajuns să bea pe
spatele lor]."[31] A native of the town, living his entire life in one of its working-
class districts and having extensive kin in the neighboring villages, G. F. might
have been inclined to adopt a more tolerant attitude toward work discipline.
However, this is not the key factor explaining poor enforcement of disciplinary
regulations; a better explanation is offered by the structural scarcity induced by

the command economy at the time. Supervisors faced the same constraints in the official economy and had to make a living under the same conditions as their subordinates. Tolerating small acts of indiscipline and various forms of petty theft in exchange for favors from those under their control was their own way of "adapting" to the system.

The second economy being premised on intense circulation of alcohol; the multiple conversions among diverse commodities, favors, and valuables; and the performative drinking in ritualized social settings all facilitated manipulation of resources and social relations for creation of value. In spite of harsh political repression, the Ceauşescu regime also tolerated the second economy to a certain extent as it provided a necessary corrective for scarcity. This was even more critical during the 1980s, when Ceauşescu imposed measures of extreme economic austerity in order to pay off Romania's burgeoning debt. The rampant black market that resulted heightened the importance of reputation— the basis of trust that facilitated exchange of drinks, things, and valuable information. In such circumstances, reputation constituted a key ingredient of social action, a valuable resource to be pursued and employed to ensure one's success in the second economy.

Reputation and Gender in the Second Economy

Although the informal arrangements of production inside state facilities were important for supplying goods to the second economy, places of leisure are even more critical in understanding alcohol consumption and exchange. The tavern and the household, two social spaces profoundly reshaped under the impact of socialist policies, became increasingly important for the subsistence strategies functioning under a "shortage economy."[32] They not only facilitated circulation of goods and exchange of services but constituted key settings for transferring information.[33] In a socialist economy, premised on the principles of central planning and rational redistribution, control of information by state authorities became the preferred mode of governance.[34] Under these circumstances, many of the local practices usually associated with the second economy amounted primarily to a search for information about the location of resources, and available channels of access to them through trustworthy partners of exchange. Significantly, alcohol and social drinking aided the flow of information and building of trust among involved parties. Alcohol was both an item of ceremonial and social consumption and one of the preferred means of payment. The village tavern, known by all as MAT,[35] functioned much like a clearinghouse for circulation of information and material commodities escaping the control of the state as well as for settling debts. Since the nationalization of industry and commerce in 1948, MAT remained the only legal outlet where alcohol could be sold and consumed. The village store (Cooperativa, as most remember it) also sold various low-alcohol beverages until the mid-1980s, when they suddenly disappeared. Generally located in the center of the village, the MAT and the village store were physical symbols in the built landscape of socialist attempts at collectivized consumption.[36] But the reality of alcohol consumption was considerably more diffuse, especially during the last decades of socialism, when an increasing number of villagers purchased small alcohol distilling installations (cazane), usually from Roma craftsmen. Homemade țuică was secretly sold to relatives, neighbors, or trusted villagers since at the time it was illegal to sell privately produced alcohol. The advantage of such an arrangement was that villagers usually sold on credit, and money was often collected weeks or months later. Debts could even be settled by means of a service or provision of another scarce good by the debtor. However, one category of villagers that was against such a practice was the wives of the debtors, since they saw family revenues vanish on payday, when these debts were usually settled.

Incorporating the cultural premises and political-economic constraints of the socialist second economy in Romania in the 1980s, practices that involved production, circulation, and consumption of alcohol also created contingent gender configurations. Under socialism, MAT was the meeting place for exclusively *male* villagers who worked in the factories in the nearby town, the local collective farm (CAP), the agricultural state farm (IAS), and the mechanical section (SMA). In addition, it was the primary leisure venue for men working for the administrative and Party apparatuses of the village. Though MAT was frequented daily, its opening hours were shortened during harvest season or when the most important agricultural work had to be carried out. It was generally very crowded on paydays, when people would even take their drinks out in front of the tavern or to the backyard if they could not find seating inside. Like most of the working-district taverns in Oltenia at the time, MAT was a rather dirty establishment, smelling heavily of cheap alcohol, tobacco, and lamp oil, the main commodities for sale inside. The most popular drinks sold there were cheap brandies, vodka, and other spirits such as *Verdele* (peppermint), nicknamed "Adio Mama!" for the side effects of the intoxication it could cause; *Secărica*, nicknamed "I have seen your grave" (*Te-am zărit printre morminte*); and "blue eyes brandy" (*Țuica doi ochi albaștri*), from the two plums drawn on its label. These nicknames speak to the often playful male camaraderie that characterized the shared experience of consumption in the MAT environment.

Conversation was lively among friends and acquaintances, although considerably more reserved in the presence of strangers. Discussions were mostly

FIGURE 10.1.   Worker commuters drinking at the village MAT sometime during the mid-1980s. From the personal collection of one of the author's informants from the village of Dobrosloveni.

about family life, work, and relations with supervisors and Party secretaries, or the details of reciprocal services and informal transactions among those drinking together. Drinking also offered an occasion for celebrating a bargain that was struck, or for an unlikely exchange taking place (*cinstea*), or for a payment-in-kind among friends who did not take money from each other for services. Generally broad political or social issues were not topics of conversation at the MAT, though banal conversation was often laced with politics as jokes subverted official positions and created a mood of playfulness. Subtle subversion was necessary to obscure relations and responsibilities since arrangements discussed at the MAT in one way or another involved resources stolen from state factories. Because Romania was struggling with pervasive scarcity in the attempt to repay all foreign debt during the 1980s, acts of petty theft were classified as speculation (incriminated by the communist penal code), and even sabotage in the case of key commodities, and they could be severely sanctioned. Indeed, "tables and chairs could have ears"; many among the villagers turned out to be informers for the militia or for the local organizations belonging to the Communist Party.[37] Reservation and coded speech were some of the strategies used at the MAT, just as at other public venues in that period.

Socialist taverns thus functioned like clearinghouses for exchanging information and settling debts accumulated in the second economy, like other drinking establishments elsewhere in Eastern Europe.[38] However, the shortages and extensive surveillance under late socialism in Romania gave MAT a crucial role in creating and enforcing informal transactions. Because information was scarce and tightly controlled by the state, the flow of alcohol made transfer of information more fluid as well. MAT drinking sessions were practices constitutive of trust (*încredere*) and reputation (*reputație*), key ingredients for a sphere of exchange lacking a formal enforcement mechanism. Reputation was not only the epiphenomenal effect of past transactions but a fundamental dimension of personhood and a key ingredient of social action. It was strategically pursued and constructed continuously in a public and performative way where the gendered character of speech and consumption was conspicuous. The most valuable forms of talk, ensuring inclusion in a circle of friends, were based on wit and allusion, where a pun or a good joke was as appreciated as one's ability to keep a promise. This stood in contrast to what was often perceived by men as women's talk—gossip, discussion of private life, complaints about everyday life. Although repeatedly derided by men, conversation among women was, in practice, at least as important as that among men, allowing circulation of knowledge not accessible otherwise, facilitating reconciliation after quarrels among families, or exchanging information about things men considered to be "unimportant."

In addition to being the site of information flow, MAT was also the key entry point for money to make its way into the circuits of the second economy, where it mediated diverse transactions easily recognizable by those intimate to the tavern world but hardly visible to outsiders. The traces of such transactions were acts of commensality during which a bargain would be struck and cemented because treating someone to a drink could be used as a payment-in-kind for agreed services. Moreover, getting drinks on credit from the tavern keeper meant that one was reliable and that one would not report the tavern keeper (liable for speculation); it also meant that one had the means to pay back the credit. This was converted into symbolic capital and *reputatie* in front of those who witnessed the arrangement.

The MAT was an essentially gender-segregated space, one of the privileged arenas of manhood. Women and children seldom entered, and when they did it was to buy something or look for someone. They did not usually stay long. Young and mature women had to be especially careful because a bad reputation was easily acquired but very hard to quell. Epithets such as whore (*curvă*, *stricată*) or loser (*căzătură*) had currency among the regulars of the tavern and could affect the social identity of local women seen in or near MAT. Taking as natural women's avoidance of the tavern, men from Dobrosloveni remembered how they were amazed to see women drinking with their husbands in taverns in other areas of Romania (especially in Banat, Transylvania, and large cities). As one of them put it, "I found it shocking to see that in Vâlcea women enter the tavern and sit at the table—as it happens in towns, at restaurants, where it is *normal* for a woman to sit at the table with her husband."[39] This confession of personal astonishment was made by C. F., a mechanical engineer born in Dobrosloveni who worked for the state railway construction enterprise his entire life. Retired at the time of his interview, he remembered with nostalgia that he had to live far away from home for most of the year and had the chance to witness a variety of drinking practices. He considered this a form of invaluable cultural capital he was proud of, and he was very happy to share some of his life experiences. Such culture shock confessed by several other men from Dobrosloveni and Caracal converges with a sense of embarrassment for those whose female relatives did not respect the MAT avoidance taboo. Thus men whose wives or partners came to the tavern became the butt of jokes. Especially derided were those whose wives came to take them home or to stop them from drinking. Hence, categories of masculinity and femininity were mutually constituted in wits and words.

Although almost every man in the village drank at MAT, there were few known alcoholics (*alcoolici* or *alcooliști* in local argot) during the socialist period. Such a pejorative tag was attached only to those who were not able to control themselves when drinking in public. M. N., an agricultural engineer at the Dobrosloveni collective farm for more than twenty years, explains "the more often one was seen dead drunk, I mean staggering [*împleticit*] and 'measuring the road with his feet' [*măsura drumul*], one was tagged as a drunkard [*bețiv*], a loser [*stricat*]." This assessment should take into account the various occasions in which inebriety was tolerated, such as important events in one's life, periods of mourning, or religious holidays. At weddings, even women could drink more in public. M. N. further remembers that, at each wedding, out of 100 or 150 guests "there were always three or four women that did not get to the steak as their husbands were forced to carry them home dead drunk."[40]

Local narratives associated moderate drinking with health (*om sănătos*), hard work and skill (*om muncitor, meseriaș*), affluence (*stare*), and respectability (*om serios*), while lack of self-control (both with regard to holding one's liquor and performing the poetics of social drinking) could become a permanent stigma with serious consequences for the professional and economic standing of the person. Even local officials seemed to be aware of the importance of drinking for local social life. During one of the meetings of the local People's Council, the collective administrative organism governing Romanian towns and communes during late socialism,[41] someone suggested that the terrace in front of the MAT was in need of repair: "Comrades, we must do something to repair the terrace outside the MAT. When the tractor driver Vasile Mincă comes from the field, from the harvest, he would enjoy sitting out there and drinking a beer." "A very good initiative!" the other participants were quick to agree.[42]

Alcohol and drinking, though, were not limited to the world of the tavern; they were important pillars of the household economy as well. Alcohol was a necessary element of rituals and celebrations and was used by many as an important economic resource to supplement other modest sources of income. People working for the village collective farm, always paid poorly and mostly in produce, were especially willing to take the risk of buying a handcrafted still for distilling *ţuică*. Legal throughout the socialist period, installing alcohol distillation equipment required a license from the local authorities that became difficult to get during the 1970s and 1980s. Many chose instead to use an undeclared still and run the risk of being caught and prosecuted for speculation. Moonshine alcohol was in even greater demand following the restrictive measures adopted during the 1980s, which limited access to alcoholic beverages in the official sector; the restrictions were the result of both Romania-specific austerity measures as well as regionwide emulation of Gorbachev's anti-alcohol campaign in the Soviet Union.[43] Moonshine was the preferred drink of less-well-off people who could not afford the more expensive beverages sold at MAT. Some of them were given credit by neighbors running a still, credit that could extend anywhere from a few days to half a year or even longer. Many would get drinks in exchange for goods stolen from state factories (fodder from the pig-fattening complex, welding rods from the wagon factory, a shirt from the garment factory) or services performed with state resources (a piece of furniture made at the factory, plowing one's personal plot with one of the SMA tractors). Most clients, of course, preferred discretion when it came to such transactions.

Selling moonshine brandy was a risky enterprise. Although in high demand among many of the villagers and usually tolerated by local militia and Party secretaries in the village, the practice was the object of a certain moral ambivalence. Villagers generally understood it as a way to make ends meet, similar to many other underground economic practices in socialism; but its potential for diverting money away from the families of customers attracted moral condemnation from those who owned stills. One woman ran a still in her backyard throughout most of the eighties after her husband had a heart condition and was unable to work—or drink, for that matter—and she had to take care of the household.[44] Because she was working for the collective farm and receiving an inadequate salary, A. T. had to engage in moonshining, partake of petty theft from the collective farm, and employ an extensive web of reciprocal exchanges. She sold a large part of the *ţuică* she produced to the tractor drivers at the SMA next to her house—in exchange for oil, plowing of her personal plot, cutting of some firewood, or money she would collect on payday toward debts she recorded carefully in a notebook.

FIGURE 10.2.   Copper still used for plum brandy moonshining in the Oltenia Region. Highly prized under socialism, this type of artisanal distilling installation was an essential source of revenue and a valuable resource fueling the second economy during the 1980s. Author's collection.

A serious and abstinent woman, managing to stay on top of hardships thanks to her industriousness, A. T.'s production of alcohol did not affect her reputation as it was done for a moral cause: to make ends meet. Her age also meant she was not the subject of sexual jokes among men or gossip among other women. She was not approached by the militia in spite of the fact that most of the villagers knew about her small enterprise. Her practice became an issue only once the wife of a tractor driver filed a complaint with local authorities claiming her husband did not bring his salary home and instead spent it on brandy sold by A. T. The militia consequently confiscated the still, although the woman was not prosecuted, given her condition. She did have to pay a small fine, however, on top of losing her investment in the confiscated equipment. Not able to run a still anymore because of supervision by the militia, she had to intensify reciprocal exchanges with the villages and theft from the collective farm to make up for the lost revenue from moonshine.

Drinking became ever more important during the 1980s both for the villagers working in Dobrosloveni and for those commuting to the factories in Caracal. It was seldom absent from transactions of the second economy centered around the household, yet dependent on the tavern for negotiation of exchanges and settling of debts. One of the paradoxes of the shortage economy run by the socialist regime in Romania was that in spite of ideologically driven efforts to unsettle older forms of social dependence—through speedy modernization, industrialization, and new settlement patterns—it managed to reinforce kinship and promote dependence on extensive networks of relatives, acquaintances, and friends in everyday life. Oltenia's world of drink indicate that, far from being associated with transformative forces linked to individualization and a modernist separation of work and leisure, alcohol consumption based on the second economy was articulated via wide webs of reciprocity continuously reinforced by commensality and social drinking.[45]

Most of those living in Oltenia under socialism and taking part in the second economy would remember with nostalgia the drinking and the forms of sociality built around it. Alcohol seems to have created a universe of meaning and relative security, facilitating informal transactions and a kind of solidarity among drinking buddies that made life easier under the shortages of the command economy. Those intimate with village life, however, confirm that moderation influenced the well-being of families in the village: "In time, moderation had visible effects. Those that did not drink had bigger houses, their children went to school, and they made it in life."[46] Indeed, in spite of alcohol's role in binding local social worlds, it also had the potential to prompt conflict between family members and fellow villagers. The prevalent claim that "those that did not know how to drink together did not have friends to help them,"[47] heard time and again in the village, can be contrasted to the equally common knowledge that "inveterate drinkers progressively lost all of their friends."[48]

Drinking in taverns situated in villages and working-class neighborhoods was constitutive of a sphere of material and symbolic exchange during Romania's late socialist period that was essential for the emergence of the second economy. Taverns functioned like clearinghouses for circulation of information and commodities, and for settlement of debts accumulated in informal transactions. Alcohol was deeply embedded in the lives of those exchanging and consuming it, which was further linked to the wider social and economic processes that constituted late socialism. Alcohol consumption directly stimulated the growth of the socialist second economy and the burgeoning forms of sociability that enabled it. Circulation of alcohol was channeled by the interplay between the ever-growing state regulations against it and its important role in diverse spheres of social and economic life. Coming at a time when many other Bloc countries liberalized their economies, the ever-stricter control of consumption by the state and the expanding second economy driven by alcohol

particularize the Romanian socialist regime during the 1980s. During this period, Romanian communist leaders turned to autarchy and implemented rigid
control on consumption, based on rational satisfaction of needs, to make possible the accumulation of economic surpluses needed to repay foreign debts to
Western banks whose interest rates were rising.

In Romania, this interplay between regulations and local acts of consumption and exchange has been ongoing for its entire modern history.[49] Given its
centrality in the interaction between the state sector of the economy and local-
ized spheres of exchange, the social life of alcohol reveals cultural premises
and grassroots articulation of power in successive political regimes. During the
late socialist period, however, alcohol came to play a particularly important role.
What gave alcohol such a prominent place was the state's own ambivalence
toward drinking: controlled so as to curtail disobedience yet tolerated to increase
state revenues and alleviate consumer shortages. Most important, state actors
were complicit in the wide webs of illicit exchanges of alcohol, which were in
fact a constitutive element of Romanian late socialism.

NOTES

1. The police forces were called militia in socialist Romania. I use the terms
militia and *militiamen* (the word also used by my informants in formal interviews and
discussions about the past) throughout this chapter for historical accuracy.

2. See Vasile Surcel, "Ştefănescu—'naşul' filierei Bachus (Ştefănescu, the
"godfather" of the Bacchus network), in *Jurnalul National*, Aug. 16, 2004; and Marian
Ghiteanu and Laszlo Kallai, "Ana Ştefănescu-Bachus: 'L-au omorât degeaba!'" (Ana
Ştefănescu-Bachus: "They killed him for nothing!") in *Ziua*, Apr. 6, 2009. A movie
about Bacchus was released a few years after his execution. Produced to convey a
clearly propagandistic message, the movie is actually a very good comedy; it enjoyed a
large audience even at projections after 1989. See Geo Saizescu, *Secretul lui Bachus*
("The Secret of Bacchus"), Romania, 1984.

3. Here the concepts of *commodity* and *politics* are those defined by Arjun
Appadurai in "Introduction: Commodities and the Politics of Value," in *The Social
Life of Things: Commodities in Cultural Perspective*, ed. Arjun Appadurai (New York:
Cambridge University Press, 1992). *Commodity* is defined as "any thing intended
for exchange," 9, while "*politics* (in the broad sense of relations, assumptions, and
contests pertaining to power) is what links value and exchange in the social life of
commodities," 57. Excellent analyses of states' engagement with alcohol in a
historical perspective are Joseph R. Gusfield, *Symbolic Crusade: Status Politics and
the American Temperance Movement* (Urbana: University of Illinois Press, 1986);
David Christian, *"Living Water": Vodka and Russian Society on the Eve of Emancipation* (Oxford: Clarendon Press, 1990); and Erica Richardson, *The Struggle for
Sobriety: Anti-Alcohol Campaign Under Gorbachev and Yeltsin* (University of

Birmingham, Research Papers in Russian and East European Studies, no. 99/1, Mar. 1999).

4. According to Susana Barrows and Robin Rooms, Engels emphasized the importance of family, religion, and leisure for the working class in his *The Condition of the Working Class in England*, published in 1845. See their "Introduction" in *Drinking: Behavior and Belief in Social History*, ed. Susana Barrows and Robin Rooms (Berkeley: University of California Press, 1991), 3.

5. See for example, Mary Douglas, "A Distinctive Anthropological Perspective," in *Constructive Drinking: Perspectives on Drink from Anthropology*, ed. Mary Douglas (Cambridge: Cambridge University Press, 1987), 3–15; and Dimitra Gefou-Madianou, "Introduction: Alcohol Commensality, Identity Transformations and Transcendence," in *Alcohol, Gender and Culture*, ed. Dimitra Gefou-Madianou (London: Routledge, 1992), 1–34.

6. See Gerald Mars, "Longshore Drinking, Economic Security, and Union Politics in Newfoundland," in Douglas, *Constructive Drinking*, 91–101; Mars and Yochanan Altman, "Alternative Mechanism of Distribution in a Soviet Economy," in *Constructive Drinking*, 270–79; and Adrian Peace, "No Fishing Without Drinking: The Construction of Social Identity in Rural Ireland," in Gefou-Madianou, ed., *Alcohol, Gender and Culture*, 167–80.

7. See the special issue of *East European Quarterly* 18(4) (1984). See especially Charlotte Chase, "Alcohol Consumption—an Indicator of System Malfunction in Contemporary Poland," *East European Quarterly*, 18(4) (1984): 415–29; Barbara Kerewsky-Halpern, "Rakija as Ritual in Rural Serbia," *East European Quarterly*, 18(4) (1984): 481–94; and David Kideckel. "Drinking Up: Alcohol, Class, and Social Change in Rural Romania," *East European Quarterly*, 18(4) (1984): 431–46.

8. See Gregory Grossman, "Notes for a Theory of the Command Economy," *Soviet Studies* 15(2) (1963): 101–23; Alain Besançon, *Anatomie d'un spectre. L'economie politique du socialisme réel* (Paris: Calmann-Levy, 1981); and Steven L. Sampson, "The Second Economy of the Soviet Union and Eastern Europe," *Annals of the American Academy of Political and Social Science* 493 (1987): 120–36.

9. Janine Wedel in *The Private Poland* (New York: Facts on File, 1986) analyzes the creativity within the second economy; most other anthropologists emphasize its functional dimensions. See Katherine Verdery, "Theorizing Socialism: A Prologue to the 'Transition,'" *American Ethnologist* 18(3), Representations of Europe: Transforming State, Society and Identity (1991), 419–39; Katherine Verdery, *What Was Socialism, and What Comes Next?* (Princeton, NJ: Princeton University Press, 1996); Gerald Mars and Yochanan Altman, "The Cultural Bases of Soviet Georgia's Second Economy," *Soviet Studies* 35(4) (1983): 546–60; and Mars and Altman, "Alternative Mechanism of Distribution in a Soviet Economy," 270–79.

10. See Law no. 119 of June 11, 1948, regarding nationalization of industry, banking, insurance, mining and transportation; *Official Bulletin of Romania* no. 113bis of June 11, 1948.

11. The alcohol monopoly was administered by MAT (*Monopolul Alcoolului şi Tutunului* [Alcohol and Tobacco Monopoly]), a division within the Ministry of Finance.

See Augustin Vişa, *Monopoluri şi carteluri în România* (Monopolies and Cartels in Romania), Ph.D. diss., (Bucharest: University of Bucharest, 1943).

12. See Decree no. 504 of Oct. 17, 1957, regarding production, sale, distribution, and retail of alcoholic beverages; *Official Gazette of Romania*, no. 29 of Oct. 21, 1957.

13. See "Dare de seamă a Comisiei de Partid şi de Stat referitoare la activitatea Cooperaţiei de Consum (Centrocoop)" (Report of the Party and State Commission regarding the activity of the Cooperative for Consumption, Centrocoop), *Archives of the Central Committee of the Romanian Communist Party, Economic Section*, File no. 143 (1952), National Archives of Romania, Bucharest.

14. Caracal is a small town of approximately forty thousand located two hours from Bucharest in the Oltenia region. Dobrosloveni, the village where I conducted interviews and observation, is situated seven kilometers north of Caracal.

15. After 1965, a series of factories and industrial facilities were built in Caracal in an attempt to transform the former agricultural region into an industrial one. Thus, factories producing canned vegetables (1965), milk products (1967), furniture (1968), garments and knitwear (1973), freight wagons (1973), and tires (1985) as well as a large pig-fattening complex, an abattoir, and a forage factory on the outskirts of the town were constructed in a short period of time, providing almost twenty thousand new jobs for the region. At the same time, five new social housing districts were built to accommodate part of the workforce, increasing the number of apartments from 250 in 1965 to more than 7,000 in 1988. See Rodica Şerban, "Pe temelia creşterii puterii industriale—schimbări profunde în in viaţa locuitorilor oraşului" (Profound Changes in the Lives of City Dwellers Caused by the Increased Industrial Power), *Scînteia*, May 6, 1988.

16. In the local idiom, every person who was stubborn and hard to persuade to change her idea would be euphemistically called a "Tartar." The meaning is probably related to the image of cultural and linguistic difference represented by Tartars in the minds of the people of Oltenia.

17. T. I., interview by the author, Caracal, Apr, 22, 2003.

18. See Sîrbu, *Adio, Europa!*

19. See "New 'Hooligan Law' to Curb Youths' Excesses," in *Radio Free Europe/Radio Liberty Research Report* (Budapest: Open Society Archives, 1957), 2.

20. Ibid.

21. On the basis of limited official data available in the 1981 edition of *Romania's Statistical Yearbook*, Paul Gafton shows that between 1950 and 1980 the quantities of alcohol consumed in Romania increased substantially: beer quantity rose by a factor of 11, wine 4.3, natural brandy 2.2, and other alcoholic beverages 5.7 times, while the adult population increased from 11 million to approximately 15 million during the period. See Gafton, "Heavy Drinking and Alcoholism in Romania," in *Radio Free Europe/Radio Liberty Research* (Budapest: Open Society Archives, 1984). Increased consumption in the region has been attributed to class mobility under socialism, to regular access to cash on the part of larger segments of the population, and to resignification of drinking as a "modern" form of consumption. See David A. Kideckel, "Drinking Up: Alcohol, Class, and Social Change in Rural Romania," *East European Quarterly* 18(4) (1985), 431–46.

22. See Ilves and Pompey, "Alcoholism in Eastern Europe," in *Radio Free Europe/ Radio Liberty Research* (Budapest: Open Society Archives, 1987), 40.

23. Decree no. 76 was part of a set of planned measures that included closing almost two thousand drinking establishments in the vicinity of factories and schools by the end of 1976. See Ilves and Pompey, "Alcoholism in Eastern Europe," 40.

24. Decree no. 76 of 1975 regarding some measures concerning retail sale of alcoholic beverages in the units of socialist commerce, in the *Official Bulletin of Romania* no. 73 of July 15, 1975.

25. Law no. 5 of 1985 for the increase of labor productivity and improvement of the organization and standardization of labor and production, in the *Official Bulletin of Romania* no. 71 of Dec. 20, 1985.

26. For a brief yet suggestive analysis of Romania's modernization during Ceauşescu as well as its economic and social effects, see Pavel Câmpeanu, *Axul prăbuşirii. Ceauşescu, anii numărătorii inverse (The Axle of Decay: Ceauşescu, the Years of the Final Countdown)* (Bucharest: Polirom, 2002), 241–92.

27. Decree no. 400 regarding rules of operation and maintenance of installations, hardware, and machinery, and for strengthening order and discipline in factories with continuous production or with dangerous installations, in the *Official Bulletin of Romania* no. 112 of Dec. 29, 1981.

28. See Ilves and Pompey, "Alcoholism in Eastern Europe," 41.

29. M. O., interview by author, Dobrosloveni, May 16, 2003.

30. See David A. Kideckel, *The Solitude of Collectivism: Romanian Villagers to the Revolution and Beyond* (Ithaca, NY: Cornell University Press, 1993); Wedel, *Private Poland*; Sampson, "Second Economy;" Verdery, *What Was Socialism?*; and Katherine Verdery, "Anthropology of Socialist Societies," in *International Encyclopedias of the Social and Behavioral Sciences*, ed. Neil Smelser and Paul B. Baltes (Amsterdam: Pergamon Press, 2002), http://web.gc.cuny.edu/anthropology/fac_verdery.html.

31. G. F., interview by author, Caracal, Apr. 22, 2003.

32. The concept was proposed initially by the Hungarian economist János Kornai and adapted for the case of Romania by Katherine Verdery in her classic ethnographies. See János Kornai, *Economics of Shortage* (Amsterdam: North Holland Press, 1980); and Verdery, *What Was Socialism?*

33. Information economics became one of the dominant paradigms during the last decades, economists such as George Akerlof or Joseph Stiglitz being well known even outside the world of specialists. Relaxing the assumptions of economics, anthropologists such as Clifford Geertz and Katherine Verdery have outlined the role of information in organization of non-Western economies. See Geertz, "The Bazaar Economy: Information and Search in Peasant Marketing," *American Economic Review* 68 (1978); and Verdery, "Anthropology of Socialist Societies."

34. See Câmpeanu, *Axul prăbuşirii*; and Katherine Verdery, "Anthropological Adventures with Romania's Wizard of Oz, 1973–1989," *Focaal: European Journal of Anthropology* 43 (2004): 134–45.

35. The acronym stands for *Monopolul Alcoolului şi Tutunului* (Alcohol and Tobacco Monopoly), a division established within the Ministry of Finance in 1932 to administer the monopoly over the sale of alcohol. With nationalization of commercial

establishments under socialism, the only remaining tavern in the village continued to be referred to as MAT. See Vişa, *Monopoluri şi carteluri.*

36. For a further analysis of architectural symbols as reflecting the ideology under socialism, see Sigrid Rausing, "Drink and Leisure: The Semiotic Significance of Two New Enterprises on a Former Collective Farm in Estonia," *Anthropology of East Europe Review* 16(2) (1999), *Special Issue: Out of the Ruins: Cultural Negotiations in the Soviet Aftermath.*

37. Militia use of informants among the consumers in taverns to find about thefts from state factories was widespread in all Romanian towns and villages during the entire socialist period. See "Department Stores, Specialty Shops, Service Stores: Bureaucracy Prevents Improvement," in *Radio Free Europe/Radio Liberty Research Reports* (Budapest: Open Society Archives, 1962).

38. See Mars, "Longshore Drinking," 91–101; and Peace, "No Fishing Without Drinking," 167–80; and Sándor Horváth, "Everyday Life of Workers in the First Hungarian Socialist Town," paper presented at the Fourteenth European Social Science History Conference (ESSHC), the Hague, Feb. 27–Mar. 2, 2002.

39. C. F., interview by author, Dobrosloveni, Dec. 29, 2002. Emphasis added.

40. M. N., interview by author, Dobrosloveni, Aug. 28, 2002.

41. See Law no. 2 of 1968 regarding the administrative reorganization of Romania, *Official bulletin of Romania* no. 54–55, Part I, of July 27, 1981.

42. This episode and the verbatim conversation happening at the meeting were told to me by M. N. in the interview quoted above.

43. For a detailed analysis of the circumstances of Gorbachev's campaign against alcoholism, see Tarschys, "Success of a Failure," 12; and Erica Richardson, "The Struggle for Sobriety: Anti-Alcohol Campaign Under Gorbachev and Yeltsin," *Research Papers in Russian and East European Studies* (Birmingham: University of Birmingham, 1990).

44. A.T., interview by author, Dobrosloveni, Aug. 18, 2002.

45. See Sam Beck, "Changing Styles of Drinking: Alcohol Use in the Balkans," *East European Quarterly* 18(4) (1985), 395–413; and Kideckel, "Drinking Up."

46. M. N., interview by author, Dobrosloveni, Aug. 28, 2002.

47. M. O., interview by author, Dobrosloveni, May 16, 2003.

48. Interview with M. N. quoted above.

49. Similar accounts, of course, could be written about other Eastern European countries such as Russia, Poland, Hungary, or Serbia, where alcohol is a key ingredient in social life.

II

The Extraordinary Career of *Feketevágó Úr*

Wood Theft, Pig Killing, and Entrepreneurship in Communist Hungary, 1948–1956

Karl Brown

In February 1955, a recent escapee from Hungary was interviewed at length by a Radio Free Europe staffer. The informant, János S., had fled fearing arrest and interrogation by the secret police, but this was not due to any conspiracy or overt anti-regime activity on his part. In the course of his interview, it came to light that

> János couldn't complain about his livelihood. . . . Every month he brought home 3–4,000 forints. How was this possible? He perpetually had one foot in prison because of his illegal slaughtering [here *fekete vágás*, more commonly *feketevágás*]. It was common knowledge that the penalty for illegally slaughtering one calf was six months in prison; as János did it regularly, he opined that he would be sent up for no less than five years if caught. . . . János was well-known to the population of the countryside for his illegal slaughtering and meat selling. When a farmer had a cow ready to calve, he would call around: "You may sharpen your knife in two weeks, János."—"Okay, bring it at night, when it's born"—was the response. The illegal slaughter took place at night, and János would be distributing the meat by daybreak.[1]

According to János, he had cornered the meat market in his small town; he also dealt profitably in wood harvested illegally from the nearby state forest. In addition to a number of his family members and fellow villagers, his clients included the two local priests, the wives of the local Party secretary and collective farm president, and the local ÁVH (secret police) lieutenant as well as two of his informers. János's income from *feketevágás* and other illicit activities may have been more than twice what a skilled worker could expect to make, and his status in the underground economy was such that his ÁVH customer jokingly addressed him by the mock honorific nickname of *"feketevágó úr,"* or "Mr. Pig-killer."[2] Although János's experience was almost certainly atypical, it illuminates the peculiar mix of historic precedents, informal social networks, and commodification that characterized illegal consumption during the Stalinist period in Hungary.

Stalinist Hungary was not a consumer-friendly environment. The communist regime sought to control all aspects of economic life, strictly curtailing any exchange that did not occur under official auspices. Bent on transforming the nation into "a country of iron and steel," the Party-state channeled the vast majority of investment into heavy industry at the expense of both consumer goods and wages. The result was an economy of scarcity only marginally better than what characterized World War II. The standard of living improved somewhat during the late 1940s—but only in comparison to the postwar devastation of the winter of 1945–46, when denizens of Budapest somehow survived on an average of 1,000 calories per day.[3] The rationing of meat, butter, flour, sugar, and bread that remained in effect into 1949 was reimposed in late 1951. Meanwhile, real wages—having risen to 90 percent of their 1938 level by 1949—fell back down to 66 percent of that mark by 1952.[4] Those Magyars (ethnic Hungarians) who sought to procure, produce, or distribute goods outside of the strict confines of state-sanctioned consumption (i.e., in state-run stores, cafeterias, and so forth) ran the risk of being tried for speculation, black marketeering, or the portmanteau category of "crimes against the public supply" (*közellátás érdekét veszélyeztető bűncselekmény*). Despite these risks, hunger, opportunity, and profit drove Hungarians to operate outside the legal economy.

Although practically all Hungarians participated in some form of illicit economic activity, this was much more feasible in rural Hungary, as the countryside was much less closely policed than Budapest and other urban areas. Most scholars now concur that Hungarian peasants managed to subvert the Party-state's centralization of the economy to some degree: they bargained with and co-opted local officials, used informal social networks based on local and professional connections, and otherwise evaded the state's proscriptions.[5] However, the root causes of this *sub rosa* activity are a more contested issue. Although some scholars hold that the second economy ran on the efforts of a class of interwar "incipient entrepreneurs"—in essence a sort of proto-bourgeoisie, whose development into full-blown capitalists was derailed by the onset of communism—others aver that this economic activity was present at all levels of the Magyar peasantry, and that the values driving it (namely "rampant individualism and utilitarianism" and "a bootstrap mentality") actually evolved in response to the intrusions of the socialist state.[6] Regardless of its origin, the effects of this criminal consumption and entrepreneurship are apparent. As historian Elena Osokina argues for the Soviet case, "The black market pumped goods and raw materials from the legal socialist economy and, to some extent, acted as its parasite in what could be viewed as a kind of economic revenge."[7] In the context of a Stalinist state bent on strictly controlling the economy, this "parasitism" and "economic revenge" became a subtle form of resistance.

This chapter contends that wood theft, pig killing, and the trade in illegal wood and meat reveal three important aspects of economic life under communism. First, the explosion of illegal consumption and entrepreneurship in the countryside grew organically out of both historic practices and responses to state intrusion. Wood theft was a perennial mode of peasant resistance in Hungary as elsewhere; pig killing, on the other hand, was a legal and well-established custom prior to the communist period. Second, all members of rural communities were active participants. János S.'s preeminence in the black market suggests that the "proper peasants"—with their extensive kinship, village, and other connections—were probably more likely to succeed in procuring scarce resources and making a profit on the black market, but the presence of Roma ("Gypsies")[8] in these illicit dealings suggests that opportunities were indeed open to anyone bold enough to seize the opportunity. Finally, and ironically, the attempted centralization of the Hungarian economy not only failed to extirpate but even encouraged economic deviance: both wood theft and pig killing became commodified under communism as never before, and the black market became the site of vibrant, hypercapitalist exchange. Economic life thus acquired a political valence it would have lacked otherwise. Although the black economy did not pose a direct or deliberate challenge to communist rule, it severely complicated—and, arguably, eventually confounded—the economic element of the communist regime's aspiration to total control.

Collectivization and Its Discontents

The communist regime sought to directly control all aspects of economic life in the late 1940s and early 1950s. In the countryside, this took the form of collectivization. Large agricultural enterprises owned and controlled by the state promised control over both agricultural production and the rural population; the surplus labor freed up by the mechanization of agriculture could then be channeled into the cities to swell the ranks of the proletariat. In Hungary, as throughout the rest of East-Central and Eastern Europe, the primary goal of the communist regime was to force peasants off their privately owned farms and into state and collective farms (*termelőszövetkezeti csoport*, or *tszcs*).[9] It did so by a number of means. The communist regime imported the concept of the "kulak" (*kulák* in Hungarian), or the rich peasant who exploits his poorer compatriots, from its Soviet context relatively unchanged.[10] Kulaks were demonized as rentiers, parasites, and holdovers from the bourgeois past; they were singled out for persecution, expropriation, and internment. In Hungary, any peasant who owned more than 25 holds (14.25 hectares) of land fell into this category.[11] More than 140,000 holds of rented land were seized outright from kulaks in September 1948, and the "kulak list" included some 71,600 families altogether.[12] Although kulaks were singled out for special attention by the regime, it made life difficult for all peasants who tried to remain outside the collective farm. Delivery quotas, reestablished in 1946, required richer peasants to yield a greater percentage of their produce to the state than their poorer neighbors.[13] Taxes on private farms were also revised drastically upward, multiplying threefold between 1949 and 1953.[14] When regressive taxation and legal oppression were inadequate, ÁVH troops and Party activists would descend on the village and bully peasants into signing over their property, tools, livestock, and labor to the newly established collective farm. Open resistance, such as strikes and attacks on the agents of state, was the exception rather than the norm.

The court records of rural crime in communist Hungary reveal that this struggle between the state and its unruly subjects was, for the most part, geared toward forcing peasants into the centralized communist economy. Of the four hundred thousand peasants put on trial during the period 1948 to 1950, the bulk were guilty of crimes against the public supply.[15] In 1951, almost three-quarters of all trials were for hoarding grain, illegal trading, and failure to deliver crops, pork, chickens, or eggs; the remainder were for failing to participate in harvesting or sowing.[16] Kulaks were disproportionately represented on this list, accounting for just over half of all these crimes; they also drew stiffer sentences. Of the twenty kulaks tried in the autumn of 1950 by the Kaposvár district court for not delivering their full quota, all drew a one-to-two-year sentence.[17] One Csongrád kulak was found guilty of attempting to hide three quintals (300 kilograms) of grain; he was sentenced to three months in prison and a 1,000 forint fine, a sentence the assessor found "too lenient."[18] Another kulak failed to bring his tractor to the harvest on time; he was sentenced to "only" three months in prison, a 2,000 forint fine, and five years' exclusion from public affairs.[19] By summer 1952, this oppressive system had also provoked what János Rainer terms the first signs of "*mass* rural resistance," in the form of threshers' strikes, refusal to surrender quotas, and even some isolated acts of violence against collections officers[20]—but for the most part, the resistance provoked by the state centered on its attempt to force the rural economy into its top-down, regimented consumption scheme.

"Passive" or covert resistance was a much more viable option than open rebellion, and the Magyar peasantry practiced it assiduously. Nonconfrontational and subtle acts such as theft, sabotage, and dissimulation have been used throughout history by peasants, slaves, and other marginalized or subject populations. These covert practices, or "weapons of the weak," have certain advantages in common, as they eschew direct confrontation with authority and instead employ subterfuge, spontaneity, and informal social networks.[21] To take just one example, arson was a common crime throughout the period. Burning something to the ground—a shed or other building on a collective farm, an unguarded harvester or another piece of state-owned farm machinery, or even the house of a particularly disliked official—could be done covertly at night, with very little chance of arrest or other repercussions. Nationwide, 12,649 arson cases were investigated in the period 1951 to 1955. At the peak of repression in 1952, there were 4,539 arson incidents investigated, or an average of roughly twelve fires per day.[22] Arson was the most spectacular of the weapons of the weak used by Hungarian peasants, but other tactics were more prevalent in their subtle yet effective opposition to the regime.

The Party-state's objectives in the countryside were complicated by two key factors: its presence was relatively weak, and functionaries were unreliable. Villages of three thousand or fewer inhabitants seem to have been visited by police officers only weekly, while towns of up to fifteen thousand had perhaps one or two policemen.[23] The ÁVH was also spread thin in the countryside.[24] In many villages and smaller towns, the Party-state's local representatives consisted of only a handful of beleaguered functionaries and administrators, and as a result these agents of the state often found themselves complicit in circumventing its intentions. One 1956 émigré, a mechanical engineer at a tractor station near Pécs, recalled that "cheating was commonplace at the tractor station, when it came to fulfilling the prescribed norms." Regular machinery inspections were routinely foiled by members of different tractor stations working in cahoots, as "faulty machines were hidden and another station was contacted for the purpose of borrowing repaired machines," which were then "transferred from tractor station to tractor station, preceding the committee of inspectors."[25] Another tractor station worker, this one an agronomist from the Harkány region, recounted the exact same manipulation at his workplace: "Frequently the same machinery was borrowed from station to station, [and] the equipment was then returned after the inspection." This source also echoed the relatively lax enforcement of the administration's will: "Peasants disregarded work contests, paid their taxes late, evaded compulsory jobs and contributions," and stole from the fields on a regular basis.[26]

Over and above whatever sympathies local administrators might have had for their local subjects, they were often simply unable to enforce the regime's program. In short, it was in the vested interest of everyone involved—both members of the administration and the peasants they purportedly controlled— to resort to subterfuge. As István Rév states:

> Those [Party functionaries] who really cooperated with the peasantry
> had the best chances. They allowed the peasants to sell their cows
> on the black market and reported the sudden loss of animals in the
> village; helped the peasants falsify their birth certificates so that
> the population suddenly grew old, and those above 65 years of age
> could qualify for quota reductions; shut their eyes when the peasants
> organized pseudo-cooperatives; tolerated the division of land among
> family members; contributed to hiding animals in the woods or grain
> under the ground. . . . For the members of the apparatus to survive,
> the survival methods of the producers were indispensable.[27]

Thus, in broad terms, rather than a supine and helpless peasantry at the mercy of an omnipotent state, collectivization in Hungary was a complex function of state centralization clashing with peasant interventions complicated by administrative malfeasance. Collectivization was indeed characterized by a large degree of violence and oppression, but it also generated opportunities for autonomous activity and even illegal entrepreneurship—and, because consumer goods were scarce, state policy actually encouraged Hungarians to take matters into their own hands by dealing on the black market. As János S.'s experience reveals, some peasants managed to not only get by but even profit by picking up where the state left off.

János S.'s background and early biography are almost a stereotype of the "proper peasant," and his experience of Stalinization was also typical. Born in 1928, he grew up in the small town his family had lived in for two hundred years.[28] His father had fought in World War I and then entered business as a livestock buyer and dealer in other commodities. János was just young enough to avoid the draft in World War II, and he trained as a butcher's apprentice from 1946 to 1949. He then drifted to Budapest, where he worked a stint in the Mátyás Rákosi Ironworks in Csepel. János returned to his hometown in 1951, when he married and began to dabble in the black market. During this time, one of his cousins was arrested for black marketeering; one of his uncles, labeled a kulak despite his legal status as a working peasant (he owned only 20 holds), was arrested for not fulfilling his delivery quota. János's first run-in with the state apparatus also occurred in that year, when local Party officials seized half of the plot of land left to him by his aunt in America; he was forced to swiftly sell off the other half before it was expropriated as well. To avoid the draft—and possibly the unfriendly attention of the local authorities—he went to work in the mines in Miskolc; he ended up serving a few months in an ÁVH border unit anyway but managed to get himself dismissed as unfit for service after a few months.[29] Returning to his hometown in mid-1953, he devoted himself fully to the profitable, and entirely illegal, trade in wood and meat.

Wood Theft

In Hungary as throughout Europe, the right to harvest wood and other forest resources was a perennial source of conflict between peasants and their landlords. Over time, nobles and other landholders gradually managed to arrogate to themselves all uses of wooded areas, usurping peasant hereditary or customary forest usage rights in the process. The pattern observed by E. P. Thompson in early modern England was prevalent throughout Europe; as the courts regularly ruled in favor of landholders, "the peasantry and the poor employed stealth, a knowledge of every bush and by-way, and the force of numbers." Between the two extremes of the rural hierarchy, the "forest-keepers and under-keepers, who had long supplemented their petty salaries with perquisites, made inroads into the venison, sold off the brushwood and furze, [and] made private arrangements with inn-keepers and pastry-cooks, butchers and tanners."[30] The same patterns are apparent in Hungary, where, by the early nineteenth century, the legal battle over enclosure and forest use had shifted conclusively in the nobles' favor. During the 1848–49 revolution, peasants attempted to reassert these traditional prerogatives; like the Habsburgs, the Hungarian revolutionary government responded with propaganda, arrests, and when those failed, executions.[31] After World War I, the independent and truncated Hungarian state began to encroach on noble prerogatives, setting the precedent for the postwar takeover of all forested land in 1948. Thereafter, Hungarian forests fell under the jurisdiction of the Ministry of State Farms and Forests (*Állami Gazdaságok és Erdők Minisztériuma*, or AGEM). Wood harvesting was restricted and carefully monitored, and forest wardens prowled the forests in pursuit of wood cutters and poachers.

The problem for the regime was that peasant households still relied on wood for heating, cooking, building houses, smoking meat, curing tobacco, and a host of other uses—and forestry workers were poorly paid and no more reliable than the tractor-trading agronomists. Denied the opportunity to harvest wood legally, peasants predictably sought out illegal sources for this necessity. Wood theft swiftly became widespread, to the point where even urban authorities took note: the Budapest police report for autumn 1954 stressed the importance of cracking down on wood thievery and called for closer coordination with the forestry department as well as joint actions by the district investigative forces and the ÁVH.[32] The regime's public portrayals of wood theft suggested that the state forests were closely policed, and its agents reliable monitors. One 1949 photographic essay in *Magyar Rendőr*, the official police magazine, revealed how effective cooperation between the forest warden and police resulted in the swift arrest of the wood thief (a kulak, of course); another story, this one from 1952, involved two kulaks who were likewise collared swiftly and efficiently.[33] Throughout, the official line on forest-resource-related crimes repeatedly drove home these two key themes: that the usual suspects and most likely culprits were almost invariably kulaks, and that AGEM officials, the police, and the courts acted swiftly and efficiently in dispensing justice to these antisocial elements. But the archives tell a different tale. In marked contrast to these success stories, a report issued following a 1952 internal survey of AGEM's operations lamented the widespread corruption, wage fraud, glossing over of mistakes, and other deviations that ran rampant among the forest ministry workers. It closed with a recommendation to monitor ministry activities at least quarterly.[34] A later report, from February 1956, reveals very little improvement, as well as the fact that the majority of forestry workers were untrained and knew very little about forestry science and forests in general. Implicitly, the previous regulatory scheme was inadequate since the latter report ends with a suggestion for monthly rather than quarterly evaluations.[35] In short, peasants continued to steal wood from the state, much as they had from nobles and other local authorities for centuries previously.

János became involved in this illicit wood trade at an ideal time for him and his fellow villagers. The winter of 1953–54 was brutally cold; there was no place in his village to buy wood legally, and even when someone could make the trip to the state store in nearby K., there was often no wood available for purchase. Thus János started scheming well in advance of the 1954–55 winter:

> At the start of September 1954, I happened to make the acquaintance
> of a young forester at the P. state forest. . . . The young forester seemed
> like quite a decent guy [*nagyon rendes embernek látszott*], so I broached
> the topic with him. First I asked him if he wouldn't like to make a little
> extra money. The young forester jumped at the opportunity, and went
> on to tell me that he had already sold wood from the state forest to

many people. He was only concerned that nobody learn his name. The
deal was settled, and I bought 15 quintals [1.5 tons] of wood from him
for 600 forints, which my uncle brought home that very night.

As János tells it, this would have been a one-time deal; however, as the winter
progressed his friends and acquaintances started approaching him for the
scarce commodity—and offering cash up front. He contacted the young forester
once more, who was amenable to further dealings, and so a mutually beneficial
illicit trade in firewood commenced. The young forester harvested 1.5 tons of
wood at a time, for which he received 500 forints per load. János's uncle—who
had access to a truck, probably via a state job—would then transport the wood to
the consumer, for which he would receive 100 forints. János retailed each load
at 800 forints, and therefore grossed 200 forints per trip, only slightly less than
an average week's wage. They sold ten truckloads, or 15 tons, of wood in this
manner over the course of the next few months.[36] This wood theft was carried
out on a massive scale, with relative impunity, and with the collusion of a member of the organization tasked to patrol precisely this type of deviant behavior.

The irony should be clear: rather than crushing this perennial mode of
peasant resistance, the centralized command economy inadvertently enabled
and even encouraged it. Prior to communist rule, peasants stole wood primarily for their own use, and generally only as much as they could carry. Under
communism, they continued stealing wood, but now from state forests rather
than their feudal predecessors—and, in János's case, by the truckload. In essence, the AGEM and rural administration inadvertently encouraged illicit
behavior on the part of the underpaid men and women who worked for them.
Wood was scarce in the first place; its unavailability to the rural population was
compounded by state imperatives for rural control, which required that wood
be purchased at state retail outlets, which were few and far between. This scarcity of firewood generated demand. All that was required was an entrepreneurial middleman to connect the supplier with his potential customers. János
filled this role and thereby made a healthy profit—but only reluctantly, according to him. His reluctance is understandable. Dealing in wood was a significantly higher-profile crime than, and yet nowhere near as lucrative as, his main
source of income: *feketevágás*, or illegal pig killing.

Pig Killing

Then, as now, the pig occupied a central role in the cultural world of the Hungarian peasant. Like wood theft, pig killing was widely practiced in rural Hungary prior to communist rule; the difference was that it was not only legal but,

in the form of the annual pig-killing ceremony (*disznóölés*), a major event "at least as important as Christmas."[37] Although the custom doubtless has earlier antecedents, its widespread observance can be reliably dated back to the start of the twentieth century. One of the many attendant effects of the economic growth of the late Austro-Hungarian Empire was that the native Hungarian pig breeds were supplanted by the more fertile and fatty Serbian *Mangalica* breed. Thereafter, pig husbandry spread rapidly throughout the Hungarian country-side.[38] By the late 1930s, there were 3.1 million pigs in Hungary, as opposed to 1.8 million cattle.[39] Pigs make good economic sense, in fact, since they are rel-atively easy to raise and their feed-to-yield ratio is significantly lower than that of any other common farm animal.[40] Thus, one full-grown (160–180 kilogram) pig supplied enough pork, bacon, and lard to last a peasant family of four all year; wealthier families might slaughter four or five pigs per year.

Killing a pig had social and cultural implications over and above material necessity. The actual slaughter of the pig was a festive event. After the pig's throat was cut, the men spent the rest of the day butchering and drinking heavily, while the women washed the intestines for use as sausage casings, did the rest of the preparation for preserving the meat by smoking and salting, and cooked all day. In addition to providing a year's supply of meat, the *disznóölés* was also an occasion for a feast, generally numbering twelve people or more; although peasant families would usually restrict the guest list to family members (in-cluding some in-laws), they would also send a "taste" of the meat around to their neighbors, seizing the opportunity to strengthen nonkinship bonds—and catch up on gossip—in the process.[41] The significance of pig killing in the Magyar peasantry's *mentalité* is indicated by its regular occurrence in the popular lex-icon. It turns up as a signifier of poverty ("one who does not stick a pig is a real pauper") and also symbolic shorthand for familial closeness (a man who had successfully inveigled his siblings out of their inheritance might find that "he has the land, but can hardly find anyone to stick the pig").[42] Thus pig killings were (and in fact continue to be) a major element of Magyar peasant life, and any attempt to alter the practice was certain to run afoul of entrenched custom.

However, meat was even scarcer than other commodities in immediate postwar communist Hungary.[43] World War II had seriously depleted the na-tional livestock reserves, and collectivization only exacerbated this problem. An abundance of swine, like any conspicuous display of wealth, rendered the owner more likely to be labeled a kulak. As a result, many peasants decided to slaughter their animals instead, choosing a short-term binge (and the chance to make a significant profit, if distributed wisely) over the near certainty that the state would take away their animals. In an effort to head off wholesale slaugh-ter of livestock, the regime established the National Office for Pork and Lard

Distribution as a way to monitor meat and lard collection.[44] The regime required that any peasant slaughtering an animal receive permission from the local authorities to do so, and then turn over the bulk of the meat and other valuable byproducts of the slaughter to this bureau of meat and lard management. To require this of the Magyar peasant was to ask him not only to change one of his most significant cultural practices but also to threaten his self-sufficiency and even his survival. Despite the difficulty of concealing this process—slaughtering and rendering a pig is obviously a lengthy, arduous, and at least briefly very noisy task—collectivization and imposition of communist rule in the countryside was accompanied by a rash of illegal pig killing.

Although specific data for the entire period are unavailable, a report for the week of January 29, 1951, reveals the contours of this legally criminal but socially sanctioned behavior.[45] In that week alone, there were 180 sentences for *feketevágás* passed down: 26 defendants were labeled kulaks, the remainder working peasants. As with other crimes, kulaks got the worst of it. The gender distribution of these common criminals was also significant: fully a quarter of the recipients of sentences passed down for *feketevágás* were women, and from what specific case data are available it appears they were always arrested as part of a group, rather than operating alone. This suggests that the gendered division of labor typifying *disznóölés* carried over into the illegal practice of pig killing under the communist regime. However, in addition to now slaughtering their pigs on the sly, peasants responded to the criminalization of pig killing with at least one other major change in their methods.

Illegal meat flooded the rural underground economy. Historically, *disznóölés* meat had been salted, smoked, and then consumed sparingly by the peasant household so that it would last out the year. *Feketevágás* meat, on the other hand, was evidence of a recently committed crime; and in the meat-scarce Hungarian economy it was also a lucrative commodity on the black market. As he had in the wood trade, János swiftly established himself at the nexus of the illegal meat trade. Because the other four butchers in his town had long since been forced out of business by nationalization of the meat industry, he had no local competition. At least every other week or so, he would acquire an animal—generally a pig, veal calf, or cow—for 150 to 300 forints. He would then slaughter it and sell it off in portions of 12–20 kilos apiece. János's meat was priced to sell, at 12 to 16 forints per kilo—well below the official price of 22.50 forints per kilo. For sheep—available only on the black market in his vicinity—he was able to charge as much as 20 forints per kilo.[46] All in all, a tidy profit. Even if he did not quite make the 3,000 to 4,000 forints per month he bragged about, his illegal activities undoubtedly paid rather well.

The Black Market

Pig killing, like wood theft, was practiced for profit as well as subsistence and on a massive scale throughout the Stalinist period, despite the regime's best efforts to halt it. János's excesses were probably unique, but the available evidence suggests that similar intricate webs of illicit activity were present in most if not all rural regions of communist Hungary. A deposition given at the Sárospatak police department in summer 1951 gives some sense of how the black trade in meat was practiced in this region. G. J. testified that on an evening toward the end of 1950, his acquaintance B. showed up on his doorstep and told him to grab his coat, as they were going to purchase some meat:

> I got in the car and we drove out to M. P.'s place, where we went into a room and B. started haggling over the price with him. . . . I also recall that comrade B. and M. P. discussed the possibility of taking pigs from the neighboring [collective farm]. B. wanted to come back the next day with the car.[47]

In the absence of any supporting evidence, the motives behind depositions such as these are impossible to determine: jealousy and coercion (with ideological rectitude or guilt coming in a distant third) are equally likely. What this report does reveal is the casual manner in which these peasants discussed not only their trade but also the possibility of theft from the state farm; conversations such as these were presumably commonplace.

The available court records support the conclusion that pig killings and the trade in illegal meat were indeed widespread phenomena, persisting throughout the period despite the regime's increasingly draconian prosecution of *feketevágás* and related economic crimes. The monthly report from April 1953 reveals both the widespread nature and the more severe prosecution of the illegal meat trade. In this month, 787 sentences were passed down.[48] Hungary had almost run out of kulaks by this point; they constituted fewer than 6 percent of these convictions. As in 1951, roughly two-thirds of all sentences were for less than six months. What is different from the earlier period was that the monetary penalties were now much higher (almost half of them were over 1,000 forints; 82 percent of the prison sentences were saddled with a fine or property confiscation as well), and the penalties for the worst offenders were absurdly stringent. S. K., a Nagykálló seasonal worker, was caught selling two calves he had slaughtered illegally; he received a 2,000 forint fine, had another 2,000 forints' worth of property confiscated, and was sentenced to three and a half years in prison. J. T., a Debrecen seasonal worker and ex-teamster, was found guilty of slaughtering more than twenty animals and selling the meat; his sentence was 2,000 forints and five years. The stiffest penalty in this report—and, in all likelihood, the most extreme punishment meted out for this crime in the entire period—fell on F. V., a kulak from Nagyatád who was found guilty of killing and selling eleven veal calves. He paid a 2,000 forint fine, had all his property confiscated, and was sentenced to eight years in prison.[49] *Feketevágás* was illegal, and selling the meat gained thereby even more so—but these were also potentially lucrative practices, and they were practiced by peasants throughout communist Hungary.

The other key aspect of this illegal trade, to return to the specific case of János S., is that his individual activities were only the tip of the iceberg in his small town: everyone he knew, at all levels of the rural social hierarchy, was complicit in his and similar schemes. He recounted a number of schemes his neighbors and acquaintances used to cheat the state: peasants being forced to sell their cows or pigs to the state farm at ridiculously low prices would instead injure the animals and then slaughter them "in an emergency"; animals were reported stolen and then slaughtered, carved up, and eaten or sold off before the police arrived. Perhaps the most interesting scam János recounted took

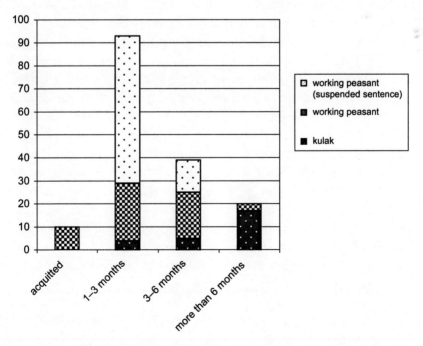

FIGURE II.I.   *Feketevágás* arrests, week ending Jan. 29, 1951.

place after disease struck a number of swine at a neighboring state farm; the peasants bought the corpses from the swineherd, reported the deaths of their animals, showed the local officials the carcasses of the diseased pigs, and then slaughtered and sold their healthy animals.[50] János, like *feketevágók* in other villages, relied on the pervasive and widespread collusion of their entire communities. Among the reasons for János's success was that his customers ran the gamut from his friends and neighbors, to priests, to the local authorities; nobody wanted to arrest the butcher who killed the golden calf. With supply and demand both accounted for by a steady stream of contacts derived from kinship ties and the village social network, all János required was a cogent distribution scheme. He hit upon the solution of using Roma as intermediaries in his illegal cottage industry, and their presence in this illicit web of consumption and entrepreneurship suggests that the criminalization of independent economic activity led to opportunities for illegal profit and consumption not only for "proper peasants" such as János but for all inhabitants of rural Hungary.

Oddly enough, during this time period the Roma had perhaps less incentive than any other group to engage in illegal activity, because they were actually beneficiaries of communist rule to some degree. Previously, the story of the Roma in Hungary—as throughout Central and Eastern Europe—is one of incessant marginality punctuated with interludes of outright oppression. They managed to eke out a precarious existence by means of various skilled and itinerant crafts (metalsmithing, woodworking, etc.) where possible. They also lived off illegal activity (theft, black marketeering, and so on), which—combined with their distinctive appearance, dress, and customs—resulted in pejorative cultural stereotypes and ill treatment by society and the courts.[51] Given the heightened and racialized nationalism of the early twentieth history, these stereotypes operated to predictable and lethal effect during World War II: large numbers of Roma were exterminated in the Holocaust (*Poṛajmos* in Romani).[52] Thus, the Hungarian attempt under communist rule to integrate the Roma into society was unprecedented in the region's history. Schooling, housing, combating anti-Roma sentiment through propaganda, and above all integration into the proletariat were the four planks of the Party's Roma program.[53] They were encouraged to join the armed forces, the ÁVH, and the local administration; schools and cultural opportunities were extended to the Roma settlements (*cigánytelepek*) on the outskirts of villages. All things considered, Roma stood to benefit from following the state's directives.

Not surprisingly, however, the regime's official policy toward the Roma was executed lackadaisically at best. A 1956 report from the legal branch of the administrative department, titled "On the Resolution of the Gypsy Question," summed up the paltry accomplishments to date: although many Roma had joined the Party and others were now working in collective farms and various other industries, very few other changes had occurred. Of the roughly 130,000 Roma then living in Hungary, fully 80,000 remained in Roma settlements, while another 8,000 had no permanent address (in itself a remarkable admission for a regime that prided itself on monitoring its populace so closely). Life in the *cigánytelep* (Roma settlement) was still far from ideal, since most were overcrowded and lacked running water and electricity. In addition, the illiteracy rate among Roma was generally still around 90 percent. According to the report, the cultural and moral development of the Roma was also a matter of some concern. Unmarried couples frequently lived together, and polygamy and incest were commonplace.[54] The regime's attempt to "civilize" the Roma met with only partial success—but this official favoritism, coupled with traditional modes of Roma behavior, opened up entirely new opportunities for illicit profit.

According to one 1955 Radio Free Europe informant, the Roma settlement at Felsőrajk was undergoing a veritable "golden age of the gypsies" ("A *cigányság aranykora*"). Although sanitary conditions remained substandard, they had improved somewhat since the war; Roma children had a school, and practically every family owned a cart and a horse or two. This community of twenty families relied on woodworking for its primary source of income until 1948, when it became impossible for them to acquire wood legally. This drove the Felsőrajk Roma entirely into the shadow economy, but after one of them was able to obtain a position on the local council at Zalaegerszeg they experienced little trouble with the law and were even able to harvest wood on the sly—from the nearby state forest, of course.[55] Another Roma, an eighteen-year-old youth from Bácsalmás, reported his successes as a peddler: despite his prior record (arrested in 1954 for selling goods without a license) he was able to obtain a trade license with very little difficulty from the local council and supported his six-person family by traveling to trade fairs throughout the region.[56]

Administrative reports on "Gypsy criminality" (*cigánybűnözés*) echo these firsthand accounts of deviant economic behavior, with officials describing Roma as prone to wood theft, robbery, work shirking, and above all being simply far too mobile, since "they acquire one form of travel documents or another and then use that to justify their going from village to village, being vagrants and stealing."[57] Accustomed as they were to operating on the margins of society and the official economy, the Roma were perhaps less disadvantaged than the ordinary Magyar peasant when, under the communist system, entire branches of the rural economy became criminalized.

János employed a number of Roma in his illicit meat-selling schemes. He used them as "front" buyers for animals when possible and also as "runners" for distributing the meat after the slaughter. In this manner he managed to

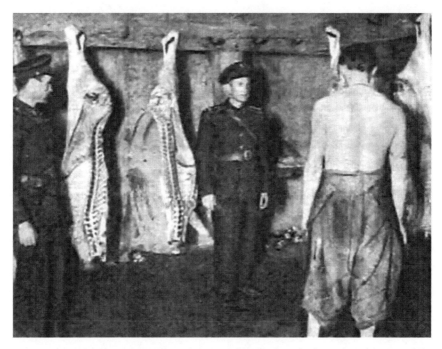

FIGURE 11.2.   A *Feketevágó* caught in the act. From *Magyar Rendőr,* Sept. 8, 1951.

divert the majority of the risk involved in pig running onto his partners in crime, much as he used the AGEM forester and his uncle as cutouts in his wood thievery. The Roma in his region were not as well off as in the communities of Felsőrajk or Bácsalmás, so they were willing to work for a few kilos of meat, intestines, and some wine.[58] The most important point is that this was a niche economic role that did not exist prior to communism; although many roles in the underground economy were based on preexisting informal social networks, this intermediary role was actually created by the regime's attempts to regulate the economy.

Consumption, Entrepreneurship, and Resistance

It was too good to last. Perhaps János S. cheated someone in a deal or was ratted out by a fellow villager. In any case, toward the end of 1954 he was getting careless. His dealings in wood had progressed past the circle of his immediate acquaintances. He became similarly nonchalant about maintaining secrecy and deniability in the pig trade, what with customers knocking on his door day and night.[59] In any case, his black-marketeering career came to an abrupt end one night in late 1954. As János tells it, a black jeep pulled up in front of his house and several ÁVH officers emerged, just as he was carving up a slaughtered calf; it was obvious the jig was up. János somehow managed to give them the slip and—abandoning his wife—walked to Nyíregyháza, caught a night train to Budapest, and from there made his way into Austria.[60] His intention, as he explained it to his RFE interviewer, was to somehow make his way to America and go into business there. With this, he vanished from the historical record forever.

What, then, are we to make of his story? János may have exaggerated his income and certain other minor aspects of his account, but his story, taken in conjunction with the archival evidence, rings true. The regime's economic policy was both unpopular and poorly executed, which legitimized and enabled illicit behavior. Peasants drew on a long tradition of stubborn resistance to outside authority and informal social networks as they responded through various means: occasionally by torching unguarded state possessions and attacking collections officers, but more often by hiding their harvests, falsifying their records, and participating in the illegal economy as both producers and consumers. Deploying these "weapons of the weak" was made much easier by collusion at the local level; administrators were far more likely to obey their immediate needs than the unrealistic directives issuing from Budapest.

More specifically, the crimes of wood theft and *feketevágás* reveal the stubborn persistence of the past and as well the unexpected consequences of postwar communist rule. Like its predecessors, the communist state was largely unable to halt the centuries-old practice of wood theft; peasants were swift to realize the limits of the state's surveillance and co-opt its local representatives. Criminalizing pig killing would have generated a cultural backlash regardless, but in the context of the meat-scarce rural economy it was tantamount to inviting the peasants to embark on lives of crime. The central irony in both of these forms of Stalinist-era peasant resistance is that they were practiced not only for subsistence, as they were in the past, but now also for exchange. Wood theft was previously small-scale, and pig killing vested with symbolic significance; under communism, the practices not only persisted but were commodified. In attempting to establish a socialist economy, the state actually provoked capitalist and consumerist tendencies among the peasantry.

As newly commodified products, wood and pork were traded on the black market. Those involved in the trade came from all walks of rural life, and although the rich or middle peasant's extended networks of kinship and village relations were conducive to his (or her) illicit interactions, criminal entrepreneurship and consumption became an option open to all ranks of the social hierarchy. The black market challenged the regime's control of the economy even as it provided scarce goods for many Hungarians. As the case of János S. shows, it even enabled some of them to prosper. It also made willing accomplices of local administrators (and agents of the secret police) as they became enmeshed in these illegal webs of exchange; their desires as consumers trumped their obligations as agents of the state.

Although wood theft, pig killing, and black marketeering were in all likelihood not practiced as a deliberate means of resistance, their results were significant to a degree that belies their quotidian character. As István Rév describes Hungary's "goulash communism" of the 1980s: "From a closer look, all the important and long-lasting economic and social reforms in all the Central European countries [after 1956] appear as nothing but the legalization of already existing illegal or semilegal practices."[61] These everyday forms of resistance never would have overthrown the state on their own, but practiced assiduously and cautiously over time they allowed many Hungarians (and other Eastern Europeans) opportunities for individual profit even as they eroded the regime's legitimacy. Thus wood theft, pig killing, black-market dealings, and other so-called weapons of the weak may not have been as spectacular as those better known forms of resistance played out in the cities of the Eastern Bloc and led by established dissidents, but they may well have been more effective in the long run.

NOTES

1. Open Society Archives, Central European University, HU-300-4-2, Master Evaluation Items (hereafter OSA/RFE Items) 1370/55, microfilm roll (hereafter "mf") 52, 5. All translations from Hungarian are my own unless otherwise noted.

2. OSA/RFE 2743/55, mf 52, 3. "Speaking Bolshevik" in Hungary would have required use of the class-conscious *"elvtárs"* ("comrade") in place of the bourgeois *"úr"* ("sir" or "Mr.").

3. József Kővágó, *Budapest on the Threshold of Winter 1945–46: Report on General Conditions in the City* (Budapest: Budapest Székesfőváros Házinyomdája, 1945), 40.

4. Ignác Romsics, *Hungary in the Twentieth Century* (Budapest: Corvina/Osiris, 1999), 280–81.

5. See especially Martha Lampland, *The Object of Labor: Commodification in Socialist Hungary* (Chicago: University of Chicago Press, 1995), Iván Szelényi, *Socialist Entrepreneurs: Embourgeoisement in Rural Hungary* (Madison: University of Wisconsin Press, 1988); Marida Hollos and Bela C. Maday, eds. *New Hungarian Peasants: An East Central European Experience with Collectivization* (New York: Columbia University Press, 1983); and Joseph D. Held, *The Modernization of Agriculture: Rural Transformation in Hungary, 1848–1975* (Boulder: East European Monographs, 1980), part VII. There are also a number of useful case studies, e.g., Ildiko Vasary, *Beyond the Plan: Social Change in a Hungarian Collectivized* Village (Boulder: Westview, 1988); Peter D. Bell, *Peasants in Socialist Transition: Life in a Collectivized Hungarian Village* (Berkeley: University of California Press, 1984); C. M. Hann, *Tázlár: A Village in* Hungary

(Cambridge: Cambridge University Press, 1980); and Edit Fél and Tamás Hofer, *Proper Peasants: Traditional Life in a Hungarian Village* (New York: Wenner-Gren Foundation, 1969).

6. See Szelényi, *Socialist Entrepreneurs*, 4, 210; and Lampland, *Object of Labor*, 333, 1–2.

7. Elena Osokina, "Economic Disobedience Under Stalin," in Lynne Viola, ed., *Contending with Stalinism: Soviet Power and Popular Resistance in the 1930s* (Ithaca, NY: Cornell University Press, 2002), 198.

8. A note on etymology: I use "Roma" throughout, as most scholars now concur that "Gypsy" has a pejorative connotation. The latter term is a corruption of "Egyptian" in Western European languages (French, *gitan*; Spanish, *gitano*), based on misapprehension of where the Roma originated; the Hungarian word for Roma, *cigány*, is derived from the Greek *athinganos*, or 'heathen,' as in German (*Zigeuner*) or many Slavic languages (*tsigan, cigan*). Donald Kendrick, *The Romani World* (Hertfordshire: University of Hertfordshire Press, 2004), 1.

9. The *tszcs* is the Hungarian equivalent of the Soviet *kolkhoz*. There were three gradations of collective organization in Hungary, ranging from sharing only tools to complete assimilation of one's goods and land into the communal pool; see Lampland, *Object of Labor*, 145 and 188, for a more detailed explanation of these differences. As Romsics notes, both state farms and collective farms were directly subject to the National Planning Office, and the distinctions between these categories are therefore largely formal for our purposes. Romsics, *Hungary in the Twentieth Century*, 278.

10. See Moshe Lewin, *Russian Peasants and Soviet Power: A Study of Collectivization* (New York: Norton, 1975), 490–91.

11. The cadastral hold was the standard unit of land measurement in Hungary after 1851; it measured 1.42 acres, or 0.57 hectares. The minimum viable area for peasant subsistence is a matter of some debate among historians of Hungarian agriculture, and it varied by region. Bell, *Peasants in Socialist Transition*, 29; and Lampland, *Object of Labor*, 38, both concur on the 5–10 hold minimum. This minimum viable area was higher on the Alföld, where extensive cereal crops were the norm; Fél and Hofer suggest 15–20 holds per family in the village of Átány; (*Proper Peasants*, 56).

12. Swain, 42; Balogh, ed., *Nehéz Esztendők Krónikája*, 30.

13. On this point see Lampland, *Object of Labor*, 141–44.

14. Romsics, 277.

15. Valéria Révai, ed., *Törvénytelen Szocializmus* (Budapest: Zrínyi Kiadó/Új Magyarország, 1991), 85.

16. Hungarian National Archive (Magyar Országos Levéltár, hereafter "MOL") M-KS-276. f. 96 (Iü) / 14 ő.e., 228.

17. MOL M-KS-276. f. 96 (Iü) / 2 ő.e., 40.

18. MOL M-KS-276. f. 96 (Iü) / 8 ő.e., 68.

19. MOL M-KS-276. f. 96 (Iü) / 8 ő.e., 77a. One quintal equals 100 kilograms.

20. János M. Rainer, "The New Course in Hungary in 1953," Working Paper no. 38, Washington, DC: Cold War International History Project, 2002, 1. My italics.

21. John C. Scott, *Weapons of the Weak: Everyday Forms of Peasant Resistance* (New Haven, CT: Yale University Press, 1985), xvi.

22. MOL M-KS-276. f. 96 (F) / 70 ő.e., 314a.

23. See, for example, OSA/RFE Items 8670/53, mf 27, OSA/RFE Items 19/54, mf 32, and OSA/RFE Items 8851/54, mf 44.

24. József Parádi, ed., *A Magyar Rendvédelem Története* (Budapest: Szemere Bertalan Magyar Rendvédelem-történeti Tudományos Társaság, 1996), 144.

25. Columbia University Hungary Refugee Project, Bakhmeteff Archive, Columbia Rare Books and Manuscript Library (hereafter CUHRP), Interview 402, Box 13, 28–29.

26. CUHRP Interview 406, Box 13, 36–37, 49, 28.

27. István Rév, "The Advantages of Being Atomized: How Hungarian Peasants Coped with Collectivization," *Dissent*, Summer 1987: 339.

28. The following is a summary of the copious biographical data collected by his RFE interviewer in OSA/RFE Items 1370/55, mf 50. János was interviewed on three separate occasions between March and May 1955.

29. OSA/RFE Items 1370/55, mf 50, 5–7.

30. E. P. Thompson, *Customs in Common* (New York: New Press, 1993), 103, 104.

31. Istvan Deak, *The Lawful Revolution: Louis Kossuth and the Hungarians, 1848–49* (London: Phoenix Press, 2001), 50, 116–17.

32. Budapest Municipal Archive (Budapest Fővárosi Leveltárá, or BFL) XXXV. 95. e / 107 ő.e., "Intézkedési terv," 3.

33. "Fát lopott a kulák," *Magyar Rendőr*, Oct. 1, 1949; "Az erdőirtó kulák," *Magyar Rendőr*, May 17, 1952.

34. MOL M-KS-276. f. 96 / 331 ő.e, 2.

35. MOL M-KS-276. f. 96 / 331 ő.e, 3, 5.

36. OSA/RFE Items 3534/55, mf 53, 2–3. János did not reveal the name of his source to his RFE interviewer either.

37. Fél and Hofer, *Proper Peasants*, 160.

38. The meatier, but also more labor-intensive, Yorkshire strain was slow to catch on in Hungary, accounting for only about 15 percent of the national stock in 1911; Romsics, 22.

39. In this regard, Hungary is unique: every other Central European country had many more cows than pigs in the interwar years. M. C. Kaser and E. A. Radice, *The Economic History of Eastern Europe 1919–1975* (Oxford: Clarendon Press, 1985), Vol. 1, 200.

40. On this point, see Richard A. Lobban, Jr., "Pigs and Their Prohibition," *International Journal of Middle East Studies* 26(1) (1994): 65.

41. Fél and Hofer, *Proper Peasants*, 119, 206. Bell notes that after one 1951 pig killing the family distributed "tastes" to twenty-three other families (*Peasants in Socialist Transition*, 226).

42. Fél and Hofer, *Proper Peasants*, 257, 276. On this point, see also Bell, *Peasants in Socialist Transition*, 76; and Lampland, "Pigs, Party Secretaries, and Private Life in Communist Hungary," *American Ethnologist* 18(3) (1991): 459–79.

43. In 1953, the average Eastern European consumed about 17.6 kilograms of meat. Although this was slightly better than in the USSR (17.2 kilograms), it was still a third less than the prewar average and compared miserably to the American standard of 70 kilograms per annum. "The 'New Course' and the Livestock Economy in the Soviet Bloc." CIA/RR IM-397, Sept. 17, 1954, 1, 10, This document is available online by searching http://www.foia.ucia.gov/ (accessed Aug. 8, 2007).

44. *Magyar Közlöny*, Sept. 25, 1948.

45. MOL M-KS 276. 96 (Iü) / 8 ő.e., 156–211.

46. OSA/RFE Items 2743/55, mf 52, 3.

47. MOL M-KS-276. f. 96 (Iü) / 5 ő.e., 123, 124–125.

48. Both the 1951 weekly and 1953 monthly figures suggest an average of about 750 *feketevágás* convictions per month, which translates to 9,000 cases per year for the period of high Stalinism.

49. These men probably did not serve their full sentences; many of them would have been pardoned in 1953, and after 1956 the Kádár regime had much larger fish to fry. MOL M-KS-276. f. 96 (Iü) / 17 ő.e., 123.

50. OSA/RFE Items 2743/55, mf 52, 9.

51. Ian Hancock neatly sums up the bind Roma found themselves in: "Forbidden to do business with shopkeepers, the Roma have had to rely upon subsistence theft to feed their families; and thus stealing has become a part of the stereotype. Forbidden to use town pumps or wells, denied water by fearful householders, uncleanliness becomes part of the stereotype." Roma culture is traditionally also very wary of outsiders, which was conducive to their self-marginalization. "Introduction," in Crowe and Kolsti, eds., *The Gypsies of Eastern Europe* (New York: Sharpe, 1991), 6.

52. As with all casualty figures for the Holocaust, this number is widely debated. Some estimates place the number as high as 1–1.5 million. See Crowe, "Hungary," 119, and Hancock, "Chronology," 21, both in Crowe and Kolsti, eds., *Gypsies of Eastern Europe*.

53. Michael Stewart, *The Time of the Gypsies* (Boulder: Westview Press, 1997), 97.

54. MOL M-KS-276. f. 96 (Iü) / 49 ő.e., passim.

55. OSA/RFE Items 7549/55, mf 58.

56. OSA/RFE Items 5459/55, mf 55.

57. MOL M-KS-276. f. 96 (Iü) / 49 ő.e., 543, 538–39.

58. OSA/RFE Items 2743/55, mf 52, 4.

59. OSA/RFE Items 2743/55 mf 52, 2.

60. According to János, he managed to distract them and then slip out the back. A bribe seems more likely. His wife did not figure largely in his story throughout. OSA/RFE Items 1370/55 mf 50, 5–6.

61. Rév, "Advantages of Being Atomized," 324.

12

Keeping It Close to Home

Resourcefulness and Scarcity in Late Socialist and Postsocialist Poland

Małgorzata Mazurek

"This is just everyday life for us," answered a Warsaw sociologist in 1982 when asked why the informal economy received little attention from the social sciences. His interlocutor was an American anthropologist, Janine Wedel, who had come to Poland to study how Poles manage their day-to-day circumstances under restrictions of martial law and shortage-driven consumption. For a curious Western observer, the seemingly banal and gray landscape of early 1980s Warsaw, with its queuing committees and the incessant finagling and hunting for basic food staples, might indeed have been an intriguing object of inquiry. "For almost everyone in Poland, even the intellectual elite, private arrangements are a way of life," wrote Wedel in her ethnographic diary. "My introduction was an education in the ways of informal give and take, in the ways of a society which is extremely sophisticated in terms of individual need and help."[1]

Wedel was struck by what others in Poland found to be commonplace during the crisis years of state socialism: the rich world of social skills based on family ties that enabled people to cope with omnipresent shortages. The "Polish crisis," a period of economic slump during the late 1970s and 1980s, was a crisis of the centrally planned regime of consumption. But at the same time it constituted the revival of other forms of provisioning and procuring goods, including that organized by one's family (together with their circle of friends) and for one's family. What Wedel dubbed "familial society" was a consumer society in which family members formed a socioeconomic unit cooperating through private arrangements in a semi-official economy.[2]

As economic collapse led to the privatization of consumption, self-help garden plots replaced self-service shops, and the informal economy became a dominant vehicle for consumption.[3] Historically, postwar Poland, devastated by the Nazi and Soviet occupations, turned toward consumption-oriented growth only in the first half of the 1970s. The Polish version of "goulash communism," encouraged by First Party Secretary Edward Gierek, led to significant material improvement. From 1970 to 1975, individual consumption increased by 50 percent and individual income by 59 percent; private farmers, who constituted almost one-third of the population, for the first time received the right to social security.[4] This short period of prosperity, credited to a large degree to foreign loans, also raised the public's expectations of the Party-state, which claimed that Poland was the tenth leading industrial power in the world. The next few years, which followed the global oil crisis, proved Gierek a skilled propagandist. Rather than getting what they had been promised, Poles faced worsening conditions.[5]

Introduction of sugar rationing in 1976 and meat, shoes, and cigarette rationing in 1981, and most importantly the emergence of the Solidarity mass movement, proved the economic and political bankruptcy of the Polish communist state. For Party officials, who introduced martial law in December 1981 under the pretense of restoring political order and combating economic chaos, it was evident that there was no way back to any previously tested forms of a centrally planned economy. But it was not clear to them what should come next. For the citizen-consumer, the "Polish crisis" of the 1980s meant continuation of or else retreat into different forms of self-help, as well as more or less legal forms of entrepreneurship. Having been thrown back on their own resources, Poles turned to their family networks, which, contrary to the Party-state, remained trustworthy and efficient. During the explosion of the unofficial economy in the 1980s, informal structures and arrangements filled the gray zone between state socialism and the grassroots market economy, contributing to fragmentation of the system.

This chapter traces family-centered resourcefulness, so central to this period in Poland as well as, in varying forms, elsewhere in the Eastern Bloc. It demonstrates how crucial it is to understanding the history of consumption in communist Poland and the gradual transition toward post-1989 economic regimes. Resourcefulness, based on "familial society," created alternative economies but at the same time soaked up Party-state resources, or certainly reshaped them, and in so doing changed the overall meaning of politics, society, work, and consumption.[6] Moreover, social patterns of resourcefulness, structured around World War II occupations and developed under the shortage economy, did not stop making sense after 1989.[7] When scarcity shifted from consumption to the job market, family resourcefulness—both as an everyday discourse and as a performative act—continued to be the most common way to cope with these difficulties. From the post-1989 perspective, the wit and flexibility associated with different ways of "jumping the queue" did not become just a symbol of nostalgia. To the contrary, the consumer flexibility of Poland's communist crisis years symbolized meaningful social practices and narratives in the post-1989 crises to come.

To be sure, the lived experience of a shortage economy is not a new topic. Eastern European economists depicted the experience as an individually chosen repertoire of social tactics or strategies within a system of politically generated waste and lack.[8] Historians of consumption in Central and Eastern Europe said a lot about how political regimes tried to forge new consumer identities and how class and gender-oriented consumption of the postwar era shifted toward the family-focused social policies of the 1970s.[9] Still, how families experienced and gave meaning to resourcefulness remains an untold story.[10] This chapter presents two family cases based on unique comparative ethnographic material, tracing how family and consumption intertwined over the past thirty years in Poland. It demonstrates how resourcefulness linked the experience of a shortage economy with the postsocialist economic crises in Poland.

The Czyżyk and the Orłowski families, whom I interviewed in 2006 together with ten other families, were an advantageous choice since rich material already exists about their everyday lives from the years 1978–1980. This chapter explores how they understood and practiced resourcefulness both as family members and as consumers. Revealingly, the notion of resourcefulness turned out to be central, not only because it was a concept frequently used by Polish sociologists since the 1980s, but also because the Czyżyks and the Orłowskis discussed their lives using the same key vocabulary of "resourcefulness," "entrepreneurship," and "creativity."

The Sociology of Lifestyles Revisited

Like most generalizations, Janine Wedel's observation from 1982 that the social sciences in Poland did not focus on the everyday economy was both right and wrong. On the one hand, it was correct since the functionalist, "quantitative sociology," consisting of large surveys and scientific forecasts, belonged to the mainstream of Polish sociology in the 1970s.[11] This kind of research provided interesting statistical evidence, based mostly on Western theoretical models, about the social values of the time. Still, it did not offer explanations about the lived reality.[12] On the other hand, Wedel's conclusion was imprecise, or rather, premature. The linguistic and antipositivist turn arrived in Polish academia in the late 1970s and flourished in the 1980s. This new paradigm brought about a revival of so-called qualitative sociology by introducing research on everyday life, explorations of hidden patterns in society, oral interviews, and ethnographic fieldwork. In this vein, Andrzej Siciński's research group on lifestyles in 1978–1980 conducted a series of interviews with and observations among seventy families from three midsized, highly industrialized cities: Bydgoszcz, Gdańsk, and Lublin.[13]

Originally the project on lifestyles was designed as a comparative study between Poland and Finland during the modernization boom of the mid-1970s. It assumed that "Poland had to be on the path towards 'consumer socialism,' 'a developed socialist society' as it was called by political-theoretical 'experts.'" "Socialist countries," Siciński explained, "were aiming at the consumption levels and patterns of the capitalist countries, though under very different sociopolitical arrangements."[14] However, what his group encountered during the fieldwork a few years later was far from scientific discourse on the "socialist way of life," which saw society determined by modern consumption, scientific progress, and social homogenization.[15] In the end, the sociologists abandoned the concept of a "socialist way of life." This allowed them to discover a social world of private arrangements, informal economies, and family-centered society.

Politically, the dossiers of the seventy Polish families, together with sociological analyses of the data, contained a lot of subversive material that, after the introduction of martial law in 1981, could not be published.[16] Siciński's research revealed the social costs exacted on families struggling to maintain their standard of living. The domination of a day-to-day routine was a feature of most people's lifestyles, whereby the logistics of coping in the everyday obliterated any planning for the future. This was even more so the case in women's lives. "They describe everyday life in Poland as 'different shades of grey,'" recalled one of the research members.[17]

Whether this landscape of "familial society" should be narrated as a waning of the state socialist project or as a historical anthropology of economic crisis is a question of perspective. My revisit to the Czyżyks, the Orłowskis, and other families from Siciński's original research pool gave me an opportunity to explore the latter path of inquiry and look for linkages between socialism and postsocialism through the lens of consumer resourcefulness. It provided a view into what had happened since 1980, that is, how everyday life had changed after Solidarity (1980–81), the consequent martial law, the liberal reforms of the last communist government (the Rakowski government, 1987–1989), the early 1990s market economy, and the contemporary era of global capitalism.[18] It also allowed me to observe, under controlled circumstances, how the experiences of the last thirty years influenced biographic narrations about the supply crisis and everyday life under a socialist economy.

The Czyżyks and the Orłowskis had much in common: the fathers belonged to a tradition of skilled labor, and the mothers came to Bydgoszcz from the village (when they were not at home with their children, these women worked in local industries and services). In both families, in 1978–79, the second generation was in their early twenties and starting adult life without children or their own place to live. In this second phase of interviews, they had their own families and houses, and so the conversations took place in their respective living spaces. Middle-aged interviewees also introduced the third generation, born in the 1980s, now teenagers and students.

The Czyżyks

In 1979 the Czyżyks lived in a family house on the outskirts of the city of Bydgoszcz.[19] Two, and sometimes even three, cars were the most characteristic element of the property since Romuald Czyżyk, his son, and his daughter's husband all worked as taksówkarz bagażowy, or "baggage taxi drivers." The taksówka bagażowa was a peculiar means of transport in communist Poland. Thanks to a lack of professional moving companies and delivery services for the public, transport of goods for individuals had to be carried out by large taxi cars.[20] Being a taxi driver became a family tradition in the 1970s, and indeed it was a very lucrative family business: "one trained the other, since everyone knew there was clearly a different kind of money [to be made with this than] at a state job."[21]

Romuald Czyżyk came from a Warsaw working-class family. He was born in Denmark before World War I, where his father had migrated, looking for work. After his return to Warsaw, his father bought a house, but soon after his savings evaporated during the economic collapse of the early 1920s. From that time on, the family remembered poverty and unemployment, but they also remembered having once possessed a house. Purchasing a property became the main purpose in Romuald's life, and his professional career was devoted to that aim. After World War II, he settled in Bydgoszcz and became a streetcar driver. On the streetcar, he met his future wife, Alicja, a trained seamstress, who moved to Bydgoszcz from a village in the Poznań district. Romuald and Alicja got married in 1949, and their children were born in the following years:

two sons—one of whom became a soldier, the other a taxi driver—and their daughter, Grażyna, who now works in the sales branch of the confection company Jutrzenka.[22]

The life of the Czyżyks was relatively modest during the first twenty years after World War II, as they lived in an apartment with coal heating. Until the mid-1960s, Alicja raised the children and earned additional money working at home assembling handbags. During the following ten years she worked for a leather industry plant, and then in a textile cooperative. As both Alicja and her daughter, Grażyna, claimed, in spite of communist prodding women's employment was not welcomed by the head of the family; women were supposed to be around the house and "serve the men." Hence, Alicja stopped working as soon as the family bought a house with a garden.

By the 1970s, Romuald had left his public service job and moved to the private sector. The main obstacle to achieving this aim was not lack of capital—it was enough to buy a used car—but an informal system of quasi-feudal corporatism: Romuald could become a member of the baggage drivers' "guild" only with a recommendation from an "insider." Once that happened, the Czyżyk family finally gained access to an independent economic life. By joining a closed group of private taxi drivers, Romuald and his family climbed socially from their former working-class status to the exclusive group of the private entrepreneur (*prywaciarz*). Being a taxi driver under communism meant the kind of profits about which their counterparts in capitalist economies could only dream. Hence the Czyżyks became the beneficiaries of an odd combination of state socialist and informal guild systems; the prior meant a deficit (but not liquidation) of private services, while the latter controlled membership and thus ensured the exclusivity of the taxi driver occupation. These two factors allowed keeping both wages and service prices high. Functioning in a privileged group allowed the family to realize their dreams and anticipate a better future.

In the 2006 interview, during my revisit to the second generation of the Czyżyks, Romuald's daughter, Grażyna, and her husband, Jerzy, stressed the importance of private entrepreneurship as a family strategy to get by and even prosper. The family's resourcefulness and determination, to use their words, protected them as consumers, though not entirely, from the shortage economy. More precisely, Grażyna and Jerzy talked about long lines, supply shortages, and food rations in connection with resourcefulness or, as they often called it, "*kombinowanie*" (loosely translated as "finagling"). *Kombinowanie* was also an inherent element of the private taxi driver's occupation; it helped, for example, in negotiating with gas stations for extra fuel or as a way to avoid taxes. According to Grażyna and Jerzy, "it was necessary to finagle in those times": in their opinion, "*chachmęcenie*" (swindling) was a typical characteristic of the Pole and not only the private entrepreneur ("private entrepreneurs might have been swindlers, but they were certainly not thieves"). *Chachmęcenie* and *kombinowanie* were persistent elements in the life stories of the second generation of Czyżyks.

In the crisis years of the 1980s, resourcefulness was applied to the realm of attaining everyday consumer products as well. According to Grażyna, having to seek out personal connections, make exchanges, and participate in other forms of "queue cutting" was the direct result of state policies, and thus she considered finagling to be legitimate. Actually, all of the 2006 interviewees viewed supply shortages as the results of the authorities' ill will rather than a deficiency of the distribution system (faulty central planning, inefficient politics of consumption, etc.). In fact, they saw them as deliberate actions taken to harm society, if not an outright conspiracy on the part of the Party against society. Grażyna, who worked in the sales department of Jutrzenka, wondered why production of consumer goods did not in any way translate to shop floor availability: "I was surprised, for instance, that [the company] Kobra produced so many shoes, but there was a shortage of shoes on the market, or that even though Jutrzenka produced so many sweets you needed food stamps to buy Irysy. I couldn't comprehend it."

According to Grażyna, social inequalities connected to supply problems resulted from the division between those who had connections and access to goods outside of normal distribution and the rest, who "not only didn't have such opportunities, but also were unable to get them because they were not resourceful." Her own supply tactic (being in the sales department, an attractive work position within the system of goods distribution) had an individualistic character and focused on the needs of her family and close friends. Grażyna did not see the causal relationship between the shortage economy and her own practice of getting goods "via the phone" from acquaintances working in other sales departments before they even entered the official distribution network.

For Grażyna's generation, as long as taxi driving remained a lucrative business, life was good. In the mid-1990s, Grażyna—who used to say that she "inherited resourcefulness from her father"—and her husband (also a taxi driver) built a new house. Part of the money for the house came unexpectedly when the employees of the confection enterprise became shareholders as a result of the company's post-1989 privatization. But problems occurred almost immediately after. The time for baggage taxi drivers, so lucrative during communism, had seemingly passed. With the rise of commercial enterprises, private shops and supermarkets increasingly offered some form of delivery. Alongside the 1990s boom in individual car purchases, the job of *taksówkarz bagażowy* became unprofitable. Hence, Grażyna's husband made the dramatic decision to give up his own business and, after twenty-one years, get a job as an employee driver at Jutrzenka.

As of the late 1990s, and especially in 2006, during an acute socioeconomic crisis in Poland,[23] Grażyna and her husband were afraid of losing their jobs at any moment. Both were employees complaining about unpaid overtime and income inequalities between the staff and the people managing the company. But they were primarily afraid of unemployment, and their potentially difficult situation on the job market: they were too old to learn something new, but too young to retire. In autumn 2006, Grażyna and her husband (both fifty-five) realized that running an independent business in the future would be impossible, and that in order to "get by" and provide for retirement in these times they had to get hold of jobs in the more secure public sector.

Functioning in the world of profitable taxi driver work was a given for Grażyna and her husband; it was something handed down from her father. Their entrance into adult life in the 1970s now seemed to have been much easier than efforts to keep their former standard of living afloat in the late 1990s and after, when outside competition in the transport services market forced Grażyna's husband to switch from an independent small business to working in a large company. Grażyna had consistently referred to resourcefulness as an intrinsic part of their prosperity in communist Poland; thanks to resourcefulness, a tough character, diligence, the willingness to realize far-reaching plans, and an unceasing drive to get ahead, the Czyżyks were assured a margin of freedom for themselves and a comfortable life "on their own." Social advances, such as the family's rise from peasant workers to private businessmen, or from living in rented premises to living in their own home, as well as the traditional (and simultaneously "luxurious") division of roles into the earning husband and the stay-at-home mother and wife, overshadowed other problems associated with everyday life in communist Poland.

Paradoxically, at the end of 1990s, when Poland entered the next economic crisis and almost a decade of severe unemployment, the main currency of success—namely, small-scale private business—underwent devaluation while work in the public sector became more attractive. In times of full-speed-ahead, neoliberal transformation, social protection in the form of a stable work contract and regular retirement payments became one of the most valuable assets, and acquiring it became proof of resourcefulness for the sake of the family.

The history of the Czyżyks—and Grażyna's statements in particular—suggests at least two meanings of family resourcefulness mobilized and actualized both under state socialism and in the post-1989 economy. First, resourcefulness in the sphere of consumption—Grażyna's domain—was not due to traditionally held views of female ingenuity in the household. Resource-fulness appeared here as a synonym for *kombinowanie*, that is, searching out gaps, loopholes, and semilegal solutions within the official distribution system.[24] Grażyna knew how to use her workplace and professional contacts to her advantage; she turned her resourcefulness into an ability to use personal connections to aid what some scholars have called family-centered egoism or "amoral familialism."[25] Application of this rule, which favored friends and one's folk over strangers (especially in the sphere of consumption), meant that the Czyżyks—thanks to their multiple resources—got on relatively well during the supply crisis of the 1980s, while for many others it was a time of torment, eternal lines, and wasted time seeking basic everyday articles. Therefore, "familial society" produced not only solidarity and familial commitment but also a lot of tension and conflict. The Czyżyks, like many other families, con-structed justifications for their participation in society based on self-interest. In their accounts, distributional differentiations, social tensions and inequalities, and the problem of unequal benefits achieved at the expense of others was neutralized by recalling the country's inefficient supply policies. Thus it is un-surprising that Grażyna assigned all supply problems to higher-up elite decision makers who, she believed, intentionally triggered deficiencies in the system. She defined her own resourcefulness as getting scarce goods through intimate, informal reciprocal relations that functioned against (and despite) unfriendly Party-state institutions.

Second, resourcefulness assumed the form of a cultivated and "natural" family virtue; it was to be passed on from one generation to the next. It was also seen as a personality trait, the presence of which represented hope and ulti-mately power during times of change—such as during the Great Depression, postwar austerity, the supply crisis of the 1980s, the transformation in 1989, or the decline of small-scale business in the late 1990s. In the Czyżyks' narra-tions, resourcefulness functioned as a family mythology of sorts, giving meaning to the past and offering optimism (whether realistic or not) for the future. They also believed that the characteristic would soon emerge in their son, thanks to his own diligence and creativity. In that sense, resourcefulness as a family tradition was a defense against negative circumstances, against the cyclic trauma caused by property loss and diminished social status. In commu-nist Poland, this psychological characteristic allowed the Czyżyks to build their own world quite apart from the social order that the Party-state tried to impose from above, where state-run property and a model class society, divided into peasants, workers, and intelligentsia, dominated. In post-1989 Poland, it allowed them a relatively smooth reorientation of their family resources from private entrepreneurship to more socially secured jobs.

FIGURE 12.1. The Orłowski family, around 1979–80. From the right: Krzysztof Orłowski, his mother, father, and younger brother Leszek. Photographed during one of the interviews by Jadwiga Siemaszko, member of Siciński's research group. Center for Research on Lifestyles Collection, Institute of Philosophy and Sociology, Polish Academy of Sciences, File 52/B/R/JS. Courtesy of the Institute of Philosophy and Sociology, Polish Academy of Sciences.

The Orłowskis

Unlike Grażyna and Jerzy Czyżyk, who willingly talked about the experiences of their grandparents and parents, Jacek, Krzysztof, and Jola Orłowski, as well as their spouses, focused on their own generation's histories, that is, on the period between 1980 and 2006 by comparing their lives in terms of past transformations and the present-day situation. In a similar manner, they too used the notions of "resourcefulness" and "creativity" in reference to family consumption to sum up the previous three decades.

Thirty years ago, the Orłowski family occupied a small apartment in a Bydgoszcz housing complex. The four children—daughters Beata and Jola, and sons Jacek and Krzysztof—were already professionally active. At the time of the interviews in 1978–1980, the elder daughter, Beata, lived with her husband outside the family house, while the rest of the siblings were looking for their own places. Years prior, Krystyna Orłowska, their mother, had retired on disability due to rheumatism. Consequently, she took care of the house and looked after her ill in-laws.

In the 1978–1980 conversations, Krystyna talked a great deal about daily problems. The sociologist from the earlier research reported: "Mrs. Orłowska buys everything that she can get: headcheese, the cheapest sausage, fish and vegetables. She recalls that there were times when she did not have anything with which to make a sandwich. The husband took only bread with margarine to work." The family lived from the husband's salary, supplemented by Krystyna's disability payments; they had no personal connections in the shops, no moonlighting possibilities, or any other sort of "side profits." Thus, family life was modest and they had no consumer aspirations, such as possessing a car. Household expenses were always precisely calculated. At the end of the 1970s, the family took out a large loan from the husband's workplace a total of three times. With the exception of their elder son, the rest of the children attended vocational schools: Beata and Jola trained as tailors, while Jacek attended culinary school. The siblings quickly started to bring money home in order to help their parents.

Krystyna's husband and the father of the family, Jan Orłowski, was a construction equipment mechanic. Friends from work called him "the eloquent one." He actively engaged in meetings of the Enterprise Council; he wrote articles about his brigade for the trade union magazine. In the late 1970s the Orłowski family defined themselves as members of the unprivileged majority, whose lives revolved around hard work and who were separate from the emerging *nouveaux riches* of the Gierek era. All around him, Jan Orłowski could see a society divided by traditional class distinctions and property privileges, meaning that many doors were closed to him.[26] As ever-growing queues indicated, it was also a society of escalating crisis. Class was the basic category for experiencing reality for the Orłowskis, and the experience of chronic shortages would soon join it. Both of these organizing frameworks seemed to offer up only a restricted space within which to maneuver.

An important event took place in the spring of 1980: Jan Orłowski departed for the USSR on a short-term work contract. Soon he recognized new opportunities to earn money by smuggling attractive and scarce goods across the border. This activity, known as consumer tourism, was practiced throughout the Bloc but was most closely identified with the Poles.[27] In the case of the Orłowskis, who had never before been involved in the second economy, it constituted a rise in their living standards and revolution in the entire family's lifestyle. The new activity now taken up by the family was to "export" knock-off Levi's jeans (sewed by daughter Jola) to the Soviet Union, where Jan distributed them. After the job contract in the Soviet Union was over, it was the younger generation of Orłowskis who took over the new family business, while the parents looked after the grandchildren or helped to sell goods brought from abroad at the market in Bydgoszcz.

The 1980s opened up a completely surprising development in the Orłowskis' lives, at least compared to the description of their life style in 1978– 1980, which was based purely on state job salaries and workplace benefits at a state company. Free trade interests turned out to be a good choice for the younger generation of the Orłowskis in the closing years of communism since they had the courage to act according to new rules that emerged alongside the erosion of state socialism. The "old" lifestyle of the Orłowskis started to give way to individual and semilegal entrepreneurship. Jan's still-at-home children—Jola, Jacek, and Krzysztof—mastered this shift to varying degrees. The biographies of Krzysztof and Jacek show that various activities carried out in the informal and private economy created for each a totally new relationship with the state.

Krzysztof, the elder son, inherited a passion for discussion, a curiosity about the world, and his father's broad interests. His parents sent him to secondary school hoping he would go on to get a higher education, a family dream that had been unattainable until then. However, Krzysztof did not adjust well to the high school in Bydgoszcz. "Krzysztof didn't fit in with the rest of the class. It was an elite school, where children primarily from the intelligentsia studied. Krzysztof was the only child in the class whose father was a physical laborer. He was not able to make friends with the others," said his mother. The class-conscious society of the late 1970s represented for Krzysztof (as for his father) a place where both social prestige and money were beyond the reach of the working class. For this reason, Krzysztof moved to the technical vocational school. Still, he tried to get accepted to the university but was unsuccessful. He had numerous interests: he enjoyed the film work of Bergman and Kurosawa and frequented the theater, and he spent time at a community center where his fiancée worked as a visual artist.

After graduating from high school, Krzysztof took the position of technical inspector at a building unit. After eight months of work in a construction company, he was laid off as part of the workforce reduction in 1979. He thus entered the 1980s unemployed and unsure of the future. Nevertheless, his worries were dispelled when the employment office sent him to a company dealing with import and repair of meat industry equipment. Krzysztof worked there for seven years. It was interesting and not stressful, and most important it guaranteed valuable meat allocations. Unexpectedly, Krzysztof found himself in a strategic place within the socialist supply system. Companies that cooperated with the consumer goods industry created intercompany distribution systems during the deepening economic crisis, and their employees gained additional consumer privileges. For many employees, access to scarce goods meant more than wages. In times of economic collapse, the workplace became a supply point, a place where the shopping was done.[28] It was also very important for Krzysztof and his family: "After the lay-off, after such a supposedly unpleasant event, I landed in a workplace where . . . I received a kilogram of meat, a kilogram of sausage or more, every week! [So] that it was very easy and convenient, the shop was at my workplace." Thus Krzysztof, by the fact of his employment in the meat industry, relieved his parents and siblings of the job of having to wait in line.

Krzysztof was also politically involved in the Solidarity movement. But being openly sympathetic to the politically independent, oppositional trade union put him in trouble following the declaration of martial law in 1981.[29] When active recruitment to new Party-based trade unions (which were supposed to compete with the underground Solidarity trade union movement) began in the mid-1980s, he refused to sign up. Small harassments began: "I was being cut out of salary increases"; "I was not sent on attractive delegations abroad." Krzysztof therefore finally parted ways with his state employer in 1987 and began working "on his own" as an independent private entrepreneur and craftsman.[30] His idea was to paint copies of the great artists' masterpieces. Krzysztof and his wife wanted to democratize the arts, "so that everyone would have [beautiful] things on the wall, not a photograph, not a reproduction, but linen, painted with a brush, [where] one can see the line, the strokes, the effect on linen."

Krzysztof defined his actions as *"kreatywność"* (creative resourcefulness/ creativity). The craft of painting united Krzysztof's businesslike activity with intellectual undertones, adding an air of high culture. His wife, a professional painter, copied the famous masters, and he sold these copies of Gauguin or van Gogh.[31] Though their new private business was an artistic activity, it was also well suited to the enterprising spirit of the late 1980s, which encompassed a spirit of initiative, a freeing up from the stiff framework of communist Poland. It was also an expression of fatigue vis-à-vis the lack of political liberties— escape from surveillance by undercover secret police and Party officials. Profit-oriented, nonpolitical work "in the crafts" was meaningful and offered a sense of freedom, as opposed to hollow busy work and political games so familiar to the state-run and state-controlled workplace.

Another instance of this same creative resourcefulness was acted out in relation to an urgent housing matter. Like many young married couples at that time, Krzysztof and his wife did not own a place of their own, although they had prepaid for an apartment that was yet to be built. Without connections, and without an apartment from his workplace, Krzysztof was doomed—like many others—to wait for years on the waiting list until he received the keys to his home. Krzysztof's idea, then, was to convert a nuclear bomb shelter among the surrounding blocks of flats into an apartment of his own. Nuclear bomb shelters were peculiar relics of the Cold War in Poland: horizontal tunnels inside blocks of flats, which were supposed to "air-out" in case of a nuclear attack, directing the shock wave into a vacancy between structures so that the building could withstand the blast. Krzysztof managed to get agreement from the apartment building cooperative and in 1984 converted the tunnel, at his own expense, into an apartment. One of his friends followed suit, and after that an entire wave of residents did the same. This form of resourcefulness had a highly social character rather than an atomizing one and went beyond narrow family interests; instead of competition, Krzysztof implemented cooperation, using available space otherwise being wasted in the housing estate.

Krzysztof's resourcefulness was in part based on an ability to sense change, to sense where a transformation in the economy would take place. The disintegration of Party-state structures associated with the deep crisis of the command economy was already clear to Krzysztof in the early 1980s, even as he was still working in the state-run enterprise. While he used the company's meat allocations, he also investigated routes for his trade business undertakings after hours. During holidays, he traveled to trade in Hungary and East Berlin. He knew that the large volume of cross-border smuggling had resulted from the flimsiness of existing formal economic mechanisms. Krzysztof observed the system's deregulation—a result of the wild expansion of the partially (although still not legalized) free market: "Production surpluses were exported from here [Poland]. Exactly what the state was unable to manage, namely, the transport [of goods], was done by citizens—on their backs, in bags—and it paid off." Both phenomena—the crisis of the state monopoly and the development of the free market—occurred simultaneously. *Kreatywność* consisted of understanding how it was possible to use the new constellation for one's own benefit in order to create something "cool," as Krzysztof liked to say, and help the family. In the times of deregulated late socialism and early free-market capitalism, the very changeability of the rules of economic activity gave him fresh ideas.

As long as the rules of emerging capitalism worked to the benefit of small-scale entrepreneurship, Krzysztof's resourcefulness—his "fondness for the free trade"—allowed him to prosper. Nevertheless, construction of supermarkets at the end of the 1990s forced Krzysztof to make the decision to return to employee status. Big business capitalism had created new barriers, a colonized space, which had previously been organized spontaneously through "sale on camp beds/trade in improvised stalls in the street and trade of all sorts." During my visit in 2006, Krzysztof and his wife (similar to the Czyżyks) felt tired, burned out, devoid of ideas, and intent on just surviving. He judged his situation at work (and the economic system more generally) negatively: he lived on credit (just like his parents in times past) and the work he did have in one of the new retail megastores gave him neither money nor time nor the conditions to be creative.

Creativity is a key word in Krzysztof's narration. On the one hand, one can treat it interchangeably with the concept of resourcefulness, which helped him find shortcuts under a shortage economy, as when he acquired consent to rebuild the nuclear shelter into an apartment or when he "was building capitalism" through his cross-border trade activities. On the other hand, however, Krzysztof's ingenuity went beyond pragmatic, everyday materialism. It was a response to an unpredictable, changing reality. Krzysztof's most creative period was between 1982 and 1992, the years of collapse of the old system and the birth of a new one. However, after almost thirty years he had the feeling that his life had come full circle. Like his parents, he lived modestly, "from paycheck to paycheck," and increasingly limited his financial aspirations ("Perhaps I should sell my car?"). If he were as old as his twenty-two-year-old daughter, he declared, he would go, as she did, to Great Britain.[32] For him, as for many others, the job-related migrations abroad of the early 2000s represented a new form of resourcefulness.

In 1980, Jacek, Krzysztof's younger brother, became a waiter in the best hotel restaurant in Bydgoszcz, located in the city center. It was an island of affluence surrounded by chronic shortages. With local customers, Jacek had informal agreements: he would let them bring their own alcohol, "something from [the hard currency luxury store] Pewex, to finagle a bit," and in exchange he would receive "access" to scarce goods.[33] During that period, an increasing number of franchise holders, small business owners, shop managers, and illegal black market currency traffickers would visit the restaurant. Thanks to his contacts, Jacek had priority access to the back doors of the city's shops and warehouses, and he knew the salesmen—who at night made up part of his clientele—in the neighborhood. These arrangements brought him not only money but above all access to goods he could exchange for other goods, hand out to members of the family, or keep at home as exchange currency:

> "If I happened to have meat, I could go to a cake shop and get sweets. If I had sweets, I could have both coffee and something else, a refrigerator or a washing machine. I knew that everything was convertible and worth buying in order to exchange it for something else. Nobody asked what the queue was for: only that there is a queue— you had to go and stand there, and take whatever there [was]. There was always something. Always something with which you could trade."

The supply crisis had the peculiar result of changing what had been a constant obstacle for his family—lack of money—into an issue of no importance. Working at the hotel restaurant, Jacek created a network of useful contacts, which he exploited to get scarce goods for himself. With characteristic energy and wits, he functioned in the world of unofficial connections as well as in the world of waiting lines (usually both at the same time). He would not turn down alcohol rations printed illegally by workers of the nearby printing house. He used to buy sweets from a shop assistant and friend who herself had a pass to wait in the separate privileged line (reserved for senior citizens, disability pension holders, and women with small children). He had an agreement with one seller that he would pass himself off as a worker of the Polish Red Cross and, after showing a phony document, would cut the line, where the "honest" stood. In this way, favorable shopping status was gained neither by resorting to "under

FIGURE 12.2.   The youngest of the Orłowski siblings, Jola and Leszek. Photo from the family album made in the late 1970s. Center for Research on Lifestyles Collection, Institute of Philosophy and Sociology, Polish Academy of Sciences, File 52/B/R/JS. Courtesy of the Institute of Philosophy and Sociology, Polish Academy of Sciences.

the counter" sales (which would certainly arouse anger in the people waiting in line) nor by backdoor sales.

The form of resourcefulness that Jacek shared with his family was shopping tourism. Together with his siblings and his wife, he traveled to various countries, beginning with communist Bloc countries, then to Turkey, finishing in India. Jacek committed himself to exchange and foreign trade, but only to "break even" and share goods with the family. In spite of contacts with the commercial underworld, he did not get drawn into large-scale activities. When the time of cross-border, individual trade ended after 1989, he kept working as a waiter, deciding to concentrate on keeping a stable family life. To date, Jacek is still a restaurant manager in the same hotel where he began his work thirty years ago, and he lives in a small apartment in a housing block on the outskirts of Bydgoszcz.

After 1989, why did this resourcefulness not lead Jacek into a business and then on to financial success? He had great potential and "the right stuff" to help make more serious money, namely, contacts with entrepreneurs, the ability to capitalize on social contacts, a strong business sense, and the courage and support of close friends and family. He was not, however, a typical *homo economicus* guided by profit. Jacek was a champion of exchange; he was interested in the process of trade, in consumption, and in sharing goods that he wangled. In addition, the scale should not be exaggerated. Thanks to connections and cleverly cutting the line, Jacek received scarce consumer commodities. A multiplication of these efforts, bordering on the daring, resulted from the extent of the supply crisis, shortages, and the deregulation of official trade channels. In committing himself to trade, making money as a goal in and of itself had secondary meaning for Jacek. He was a *bon vivant*, who used his resources and goods in order to enjoy life, and sometimes to let others earn some money. For example, at one point he ordered and paid for clothes to be made his sister's dressmaker friends, as a way to help them out, but then he never bothered to pick them up.

When, at the beginning of the 1990s, bartering goods lost its usefulness, Jacek remained a restaurant employee. Though he had functioned very well in the late socialist reality of barter exchange, he felt "bored" in the more individualistic society of the free market. Jacek valued traditional "mechanical solidarity," where everyone circulated on the same path of exchanges and favors, whereas it was harder for him to find his place in "organic solidarity," where people offered their specialized services to others in exchange for money. Over the years, resourcefulness remained for him a domain of cordial sociability, and therefore Jacek preferred to continue his job as a waiter rather than become involved in making money.

Continuities

The biographies of the Czyżyks and the Orłowskis disclose acts of resourcefulness, creativity, and efficiency, dating to the crisis times of "real existing socialism" and continuing into the period of "real existing capitalism." Both families exploited weaknesses in the shortage economy: they converted its small areas into legal private property (as with the Czyżyk family and Krzysztof Orłowski), or they became entrepreneurs and tradesmen in the gray economy (the Orłowski siblings). They played the game of consumer wit, which strengthened family ties at the cost of the state-run economy. Altogether, they contributed to the dynamics of change, which ended with a transformation in the economic system. The market reforms of the early 1990s politically legalized already existing forms of consumer resourcefulness that earlier had been defined as dubious, illicit, or contradictory within the official doctrine of state socialism.

Eventually, both families managed to get by within the realities of a new neoliberal economy—be it the "shock therapy" of the early 1990s or the mass unemployment of the years 1999–2006—by shifting their resourcefulness back from consumer wherewithal and individual private business to more secure jobs. The golden age for the Czyżyks came at the turn of the 1960s to the 1970s, when they managed to become private entrepreneurs. New opportunities opened for the Orłowskis in the crisis years of the 1980s, when bartering became widespread, socialist currencies underwent further devaluation, and goods (and access to them) became the real currency. Both families continued work as private entrepreneurs after 1989 but without exception became hired employees a few years thereafter. The capitalism of the late 1990s and early 2000s, with its high unemployment and the increasing domination of large multinational companies, meant their individual resourcefulness and ingenuity was again put to the test.

These personal trajectories, linked by the notion of resourcefulness or *kreatywność*, demonstrate continuities between everyday lives under communism and postcommunism. The consumption-directed social practices of the socialist period (cutting the line, finagling, smuggling goods, bartering) were perceived by these families as part of the broader phenomenon of social resourcefulness, which continued to exist and, even more importantly, remained crucial during the social rupture of 1989 and after.[34] Rather than negating the decisiveness of a systemic shift, this points to the simultaneity of the decline of socialism and the emergence of capitalism, as well as the ways in which people made sense of it.

Moving away from the particular cases of the two families here, my ethnographic revisit demonstrates that late socialism and postsocialism alike produced an economy that was based on everyday family ties as the only stabilizing unit. As consumers under communism in Poland, people understood family as the key socioeconomic structure of that time. Consumer resourcefulness points to how people were privatizing the social and economic resources at hand in different regimes of consumption, be it the wartime black market, postwar barter economy, or, later, the erosion of state socialism and emergence of grassroots capitalism. In this way, consumption under communism ceases to be a narrative of unique modernity, and instead a history of Poland and Poles dealing with shifting forms of an economy in crisis.

Translation: Mark Keck-Szajbel and Małgorzata Szajbel-Keck

NOTES

Special thanks to Małgorzata Fidelis, Stefan-Ludwig Hoffmann, the editors—Paulina Bren and Mary Neuburger—and the OUP anonymous reviewers for their comments. I am grateful to Beatrice von Hirschhausen and Marcel Cohen for sharing with me the idea of an ethnographic revisit. Financial support for research on this article from the German Historical Institute Warsaw is gratefully acknowledged.

1. Janine R. Wedel, *The Private Poland* (New York: Facts on File, 1986), 37.

2. Wedel, *Private Poland*, 95.

3. Steven L. Sampson, "The Second Economy of the Soviet Union and Eastern Europe," *Annals of the American Academy of Political and Social Science*, 493 (September 1987): 120–36; Katherine Verdery, *What Was Socialism, and What Comes Next?* (Princeton, NJ: Princeton University Press, 1996); Janos Kenedi, *Do It Yourself: Hungary's Hidden Economy* (London: Pluto Press, 1981).

4. Andrzej Friszke, *Polska: losy państwa i narodu: 1939–1989* (Warszawa: Iskry, 2003), 319–27.

5. Jadwiga Koralewicz, Ireneusz Białecki, and Margaret Watson, eds. *Crisis and Transition: Polish Society in the 1980s* (Oxford, New York: St Martin's Press, 1987); Jacek Kochanowicz, "Trust, Confidence and Social Capital in Poland: A Historical Perspective," in *Trust and Democratic Transitions in Post-Communist Europe*, ed. Ivana Markova (London: Oxford University Press, 2004), 63–84; Jacek Kurczewski, ed., *Umowa o kartki* (Warsaw: Wydawnictwo Trio, 2004, 1st ed. 1985); Elżbieta Firlit, Zbigniew Hockuba, and Anna Podbłaszczyk, eds. *Zakupy dóbr trwałego użytku na rynku rzeszowskim: niedobór a postępowanie klientów (raport z badań)* (Warsaw: Uniwersytet Warszawski, 1989); Wojciech Pawlik, *Prawo, moralność, gospodarka alternatywna* (Warsaw: Instytut Profilaktyki Społecznej i Resocjalizacji UW, 1988); Piotr Gliński, *Ekonomiczne uwarunkowania stylu życia. Rodziny miejskie w Polsce w latach*, Ph.D. diss., Instytut Filozofii i Socjologii Polskiej Akademii Nauk, Warszawa, 1983; Kazimierz Sowa, ed. *Gospodarka nieformalna: uwarunkowania lokalne i systemowe* (Rzeszów: Towarzystwo Naukowe Organizacji i Kierownictwa, 1990); Teresa Pałaszewska-Reindl, ed., *Polskie gospodarstwa domowe: życie codzienne w kryzysie* (Warszawa: Instytut Związków Zawodowych, 1986).

6. Borrowing from Pierre Bourdieu's concept of *habitus*, resourcefulness here means an embodied, internalized, and therefore natural and self-evident way of behavior that helped people improvise or even prosper in times of crisis and rupture. In other words, the resourcefulness may be understood in this particular case study as a set of social dispositions activated *both* in times of supply crisis and in the more recent moments of uncertainty such as during the economic "shock therapy" of the 1990s, which radically restructured the economy to speed up transition, and the mass unemployment that followed in the early 2000s. Resourcefulness understood in this way—as a culturally and existentially determined ability to act and shape one's own material world—represents both necessity and choice as a means of coping with life in times of social rupture and economic crisis. Bourdieu, *The Logic of Practice* (Oxford: Blackwell, 1990), 52–65; Bourdieu, *Outline of a Theory of Practice* (Cambridge: Cambridge University Press, 1977), 78–87. About the concept of resourcefulness in Polish sociological literature, see Jerzy Kwaśniewski, Robert Sobiech, and Joanna Zamecka, eds., *Zaradność społeczna. Z badań nad społecznymi inicjatywami w dziedzinie rozwiązywania problemów Polski lat osiemdziesiątych* (Warszawa: Zakład Narodowy im. Ossolińskich, 1990).

7. Kazimierz Wyka, "Excluded Economy," in *Unplanned Society: Poland During and After Communism*, ed. Janine R. Wedel (New York: Columbia University Press), 23–61; Jan T. Gross, "Themes for a Social History of War Experience and Collaboration," in *The Politics of Retribution in Europe: World War II and Its Aftermath*, eds. István Deák, Jan T. Gross, and Tony Judt (Princeton, NJ: Princeton University Press, 2000), 15–36.

8. János Kornai, *The Socialist System: The Political Economy of Communism* (Princeton, NJ: Princeton University Press, 1992); André Steiner, *The Plans That Failed: An Economic History of East Germany, 1945–1989*, translated from the German by Ewald Osers (New York, Oxford: Berghahn Books, 2010).

9. Małgorzata Fidelis, *Women, Communism, and Industrialisation in Postwar Poland* (Cambridge: Cambridge University Press, 2010); Mariusz Jastrząb, *Puste półki: problem zaopatrzenia ludności w artykuły powszechnego użytku w Polsce w latach 1949–1956* (Warszawa: Wydawnictwo Wyższej Szkoły Przedsiębiorczości i Zarządzania im. Leona Koźmińskiego, 2004); Antonela Capelle-Pogăcean and Nadège Ragaru, eds., *Vie quotidienne et pouvoir sous le communisme—Consommer à l'Est* (Paris: Éditions Karthala, 2010); Paul Betts and Katherine Pence, eds., *Socialist Modern: East German Everyday Culture and Politics* (Ann Arbor: University of Michigan Press, 2008); Barbara Einhorn, *Cinderella Goes to Market: Citizenship, Gender and Women's Movements in East-Central Europe* (London: Verso, 1993); Wedel, *Private Poland*, 116.

10. An exception would be a sociological work based on in-depth interviews on Soviet and post-Soviet economy of favors: Alena Ledeneva, *Russia's Economy of Favours: Blat, Networking and Informal Exchange* (Cambridge: Cambridge University Press, 1998).

11. Antoni Sułek, "'To America!': Polish Sociologists in the United States After 1956 and the Development of Empirical Sociology in Poland," *East European Politics and Societies* 24 (Summer 2010): 327–52; Małgorzata Mazurek, "Notion of Work and Sociologist Advisors in Communist Poland, 1956–1970," *Revue d'histoire en sciences humaines* 17 (2007): 11–32.

12. The most sensational data from that time showed that "family" and "nation" constituted two central collective values, leaving the sphere of intermediary institutions (Party-state, workplace, local community, or church) far behind. However, this model, thought very popular among sociologists, was not able to explain such phenomena as "Solidarity" or the informal economy. Stefan Nowak, "Postawy, wartości i aspiracje społeczeństwa polskiego. Przesłanki do prognozy na tle przemian dotychczasowych," in *Społeczeństwo polskie czasu kryzysu*, ed. Stefan Nowak (Warszawa: Wydawnictwo Instytutu Filozofii i Socjologii PAN, 2004, 1st ed. 1984), 337–80; Wedel, *Unplanned Society*, 1–20; Władysław Adamski, ed., *Sisyphus: Sociological Studies. Humanistic Sociology Revisited*, vol. 1 (Warsaw: PWN Polish Scientific Publishers, 1981).

13. In 1977 Andrzej Siciński's Center for Societal Forecasting (Zespół Prognoz Społecznych) was transformed into Center for Research on Lifestyles (Zespół Badań nad Stylami Życia) at the Institute for Philosophy and Sociology at the Polish Academy of Sciences. Siciński's shift from social planning and forecasting toward cultural anthropology can be traced in the center's publications from the 1970s and 1980s: Andrzej Siciński, Géza Kovács, and Władimir I. Starowierow, eds., *Problemy prognozowania w krajach socjalistycznych* (Wrocław: Zakład im. Ossolińskich, 1975); Siciński, ed., *Styl Życia. Koncepcje, propozycje* (Warszawa: Państwowe Wydawnictwo Naukowe, 1976); Siciński, ed., *Styl życia. Przemiany we współczesnej Polsce* (Warszawa: Państwowe Wydawnictwo Naukowe, 1978); Siciński, ed., *Styl życia, obyczaje, ethos w Polsce lat siedemdziesiątych - z perspektywy roku 1981: szkice* (Warszawa: Instytut Filozofii i Socjologii PAN, 1983); Siciński, ed., *Style życia w miastach polskich (u progu kryzysu)* (Wrocław: Zakład im. Ossolińskich, 1988). On the history of the Center for Research on Lifestyles, see Piotr Gliński and Artur Kościański, eds., *Style życia-społeczeństwo obywatelskie - studia nad przyszłością* (Warszawa: Wydawnictwo Instytutu Filozofii i Socjologii PAN, 2009).

14. J. P. Roos and Andrzej Siciński, "Ways and Styles of Life in Finland and Poland: An Introduction," in *Ways of Life in Finland and Poland: Comparative Studies on Urban Populations*, eds. J. P. Roos and Andrzej Siciński (Averbury, UK: Aldershot 1987), 2.

15. In the 1970s research on "socialist styles of life" was booming in Central and Eastern European countries. Just in the Soviet Union, one hundred books on this topic had been published by 1976. Siciński, *Styl życia. Przemiany we współczesnej Polsce*, chapter 1.

16. One of Siciński's students, Piotr Gliński, was sent as a political internee to a detention camp during martial law (1981–1983). His Ph.D. dissertation on the informal economy and family ties, based on the Siciński group research of 1978–1980, has never been published. Gliński, *Ekonomiczne uwarunkowania stylu życia: rodziny miejskie w Polsce w latach siedemdziesiątych*, Ph.D. diss. (Warszawa: Instytut Filozofii i Socjologii PAN, 1983), unpublished manuscript.

17. Elżbieta Tarkowska, "Differentiation of Life Styles in Poland: Gender and Sex," in *Ways of Life in Finland and Poland*, 134.

18. An ethnographic revisit occurs when an ethnographer undertakes participant observation, that is, studying others in their space and time, with a view to comparing his or her site with the same one studied at an earlier point in time, whether by this

ethnographer or someone else; Michael Burawoy, *The Extended Case Method: Four Countries, Four Decades, Four Great Transformations, and One Theoretical Tradition* (Berkeley: University of California Press, 2009), 75; Burawoy, "Revisits: An Outline of a Theory of Reflexive Ethnography," *American Sociological Review* 68(5) (2003): 645–79.

19. Bydgoszcz (in German, Bromberg) is a highly industrialized Polish city (the eighth largest) in the northern part of the country, midway between Warsaw and Gdańsk (Danzig). Before World War II, the town was inhabited by Poles, Germans, and Jews; after 1945 it welcomed many settlers from eastern and central Poland.

20. Here I refer to fieldwork notes written between 1978 and 1980 by sociologist Piotr Gliński, a member of Siciński's group. File 44/B/Rz/PG from the collection of Zakład Badań nad Stylami Życia at the Institute of Philosophy and Sociology PAN (henceforth, ZSŻ at IFiS PAN).

21. Conversation with the Czyżyks, August 2006.

22. Currently the department of customer service.

23. From the late 1990s until the mid-2000s, Poland witnessed an acute socioeconomic crisis. During that time the rate of unemployment stabilized at 20 percent and in the year 2005 it still represented 18.9 percent. See Stéphane Portet, "Poland: Circumventing the Law of Fully Deregulating," in *Working and Employment Conditions in New Member States*, ed. Daniel Vaughan-Whitehead (Geneva: International Labour Office, 2005), 273–338; Catherine Spieser, "Labour Market Policies in Post-Communist Poland: Explaining the Peaceful Institutionalization of Unemployment," *Politique Européene* 1(21) (2007): 100.

24. *Załatwianie* embraces accomplishment of serious objectives, from reserving a place in a hospital or kindergarten to getting an apartment or telephone, often by skirting the system. *Załatwianie* entails "arranging," or finagling commodities, services, and privileges unobtainable from the state economic or bureaucratic institutions. *Załatwianie* and *kombinowanie* are to some degree interchangeable, but the latter is shadier in connotation and can refer to larger-scale wheeling and dealing. Wedel, *Unplanned Society*, 93, fn. 2.

25. The term "amoral familialism" (*amoralny familizm*), coined by Edward Banfield, was used by the Polish sociologists Elżbieta and Jacek Tarkowscy to describe fragmentation of the crisis-driven Polish society in the 1980s. See Edward C. Banfield, *The Moral Basis of a Backward Society* (Chicago: University of Chicago Press, 1958); Jacek and Elżbieta Tarkowscy, "'Amoralny familizm,' czyli o dezintegracji społecznej w Polsce lat osiemdziesiątych," in Jacek Tarkowski, *Socjologia świata polityki*, vol. 1 (Warsaw: Instytut Studiów Politycznych Polskiej Akademii Nauk, 1996), 263–81.

26. See Winicjusz Narojek, *Społeczeństwo otwartej rekrutacji: próba antropologii klimatu stosunków międzyludzkich we współczesnej Polsce* (Warsaw: Wydawnictwo Instytutu Filozofii i Socjologii PAN, 1980), where the author interprets communist Poland in categories of social promotion of the first postwar generation.

27. A special volume (number 16) of *Cultural Studies* was devoted to precisely this phenomenon of consumer tourism in 2002. See also Chapter 15 in this volume.

28. See Tomasz Żukowski, "Fabryki-urzędy. Rozważania o ładzie społeczno-gospodarczym w polskich zakładach przemysłowych w latach realnego socjalizmu," In

Zmierzch socjalizmu państwowego. Szkice z socjologii ekonomicznej, ed. Witold Morawski (Warsaw: Państwowe Wydawnictwo Naukowe, Warszawa 1994), 60–174.

29. Introduction of martial law on December 13, 1981, brought the illegalization of Solidarity and imprisonment of thousands of Solidarity activists. In 1983–1984 the Party-state decided to set up new regime-sponsored trade unions that would compete with the underground structures of Solidarity, which survived and continued oppositional activities until they were legalized anew in 1989. Andrzej Paczkowski, *The Spring Will Be Ours: Poland and the Poles from Occupation to Freedom*, transl. by Jane Cave (University Park: Pennsylvania State University Press, 2003), chapter 8; Grzegorz Ekiert, *The State Against Society: Political Crises and Their Aftermath in East Central Europe* (Princeton, NJ: Princeton University Press, 1996), chapter 9.

30. In the Poland of the 1980s, craftsmanship was often synonymous with small-scale private business.

31. During my visit to the Orłowskis' house, Krzysztof showed me van Gogh's famous "Sunflowers" as painted by his wife. This was a professionally made copy with a striking resemblance to the original.

32. In the first two years after the accession of Poland to the European Union in 2004, about two million Poles, young people in particular, migrated to Great Britain and Ireland looking for a job and better living conditions. Janusz Sawicki, *Migration in the European Union: Grounds, Specificity and Consequences: The Polish Case* (Warsaw: Institute for Market, Consumption and Business Cycles Research, 2008).

33. Pewex was a retail chain, similar to Intershop in the GDR, where one could buy Western products with dollars and other hard currencies. For the GDR case, see Jonathan Zatlin, *The Currency of Socialism: Money and Political Culture in East Germany* (New York: Cambridge University Press, 2007).

34. Similar arguments about continuities between state socialism and postsocialism can be traced in recent anthropology to the post-1989 era. For the Polish case, see Elisabeth C. Dunn, *Privatizing Poland: Baby Food, Big Business and the Remaking of Labor* (Ithaca, NY, and London: Cornell University Press, 2004).

PART V

Constructive Criticism

A determinedly Cold War–era examination of the Soviet Bloc, titled *The Techniques of Communism*, pointed out—correctly—that "criticism and self-criticism are regarded as one and the same process by the Communists."[1] The author saw both mechanisms as having three main aims: to pave the way and build approval for radical changes emanating from the Kremlin; to ensure ideological unity within the ranks; and, finally, to recharge the larger project of building socialism. Self-criticism was undoubtedly used to great effect in the early postwar consolidation of power in Eastern Europe. When Stalin accused both Yugoslav leader Tito and Polish leader Gomułka of "ignoring the Soviet experience, [and] sliding into nationalism," he expected them to undergo a self-criticism, a public self-chastisement in which they would recant their sins and reaffirm their commitment to "the program," as was the Soviet way.[2] When Tito refused, Yugoslavia was expelled from the Bloc. At first Gomułka refused as well, but while the spotlight shone on Tito's betrayal, he had time to rethink and by August 1948 Gomułka had backtracked.

The Stalinist show trials that soon followed can be viewed as a turbocharged form of public self-criticism, a trial of false confessions put on stage for the public, the object of which, as the historian Tony Judt argued, "was not to seek or illustrate the truth but to confirm a certain version of reality."[3] The practice of self-criticism was so ingrained in some of these formerly high-ranking Party officials that, even as they recognized their confessions for the lies they were, they continued to support the idea of the Party having put them on trial—and in many cases slotted them for execution—for the larger cause of communism and its progress.[4] Self-criticism thereafter periodically reared its head following large-scale revolts against Soviet-type communism in Eastern Europe; the Prague Spring, for example, was followed by a series of self-criticisms by public figures wishing to remain in official good standing. But penned self-criticisms were also demanded from lesser folk as safeguards against any possible future dissent; these letters were placed on file, ready to be made public if necessary. One might recall how in Milan Kundera's novel *The Unbearable of Lightness of Being* the womanizing Prague doctor, Tamas, opts for demotion to a village clinic rather than write a letter of self-criticism. Ironically, with the onset of Gorbachev, glasnost, and perestroika, criticism and self-criticism came back in vogue in the Soviet Union; in this case, however, the rest of the Bloc leadership was none too happy about it and refrained from following suit until the very end.[5]

The counterpart to these individual self-criticisms was state-generated "constructive criticism" of socialist society, which can be traced back to Lenin, who insisted:

> Our first and main means of increasing the self-discipline of the
> working people and for passing from the old, good-for-nothing
> methods of work . . . must be the press, revealing shortcomings in
> the economic life of each labour commune, ruthlessly branding these
> shortcomings, frankly laying bare all the ulcers of our economic life,
> and thus appealing to the public opinion of the working people for
> the curing of these ulcers.[6]

With the ascension of Stalin, however, revealing the ulcers of socialist society was sublimated in favor of feverish applause for all things communist or, more precisely, all things Stalinist. Khrushchev brought constructive criticism back briefly, before Brezhnev's dilution of this Leninist principle. Nevertheless, during the late socialist period some form or other of constructive criticism was to be found whenever one lay open the editorial pages of the Party daily paper or switched on the radio or television.

Constructive criticism was a cagey form of "criticism," which aimed an arrow at state policies but then fired it instead at socialist citizens who were getting in the way of society achieving communism. In a typical example, a 1976 broadcast on Radio Prague noted that in the lead-up to Christmas many people were "complaining about the shortage of [certain] goods," and yet they were the ones leaving their workplaces "under some pretext" to do their Christmas shopping; the irony, the radio broadcast explained, was that the very product in short supply might well be the responsibility of those factory workers who were off shopping.[7] Hungarian historian András Mink has argued that the constructive criticism of late socialism paraded as a "substitute for a political discourse," offering the pretense of a "pluralist political community."[8] In other words, even though there were no real elections, and no contesting political candidates, this sort of state-generated debate could be cast as synonymous with democracy.

Today, socialist constructive criticism has proven to be vital source material because it reveals both the Party-state's expectations and, more important still, its anxieties over those failed expectations. Certainly, what the three chapters in this section show is that, however manufactured, it was not completely dismissed then, and it should not be dismissed now. Brigitte Le Normand's chapter offers us the evolution of public opinion on Yugoslav housing policy as a window for tracking changing attitudes toward and critiques of consumption in the postwar era. Le Normand employs various forms of state-generated criticism to draw out the conflicts over housing, from slum-level rent control to luxury ownership. A particularly rich resource she uses is the *New Yorker*-type cartoon (popular throughout the Bloc) poking officially sanctioned fun at all aspects of everyday life. In fact, entire magazines across the region were devoted to this particular art form-cum-critique. The study of jokes under communism has a history, but interestingly it is usually the jokes told privately that are the focus of attention. Yet, as a recent work on communist-era jokes concludes, ultimately the privately told jokes had no subversive effect but instead worked to let off steam.[9] It is instead the less studied officially sanctioned socialist cartoon that has far more to tell us.

Mark Keck-Szajbel, in his chapter, further demonstrates that constructive criticism could, in fact, be constructive. He shows how during the 1970s, when East Germany and Poland briefly opened their borders to one another, the Polish press, on the one hand, cajoled and chided its citizens along the path to appropriate consumer behavior abroad and, on the other, offered them invaluable advice on how and where to find sought-after goods in East Germany. Indeed, what at first had seemed like a good idea and was optimistically named the "Borders of Friendship" soon turned sour as each country's citizens bought up the others' hard-to-find goods. In research to date, the phenomenon of trader tourism is usually seen as strictly prohibited, or at best unofficially condoned. But by looking at the critical interventions of the press, Mark Keck-Szajbel shows that in the case of the Borders of Friendship Polish authorities actively encouraged cross-border tourist trade in East Germany for its convenience as a secondary market.

Tamas Dombos and Lena Pellandini-Simanyi most directly engage with constructive criticism by examining the intense "lifestyle debates" that took place in Hungary from the 1960s on. Despite the debates being carefully regulated by the various periodicals that acted as forums for these nationwide discussions, competing visions of an ideal socialist way of life surfaced. In the second half of their chapter, Dombos and Pellandini-Simanyi go on to explore the interplay between state-generated ideals of consumption and people's everyday practices. Since these lifestyle debates were an unmistakable element of the socialist public consciousness in post-1956 Kádárist Hungary, the authors attempt to gauge the response to them through a series of interviews conducted by Pellandini-Simanyi. They find that, given the ambiguous place of consumption within Hungarian socialism, "these debates seem to have had a genuine function for political and intellectual elites who were continuously attempting to map out the acceptable parameters of consumption."

NOTES

1. Louis F. Budenz, *The Techniques of Communism* (Chicago: Regnery, 1954), 106.

2. A. Kemp-Welch, *Poland Under Communism: A Cold War History* (Cambridge, New York: Cambridge University Press, 2008), 32.

3. Tony Judt, "Justice as Theatre," *Times Literary Supplement*, Jan. 18, 1991: 6.

4. Eugene Loebl, *My Mind on Trial* (New York: Harcourt, Brace, Jovanovich, 1976), 209.

5. Charles Gati, "Gorbachev and Eastern Europe," *Foreign Affairs* 65(5) (Summer 1987): 958–59.

6. As quoted in Brian McNair, "Glasnost and Restructuring in the Soviet Media," *Media Culture Society* 11 (1989): 328–29.

7. Open Society Archive, Budapest: *Radio Prague*, Dec. 11, 1976: 15:30 hrs.

8. András Mink, "A kesudió ügy," *Beszélő* 3 (1997): 7–8.

9. Ben Lewis, *Hammer and Tickle: The Story of Communism, a Political System Almost Laughed out of Existence* (Pegasus, 2009). See also Christie Davies, "Humour and Protest: Jokes Under Communism," *International Review of Social History* 52 (2007): 291–305.

13

Kids, Cars, or Cashews?

Debating and Remembering Consumption in Socialist Hungary

Tamas Dombos and Lena Pellandini-Simanyi

In the first decade after the Second World War, as elsewhere in Europe, Hungary experienced much economic hardship. But reconstruction in Eastern Europe, in contrast to the West, was exacerbated by the leaderships' strictly prioritized forced industrialization. Nevertheless, postwar recovery, the death of Stalin in 1953, and in particular the 1956 Hungarian Revolution facilitated a reprioritization of consumption over production.[1] This shift was palpable across the Bloc, but it was Hungary under the regime of János Kádár that went furthest in its embrace of consumer goods in the post-1956 period. Certainly the infrastructure necessary for a new era of consumption in Hungary underwent significant development after 1956: new department stores, such as the much admired Corvin Áruház; self-service supermarkets; and shop-window displays became an inseparable element of the urban experience.[2] Besides providing cheap basic necessities, for the first time the range of nonessential products also expanded. In 1963, the Luxus department store opened in downtown Budapest, offering high-priced, exceptional-quality goods, such as fur coats and elegant clothes, in beautiful surroundings.

The official economy was further supplemented by an expanding illegal black market of goods smuggled from abroad,[3] received in packages sent by relatives living abroad, or manufactured at home from raw materials largely stolen from one's workplace. In Hungary, unlike elsewhere in the Bloc, the black market seemed to flourish not because of scarcity but because of relative abundance; there was more available to trade and appetites were whetted for ever-larger varieties of goods. When the system failed to deliver this variety, consumers themselves came up with strategies to establish it. Differentiating between green and brown bottled beers of the same brand or having a preference for a pack of cigarettes coming from a particular factory were common practices reflecting the growing importance of consumer choice in constituting one's social identity.[4]

These developments in the infrastructure and practice of consumption were very much in line with the official Party policy of stimulating consumption, which lay at the heart of Hungarian and Bloc-wide efforts to fight the Cold War on a new front, with the purpose of consolidating legitimacy at home.[5] In this period, Soviet leader Khrushchev initiated a new policy that aimed to prove the superiority of socialism over capitalism in terms of standard of living. The "dognaty i peregnaty" (catching up and taking over) programs adopted by the 1959 and 1961 Congresses of the Communist Party of the Soviet Union served as a model for communist parties all across the Bloc.[6] Though all of these states used consumption in varying forms as a legitimating tool, this was arguably more critical in Hungary, where the revolution had so violently shaken the regime and society. After 1956, this purposeful reorientation was abundantly clear on the shelves of stores, and also in official newspapers and magazines, which were full of practical advice on how and what to consume: home decoration, fashion, cooking, cars, and DIY tips were among the most common topics.[7] By 1973, in fact, advertising meant to boost consumer demand reached an estimated 3 percent of national expenditures.[8] Perhaps more so than elsewhere in the Bloc, serious efforts were made not only to provide but to stimulate greater consumption among the public.

These post-1956 shifts in the system (later dubbed "goulash communism" after the well-known Hungarian stew) were buoyed by growing incomes. Right after the 1956 revolution, the government implemented a 20 percent increase in real wages, adding a further 3–4 percent every year until the end of the 1970s.[9] Between 1957 and 1978 real wages consequently doubled, and consumption multiplied 2.5 times, while the supply of consumer durables grew ten times. In the 1960s, for the first time in history, Hungary's general population enjoyed abundant, nutritious meals every day. Between 1958 and 1962, television subscriptions multiplied twentyfold; between 1960 and 1970, car ownership multiplied by eleven times; between 1960 and 1980, the number of flats increased by 50 percent, and new, bigger, and more modern dwellings were built.[10]

FIGURE 13.1. "A brightly colored chequered flannel suit can be sporty if worn with trousers, but it can also complement a summer dress. Depending on the length of the journey, the size of the luggage varies. The Leather Department's assortment satisfies all needs." Advertisement in a 1977 issue of the Hungarian fashion monthly *This Is Fashion* [Ez a Divat].

The gradual increase in levels of consumption, however, and particularly its increased visibility left state ideologues in an awkward position. Until that point, no known socialist models of affluence existed; the first years of Hungarian socialism were marked by scarcity, idealized notions of egalitarianism, and the notion that ascetics distinguished true socialist ethics from the bourgeois mentality. In this context, the way an affluent *socialist* society should develop remained ambiguous.[11]

This chapter explores this ambiguity by looking at how the contradiction between the original socialist ideals and growing affluence was negotiated in both public and private discourse in the period of the post-1956 decades. First, it examines how the contradiction was addressed in so-called democratic media debates on socialist lifestyles. These debates played out in various newspapers among a wide range of participants and readers. Second, post-1989 interviews focusing on the memories of everyday life during socialism are analyzed in order to understand how the contradictions and tensions were addressed, and perhaps resolved, in people's everyday lives at that time.

This work suggests that the norms expressed in the public discourse of the time remained largely in line with the original, ascetic socialist ideals. The ideal socialist way of life promoted by participants of the media debates centered on work, culture, and the community, while consumption was disdained as materialistic and individualistic. In these debates, the country's growing affluence was largely viewed with suspicion; many regarded it as a deviation from true socialist ideals. Analysis of interviews, however, reveals a more complex picture. Most people embraced the new consumption opportunities, and respondents resolved the contradiction between the official ideals and actual practices in a variety of ways, largely depending on their social position within the system. Members of the socialist elite expressed norms congruent with official discourse and yet paradoxically engaged in the highest level of consumption during this time. They solved the contradiction by legitimating their affluence with reference to hard work and cultural consumption. Working-class respondents, in contrast, saw no contradiction at all. They viewed socialism as a system that should grant equal access to a high level of material consumption on the basis of hard work and so urged even more consumption. Somewhat similarly, people who had belonged to the precommunist elite, as well as a new so-called petit-bourgeois class, formulated their version of a sophisticated and dignified way of life, replete with material possessions, in opposition to the socialist public discourse, altogether refusing the ideal of asceticism. Finally, the "socialist entrepreneurs," who financed their conspicuous and hedonistic consumption from semilegal activities, treated public discourse as a set of empty phrases, which they felt no need to reference in making sense of their own extravagant practices.

The Lifestyle Debates

If one is to analyze public attitudes toward consumption in socialist Hungary, the so-called lifestyle debates provide a nearly inexhaustible source of information. These debates formed part of a long series of "democratic media debates," which were an unmistakable element of the socialist public consciousness in post-1956 Kádárist Hungary.[12] Partly spontaneous and partly induced by the political elite, the existence of these debates might suggest a lively environment for public debate; they certainly fit in with a Bloc-wide impulse during late communism for officially sanctioned constructive criticism. But as the historian András Mink rightly points out, their main function was in fact to "substitute for a political discourse." Even though they often expressed discontent with socialist reality, thereby causing some discomfort to the regime, they "played an important role in the mental reproduction of the system by emulating the workings of a pluralist political community."[13] The sharp disagreements and heated discussions often obscured the delicate limits that the socialist regime placed on the nature of things that could in fact be discussed publicly. Governed by what was known as the "three Ts" (tűrés, tiltás, támogatás—tolerance, prohibition, support), the debates practiced a priori and post facto censorship.[14] Yet given the ambiguous place of consumption within Hungarian socialism, these debates seem to have had a genuine function for political and intellectual elites who were continuously attempting to map out the acceptable parameters of consumption.

The democratic media debates were primarily concentrated on the pages of four important periodicals: Élet és Irodalom, Kortárs, Kritika, and Új Írás.[15] Although both the forum and the contributors differed, all the debates followed a more or less common script. The journal or newspaper published an article that aimed to provoke a strong reaction in the form of letters and counteropinions. The editors then published a summary of the main questions relevant to the debate, with an open call for submissions. From the letters that were received during this round, the editorial board selected a limited number of contributions that were published on the pages of the journal in the months (sometimes years) following publication of the original editorial. The debate was officially closed with a concluding essay on the topic on behalf of the editorial board, in which the journal's "voice of authority" synthesized a "common standpoint," often linking it to the official policies of the government.

Even though the majority of the contributors were intellectuals, the editors were keen to publish letters from all social strata, including "everyday people" from working-class backgrounds. While retaining some skepticism toward the all-encompassing readership of these debates, one must emphasize that the debates did reach out to a wider audience beyond the socialist intelligentsia. The success of a particular debate in the 1970s, for example, resulted in a sharp increase in circulation for *Élet és Irodalom*,[16] and also the launch of a new weekly periodical (appropriately named *Új Tükör*, "New Mirror") to "satisfy the growing mass demand" for such a forum.[17] A wider reception of the main ideas of these debates was also facilitated by references to it and summary articles published in large-circulation daily newspapers, such as *Népszabadság*.

The earliest, most popular, and possibly most influential of the lifestyle debates was initiated by a short reaction in the fall of 1961, by poet Mihály Váci, to the new Soviet program that aimed at overtaking capitalist economies not only in industrial and agricultural production but also on the level of consumption and lifestyle.[18] In his editorial in *Új Írás*, Váci criticized the one-sidedness of the program; it was too focused on consumer goods and material well-being, while the role of art and culture was entirely left out. To correct this problem, he called for a similar program to be taken up by artists and intellectuals to reinvigorate socialist cultural life. Within a year of publication of this editorial, nearly 130 people had responded with longer articles or shorter letters expressing their opinions; 25 of these were published in the pages of *Új Írás*. The contributors ranged from artists, teachers, and economists to high school students and lamp factory workers. The official title of the debate was "Culture and Lifestyle," but in fact the debate entered the intellectual history of Hungarian socialism under the name of "fridge socialism," a term that appeared in the editors' closing remarks. Fridge socialism was a general term that pointed to the growing availability of consumer durables, among them refrigerators, and the new lifestyle they enabled.

A common theme of the culture-and-lifestyle debate was the deleterious effect of consumption on cultural life (a theme that would continue in future debates[19]), but perhaps more central still were its ill effects on collectivist socialist ideals writ large. Indeed, one of the central issues around Hungary's ever-expanding consumer opportunities was the seeming individualizing effects. As the opening essay of the "fridge socialism" debate argued:

> People who earn more can greatly extend the scope of their "personal needs." They can buy or save up for motorbikes, cars, weekend houses. . . . The desire to have personal goods is ever growing. . . .
> Is it not the struggle for personal property that is responsible for strengthening selfishness, materialism and indifference in people? If our man has achieved his desires, does it not dull him into a petit-bourgeois existence to be locked up in his flat every day watching television, isolated from the pedestrians in his car, or separated

KOMPRESSZOROS HÁZTARTÁSI HŰTŐSZEKRÉNYEK 160 ÉS 200 LITERES NAGYSÁGBAN MÉLYHŰTŐTÉR 18 LITER, −12°C ALATT

GYÁRTJA: HŰTŐGÉPGYÁR

FIGURE 13.2. "Compressor refrigerators in 160 litre and 200 litre sizes, freezer 18 litre, below minus 12 degrees. Produced by the Refrigerator Factory." Advertisement in a 1977 issue of the Hungarian fashion monthly *This Is Fashion* [Ez a Divat].

from collective social gatherings when instead spending time at his weekend home?[20]

A life that was centered on acquisition of consumer goods was considered to be necessarily individualistic, more focused on the personal fridge than the collective good. Another contributor was quick to cast off any doubts: "Does the car, the little weekend house, and the attainment of individual goods in general slide us into imitating the bourgeois way of life? Does it escalate the spread of individualism? According to my personal experiences so far, it does!"[21] Others went so far as to talk about the "moral landslide into individualism."[22]

Closely linked to this issue of individualism, contributors to the debate lamented that consumer abundance precipitated a mass turning away from public life, common affairs, and especially politics. As the opening editorial of the fridge socialism debate put it: "Some say it bluntly: on one side, there is television, the car, a vacation abroad and crinoline; on the other, there is declining political interest, a fleeting attention paid to the products of socialist culture, and the reappearance of bourgeois morality and individualization."[23] In the socialist era, this disinterest was especially problematic since the ethos of the regime was built around the common struggle for the communist future. The political activism needed for constant amelioration of socialism was contrasted with the "petit bourgeois loathing of deeds, changes and determined action [characterized by the saying] 'everything is just fine the way it is.'"[24] As a contributor to the fridge socialism debate put it clearly, "what we experience with every step—eager material demands and isolating ourselves in the individual activity of re-fashioning our lifestyle—is in complete opposition to the requirements of our future."[25] In these frequent condemnations, the term "materialistic" was contrasted with the moral, the personal, and the cultural.

The worry that consumer abundance ultimately leads to lack of motivation and laziness was vital to these debates. These issues were especially pressing in light of a communist utopia, which promised material well-being through socialist economic development. This dilemma was nicely summarized in Váci's lyrical manifesto that launched the fridge socialism debate:

What can we do to stimulate the masses to keep on making an effort
even though they are well acquainted with material goods and are
no longer forced to make an effort to survive . . . so that the people
rising from the bitter ocean of poverty, misery, travail and hardship to
the quiescent and cheerful coasts of communism do not doze off on
the tepid sandy beaches of material well-being, but remain humans,
motivated by spiritual challenges open to new sounds and aims?[26]

Váci advocated "stimulating the masses," but he also agonized over the compla-
cency that was due to their material well-being. Significantly, his concerns were
echoed by numerous contributors, while others accused him of occupying the
same platform with "the enemies and skeptical critics of socialism."[27]

Following on the heels of the fridge socialism debate, the dilemmas of
socialist consumption were further explored beginning with a 1964 discussion
in *Élet és Irodalom* that became identified with the pun "kicsi-vagy-kocsi" (translated as kid-or-car). The central theme of the kid-or-car debate grew out of a
pessimistic essay by novelist Ambrus Bor, which contrasted demographic
growth elsewhere in the world to population decline in Hungary and then
linked this deleterious trend to issues of individualism and self-centeredness,
both by-products of socialist consumption.[28] Bor blamed the country's flagging
birthrate on newly enacted liberal abortion laws, but also the growing interest
in ever greater avenues for consumption among the younger generation.
Among other things, he established a causal link among individualism, the
housing shortage, and a low domestic birth rate. According to Bor, "the relationship between the low birthrate and the shortage of housing is obvious." As
he elaborated, people do not simply want a flat in which to start a family but "a
flat with a lock on the door to build up a petit-bourgeois autarchy only concerned with cooking."[29] In other words, the pursuit of individual happiness,
defined through consumption, stood as a roadblock to the self-sacrifice and
collective commitment necessary for bringing up a child.

Moreover, even those who did bear children—but who generally (and "self-
ishly") would have only one child—practiced similarly harmful forms of consumption. Worse still, they passed these practices on to their offspring: "Parents
try to give everything to their child . . . thus loads of valuable things travel
between them as means of exchange, thereby devaluing all gifts . . . [this child
will hardly become] a communal-minded man, because his first experiences
gave him the sense of *mine* and not of *ours*."[30] One child or none, overconsumption and its fallout seemed to be undermining the collective, which, in this
case, included production of future generations.

Over the next three months, more than a hundred articles and letters
were sent to the editorial office of *Élet és Irodalom*, sixteen of which were published full-length, while excerpts from another seventeen appeared toward the
end of the debate. The genres varied from essays and personal stories to sociological accounts and policy proposals, with a range of contributors from
writers, demographers, and teachers to "proud mothers." Many of these respondents commented on the question of abortion, emancipation of women,
and social policies aimed at increasing the number of children. But significantly, a more substantial portion dealt with the changing consumer morality

of the younger generation of child-bearing age. According to many contributors, the material well-being of this generation was the cause of their seeming
immorality as well as the general decline in their reproductive and productive
capacities. As the first contributor to the debate opined: "More than a few
people greedily long for products . . . and they expect their prosperity not from
the cooperation of society, not from the state, but from individual profiteering. No matter how fast production grows, for the greedy profiteer no mathematical growth can suffice . . . he abstains from reproduction."[31] In short, as
profiteering purportedly replaced production, individualistic greed replaced
reproduction.

A later and even better known debate on the pages of *Élet és Irodalom* in
1976 pushed these issues further still. The opening essay, by Bulcsú Bertha,
a journalist on the staff of the periodical, compiled a long list of minor but
annoying discomforts (the bad quality of bread, flawed telephone lines, lazy
waiters, sloppy workers, etc.) that all came to be symbolized by the cashew
nut.[32] The cashew was considered to be an exotic, imported delicacy that was
sold for what was equal to the half-day wage of a worker, and so remained
unsold in large quantities owing to its unrealistic price. The import and sale
of such a luxury product was seen as part of a series of irrational economic
practices that made socialist life cumbersome. Responses started to pour in
following publication of Bertha's editorial, describing situations and stories
supporting or contradicting his argument. Although the debate was officially
titled "Let's Produce a Better General Mood!" the title of the original paper
("Cashew Nut") became both part of everyday vocabulary and the catchword
for the debate, which focused largely on the link between everyday discontents and the lack of motivation that resulted from material well-being.

The fact that these grievances came to be symbolized by the "cashew nut,"
a foreign product, was no accident. Indeed, identifying consumer abundance
as "foreign" to the socialist system was a recurring topic. First, the idea that
consumerism was inseparably attached to the Western world, and to America
in particular, was ever-present. This excerpt from another debate from the
1970s, the "Socialist Culture and Entertainment" debate, is a typical example:
"We are constantly bombarded from the West with ideological dilution, which
achieves its hidden ideological effect—its political aim under the cover of
pseudo-culture and kitsch."[33] Besides being a Western import, "petit-bourgeois"
mentalities further represented a stubborn remnant from the past. As articulated in one of the contributions to the fridge socialism debate, "The comfort
that our society is able to generate can result in a petit-bourgeois attitude and
lifestyle, as a result of the memories and educational practices of elder generations, or as the consequence of media products coming from the West."[34] Use

of the category "petit-bourgeois" was by no means limited to this occasion; it became an emblematic term for people characterized by the "perverted" values linked to overconsumption.[35] The term, in fact, was used in the first contributions to the fridge socialism debate, and it was then a recurrent point of reference throughout the consequent debates: "the years spent slogging for a television, a fridge, a weekend house or a car lead to a petit-bourgeois mentality";[36] "people enter the filthy station of petit-bourgeoisie and egoism on the tracks of material well-being";[37] "the civilized lifestyle, and the mass demand for it, creates petit-bourgeois weaklings out of humans."[38] Parallel to this, in the debate on Socialist Culture and Entertainment, the consumer-oriented entertainment industry that emerged in the twentieth century was described as appropriate to the "petit-bourgeois and impoverished gentry,"[39] the "carrier of a petit-bourgeois ethos."[40] In the "kid-or-car" debate, having one or two children, or even none, was described as "the preferred family model for the petit-bourgeoisie."[41]

Even though the critique of this petit-bourgeois way of life was far-reaching, it never went so far as to draw larger conclusions about the system as such. Instead, the axe inevitably fell on the individual, that is, the individual without the appropriate socialist moral compass on hand, who was consequently wallowing in the materialistic miasma of petit-bourgeois behaviors. He was a sorry sight, all the debates agreed. No matter how widespread it might have become, the petit-bourgeois mentality was understood as innately foreign to the system, in direct conflict with values that the socialist majority were said to share. As the editorial board's conclusion to the fridge socialism debate very expressively described: "It is possible that a doctor or an artist, even a miner, imagines himself to rise above society by having a car, and he steers his world along the road of bourgeois illusions. But on this road he bumps into the ethical iron wall of the community . . . and in that clash, there can only be one loser."[42] Thus, even though problems did exist, they were the result of individual fallibility, with no systemic cause.

The petit bourgeois mentality was the outcome of "individual, subjective distortions that happened during the process of the application [of state policy]."[43] By juxtaposing the "iron wall of the community" with the "deviance" of everyday consumers, these debates institutionalized a moral framework aimed at regulating, channeling, and domesticating consumer desires in socialist Hungary. At the center of this framework was the socialist ethos of hard-working people who resisted the temptations of their egoistic urges and instead devoted their lives to building a better future. This ("correct") ethos was contrasted with the practices of petit-bourgeois consumers who worked for material well-being and ignored their communal obligations.

Consumption Remembered

These debates on consumption clearly attempted to delimit the parameters of legitimate consumer practices on the basis of an ideal of socialist life centered on work, culture, and community as opposed to the materialistic, egotistical, and superficial petit-bourgeois way of life. From this point of view, the desire for affluence was a departure from socialist ideals, even a personal moral failure. But with such a binary in place, carefully delineated through these debates, the question still remains: How did the wider public define their place within the socialist-bourgeois divide? To what extent did these concerns inform everyday understandings and consumption norms and practices in socialist Hungary? And, perhaps even more important, how did people themselves experience and resolve the contradiction between these ideals and their growing access to material goods?

This question can be answered, to some extent, through analyzing interviews with Hungarians of diverse class backgrounds, born during the 1950s and early 1960s.[44] These interviews, in which respondents recalled their everyday life and consumption during socialism, suggests that people from different social backgrounds and political orientations solved the contradiction between official ideals and a growing level of consumption in everyday life in a variety of ways, drawing selectively and appropriating only particular elements of the official discourse into their views.

In general, the "socialist elite," broadly defined as interviewees who prospered within the "official structures" of socialist Hungary, tended to be the most sympathetic to the values valorized in the public debates. Indeed, many of these accounts shared the emphasis of Váci and other public intellectuals on socialist asceticism. This ethical stance, in tune with the official socialist ideal, was centered on principles of intellectual development, aesthetic refinement, and a broader, everyday vision of living in a "cultured," as opposed to materialistic, way. A similar sort of ethics is captured by the concept of *kulturnost*, used by Jukka Gronow in the Soviet context to describe the "special cultural consciousness" favored by the Stalinist regime, encompassing a wide range of practices, from theater going and music to good manners. Gronow associates *kulturnost* with the Stalinist making of a "civilized" and modern society via urban modes of consumption in the Soviet Union in the 1930s. Part and parcel of such consumption, however, was encouragement of a certain consumer modesty and restraint as well as appreciation for and consumption of high culture.[45]

Zsuzsa, a researcher who used to work for a research institute in Budapest, adopted many of the official norms of consumption.[46] She recalls that when she was young, in the 1960s, she used to spend her limited pocket money on inexpensive cinema tickets in Budapest's art cinemas: "I used to go to the cinema, sometimes three times a day; we used to run from one cinema to the other. There used to be these cheap cinema passes, I liked those—and to go to events or just to walk around." She continued to draw a clear normative distinction between cultural edification and materialistic consumption throughout her adult life. She recalled, for example, that during a trip to Italy in the 1980s they went to "all the museums in Rome, including the Vatican," but stayed in the cheapest hostel, never went to cafés or restaurants, and even walked to save on transport. She explained that this was "not because I couldn't afford it in principle, but because I felt bad about spending money on it. According to my value system . . . I never begrudged money spent on entry tickets and things like that, but I would prefer to walk two kilometers to avoid spending money on expensive transport."[47]

People grouped in this general category of the socialist elite classified goods outside the field of culture, and those that were seen to be excessive or showy, as materialistic consumption, a theme also central to the "conclusions" drawn in both the fridge socialism and the cashew nut debates. They tended to emphasize that their choices were always modest, even if they could afford more. Significantly, the main reason "excessive spending" and ostentation were rejected was that both were considered a characteristic of people who were not entitled to their affluence. This judgment was based first on the view that hard work, and gradual accumulation of its rewards, represented the only legitimate entitlement to goods; and second, on the assumption that money earned through honest hard work must necessarily be spent in a restrained and modest way. In other words, socialist asceticism, even when not linked to pursuit of high culture, was invariably linked to work ethic; again, this connects with public critiques of laziness and entitlement.

The link was customarily established through a narrative in which interviewees achieved everything they had "from zero," reputedly through the force of their own hard work and thriftiness, and even by denying themselves their desires and budgeting what they did have. Ilona, for example, a biochemist, recalled that in the 1970s, even when she was better off, continued budgeting, bargaining at the market, and refraining from purchasing expensive clothes, although she could afford them. In her view, being willing and able to give up material desires was the true mark of having come from a poor background and achieving one's position legitimately through hard work:

I was born after the war. All the hardship is there in me, in my subconscious . . . not my subconscious, rather on the surface . . . no, somewhere in between. So I remember that we could only heat one

room, and that kind of thing. And that the butter and jam sandwich was the absolute best, the butter and mustard sandwich not so
good. There was no ham . . . these were the 1950s. For us it was very
natural, and in fact I think that for my entire generation, if life is like
that then we have to tighten the purse-strings and we will not get
depressed. As far I am concerned, I won't. We have learned well how
to live on pennies. And to get somewhere from there.[48]

In contrast, people who spent recklessly, in her opinion, "must either steal or
cheat, or live on daddy's money, who either steals or cheats," because "if someone gets somewhere on his own steam, he is not like that [i.e., wasting money]."[49]

A similar view was expressed by János, the former head of an agricultural
conglomerate. In his account, hard-working people and real experts in their
field were naturally inclined to modest consumption. For him, these qualities
distinguished people who legitimately achieved what they had from the presocialist incompetent elite: "In the old aristocratic world, when the monkey [i.e.,
pretentious, vain] count came, he could hardly speak he was so stupid, but still
he was the count, and he was dressed up in pomp and came in a pompous
horse-drawn carriage."[50] In a tone still brimming with postwar communist disdain for a bygone aristocratic world of nobles and peasants, János, like Ilona,
posited modest consumption as an identifying characteristic of people who had
achieved their success according to the socialist ideal of hard work and gradual
advancement, as opposed to flimsy noble birthright.

Yet the paradox of this stance is that although it emphasizes egalitarianism
and asceticism, it is held only by interviewees who, thanks to their well-placed
positions during socialism, engaged in the highest level of consumption in Hungary. Interviewees, recognizing this, were often uneasy about the contradiction,
and eager to resolve it. János, for example, explained that he was always modest
in his consumption except in the case of the large house that he built when he
thought both his children and his elderly parents might move in there some day:

At that time, we thought that my son would need it [a home] as well.
It used to be different in those times. My parents were alive, and during those years we always thought that we might need to move them
in to live with us, and so on. . . . But it doesn't mean [that we were
posh]. This was the only thing; there was nothing extravagant other
than the house.[51]

Here the presumed needs of the family, rather than the individual, justified
"extravagant" acquisition of the large house.

But generally the emphasis on framing one's life according to a socialist narrative—in which consumer abundance was the result of hard work—was one of the main discourses that helped to legitimize elite consumption as "well-deserved":

> ZSUZSA: When I was a university student, I had already been working from the age of sixteen every summer. So, the point is that I earned very well; I worked fourteen to sixteen hours a day and didn't take holidays. Others worked three days, then took three days off. . . . The others were happy because they could go visit the family [during their breaks]. . . . So we had much more money at that time for furniture and we planned and chose it together. At that time, the *koloniál* style was cool and we [she and her husband] chose *koloniál* furniture, and we wanted paintings and *majolinka* vases and all that. So I shopped many times in the pawn shops in the 1970s—we frequented the pawn shops all the time; we always visited them to see if we liked something. The aim was always to buy something.
> LÉNA, INTERVIEWER: The way you furnished the flat, did it count as special?
> ZSUZSA: Yes. The kitchen-living[52] room [where we were living] and the house itself was shabby, but when we wanted to sell it and they [potential buyers] came in and saw the room, usually they remarked "wow!" because at that time it was cool, this oak *koloniál* furniture. And, obviously, these buyers didn't expect to see it there. Especially in those days.[53]

Zsuzsa could not ignore the fact that the *koloniál* furniture was special and expensive, and it could be bought by only a few people, which contradicted her usual narrative in which she wished to avoid making distinctions between groups. This contradiction was resolved through Zsuzsa's long explanation of how she worked hard to be able to buy the *koloniál* furniture. It was only a legitimate purchase because Zsuzsa and her husband worked harder than others; therefore, they had earned not just the furniture but the right to it. In this way, *koloniál* furniture was associated with an elevated lifestyle, and in fact the very idea of having a "higher" lifestyle was construed as possible and legitimate when deserved by people who were the most hard-working and ambitious in *socialist* terms. This suggests that although the socialist elite shared the moral framework identified in public discourse, the norms propagated there were not in fact translated into lower consumption, let alone asceticism, on their part. This discomfiting contradiction was resolved by deploying the ideals of culturedness and hard work, which were also emphasized in public discourse, to legitimate their relatively higher wealth and consumption.

Within the working class (understood here as people involved in physical labor), there was an even greater discrepancy between official ideology and how consumption is remembered. These interviewees often formulated their own lives using commonplace socialist platitudes such as "we worked for socialism" or "we built the country."[54] Yet, unlike in the case of public discourse as echoed in the remarks of the socialist elites, the norms of modesty and restraint were absent from the working-class accounts. Instead, their memories were centered on the desire for—and occasional achievement of—goods that were condemned in public debates as materialistic: elegant clothes with which to impress the neighbors or "lovely" home decorations that were officially labeled as petit-bourgeois kitsch.

However, unlike the socialist elite these respondents did not recognize these desires as incompatible with the official version of a socialist ideal; for them, the essence of socialism as a workers' state meant precisely that the regime provided access for workers to consumer goods that were previously the privilege of the higher classes. The Téglásis, a family of unskilled manual workers, for example, remembered that they greeted every new consumption opportunity during socialism with enthusiasm. They recalled with pride that in the 1960s they could afford to go to the local restaurant every Friday, that they bought living room furniture and elegant maternity dresses in the 1970s, and that they moved into a larger flat offered by the city council in the 1980s.

Among all of the interviewees, the Téglásis expressed the clearest nostalgia for the socialist regime, while feeling no need to couch their memories of consumption within a framework of modesty or restraint. Here, their nostalgia is arguably more than just a positive reading of socialist times or the desire to bring them back. Rather, nostalgia is simultaneously a way of framing memories of the past and a means of expressing criticism of the present by projecting ideals to the past.

This definition of nostalgia provides a clue to understanding the Téglásises' nostalgic view of the past. They often contrasted socialism with post-socialist Hungary, where inequality grew and access to goods crucial for providing a basic level of material existence and dignity became uncertain. Although they used to be very poor, they still remembered socialist times as an era of security, when they could always find work and they could take the basics—food, medicine, and shelter—for granted. For them, the fact that the state provided for some of their major expenditures, such as their flat and health care, meant they did not have to worry about saving for their future but could build a relatively happy everyday life structured around Sunday lunches and holidays. In their account, the state was akin to a kindhearted uncle who kept track of family occasions and helped them when they needed it, providing free beer on May Day and milk tickets for expectant mothers. Indeed, in many ways their personal experiences match the picture painted by official socialist discourse of happy workers enjoying the May Day celebration with their families amid the calm of everyday life:

> MÁRIA TÉGLÁSIS: Later there were these company May Day celebrations, the workers went to the Népliget [People's Park] with their families. We got sausage and beer tickets for free; they encouraged the families with that, so that when there was a celebration, we went to the Népliget. And we met colleagues there, everybody with their family, a little beer, a little sausage; these didn't cost money, but still, we relaxed there.[55]

In general, a conscious asceticism, or refusal to show off possessions, was entirely absent from the Téglásises' memories. They were much poorer, so consumer opportunities dismissed by the elite as deplorable commodity acquisition were experienced by them as an entry into "decent" society. In her recollections, Mária often referred to the importance of "living up to the larger world," the world of "decent people." She recalled regularly staying up late at night washing and ironing clothes, polishing shoes, and curling her hair so "that the neighbors can see that we are impeccably tidy and clean."[56]

These views constitute an interesting contrast to those of the socialist elite, who tended to valorize working-class poverty as down-to-earth unpretentiousness, nobler than blind pursuit of goods. This story (told by another interviewee) about a poor neighbor whose son became a noted poet during socialism captures this difference well:

> Once [the neighbor] came home and said to his wife: "We will no longer close the attic door with a corn cob. I will buy a lock!" And for him this brought genuine happiness. He was very proud that he had provided a lock. Later, his son [the poet] was boasting with that corn cob—that his father used to close the attic door with a corn cob. When this son received an award, Comrade Kádár said to the father that he can be proud of his son. The man answered, "I would be proud, but I wish he wouldn't emphasize the pitiful poverty all the time! I haven't been such a *rongy* [miserable, useless] man that I couldn't even provide for my family!" This was shameful for him. All

he understood from this and tried to say was that he was not a hopeless person, someone who could not even provide for the family![57]

Contrary to the socialist elite's (including the poet-son's) romantic vision of modest working-class life, the Téglásises, like the father in the story, found nothing uplifting about poverty; if anything, it was experienced as shameful, as a failure to live a decent life. For them, acquiring better living standards—in terms of accommodation, clothing, and food—were not taken for granted; they represented an unquestionable aim.[58] Though this aim was not incompatible with socialism per se, the emphasis on material acquisitions represents a marked difference from the accepted ideological parameters that the socialist elite used to frame their consumer experiences. Yet because these working-class interviewees saw growing consumption as entirely compatible with socialism, for them the contradiction between ideology and consumption seldom arose; when it did, it did so quite differently—in terms of why socialism was not able to provide an even higher standard of living.

Working-class respondents saw their material desires as attuned to "socialist values," but a large number of interviewees adopted what one might call an oppositional or even "antisocialist" stance that was articulated explicitly in contrast to official ideology. This stance involved rejection of the socialist emphasis on antimaterialism and equality, instead emphasizing the importance of possessions in being able to live a dignified life. This view was apparent not only in accounts of those whose families had lost property and privileges during socialism but also among participants from poor presocialist backgrounds who became relatively better off—one might say petit-bourgeois—during socialism. For them, socialism offered an opportunity to realize aspirations according to presocialist ideals.

Sára, for example, a quality controller whose father was an army officer from a peasant family, belonged to this latter category. She recalled that her family placed significant emphasis on teaching her "ladylike" behavior, which included mastering an elegant style of clothing and table manners. In her recollections, even during socialism she tried to look appropriate to her social standing (for example, having the appearance of a "degree holder") in how she dressed, furnished her home, and held formal family lunches. For her, a modest, egalitarian society—where differences disappear in general, and in terms of consumption in particular—was neither a reality nor an ideal to which one should aspire.

At the same time, Sára agreed with many of the elements of socialist discourse, such as rejection of individualism. Yet she saw the socialist system as counterproductive to these very values:

KIDS, CARS, OR CASHEWS?

Look, polgári[59] [presocialist bourgeois] society had a value system. I
did not grow up in the polgári society but in the socialist. It was all
about alienating people from one another as much as possible, putting them into 50 square meter flats and putting their parents into
elderly homes. The poorer people are, the better it is so that they do
not have time to think: only that they have the cheap schnapps, beer,
a TV and nothing else. . . . One should only be a worker, exist only at
that level. In a 50 square meter flat in which you cannot have family
celebrations, because where would you seat people?[60]

This view was elaborated by Otto, an engineer from a wealthy peasant family
whose property had been nationalized:

In the 1950s, when one was not allowed to own anything and one
was called a "kulak"[61] or an "exploiter," it is back then that people
used to live like that (one day to the next, drinking away their wages
every day). There were lots of pubs and that sort of thing. One used
to own one jacket, just a cap, not even a hat, and what one earned
was spent immediately. People used to go to the pub and drink because there was nothing else to do. Also, it would have been frowned
upon to save. They would have been asked where they'd stolen what
they'd accumulated. This was the mentality. If one was a bit thrifty
and wanted to achieve something, one was frowned upon, especially
at the workplace.[62]

In Sára's and Otto's accounts, the modest and even ascetic socialist consumer
norms did not contribute to a fuller life as painted in public debates. In Otto's
recollections, it was precisely this norm—as well as the poverty it obscured—
that prohibited long-term planning, genuine hard work, and formation of community feeling. In this sense, the underlying values behind this antisocialist
stance share some of those similarly propagated in socialist public discourse,
except that those who adhere to this point of view also reject the idea that these
values could be, or ever were, realized through the socialist path. Instead, these
respondents promoted a different ideal, where private property, wealth accumulation, and consumption in general were the indispensable elements of a
proper, full life. These respondents therefore viewed the growing affluence in
later socialism—as opposed to the lean 1950s, which they described as empty
of values—with approval.

Similarly—and again in contrast to the socialist elite—interviewees who
had realized most of their income through the so-called second (unofficial)

economy framed their own consumer practices against the grain of official socialism. Interestingly, these respondents employed a certain level of ignorance about socialist-era public debates on consumption as well as a sense of irony about the same. Though many were aware of some of the elements of socialist public discourse, such elements were almost entirely absent from their own accounts of the socialist era; for them these were nothing more than empty phrases. In fact, these interviewees were convinced that *everybody* tried to navigate their way through socialism as best they could, without taking the public discourse on consumption seriously at all. Instead, like the working class (although with significantly greater means at their disposal), this group recalled a carefree and eager approach to spending and made no mention of self-restraint or normative considerations in relation to consumption. In addition, like many in the working class, they did not see their consumption habits as specifically opposed to socialist ideology.

In fact, many in this group often explained excessive spending practices as a direct consequence of socialism. Olga, who worked in a cooperative but earned large sums of unreported revenue, remembered socialism as follows:

> When I was young, I also experienced this [habit of excessive buying].
> I used to have many clothes that I never wore. In fact, I experienced
> this when I divorced and we moved out of our former flat; the majority
> of the things—furniture, books, kitchenware—we shipped over to the
> new flat over several weeks. I was putting the clothes that we had never
> ever worn in our entire life into bags. We hadn't even taken them out
> of the wardrobe! And it was not only clothes, but there were also pots
> which were not even unpacked. . . . So I too went through this. In my
> opinion, almost everybody did: that you see something, and you want
> it immediately, you take it home, and you have a look at yourself in the
> mirror, and you say: "Jesus Christ! How is that possible?! I liked this?!"
> It happened. And you know, earlier [during socialism] it was because
> you couldn't buy that many things. . . . And then I would see some-
> thing that I was convinced I had been longing for for a thousand years.
> I tried it, it was all right, I came home and . . . What could you do with
> it? You could not take it back. You put it into the wardrobe.[63]

Olga linked her behavior to scarcity, which for her (as for most people) meant longing for specific goods and being in a constant state of searching. In this state, if one had the rare opportunity to buy something nice, one had to grab it.[64] But Olga's glut of personal goods seemed to directly contradict the notion that she lived a life of scarcity. Perhaps more important, Olga did not see her practices as in any way irregular; in fact, she was convinced that everybody thought and lived the same way she did.

Miklós, who set up his private textile company in the 1970s, took a similar approach to consumption. After an initial period of budgeting, he started buying expensive jewelry and fashionable clothes for himself and his family. He explained that the new entrepreneurs were highly competitive in their consumption, and success was measured by possessions. In his account, it was not a reaction to the shortage economy, but rather a way of asserting his status and gaining access to informal channels that allowed his business to thrive. He explained that during socialism he could buy raw materials only "under the counter" (that is, illegally), and he recalled that once, when he approached shop assistants in a modest outfit, parking his cheap Eastern Bloc car, a Trabant, outside the shop, he was met with refusal. It was only when he tried again, wearing visible signs of his wealth, that he was able to buy the scarce raw materials he needed. Unlike Olga, he was aware that his practices were vilified in socialist public discourse, but as he recalled it, these norms were so distant from his everyday experiences that he could not take them seriously.[65]

Conclusion

In 1969, during a meeting of the Hungarian Communist Party's Planning Commission, a cadre member voiced his concerns about a document that set out the direction of Hungary's development for the next fifteen years:

> It is somewhat disheartening that the forecasts of a socialist country up to 1985 . . . do not say much more than that the structure of consumption will follow a pattern very similar to that of more developed countries. If we want more than just to create a kind of bourgeois welfare, then we have to take into account more seriously the specific nature of a socialist country.[66]

The question of whether material well-being was the hallmark of success of the socialist system or if it threatened the very essence of the socialist ethos remained one of the system's central ideological dilemmas. The predominantly intellectual contributors to the lifestyle debates tended toward the latter position and put forward a vision of socialist society that was not simply more affluent but more "moral" than its capitalist counterpart. According to this ideal, people were supposed to find satisfaction in hard work, and in engagement with public life and culture as opposed to materialism—a term that stood for a complex set of condemnable phenomena of egoism, individualism, laziness, and superficiality. For them, growing affluence constituted a threat to the socialist ideal.

However, analysis of memories of socialism reveals that the worry about rampant materialism and its incongruity with socialist ethics, which constituted the central theme of these debates, was hardly shared by all people at the time. The socialist elite were the only group discomfited by the contradiction between material wealth and socialist norms. "Socialist workers," on the other hand, proposed a different ideal of socialism as a system that permitted equal access to material abundance. The only group that formulated its views explicitly in opposition to socialism (as both a system and a set of ideals centered on asceticism and equality) is that of antisocialist respondents with petit-bourgeois and wealthy presocialist backgrounds. Finally, "socialist entrepreneurs" were either unaware of the public discourse that derided their lavish purchases or simply treated it as empty ideology.

These stances allowed people in diverse positions within the social hierarchy to resolve the contradiction posed by the widening gap between the official ideal of modest consumption and the reality of a rapidly developing consumer culture. Although all of them contained elements of (or at least references to) the socialist ideals, none of these stances, not even self-declared socialist ones, involved full commitment to the official socialist ideals of ascetism and egalitarianism. This tension between official ideology and discourse on the one hand and people's actual practices and views on the other represented an internal and seemingly perpetual contradiction of the system.

NOTES

1. Most recently by David Crowley and Susan Reid, "Introduction," in *Pleasures and Socialism* (Evanston, IL: Northwestern University Press, 2010).

2. Sándor Horváth, *Kádár gyermekei* (Budapest: Nyitott Könyvműhely, 2009), 128; Tamás Valuch, *A hétköznapi élet Kádár János korában* (Budapest: Corvina, 2006).

3. Anna Wessely, "Travelling People, Travelling Objects," *Cultural Studies* 16 (2002): 3–15.

4. Ferenc Hammer and Tibor Dessewffy, "A fogyasztás kísértete," *Replika* 26 (1997): 31–46.

5. Miklós Vörös, "Életmód, ideológia, háztartás: A fogyasztáskutatás politikuma az államszocializmus korszakában," *Replika* 26 (1997): 17–30; Ákos Róna-Tas, *The Great Surprise of the Small Transformation: The Demise of Communism and the Rise of the Private Sector in Hungary* (Ann Arbor: University of Michigan Press, 1997), 66.

6. Tibor Dessewffy, "Az ántivilág," in *A kocka el van veszve* (Budapest: Infonia-Aula, 2002), 141–59.

7. Horváth, *Kádár gyermekei*, 128.

8. MSZMP KB. Agitációs és Propaganda Osztály, *Jelentés a reklámtevékenységről*, Apr. 11, 1973, as cited by Horváth, *Kádár gyermekei*. In theory, socialist advertisers focused on providing "truthful" information about the products' price and use value. See István Bessenyei and Mária Heller, "A reklám: a csereérték ügynöke vagy a fogyasztás szolgálólánya?" *Jel-Kép* 2 (1980): 118–34. As Bessenyei and Heller point out, however, socialist marketing used the same strategies of symbolic differentiation as its capitalist counterpart. According to them, its strategic role was to enhance the factories' position in the struggle for scarce resources, as the demand generated by advertisements for the company's products served as a basis of claims for further subsidies and resources from the state. The same tension between socialist advertisers' self-image and their practice is more thoroughly analyzed by Patterson in the case of Yugoslavia. See Patrick Hyder Patterson, "Truth Half Told: Finding the Perfect Pitch for Advertising and Marketing in Socialist Yugoslavia, 1950–1991," *Enterprise & Society* 4 (2003): 179–225.

9. Ferenc Hammer and Tibor Dessewffy, "A fogyasztás kísértete," 37–38.

10. Zsuzsa Ferge, *A Society in the Making: Hungarian Social and Societal Policy, 1945–1975* (Harmondsworth: Penguin, 1979); Hammer and Dessewffy, "A fogyasztás kísértete"; Tamás Valuch, *Magyarország társadalomtörténete a XX. század második felében* (Budapest: Osiris, 2005); Valuch, *A hétköznapi élet Kádár János korában* (Budapest: Corvina, 2006).

11. Part of the problem was the ambiguity of the Soviet model, in which core socialist values of egalitarianism and asceticism were in tension with Stalin's creation of a Soviet political elite and a technocratic "middle class" in the 1930s. Still, Stalin's consuming classes had been constrained both by the limits of the Soviet economy in the 1930s and, more critically, the austerity required during World War II. See David Hoffman, *Stalinist Values: The Cultural Norms of Soviet Modernity, 1917–1941* (Ithaca, NY: Cornell University Press, 2003); and Jukka Gronow, *Caviar with Champagne: Common Luxury and the Ideals of the Good Life in Stalin's Russia* (Oxford: Berg, 2003).

12. In past years, these debates were often the object of historical and sociological analysis. Most authors use them only to illustrate the limited nature of the socialist "public sphere." András Mink, "A kesudió ügy," *Beszélő* 3 (1997): 7–8; István Rév, "Retrotópia: A kritikai gondolkodás primitív fordulata," *Beszélő* 12 (1998): 40–54; Heller et al., "Nyilvános stratégiák és nyilvános szabályok," *Szociológiai Szemle* 4 (1992): 53–60. Others used these debates to document certain trends in the socioeconomic history of Hungary; Iván Berend, *Gazdasági útkeresés 1956–1965: A szocialista gazdaság magyarországi modelljének történetéhez* (Budapest: Magvető, 1983). Passing references to these debates are often made in the literature on socialist consumption and material culture (Vörös, "Életmód, ideológia, háztartás"; Krisztina Fehérváry, "Goods and States: The Political Logic of State-Socialist Material Culture," *Comparative Studies in Society and History* 51 (2009): 426–59.

13. Mink, "A kesudió ügy."

14. See Timothy Garton Ash, "A Hungarian Lesson," in *The Uses of Adversity: Essays on the Fate of Central Europe* (New York: Random House, 1989), 143–56; Gábor

Murányi, "A magyar sajtó története 1948-tól 1988-ig: Vázlatos áttekintés" in *A magyar sajtó története*, ed. György Kókay, Géza Buzinkay, and Gábor Murányi (Budapest: Sajtókönyvtár. 1994), 218–21.

15. *Élet és Irodalom* was a biweekly newspaper that contained political and social commentary, feature articles, longer analyses, and belles lettres. *Kritika* was published monthly and defined itself during the socialist period as "a journal of cultural policy." *Kortárs* and *Új Írás* were literary journals with social commentary columns.

16. László Zöldi, *Az ÉS vitái* (Budapest: Múzsák Közművelődési Kiadó, 1983), 81.

17. Murányi, "A magyar sajtó története 1948-tól 1988-ig," 222.

18. Mihály Váci, "Se atombomba, de az isten!" *Új Írás* 7 (1961): 579.

19. Although more limited in scale and importance, a debate on Socialist Culture and Entertainment took place in *Kritika* from 1972 to 1973, which reflected a series of public discussions about popular culture, mass culture, and "light art" that were present in other periodicals as well throughout the socialist years.

20. Váci, "Se atombomba."

21. János Földeák, "Hűség a néphez és a marxizmus-leninizmushoz!" *Új Írás* 1 (1962): 50–51.

22. Imre Gerelyes, "Huszonegy karóra," *Új Írás* 9 (1961): 839–42.

23. Editorial Board of Új Írás, "Kultúra és életforma," *Új Írás* 8 (1961): 736–37.

24. Gyula Fekete, "Árnyékboxolás—tizenkét menetben," *Élet és Irodalom* 13 (1964): 5–6.

25. István Márkus, "Már ma is a holnap készül," *Új Írás* 4 (1962): 358–61.

26. Váci, "Se atombomba."

27. Márkus, "Már ma is a holnap készül."

28. Ambrus Bor, "Több kenyér, kevesebb gyermek?" *Élet és Irodalom* 50 (Dec. 14, 1963): 5; József Pálfy, "Az emberiség kenyeret kér. Népesség, szaporodás—és távlatok," *Élet és Irodalom* 47 (Nov. 23, 1963): 1–2.

29. Bor, op. cit.

30. Éva Bozóky, "Közügy vagy magánügy?" *Élet és Irodalom* 2 (Jan. 11, 1964): 7–8.

31. Bor, "Több kenyér, kevesebb gyermek?"

32. Bulcsú Bertha, "Kesudió," *Élet és Irodalom* 9 (Feb. 28, 1976): 3–4.

33. Gyula Virizlay, "Kultúra és szórakozás: Megjegyzések Agárdi Péter cikkéhez," *Kritika* 10 (1972): 16.

34. József Bőgel, "(Olvasói levél)," *Új Írás* 4 (1962): 361–62.

35. The use of the term "petit-bourgeois" to mark problematic tendencies in socialist lifestyle is not limited to the case of Hungary but appeared in all countries throughout the regions facing a similar socioeconomic situation. For the case of Czechoslovakia, see Paulina Bren, "Mirror, Mirror, on the Wall . . . Is the West the Fairest of Them All? Czechoslovak Normalization and Its (Dis)Contents," *Kritika* 9 (2008): 846–47.

36. Editor Board of Új Írás, "Kultúra és életforma," *Új Írás* 8 (1961): 736–37.

37. Imre Gerelyes, "Huszonegy karóra," *Új Írás* 9 (1961): 839–42.

38. Eta Ádám, "Sok a tisztáznivaló," *Új Írás* 6 (1962): 626–27.

39. Agárdi, Gábor, "Szocialista kultúra és szórakozás." *Kritika* 6 (1972): 11–12; Róbert Rátonyi, "Mitől 'könnyű' az, ami nehéz?" *Kritika* 9 (1972): 15.

40. Virizlay, "Kultúra és szórakozás."

41. Edit Erki, "Ok vagy okozat?" *Élet és Irodalom* 12 (1964): 5–6.

42. Editorial Board of Új Írás, "Kultúra és életforma," 903–5.

43. Ibid, 903–5.

44. The empirical data were collected in the form of interviews conducted by Léna Pellandini-Simányi between July 2005 and June 2006, as part of a research project that looked at changing consumption norms in Hungary.

45. Gronow, *Caviar with Champagne*, 146–47.

46. Interview with Zsuzsa by Léna Pellandini-Simányi, Budapest, Feb. 10, 2006. (All interviews were conducted in confidentiality, and the names of interviewees are changed by mutual agreement.)

47. Ibid.

48. Interview with Ilona by Léna Pellandini-Simányi, Budapest, Sept. 23, 2005.

49. Ibid.

50. Interview with János by Léna Pellandini-Simányi, Budapest, Sept. 30, 2005.

51. Ibid.

52. The flat consisted of one room and a kitchen.

53. Interview with Zsuzsa by Léna Pellandini-Simányi, Budapest, Feb. 10, 2006.

54. Interview with Ábel by Léna Pellandini-Simányi, Budapest, Mar. 13, 2006.

55. Interview with Mária by Léna Pellandini-Simányi, Budapest, Mar. 24, 2006.

56. Ibid.

57. Interview with Sándor by Léna Pellandini-Simányi, Budapest, Nov. 10, 2005.

58. The contradiction between this view and the official ideology, which emphasized the opposition between inner richness and material desires and praised material simplicity, offers important parallels with other antimaterialist projects. Beyond the obvious parallels with other socialist countries, connections can be drawn with Western trends of mass culture critique on the part of the 1960s counterculture, the voluntary simplicity movement, and academic critique of materialism. But as Daniel Miller points out, laudable though the aims of these antimaterialist movements may be, they should not run counter to what he calls "a quite different morality, an ethics based on a passionate desire to eliminate poverty." Although the antimaterialist stance may well hold in Western, middle-class contexts, he suggests that "most human suffering is the direct result of the lack of goods. What most of humanity desperately needs is more consumption, more pharmaceuticals, more housing, more transport, more books, more computers." Miller, "The Poverty of Morality," *Journal of Consumer Culture* 1 (2001): 227–28.

59. The word *polgári* originally means citizen, and it has a long history of denoting ideas related to citizens' rights and duties as opposed to the aristocratic and socialist organization of society. Recently it has been appropriated by the conservative party, called Fidesz (Party of Young Democrats)—Hungarian Polgári Party, to emphasize continuity with presocialist Hungary and tradition as opposed to the Socialist Party. The word conveys anticommunist overtones, nostalgia for presocialist times and positive associations of peaceful development, and bourgeois civilization. Here she uses the term to refer to the society before socialism.

60. Interview with Sára by Léna Pellandini-Simányi, Budapest, Apr. 09, 2006.

61. *Kulak* is a derogatory term for a wealthy land owner.

62. Interview with Otto by Léna Pellandini-Simányi, Budapest, Apr. 14, 2006.

63. Interview with Olga by Léna Pellandini-Simányi, Budapest, May 15, 2006.

64. This phenomenon is described by Katalin S. Nagy as the "scarcity game of socialism" ("when, where, what can be bought at the moment"), a consumer strategy based on rapidly recognizing and grasping unexpected and elusive consumption opportunities. Nagy, "Fogyasztás és lakáskultúra Magyarországon a hetvenes években," *Replika* 26 (1997): 47–53.

65. Interview with Miklós by Léna Pellandini-Simányi, Budapest, May 22, 2006.

66. Unnamed Party cadre member, quoted in Ferge, *Society in the Making*, 306.

14

The House That Socialism Built

*Reform, Consumption, and Inequality
in Postwar Yugoslavia*

Brigitte Le Normand

Socialist Yugoslavia held a unique place within the spectrum of state policies and consumer cultures that characterized postwar Eastern Europe. Although outside the Bloc as of 1948, Yugoslavia followed the Bloc pattern to a surprising degree. At the same time, it was never constrained by Soviet policy or oversight. This had far-reaching consequences as Yugoslavia was more openly able to prioritize consumer needs and curtail central planning in favor of a consumer-driven economy. Starting in 1957, personal consumption went from being last on the list of priorities to occupying the middle position in the social plan for 1957–1961, which set out the economic goals for this period.[1] It shortly rose to the top priority, culminating in the major reforms of July 1965, during which Yugoslav policymakers fundamentally altered the central planning system, gradually turning it into a "mixed economy." In this system the market played a greater role, and enterprises (though the vast majority were still socially owned) vied for clients. As a result, in contrast to the queues and empty shelves that were common in the Eastern Bloc for much of the period, shops in Yugoslavia were overflowing with products, domestic and foreign, common and luxurious.

Yet Yugoslavia, like the rest of the Eastern Bloc, was still a socialist country, with a one-party state, social ownership of production, and a

Marxist program of social and economic transformation. Economic priorities and consequent reforms thus echoed concerns elsewhere behind the Iron Curtain, where policy shifts of the 1950s also meant a turn toward consumption and a higher standard of living. But in Yugoslavia, as elsewhere, did this prioritization of consumption, and the new role of consumer preference in guiding the economy, produce more contented consumer-citizens? Or did these citizens reject the more onerous outcomes of market liberalization, most palpable in Yugoslavia, which effectively led to serious price increases in 1965?

From an ideological perspective, consumption's newly prescribed role in the economy created certain conundrums for the Yugoslav regime and its citizens. One major problem was harmonizing consumption and consumer culture with socialist values that, in spite of appearances, had not been discarded.[2] Such tensions arguably pervaded all sectors of the Yugoslav economy to an even greater extent than in the Bloc. Because Bloc states had both less economic liberalization—including its visible inequitable effects—and a lower tolerance for critique of state reforms, in Yugoslavia patterns of provision and consumption provoked far greater public scrutiny and official debate. As a result, the Communist Party goals of consumer-driven economic modernization and creation of an egalitarian workers' state led to open conflict and negotiation.

The realm of urban housing, in particular the housing economy in Belgrade, offers an instructive example for tracking the predicaments of Yugoslav consumption. Most studies of consumption in Eastern Europe have tended to focus on disposable goods, such as clothing, plastic goods, and home furnishings; shifting attention to a costly durable good such as housing offers a useful corrective to the image of a society of abundance in the 1960s. Whereas almost everyone could take part in the consumer feast of foods, clothes, and home furnishings, acquiring a home was a costly proposition, one that was not within everyone's reach. At the same time, it was a more essential need than many of the consumer goods that had become readily available. European socialist states, Yugoslavia included, resolved this dilemma by committing themselves to renting affordable housing to their citizens, but in most cases they were able to provide rentals to only a fraction of their populations. Thus, whether bought or rented, housing offers a useful barometer of distribution practices and experiences of inequality in these states. In Yugoslavia, the visibility of inequality in urban housing—more so than for any other available consumer good—turned it into a litmus test by which the press and the public assessed the outcomes of consumer policy and economic reform.

From Egalitarian to Self-Managed Consumption (1944–1964)

As the Communist Party of Yugoslavia consolidated its power at the end of the Second World War and into the 1950s, Yugoslavia's federal government passed various laws and regulations related to housing. Operating on the model of the Soviet Union and the newly forming Eastern Bloc, socialist policymakers rethought the role of housing on the basis of a critique of its place in the capitalist system and expressed their desire to transform its role in line with the twin goals of industrialization and creation of an egalitarian society. First, the Yugoslav regime limited the rights of landowners, operating on the Marxist assumption that real estate ownership was a means for an idle privileged class to exploit the working class. Authorities moved to gradually eradicate this form of exploitation by freezing rents at half their 1939 levels, which they would reach again only in 1952.[3] As far as distribution of existing housing was concerned, Yugoslav officials identified excess space in privately owned apartments and redistributed it to inhabitants in need of lodging. Local authorities also managed and rented out state-owned housing stock (mostly properties confiscated from collaborators after the war) according to "objective criteria," though in practice there were serious irregularities.[4] Beyond serving the egalitarian agenda of consumption according to one's needs, assigning apartments also reinforced the state's power, contributing to forming a network of patron-client relationships.[5]

In pursuit of its egalitarian agenda, the state took over not only distribution of housing but also financing and production. Architects and urban planners with explicitly egalitarian visions were charged with producing models and concepts for standardized apartments, buildings, and even housing settlements that could be reproduced all over the country.[6] Competitions were held to find the best possible design for an apartment, largely defined as one that maximized the use of resources—especially space and building materials.[7] At the same time, in the interest of industrialization, investment in housing as with other consumer goods was strictly limited. Indeed, according to economist Ljubo Sirc's calculation, consumption of virtually all goods more or less stagnated in the period between 1948 and 1955, actually decreasing in 1950 and 1952, and growing by an average of only 2 percent per year between 1944 and 1955.[8] There was an initial period of intensive housing construction in the Yugoslav capital, as authorities in Belgrade urgently needed to replace some of the stock that had been destroyed in the war, nearly half of which (12,889 out of 30,000 buildings) was either damaged or totally destroyed.[9] But after this initial building boom, the number of apartments built each year stabilized at approximately 1,200–1,300 between 1950 and 1953, in spite of the population of the city growing by an average of 18,800 new inhabitants per year.[10] This came to an average of about one new apartment built in Belgrade per fifteen new inhabitants during these years, which was clearly insufficient to meet demand.

Having split from the Bloc in 1947–48, Yugoslavia shifted in 1953 to the policy of "self-management," the cornerstone of the famously unique Yugoslav "path to socialism." Yugoslav officials claimed that self-management was "true" socialism, where workers ran their own factories through elected workers' councils. This system would also be applied to the "noneconomic" sector—which included schools, hospitals, and the civil service—and all other dimensions of organized social and political life, including the governing of apartment buildings. In the housing sector, self-management was initially put to the service of the state's egalitarian agenda. Management of apartment buildings was placed directly in the hands of the inhabitants, with building owners retaining only the right to receive a percentage of rents or sell or bequeath their property. Buildings containing more than two large apartments or three small ones were subjected to the new system, and real estate owners' ability to profit from their property was further limited.[11]

In the midst of Yugoslavia's move to self-management, the death of Stalin in 1953 and resultant shifts in Soviet leadership precipitated normalization in Soviet-Yugoslav relations. Khrushchev's "Peaceful Coexistence" opened diplomatic and trade relations between Yugoslavia and the Bloc, though Soviet intervention in Hungary in 1956 meant that tensions continued and Yugoslavia was never formally reincorporated into the Eastern Bloc. Still, a "thaw" in relations lessened the pressure on Yugoslav military investment and brought a shift toward more investments in production of consumer goods at the expense of investment in heavy industry. Significantly, this was precisely the period when a similar shift, though admittedly less dramatic, was taking place within the Eastern Bloc.[12] For Yugoslavia, as for the Bloc, the notion of keeping up with the "West" was central to domestic legitimacy in this period, and incentives for workers were meant to encourage productivity and thus further the building of socialism.[13] Indeed, more than elsewhere in the Bloc, in Yugoslavia consumption and production were meant to propel each other forward as an "engine" of the economy. In short, workers would finance their heightened consumption through increased productivity; incentives would jump-start the sluggish economy.

The Yugoslav approach to the consumer sector prioritized an increased standard of living, as reflected in a series of proclamations and decisions between 1955 and 1957. In 1955, Tito indicated in a speech in Karlovac that the state would reduce its capital investments and increase investment in production of consumer goods, a reorientation that was reflected in the 1957–1961 economic plan. Whereas increasing the standard of living had achieved only fourth and last place among the goals of the 1948 Five Year Plan, by 1964 it moved to first place.[14] As a result, consumption increased by an average of 8.5 percent per year between 1957 and 1964.[15] Curiously, this coincided with an almost identical shift in the parallel universe of the Eastern Bloc, where precisely an "increased standard of living" became a priority enshrined in state policy. Across the Bloc, in the area of housing, states recognized the urgent need to attend to housing crises, a key element in affecting change in living standards.[16] This was by no means seen as antithetical to Yugoslav self-management, wherein self-managed enterprises redistributed to workers a large proportion of their "profits" through rewards, including new housing.

Perhaps this shift in Yugoslavia as elsewhere was less about ideology than the possibility for greater consumption given actualized postwar recovery. After all, economic policymaker Edvard Kardelj had been arguing since at least 1947 that workers would be motivated to work harder by the prospect of pay according to productivity, translating increased effort into a higher standard of living.[17] This is to be distinguished from the practice in the 1930s in the Soviet Union of rewarding exemplary employees—shock workers—with privileges.[18] Rather, Kardelj's idea was to reward the enterprise as a whole in a manner commensurate with its productivity. This was a hollow promise in the context of consumer goods shortages, but it came to have real resonance as the potential for more consumer goods expanded in the late 1950s. By this time Yugoslav policymakers made an explicit connection between production and consumption. In the second Party plenum of 1959, for example, Mijalko Todorović justified the shift to greater incentives in stating that workers were motivated to be more productive by the "dream of consuming."[19]

This consumerist shift had important long-term consequences, although in the short run the Yugoslav state did not abandon its egalitarian mission. Far from privatizing, the Yugoslav state continued to manage housing in a truly "socialist" fashion, and by 1958 all residential buildings were nationalized. Each Yugoslav continued to have the right, however, to own and occupy a building containing a maximum of two large apartments or three small ones; legislators considered this amount of real estate to be sufficient for fulfilling an extended family's needs, anything beyond this being considered rental property.[20] Though policymakers did not oppose private ownership of real estate per se, they discouraged its spread, promoting instead the growth of the "social" sector, which would finance, own, and manage the majority of new housing in urban centers and control distribution, as elsewhere in the Bloc.[21] Moreover, the new commitment to improving the standard of living did not translate into ramped-up housing production. In 1956, a year in which Belgrade's population alone increased by fourteen thousand inhabitants, the total number of apartments built across Yugoslavia was a mere 14,375.[22] Given the chronic shortage of housing, distribution continued to be a tool for maintaining state power.

At the same time, the consumerist shift resulted in new policies, aimed at resolving the housing crisis, that set the stage for gradual privatization of the housing sector. Having subsidized the cost of housing for all these years, Yugoslav policymakers suddenly sought to make its consumer-citizens foot the bill. To put the housing sector on sound financial footing, the state had to rethink how it should go about financing construction of housing for ordinary citizens. In 1955, Funds for Housing Construction were created in select Yugoslav cities, including Belgrade. According to this new system for financing housing, 4 percent of workers' wages would be deposited into these funds. Because the funds were locally administered, policymakers believed it would encourage firms to improve their productivity and local government to invest in economic development since increased revenues would benefit workers and local citizens directly. The reforms of 1959 institutionalized this practice on a national scale and also raised rents to reflect the cost of amortization and maintenance so that depleted housing stock could be replaced. Moreover, the reforms introduced a new concept: the idea that people could purchase an apartment through a prepayment system, which allowed them to make monthly payments to a construction company to finance construction of a new home. For the first time, policymakers actively sought to mobilize personal savings in order to increase the housing stock. In a limited way, they had introduced market mechanisms, tying access to housing to enterprise productivity and allowing construction firms to sell to individuals. Through their reforms, they made housing an "investment" for Yugoslav citizens by giving them a personal stake in purchase and maintenance.

After a few years, however, it became apparent that this new system favored certain strata of the population over others, compromising the still-prominent state objective of creating an egalitarian workers' state. Namely, even though all employees in the social sector were obliged to contribute a fraction of their income toward construction of housing, only a small proportion actually obtained a state-owned apartment. Making matters worse, these lucky few were not always chosen according to need and precedence. Although they were not supposed to do so, employers used apartments to lure scarce skilled labor and management to their enterprises. Those who obtained apartments were further privileged in relation to those who did not because rents set by the state were subsidized and thus substantially lower than the cost of subletting or building one's own home.

Subletting a room or a bed in an apartment was a very expensive proposition. Landlords could charge whatever price they wanted, thanks to the endemic housing crisis, the constant influx of workers to Belgrade, and the fact
that subletting, even if legal, was not regulated by the state. Frequent articles on
the subject of the housing crisis in the weekly newspaper *Beogradska nedelja*
juxtaposed the haves and the have-nots in the Belgrade housing arena. One
article, for example, described exploitation of single renters at the hands of
unscrupulous landlords through a series of anecdotes.[23] In one case, a woman
was renting seven beds to fourteen girls, and the housing council for her
building could do nothing about it because it was headed by her relative. In
another instance, a landlord rented a room, with no access to a bathroom, to
six girls who paid 4,500 dinars apiece. One cartoon made light of the cramped
living situation of such young people, depicting two well-dressed landlords
standing in front of their apartment entrances, each one covered with more
than ten nameplates: one landlord asks the other, "Wouldn't it be something
if our sub-letters played a soccer match?"[24] Newspapers also regularly published articles on people forced to live in the most abject living conditions—
slums, converted pig sties, or hastily converted cargo train wagons.[25] Such
articles and cartoons, which appeared in virtually every issue of the Belgrade
weekly, attest to the prominence and visibility of housing inequities in the
Yugoslav capital. Indeed, a number of predominantly low-income households
headed by unskilled or semiskilled workers opted to resolve their need for
housing by building their own home without official sanction, a phenomenon
that was described as "wild construction." Self-builders would erect a house
illegally, frequently on land reserved for other purposes. They used their own
savings to build these homes, which they tended to complete in stages, moving
in as soon as there were four walls and a roof. In 1961, it was estimated there
were twenty-four hundred illegally erected buildings standing in Belgrade,
including housing as well as sheds.[26]

Though a dearth of housing construction by the state and the social inequalities that resulted from it were not unique to Yugoslav socialism, citizens
were entitled to discuss the problem more openly than elsewhere in the Bloc.[27]
Although it is unclear how most people actually understood housing questions,
the Yugoslav press began to frame these issues as a problem of inequality—a
discourse that was both engrained and politically acceptable. In *Beogradska
nedelja*, for example, journalist Živorad Živković pointed out that only 5.2 percent of apartments built in the first half of 1961 were in the most-affordable
category IV. Apartments during this period were classified in four standard
categories, with category I apartments using the highest-quality materials and
having the most luxurious amenities, and category IV apartments as most

basic. Živković denounced the fact that the majority of apartments built were category II, an irresponsible choice in view of the chronic shortage of housing and the fact that two category IV apartments could be built for the cost of producing one in category II. Initially, Živković and others faulted urban planners for aspiring to build only luxurious, cutting-edge, and expensive housing, to the detriment of more modest, less ambitious homes.[28] As another reporter also complained, "No one is asking urban planners to build [inexpensive apartments] in New Belgrade but why can't they lower their expectations in the periphery of the city?"[29] He claimed to have interviewed a number of people who had not had an apartment for years, who all endorsed lower-standard apartments because "what is buying coal and a ceramic stove in comparison to living in humid rooms, little shacks, apartments with roommates, or bachelor's rooms for 14,000 dinars and rent paid a year in advance?"[30] Surprisingly, many federal policymakers tended to agree with this articulation of the problem, revealing deep discomfort at the higher levels with the effects of housing reform. Momčilo Marković, a member of the Federal Executive Council, appeared to reiterate Živković's criticism when he stated that "we are building apartments that are more expensive than what our standard and national income can allow." He put pressure on urban planners to lower their requirements for quality or luxury in order to bring down the cost of apartments.[31]

Later discussions of the problem grew more critical of the Yugoslav state itself, rather than merely its urban planners. Critics found fault with both the housing funds and the economic system in general. In a 1963 article, for example, Živković accused the state of having set up a system that consistently discriminated against workers. He opened dramatically:

> In our city, every third apartment is NEWLY BUILT. [. . .] [From 1946] to the first day of January of the year, 48,064 new apartments were built.
> Only 3,460 workers moved into a new apartment.
> Of each 100 keys, workers obtained SEVEN.
> Of every thousand, but SEVENTY.[32]

But if workers were not getting the apartments, then who was? "That's right," Živković answered, "those apartments were obtained by specialists, we resolved THE CADRE PROBLEM, the apartments were obtained by those upon whom production depends the most." It is tempting to read into this a reference to the new "red bourgeoisie" condemned by Milovan Djilas in *The New Class*, but Živković was in fact talking about engineers and managers, whose privileged position resulted not from Party membership but from demand for their scarce skills. At the same time, because connections or party membership seem to have determined access to top positions, we cannot completely write off Djilas' argument.

This was a "new class" of technocrats who formed a broader-based group of consumers than Djilas's narrow communist elite.[33] As Živković observed, these cadres had privileged access to housing, while certain workers had significant disadvantages. Various economic branches—among them the textile industry, building construction, the leather and shoe industry, the wood industry, hostelry, and retail commerce—contributed much larger sums to the Funds for Housing Construction than they were able to retrieve. Construction workers, for example, paid 730 million dinars into the funds and retrieved only 31 million dinars. According to Živković, firms working in large-scale commerce, import-export, and electrical energy faced no such problems. Small firms were also discriminated against. They paid in 1.2 million dinars and retrieved only 200,000 dinars. Finally, Živković noted that corruption was a problem, suggesting that some workers' council members had managed to convince the councils to invest in luxury apartments for their own use. Once again raising the issue of overproduction of costly apartments, he condemned the policy in no uncertain terms: "There are no valid arguments to justify such a housing policy."

An article the following November suggests that Živković was not just stirring up trouble but was expressing commonly shared frustrations. The municipal committee of the Communist Party, in collaboration with other organizations, invited the employees of eighteen firms in Belgrade to send in questions addressed to their local political leaders. The 1,885 responses indicated that workers were most preoccupied with "food, apartments, the cost of transportation; in other words, the price of consumer goods in general." The author of the article noted that workers in small companies sought a greater share in the apartments built, and that workers in large factories expressed frustration that management was getting most of the apartments.[34]

The Funds for Housing Construction, introduced in 1955 in Belgrade and throughout Yugoslavia in 1959, were a first effort to rationalize production of housing and encourage local economic development. But the program basically led to preferential distribution of housing to managers because they were considered to be the most valuable for production. Hence, even with its seemingly socialist form of pooling of resources for housing, the result of the policy was to increase visible inequity in housing practices. Yugoslav commitment to creating a more egalitarian society remained strong, but in practice certain segments of the population—technical specialists, in particular—benefited from the new system, while workers continued to live in relative squalor. As Yugoslav reform exacerbated social difference, popular frustration as well as intellectual critique multiplied.

Market Socialism

In spite of his attacks on the new system, Živković stopped short of advocating a return to the old system of assigning housing according to precedence and need. Even though policymakers agreed with Živković in many respects, they argued that the best way to reduce inequality was not to return to a system of egalitarian redistribution but to push ahead toward a market-driven system and so increase the personal stake of consumers in the housing market. Yugoslavia was not the only socialist state to begin promoting private construction as a "more economical" alternative to the state housing sector; Poland, Hungary, Czechoslovakia, and Bulgaria did the same to varying degrees.[35] Whereas in Poland and Czechoslovakia private housing was mostly built in villages and small towns, in Yugoslavia this solution was even advocated for the cities.[36] Privatization of urban construction was uniquely Yugoslav; so too was the manner in which private ownership was depicted as a tool for achieving social equality.

Hints of this radical redefinition of the notion of "equality" in the sphere of housing were visible as early as 1962, when Marković argued that "an apartment is a consumer good—a possible object of personal ownership, and it's helpful to aid every person who has the means to build or buy an apartment."[37] Instead of everyone having the right to housing of equal standard, equality meant that everyone would have equal access to the *opportunity* of acquiring a home—although the size, form, quality, and location of this home would vary according to the budget of the household. He argued that opportunity should be broadened through a wider variety of available apartments with regionally specific characteristics. Also, more of the most basic apartments should be built in concentrated multistory constructions that could later be improved or renovated. Finally, there should be more opportunities for people to build their own homes. In short, standardization was thrown out the window, in favor of flexibility, adaptability, and variety.[38]

This rearticulation of housing strategy was pursued in the context of the much broader shift toward market socialism in 1963, culminating in the reforms of July 1965. These reforms aimed to further restrict the state's interference in the economy, primarily by liberalizing prices and creating an effective banking sector. In line with this new approach, the state tried to withdraw from management of housing provisions and encourage private acquisition of housing through the market, with the financial support of the banking sector. Edvard Kardelj, one of the architects of the economic reforms of this period, pointed to the need to change popular attitudes about the nature of housing: "We have to get rid of the vulgar understanding, which still exists in some places, according to which producing shoes is a useful activity, and housing construction is some sort of social activity [in the sense of a social service] or a necessary evil that drags us behind in economic development."[39] Kardelj made it clear that collective ownership would continue to exist not because it was the state's obligation to provide housing to the population but rather because, under certain circumstances, collective ownership was more efficient than personal ownership.

In the first half of the 1960s, policymakers at the federal and municipal levels undertook experiments with the goal of implementing these reforms. As in the case of the Funds for Housing Construction, several Yugoslav cities had been experimenting since 1959 with schemes for increasing production of housing and decreasing costs; some of these approaches were then adopted on a national scale in 1965. The city of Belgrade was at the forefront of developing new solutions. By 1965, in Belgrade 167,000 people lived in category VI apartments, meaning ones considered of too low a standard to be lived in.[40] According to Miodrag Stevović, fifty thousand of the city's households in 1964 shared an apartment with another family.[41] In 1964, the president of the district of Zvezdara estimated there were six thousand illegal housing constructions in Belgrade, probably sheltering some twenty-four thousand inhabitants.[42] Belgrade's mayor, Branko Pešić, estimated in 1965 that the number had increased to ten thousand illegal homes, housing some fifty thousand people.[43]

As early as 1962, it was announced that in the near future construction companies would sell new housing directly to customers in Belgrade, with the goal of increasing the share of private investment in construction of new housing.[44] The notion of "selling on the market" was an extension of the idea, introduced in 1959, of private purchases of apartments through prepayment—but with a major difference. Whereas the old system presumed that demand had to precede supply, the new system was based on the idea that supply should be used to stimulate demand. Construction companies would actually attempt to create demand by advertising to the public. Because they would compete for clients, it was believed they would be encouraged to improve the quality of their products and lower prices. In this manner, arousal of consumer fantasies could be used to drive the construction industry. In theory, the stimulation of consumer demand would encourage worker productivity by giving them a reason to increase their earnings, as well as enable the construction sector to mechanize.

Although production of apartments for the market was announced in Belgrade as early as 1962, it does not appear to have been translated into policy until 1964. In view of the high cost of apartments in relation to personal income, a suitable financing mechanism had to be found. A proposal was finally discussed in Belgrade's municipal council in May 1964, specifying that people would be able to apply for a bank loan to purchase a home—if they could make a down payment amounting to half of its value. According to the proposal, this financing scheme would also be available to individuals wanting to build their own home. Encouraging self-building was another way of resolving the housing crisis by involving personal investment, a strategy Hungarian economic planners had also employed.[45] However, it promised none of the positive effects associated with the plan to sell housing on the market. It would not encourage the construction industry to cater to consumer needs, lower prices, industrialize, or operate more efficiently in any other way. Instead, the self-building scheme was targeted at resolving the problem of wild or illegal construction. In essence, these builders had already redefined housing as a consumer durable; the authorities' main concern was to regulate their activities. In trying to encourage self-builders to build legally, authorities proposed opening up 20,000 new parcels for self-building over the next seven years. Added to the plan for 80,000 new apartments, this meant 100,000 new homes for Belgrade's inhabitants in the next seven years, or an average of more than 14,000 new apartments per year. Given that 7,512 apartments were built in Belgrade in 1963, the proposal implied that adopting these two strategies would double housing production.[46]

Several participants in the Belgrade city council debates expressed serious reservations about the proposal, some of which centered on whether the financing scheme would really help to resolve the housing crisis, and whether it would help those hit hardest by the crisis. The president of the municipal council of trade unions pointed out that if banks required a 50 percent down payment on behalf of loan applicants, workers in low-profit sectors of the economy would still not be able to finance purchase of a new home. He predicted that the eighty thousand new apartments put on the market would be purchased by people living in the interior of the country, who had not contributed to the city's economic growth.[47] Others, including the director of the urban planning office, argued that it made no sense to encourage low-income families to build single-family homes.[48] The presumed suitability of these homes for low-income households in comparison to apartments in mass-produced apartment buildings had to do with their supposedly lower cost. This assumption implied that people would be expected to build homes with absolutely minimal amenities, and that the local authorities would build only the most basic infrastructure. Setting aside any preoccupations relating to spatial planning, this part of the proposal implied a dual-tracked standard of living. Whereas one part of the population, which earned higher incomes, would be allowed to invest in apartments of higher quality and lower price; another part, which earned lower incomes, would be encouraged to channel its savings into substandard housing in primitive settlements. In spite of such reservations, the fact that Marković, a member of the Federal Executive Council, was present at the meeting and strongly endorsed the proposal suggests that the municipal council was under serious pressure to adopt it, which in effect is what happened.

A year later, in April 1965, the federal government adopted a series of reforms that mirrored the Belgrade proposals.[49] The reforms sought to resolve the housing crisis by improving the efficiency of the construction sector and by shifting a large part of the cost of housing onto the shoulders of consumers. They sought to achieve the latter goal, on the one hand, by encouraging personal consumption and, on the other, by bringing rents and fees in line with the actual costs of maintaining buildings and replacing infrastructures. Applying the principles of self-management, the reforms sought to closely tie the standard of living within a political-territorial unit to its economic development and productivity, which reinforced a certain kind of inequality: differences in living standard between locales. Moreover, the reforms also appeared to endorse a second type of inequality, one that had already been presaged in the Belgrade proposal. Leaving behind the egalitarian project of mass producing standardized housing and distributing it according to objectively measured need and priority, the reforms aspired to give citizens the opportunity to purchase apartments according to personal choice and income. But a person's income depended first on the value of the product produced, and second on the value of the person's skill in the production process. Thus, by the mid-1960s policymakers had retreated at least in practice from the goal of creating an egalitarian society, opting instead to move toward a Western-style consumer society in which manufacturers would thrive by creating consumer demand.

Failed Promises of Redefined Equality

Ultimately, the increased emphasis on personal consumption did not diminish inequity in socialist Yugoslavia. This is not because it provoked a spiral of conspicuous consumption, as happened in the United States in the second half of the twentieth century, but rather because the minimal cost of a dwelling continued to exceed the incomes of a significant proportion of the urban population. With this in mind, popular frustration with the failure of the reforms to deliver affordable homes translated into hostility toward flagrant inequalities in housing consumption. The fact that in Yugoslavia such critiques were both more possible and effective than elsewhere in the Bloc meant that the radical nature of the Yugoslav experiment was always constrained by the continued primacy of socialist sensibilities. Discontent among the populace over visible inequities translated into limits on the consumer-driven economy as well as pressure on policymakers to find solutions to the continued problems in the housing sector.

Toward the start of the 1964–65 housing reforms, public opinion makers seemed to be willing to accept policymakers' arguments that what was needed was not more government intervention in the market but less. Even Živković, the most vocal critic of housing policy in *Beogradska nedelja*, registered his approval of the new policy, applauding replacement of the Funds for Housing Construction with a system of bank credit that would allow workers to buy their own homes.[50] However, policymakers' claims that the reforms would reduce inequality by increasing opportunity quickly lost credibility. Following liberalization, prices rose sharply and inflation climbed from an average rate of 1.5 percent annually between 1954 and 1964 to 10.4 percent annually between 1965 and 1975.[51] As apartments rose in cost, the population began to seriously doubt the notion that competition would help bring prices down. Whereas in 1964 apartments cost between 72,000 and 92,000 dinars per square meter, by 1966 their cost had risen to 170,000 dinars per square meter.[52] Along with prices, salaries increased, but at rates depending on the economic branch and occupation.[53] This meant that apartments continued to be too expensive for a significant segment of the population. As an article published on May 8, 1966, in *Beogradska nedelja* claimed, "the scope of apartment construction and the cost of an apartment today are the most serious problems in Belgrade," adding that fifty thousand inhabitants did not yet have an apartment, and that 60 percent of households were forced to share their accommodations.[54]

In Belgrade, the program for promoting self-built housing also proved a failure in terms of its capacity for helping the city's low-income families. As early as September 27, 1964, *Beogradska nedelja* reported people shunning the parcels of land that had been opened up for self-building. One problem was that bank credit had not yet become available, so workers had to rely on obtaining loans from their employers, which was a slow and expensive proposition. This difficulty would be addressed shortly by introducing bank credit, but the cost of readying parcels for construction posed a much larger problem. A number of tasks had to be carried out, among them connecting the plot to local electric and water supplies as well as road networks, and installing some kind of system for dealing with waste. To pay for this work, home builders had to pay between 400,000 and 2 million dinars, or nearly twice the cost of a house.[55] An article quoted the cost of communal infrastructure installation as ranging between 1 million dinars in the distant periphery of Krnjača, across the Danube River, and a whopping 11 million dinars in the luxurious settlement of Jajinca, on the southern periphery of the city.[56] Considering that a worker in a foundry might earn 22,000 dinars a month, and a worker for the municipal water supply might earn 31,000 dinars monthly, it was clear that such low-income families could hardly afford to invest in a parcel even in the most modest settlement.[57] One cartoon in *Beogradska nedelja* expressed the incredulity of Belgraders at the enormous cost of readying a parcel for construction: a disgruntled bare-chested man, holding a shovel, confides to another, "And now I barely have enough to build a shed, because the plot cost me 11 million dinars!"[58]

In explaining the high cost of this fee, one district official pointed out that the previous fee, which amounted to 100,000 dinars plus 10 percent of the value of the home, up to a maximum of 500,000 dinars, had not met the basic costs of building local infrastructure and resulted in creation of neighborhoods without paved streets and other necessities. Inhabitants subsequently demanded this problem be corrected, but the district coffers were empty. Under pressure from the government of the Serbian republic and the Belgrade municipality, districts opted instead to demand that future inhabitants cover the total cost of building and installing necessary services. He added, "We are aware that, in this way, owners of detached homes need to be citizens with higher incomes." Another official added what had seemed obvious to urban planners in 1964: "We have only now come to realize that family home construction must be more expensive than construction in blocks."[59] The author of the article concluded that even though having homeowners carry such costs was a rational answer, it did not satisfy him, "for such a housing policy cannot in any way help to lessen the housing crisis that is so present in the capital city."[60] This episode illustrates a striking fact: in the context of the economic reforms of the 1960s, equality (however it was defined) took a backseat to fiscal responsibility, which was part of the broader plan to improve the efficiency of the economy.

The project of enabling families to buy or build their own housing was not the only policy to come under public scrutiny. Articles and cartoons in *Beogradska nedelja* and other newspapers continued to emphasize the state's incompetence in providing state-owned rental housing to its working people. One reporter tracked down former residents of Prokop, a slum, in their new high-rise apartments. The inhabitants (whose names suggest they were of Roma ethnicity) complained they could not afford the costly rent of these apartments on their modest salaries.[61] Numerous cartoons emphasized the inherent inequality of access to housing, and they even accused white-collar workers of securing their homes on the back of the working man. In one, a fellow with a housing allocation document in his pocket leapfrogs over another in working-class attire (a cap on his head, a wrench in his pocket).[62] In another, similarly attired workers deposit money into a barrel labeled "housing fund"—and below, men wearing suits and ties draw money from the bottom of the barrel.[63] A third cartoon, entitled "equality," shows two men separated by an equal sign. When it begins to rain, one man takes the equal sign and makes a tent with it, leaving the other soaked.[64]

FIGURE 14.1.   Cartoon highlighting popular frustrations with the Funds for Housing Construction. Caption reads, "Without Words." From *Beogradska nedelja*, Feb. 20, 1966.

Significantly, popular frustration provoked by the failure of these policies to diminish inequality ultimately constrained the authorities' freedom of action. The case of Block 30 in New Belgrade is a good example of this. In 1967, Belgrade's urban planning office commissioned architect Uroš Martinović to develop a detailed plan for a luxury development in New Belgrade, the city's new city center and model settlement. It was aimed first and foremost at diplomats, but also at "citizens who are looking for comfort."[65] In an attractive color brochure promoting the planner settlement, titled simply "catalogue of apartments—block 30," prospective buyers could look at generous floor plans and admire stylish renderings of open-plan apartments decorated with trendy furnishings. The buildings would contain various sizes of apartments, among them units with six and a half bedrooms—unheard of in the rest of Belgrade, where new apartments rarely exceeded two bedrooms.[66] The director of the urban planning office, Aleksandar Đorđević, advanced the idea that "there is an interest in apartments for 150 million dinars," adding, "Whose money this is, how they obtained it and what I would do with that money, don't ask me that because I'm just an urban planner."[67] On the one hand, this project made sense within the framework of the reformed housing policy. It enabled people to acquire the kind of home that they judged "best corresponded to them," and in the process channel large sums of money into the housing industry. Although such a project would not likely prompt the construction industry to lower prices, it was an excellent exercise in finding ways to stimulate consumer demand by feeding consumer fantasies.[68]

Public opinion was decidedly hostile to the lavish idea precisely because housing remained out of reach for a large portion of the population. Having described the wondrous amenities that would be available to the inhabitants of this luxury settlement—ranging from car garages immediately below their multistory apartments to covered passages allowing inhabitants to navigate the block undisturbed by poor weather, and kitchens equipped with the most desired appliances—journalist Andeljko Dragojević asked:

> Who here will be able to pay such high prices? It is hard to believe at the moment that it will be those working people and civil servants without apartments who, in spite of their mainly modest means, are by rule referred to the most disadvantageous [financial] conditions: personal participation or a loan from their employer—75% of the value of the apartment—plus 25% bank loan with a 25 year repayment schedule.[69]

In spite of the apparent demand for luxury apartments, the project to build the luxurious Block 30 was never realized. The economic slowdown of the early 1970s played a role in ultimately shelving the project, but the controversy it provoked is a direct testament to the limits of market reforms in a country whose population still believed quite strongly in the egalitarian socialist program.

During the same period, Belgrade's municipal government finally acknowledged the limitations of a liberalized housing economy when it came to giving everyone an opportunity to obtain a home. On October 17, 1968, the city council passed a resolution that created a social housing program aimed at those who had been marginalized by the housing reforms. Recognizing that "our socialist laws have bypassed the issue of providing the lowest categories of workers with a manner to participate in the distribution of housing in some manner," the resolution set up a mechanism for financing construction of two thousand apartments per year for the next five years, aimed specifically at low-income workers, in addition to the projected ten thousand apartments per year that were to be built for the usual distribution channels. Construction of these "solidarity" dwellings would be financed in part by employers and in part by other organs, as well as by wealthier economic branches that had succeeded in furnishing housing to their workers. The intended recipients were concentrated especially in the textile, leather, wood, agricultural, and delivery industries and parts of the metal, construction, and transportation industries. The intention was not to segregate these new homes (which would average 50 square meters in size, or approximately 540 square feet) but to integrate them into existing projects.[70]

In a sense, this represented a continuation of the egalitarian rationale of socialism—a program for distributing housing not on the basis of productivity but need and precedence. Yet this program catered only to the neediest (and

ДУШАН ПЕТРИЧИЋ: Једнакост

FIGURE 14.2.   By the late 1960s, the issue of housing had become a powerful symbol of the generalized erosion of equality in Yugoslav society. From "Equality," *Borba*, Dec. 14, 1968.

arguably only one segment of the needy population), while the rest of society was expected to obtain its dwellings through the approved channels: buying or building a home using their own resources and bank loans, or renting apartments that were built from their incomes. In this sense, the initiative had much in common with social housing programs that existed in Western Europe as of the late 1960s, aimed at those who, owing to poverty, simply could not enter the housing market.[71] Policymakers opted to persevere with the new economic orientation, merely offering assistance to those consumers at the margins.

At the end of the Second World War, when the socialist regime consolidated its control over Yugoslavia, economic policymakers implemented a Stalinist-type model for financing, building, distributing, and managing new housing. Though they respected the right to own real estate, they made it difficult to acquire it in the future, and nearly impossible to earn income through property rentals. Moreover, they gave the state a central role in provision of housing, which was understood as a kind of social service. As Yugoslavia embarked on its "own path" to socialism, policymakers did not, however, renounce their management role in the housing economy. Rather, they sought to tie housing to productivity, moving away from the earlier conception of housing as a social service.

Building on this, in the mid-1960s economic policymakers decided that a larger proportion of housing investment should come from private savings. They did not, however, portray this as a retreat from egalitarianism; instead they redefined equality not as access but as opportunity. The first outcry came from specialists working in the area of housing, in particular urban planners, who objected that the desire to mobilize personal savings had overwhelmed any consideration of what was economically viable or socially desirable. Over time, the citizens of Belgrade became disenchanted with this new definition of equality, which seemed to work only for the wealthy. Yugoslavs were not ready to abandon their egalitarian ethos.

In a sense, the experiments with the market and with redefining equality gave Yugoslavs a taste of the future—not the glorious future of socialism, but the hard realities of postsocialism. They learned early on that a market system did not mean a world where everyone could live in a luxury home. They enjoyed the consumer abundance that came with the market reforms, but perhaps more than their Eastern Bloc neighbors Yugoslavs realized they had a real stake in preserving socialist values and institutions. Yugonostalgia—the fascination the inhabitants of Yugoslavia's successor states have for the socialist era and its material culture—is in large part rooted in this paradoxical appreciation for both socialism and the market.

NOTES

1. Ljubo Sirc, *The Yugoslav Economy Under Self-Management* (London: St. Martin's Press, 1979), 36.

2. Patrick Patterson has described, for example, the dilemmas of developing a marketing industry when marketing was seen by Marxists as artificial creation of illusory needs. His research suggests that these tensions were never truly resolved, which hobbled the marketing industry's self-confidence and limited its effectiveness in promoting Yugoslav products. Patrick Hyder Patterson, "The New Class: Consumer Culture Under Socialism and the Unmaking of the Yugoslav Dream, 1945–1991." (Ph.D. diss., University of Michigan, 2001).

3. Jack C. Fisher, "City Planning and Administration in Yugoslavia," *Urban Affairs Quarterly* 1(2) (1965): 68.

4. Svetislav Aranđelović, *Stambena Svojina u Jugoslaviji* (Belgrade: Institut društvenih nauka, 1967), 12–14, 24.

5. On this phenomenon elsewhere in the Bloc, see Katherine Verdery, *What Was Socialism, and What Comes Next?* (Princeton, NJ: Princeton University Press, 1996), 25–26; Stephen Kotkin, *Magnetic Mountain: Stalinism as Civilization* (Berkeley: University of California Press, 1995), 163.

6. This approach was not unique to Yugoslavia. For the Czechoslovak case, see Kimberly Elman Zarecor, "Manufacturing a Socialist Modernity: The Architecture of Industrialized Housing in Czechoslovakia, 1945–1956" (Ph.D. diss., Columbia University, 2008), 145–46.

7. See, for example, "Rezultati konkursa za izradu tipskih stanbenih zgrada u Beogradu," *20. Oktobar*, Mar. 14, 1947; "Iskoristimo što bolje prostor pri gradnji većih stanova," *20. Oktobar*, Mar. 28, 1947; "Najmanji I najjeftiniji stan sa više udobnosti," *20. Oktobar*, July 18, 1947; "Problem racionalnog stana," *20. Oktobar*, July 11, 1947.

8. Based on Sirc, *Yugoslav Economy*, 240–41.

9. Izvrsni odbor N.O. Beograda, *Beograd: Generalni urbanisticki plan 1950* (Belgrade: Izdanje izvrsnog odbora N.O. Beograda, 1951), 51.

10. The estimates of homes destroyed in the war were taken from IAB, FSGB, Zapisnici sednice NO Grada Beograda, 17.10.1968: 53. For data on the population, see "13.4 Stalno stanovištvo Beograda po stanbenim zajednicama i samostalnim naseljima," *Statistički godišnjak grada Beograda 1969 (Belgrade: Zavod za statistiku, 1969)*: 153; for the number of apartments built per year, "6.4 Broj i površina izgradjenih stanova po godinama," ibid., 87.

11. Peter Bassin, "Yugoslavia," in *Housing in Europe*, Martin Wynn, ed. (New York: St. Martin's Press 1984), 16.

12. On the Hungarian case, see Krisztina Fehervary, "In Search of the Normal: Material Culture and Middle-Class Fashioning in a Hungarian Steel Town, 1950–1997" (Ph.D. diss., University of Chicago, 2005), 260–81.

13. See, for example, Paulina Bren, "Mirror, Mirror, on the Wall . . . Is the West the Fairest of Them All? Czechoslovak Normalization and Its (Dis)Contents," *Kritika: Explorations in Russian and European History*, 9(4) (2008), 831–54; David Crew, ed. *Consuming Germany in the Cold War* (London: Berg, 2004); Susan E. Reid, "'Our Kitchen Is Just as Good': Soviet Responses to the American Kitchen," in Ruth Oldenziel and Karin Zachmann, ed., *Cold War Kitchen: Americanization, Technology, and European Users* (Cambridge: MIT Press, 2009), 83–112.

14. Predrag Marković, "Ideologija standarda Jugoslovenskog režima 1948–1965," *Tokovi Istorije*, no. 1–2 (1996): 7–20, 14–16.

15. Sirc, *Yugoslav Economy*, 240–42.

16. In addition to investing more in housing, states adopted new approaches, with Poland, Czechoslovakia, and the GDR introducing housing cooperatives in the middle to late 1950s, which came to play a central role in fulfilling housing needs. David Short, "Housing Policy in Czechoslovakia," in J. Sillinge, ed., *Housing Policies in Eastern Europe and the Soviet Union* (London: Routledge, 1990), 91; Andrew Dawson, "Housing Policy in Poland," in Sillinge (ed.), 62–63; Hanns Bucholz, "Housing Policy in the German Democratic Republic," in Sillinge (ed.), 342–43.

17. Susan Woodward, *Socialist Unemployment: The Political Economy of Yugoslavia, 1945–1990* (Princeton, NJ: Princeton University Press, 1965): 141.

18. Stephen Kotkin provides a good description of how Stakhanovism functioned in Magnitogorsk. Kotkin, *Magnetic Mountain*, 207.

19. Marković, "Ideologija standarda Jugoslovenskog režima," 14–16.

20. Aranđelović, *Stambena Svojina u Jugoslaviji*, 33.

21. Romania and Bulgaria at first invested so little in housing that private construction remained de facto dominant in the early postwar period. But even there, the state sector gradually overtook private construction in cities in the 1960s, ironically at the very moment when Yugoslavia, Poland, Czechoslovakia, and the GDR were looking to reduce their investment in the housing sector by encouraging other approaches, such as cooperative and private investment. See David Turnock, "Housing Policy in Romania," in Sillinge (ed.), 138–39. On housing in other Bloc states, see Short, "Housing Policy in Czechoslovakia," in Sillinge (ed.), 90; Dawson, "Housing Policy in Poland," in Sillinge (ed.), 62–63; Gerlin Staemmler, "East Germany (the German Democratic Republic)," in Sillinge (ed.), 236.

22. For Belgrade's population, see Zdravko Antonić and Nikola Tasić, *Istorija Beograda*. (Belgrade: Srpska akademija nauka i umetnosti "Draganić," 1995), 490–92; for statistics on housing construction in Yugoslavia between 1956 and 1963, see *Statistički godišnjak Jugoslavije* (Belgrade: Savezni zavod za statistiku, 1964), 205.

23. "Samac—gradanin drugi red," *Beogradska nedelja*, Sept. 2, 1962.

24. "Pod-utakmice," *Beogradska nedelja*, May 31, 1963.

25. "Putujte? Ne, stanujemo" *Beogradska nedelja*, Oct. 29, 1962; "Milicionar adaptor," *Beogradska nedelja*, Mar. 31, 1963; "Skloni se da prodem," *Beogradska nedelja*, Aug. 25, 1963.

26. IAB, FSGB, Zapisnici sednice NO grada Beograda, 18.10.1961, 5.

27. On the relationship between inequality and housing in the Eastern Bloc, see Ivan Szelenyi, *Urban Inequalities Under State Socialism* (Oxford, New York: Oxford University Press, 1983).

28. "Zašto se ne gradi jeftini stanovi," *Beogradska nedelja*, Sept. 24, 1961.

29. "Krov nad glavom," *Beogradska nedelja*, Nov. 4, 1962.

30. Ibid.

31. "Prednosti jeftini stanova," *Beogradska nedelja*, Dec. 30, 1962.

32. "Na ruke tvorcima stambene politike," *Beogradska nedelja*, Mar. 24, 1963. Emphasis is in the text.

33. See Patrick Patterson for discussion of a "new class" of Yugoslav consumers, which he argues encompassed the "ordinary Yugoslav citizen." Patterson, "New Class," 2–4.

34. "Ekonomske cene ekonomske plate," *Beogradska nedelja*, Nov. 3, 1963.

35. The GDR and Romania, in contrast, attempted to strengthen their state building programs and placed limits on private ownership by 1970. Frank Carter, "Housing Policy in Bulgaria," in Sillinge (ed.), 187–90; Bucholz, "Housing Policy in the German Democratic Republic," 343–44; Short, "Housing Policy in Czechoslovakia," 101; Dawson, "Housing Policy in Poland," 66–67; Turnock, "Housing Policy in Romania," 138–39.

36. The Hungarian state created a program to allow mining workers to purchase their own cottages in the early 1950s, although its motivations were to settle the workforce and eliminate discipline problems, in a sense looking back to nineteenth-century paternalism rather than forward to the late-twentieth-century conviction that everyone should own a home. Mark Pittaway, "Stalinism, Working-Class Housing and Individual Autonomy: The Encouragement of Private House Building in Hungary's

Mining Areas, 1950–54," in *Style and Socialism: Modernity and Material Culture in Postwar Eastern Europe*, eds. David Crowley and Susan E. Reid (Oxford: Berg, 2000), 49–64.

37. "Prednosti jeftini stanova," *Beogradska nedelja*, Dec. 30, 1962.

38. Ibid.

39. "Stambena izgranja i stanarina," *Beogradska nedelja*, Jan. 5, 1964.

40. "Preskupa je kučica u cveću," *Beogradska nedelja*, June 20, 1965.

41. IAB, FSGB, Zapisnici sednice NO Grada Beograda, 15.5.1964, 59–60.

42. Ibid., 91.

43. IAB, FSGB, Zapisnici sednice NO Grada Beograda, 15.5.1964, 91; Zapisnici sednice NO Grada Beograda, 4.11.1965, 52–53.

44. "Kombinat za montažne i opšte građevinske radove Trudbenik Beograd," *Beogradska nedelja*, June 10, 1962.

45. Fehervary, "In Search of the Normal," 277–80.

46. "6.4 Broj I povrsnia izgradjenih stanova po godinama," *Statistički godišnjak grada Beograda 1969*, 87.

47. IAB, FSGB, Zapisnici sednice NO Grada Beograda, 15.5.1964, 71.

48. IAB, FSGB, Zapisnici sednice NO grada Beograda, 15.5.1964, 105–8, 158–59.

49. *Jedinstvena terminologija najčešće pojmova korišćenih u oblasti stanovanja* (Belgrade: Savezni zavod za urbanizam i komunalna i stambena pitanja Beograd, 1968), 28.

50. "Povećanje stanarina i više stanova," *Beogradska nedelja*, Dec. 20, 1964.

51. Martin Schrenk et al. *Yugoslavia: Self-Management Socialism and the Challenges of Development* (Baltimore: Johns Hopkins University Press, 1979), 32.

52. "Gradi se sporo i skupo," *Beogradska nedelja*, Apr. 10, 1966.

53. Data are taken from "16.1 Prosečan neto lični dohodak po jednom zaposlenom po granama delatnosti" *Statistički godišnjak grada Beograda 1969*, 172.

54. "Cena stana iznad materijalnih mogućnosti građana," *Beogradska nedelja*, May 8, 1966.

55. "Gradjani ne gradi stan," *Beogradska nedelja*, Sept. 27, 1964.

56. "Preskupa je kučica u ćveću," *Beogradska nedelja*, June 20, 1965.

57. The salaries that are given as examples are taken from "Stan nije sve," *Beogradska nedelja*, Apr. 8, 1965.

58. "Preskupa je kučica u ćveću," *Beogradska nedelja*, June 20, 1965.

59. "Zasto je preskupo kucica u cvecu?" *Beogradska nedelja*, June 27, 1965.

60. Ibid.

61. "Kule u vazduhu," *Beogradska nedelja*, Apr. 18, 1965.

62. "Senke kolektivnog trošenja," *Beogradska nedelja*, Feb. 6, 1966.

63. Untitled, *Beogradska nedelja*, Feb. 20, 1966.

64. "Equality," *Borba*, Dec. 14, 1968.

65. Urbanistički zavod grada Beograda (henceforth UZGB). G 0/4/71-110, GL 84, "Zapisnik XV sednice Saveta za urbanizam Skupštine grada Beograda, održane da dan 27.3.68. godine u prostorijama urbanističkog zavoda grada Beograda," 27.3.1968.

66. UZGB. G 0 4, 71-110, "Katalog Stanova—Blok 30."

67. "Eksklusivni blok 30." *Borba*, Aug. 10, 1968, 6.

68. UZGB. G 0/4/71-110, GL 83, "Katalog stanovanja blok 30," undated.

69. "Eksklusivni blok 30," *Borba*, Aug. 10, 1968.

70. IAB, FSGB, Zapisnici sednice NO Grada Beograda, 17.10.1968.

71. Michael Harlowe has investigated this trend in five countries: Britain, France, Germany, the Netherlands, and Denmark. Harlowe, *The People's Home? Social Rented Housing in Europe and America* (Oxford: Blackwell, 1995.)

15

Shop Around the Bloc

Trader Tourism and Its Discontents
on the East German–Polish Border

Mark Keck-Szajbel

Late in 1971, citizens of East Germany and Poland awoke to the news that, starting on New Year's Day 1972, travel regulations would be eased. In a project called the "Borders of Friendship," ordinary Poles and East Germans were to be allowed to travel to "socialist brethren countries" without a visa and without a passport. In the years that followed, border guards in both states registered a huge increase in tourist traffic: whereas in 1971 1.6 million visitors had come to Poland from socialist countries, the following year this number jumped to an astounding 8 million.[1] East German and Polish citizens were handed the unprecedented possibility to travel relatively freely and—perhaps most importantly—in an unorganized (and untethered) fashion, engaging in a variety of activities along the way.

As a result of the decision to liberalize travel, otherwise peripheral cities such as Zittau or Zgorzelec on the East German-Polish border became tourist centers as millions of travelers crossed one another's borders. In these cities, Poles and Germans mingled freely, and it was here that most gained their first experience of life in another socialist state. But they moved on to the more enticing locations of Berlin and Warsaw, selling and buying as they went, becoming what scholars of this period have dubbed "trader tourists."[2] The trader tourist was a socialist chimera: derisively accused of Western modes of consumption, the trader tourist used the ability to travel to search for scarce goods,

FIGURE 15.1.   A modern landscape in Dresden. From *Swiatowid* 775, October 1973, 18.

"abusing" the socialist marketplace through mass purchases. As opposed to organized smuggling rings of the early 1990s, however, the vast majority of travel tourists went abroad individually or in small groups, and they usually filled their bags (or trunks) with goods purchased legally abroad. Although the scope of "customs infractions" grew in the 1980s, in prior decades the primary aim of trader tourism was to satisfy needs that could not be fulfilled at home.[3]

The decision to pursue an open border project was the direct result of changed leaderships in both states in early 1970. In theory, Party Central Committees in Warsaw and Berlin hoped that the liberalization of travel regulations through Borders of Friendship would usher in greater integration along the lines of "international proletarianism" between states. In practice, the open border project was a logical extension of attempts to raise the standard of living in the Eastern Bloc. In the 1960s and 1970s, workers' wages grew in almost every socialist country, and historians consider this period one of relative abundance (albeit with intermittent shortages), alongside a new consuming citizenry. Likewise, other Bloc countries pursued open border projects with some of their neighbors. Czechoslovakia had agreements with Hungary and (after a delay) with other Bloc countries, such as Poland, East Germany, and Romania, as well.[4]

But despite these similarities, the open border project between Poland and East Germany was unique because it offered what was for the East Bloc an unprecedented level of untethered travel. East Germany could never agree to drastically liberalized travel with the West (after all, it had built the Berlin Wall in 1961 precisely to prevent such movement), and Poland was landlocked by more orthodox communist regimes that tried systematically to reduce contact with Westerners.[5] But the East German Politburo was willing to offer its citizenry "vacationscapes" in Poland, recognizing that by allowing East Germans to pack up their Trabant cars and putter off to Pomerania or Silesia they could promote a form of individual tourism that placated its citizens through offering the possibility of visiting former German homes in what was now Poland; maybe it was a poor substitute, but nevertheless a substitute, for visiting family members in the West, which was not allowed. For the Polish authorities, promoting unorganized travel to East Germany meant allowing their citizens to travel to a coun try perceived—both by the powers that were and by everyday citizens—as a "showplace of socialism" and of modern living standards, and a shop ping Mecca. East German cities were well planned and organized, and the visitor would (presumably) be welcomed in museums as well as the marketplace.

That the Polish and East German tourist could now travel "freely" was itself quite remarkable. Real, or certainly perceived, surveillance was temporarily lifted (even if the individual was exchanging one secret police for another across the border); individuals were no longer required to put their names on lists for organized travel (since no one could be denied the personal identification card required at home and now sufficient to travel abroad); and this new travel route was understood by both officials and citizens as participation in an open market. Particularly in Poland, the Borders of Friendship program was consciously seen as a measure to prevent social unrest by providing a secondary marketplace beyond the Oder. The result was a stark imbalance between the number of East Germans coming to Poland as tourist traders and the number of Poles who poured into the GDR to shop.

The resulting animosity between national communities competing for scarce goods at a transnational level has been described by historians as emblematic of (failed) attempts to liberalize across the East Bloc. On the one hand, open borders immediately provided individuals with otherwise hard-to-find commodities (and, in the case of Romania, as Christina Petrescu writes, represented a system-stabilizing factor), but on the other hand the unmatched extent of scarcity brought disgruntled citizens to protest foreigners and the regime.[6] In part, the animosity toward new consumers was part of larger, historical trends of hatred toward foreigners: citizens readily picked up "old vernacular," as Jonathan Zatlin writes, which was greatly reinforced in light of the postwar redrawing of nations.[7] Although responses at the national level are well docu-mented and analyzed, historians have been slow to consider homegrown im-ages of foreign societies.[8] In other words, what informed local communities to travel abroad and mass-buy? Did national governments condone—implicitly or explicitly—the actions of their citizens abroad?

This chapter demonstrates how Polish officials were not only aware of the "trader tourist" imbalance between Poland and East Germany but actually encouraged Polish citizens to take advantage of foreign abundance. Of course, there were periodic admonishments, but as the East Germans joked in the 1980s, "Why is Pope John Paul II soon going to the capital of the GDR? Because he's the last Pole who hasn't shopped at Alexanderplatz."[9] Poles flooded Ger-man cities, emptying stocked shelves and loading their cars with goods to take home for family and friends, with their government's general approval. Indeed, Polish authorities viewed the open border much like a consumer pressure valve to alleviate its own supply problems. But increasingly, rampant and uncon-trolled consumer activities across the border also made it clear to both govern-ments that the open border threatened social control. In response, officials would have to admonish "bad travel," while endorsing correct, normative modes of travel and consumer restraint. But this seemed unrealistic once the open border had attained the semiotic potential of a secondary marketplace.

Open Season

Toward the end of 1971, as this new border treaty first dawned, the Polish and East German press began to publish short articles concerning the future of mass travel to and from other communist countries.[10] It was reported that the East German and Polish governments had agreed to lift travel barriers as of January 1, 1972; all that was now needed to cross the border was a standard personal identification card. National newspapers on both sides of the border called the decision a "revolution" in coexistence between socialist states.[11] Importantly, however, the Polish press was equally interested in practicalities: "The essential novelty is that the tourist fee assessed by the exchange office to all Comecon countries was lowered from 50 to 30 percent" and that "limits on the frequency of travel and on the exchange of currency have also been repealed."[12] According to the changed travel regulations, citizens of both countries were now allowed to exchange unrestricted amounts of East German marks and Polish złoty while visiting their socialist neighbors.

While Polish journalists reported on practicalities, they were also the first to openly articulate the expected results of the Polish shopping frenzy in Germany.

Mieczysław Rakowski, the editor of *Polityka* [Policy] and later prime minister of Poland, wrote with foresight:

> On 1 January, the treaty between Poland and East Germany on passport-free border crossings was enacted. The exchange of [Polish] złoty for [East German] mark (1 zł = 4.78 marks) is unlimited. According to first reports from the GDR, our citizens are storming the stores in Berlin and other cities. It'll be interesting when the Germans start to protest empty shelves.[13]

Like Rakowski, the German press predicted throngs of Polish shoppers and was quite aware that this did not bode well for Germans, whose consumer supply was potentially in jeopardy. As the *Neues Deutschland* (New Germany) delicately put it, there were fears that some "problems would occur from the start," potentially leading to "impairments in foreign currency balances" and, more importantly, to "temporary impairment" of the "continuous maintenance of certain goods in our lands."[14] But GDR journalists and officials also expected problems in consumption to subside as the ability to travel normalized and as the chance to buy goods across the border became less novel.

By contrast, from the Polish perspective the opening of the border was immediately acknowledged and welcomed as a boon to the Polish economy and the Polish consumer. Certainly, the Polish Central Committee initially feared the consequences of an open border and the return of some estimated seven to eight million Germans expelled from Poland from 1945 to 1948 following World War II and the redrawing of borders.[15] But fears of property reclamations or explosive tensions between Poles and Germans on Polish soil dissolved in the face of the economic benefits. As future First Secretary Stanisław Kania reported, individual tourism was a "priceless" form of "economic cooperation." He noted how tourism to East Germany "aided the [Polish] national economy" by giving everyday citizens new shopping venues (and filling government coffers through exchange commissions).[16]

The Polish press was exceedingly positive about the opportunity and outcome for travel to East Germany. Journalist Jerzy Urban, for example, lauded the opening of the border between the two states as a historic corrective to trade barriers introduced in the twelfth century and passports in the sixteenth. As he elaborated, the open border project was perhaps the single most important move toward interpersonal understanding across borders.[17] The press documented how Polish travelers were enjoying the old towns of Plauen, Görlitz, and Leipzig, but especially German restaurant food, which was less expensive than Polish fare. Big cities were also high on the Polish itinerary, even in official publications. Dresden was a lively city of sounds and restaurants; Leipzig was "so full of people, one could not make it through the market"; Berlin was not

FIGURE 15.2.   Zgorzelec border. From *Swiatowid* 19, no. 733, May 7, 1972, 3.

only a "triumph of the idea of socialism" but also an "active city," with "modern architecture," especially at Alexanderplatz, where one found the shopping extravaganza Centrum-Warenhaus (Central Department Store).[18]

Indeed, the Polish press not only depicted the vast opportunities but gave practical tips on shopping in East German cities, including details as new shopping centers were established, with their opening times and the variety of goods to be purchased there. The Germans seemed just as eager to point to their state as a cornucopia for socialist consumers. As with 1960s Yugoslavia, where Western models were used to advertise home-grown industries, Poles were encouraged to experience a modern (consumer-friendly) East German state.[19] In East German cities one could always find (according to tourist advertisements and journal reports) a mall, a boardwalk, or simply well-supplied shops. In an interview conducted while he was visiting Poland, Peter Koehli, the director of the East German state-run airline Interflug, reminded Polish readers that "prices in Germany [were] attractive" and significantly lower than in Poland for frequently purchased goods. A bottle of beer, for example, cost 60 pfennigs in German restaurants, and cigarettes cost only 1.60 GDR mark per pack.[20] The result, as the well-known Polish reporter Andrzej Wróblewski remarked in an interview, was that "more than one Pole goes to Frankfurt for chicken, because it is cheaper there."[21]

The presence of East Germans in Poland and Poles in East Germany brought ideology, economy, and everyday practice to convergence in the 1970s.[22] Upholding the notion of friendship, the Polish press implied that participation in this range of tourist, leisure, and shopping activities was a reciprocal relationship established through the new border politics; that is, Germans enjoyed consuming in Poland as much as the Poles did in East Germany. Certainly, Germans did buy products in Poland, especially those that were cheaper than back home or else of better quality, and they particularly took advantage of cross-border shopping on weekends when their own shops were closed.[23] In Warsaw, the government closely tracked German consumer demand, as evidenced in an official report to the Central Committee on how Germans wanted cheap(er) goods from Poland—"some types of manufactured goods/cigarettes, some higher quality smoked meats, natural coffee, vodka, polyamide covers, bikes, electric lamps, gasoline, etc."[24] And certainly Polish shopkeepers were also quick to capitalize on the quality of their goods. As the prolific journalist Andrzej Mozołowski highlighted in *Polityka*, signs in store windows along the Polish border towns advertised in German, and one sign in Słubice jumbled Polish with German in a sort of East Bloc consumer esperanto: "*Cukiernictwo— lody—Eis. Marian Kral (Polnisches Eis schmeckt besser)*" [Confectioner—Ice Cream—*Eis*. Marian Kral (Polish Ice Cream Tastes the Best)]. Mozołowski added that East Germans often bought bread in Poland because "the bread is better—and always fresher."[25]

Still, German participation in trader tourism was less extensive than Polish, and East German magazines and newspapers, unlike their Polish counterparts, stressed the fact that consumption was not the reason to travel to Poland. In part, this was a measure to work against animosity: indeed, many Bloc citizens were convinced that East Germany's economy was flourishing at the cost of other Warsaw Pact countries.[26] In general, the East German press focused on the open border as an opportunity for socialist Germans to travel and partake in recreation in areas once familiar to them. More so than shopping, it was an opportunity to return "home," to step back into a paradise lost. Trader tourist consumer activities were chided, especially when they seemed to overshadow social obligations. In one issue of the *Wochenpost*, the reporter explained that a *Jugendweihe* (the communist equivalent of first communion) was a very special occasion, and that it was "more valuable" ("*mehr wert*") to be in the company of good friends than to engage in "some type of 'consumption.'"[27] In other words, presents were less important than the presence of family members, and social gatherings should not be an excuse to travel to Poland for gifts. From the side of East German officials, even meager individual shopping trips into Poland were seen as suspect, and by no means encouraged. Consumption, when mentioned, was consistently downplayed.

Nevertheless, Germans also went east for a taste of the "exotic": the Slavic language, different (sometimes otherworldly) norms, and the possibility to experience a level of cultural liberalization foreign to GDR citizens. A young reader of the *Eulenspiegel* (The Trickster) related a telling story about how he and his parents visited Poland. He was pleasantly surprised, he reported, by the strange but charming manners of the Poles, the difficult language, and the friendly service. And indeed, unaware of the conventions of East German travel to Poland, he was taken aback when he learned that his parents had been advised not to fill up on gasoline in their native East Germany. Gas in Poland, they had been told, was much cheaper and available right beyond the border. Quite predictably, they ran out of gas just kilometers before reaching that border. But a Pole on his way back from Germany arrived and, despite the language barrier, which meant a minimal exchange of words, generously gave them several liters of gasoline hidden in his trunk. When the East Germans offered payment for the man's generosity, the Pole refused, simply responding, "*Proschim*" ("You're welcome").[28] On the one hand, this public (and thereby publicized) account of cross-border tourism seemed to highlight the "mistake" of East Germans who refused to buy gasoline on their own side of the border, or who used trips to Poland for purposes of shopping. On the other, it recalled the original purpose of the cross-border project—socialist brotherhood—suggesting that even through misplaced ideas about consumption, East Bloc socialist ties might be generated.

But brotherhood or not, the trader tourist imbalance was evident, and it soon became clear that the open border was in fact stymieing any potential economic reform in Poland by offering fast and effective, yet ultimately superficial, solutions to serious problems. Indeed, since Poles exchanged nearly twice as much money as East Germans, open border consumption aided anti-inflationary politics and offered an opportunity to close the supply-demand imbalance. In other words, Borders of Friendship was, for the Polish government, a safe—but short-term—solution to hidden inflation and empty shelves.[29]

Trader Tourism

As the two communist parties attempted to shape the new tourist industry that had resulted from the open border, "economic cooperation" remained one of the leitmotifs. Both parties anticipated a larger flow of Poles into East Germany (Poland had, after all, twice as many inhabitants), but they also assumed that consumer interests would eventually balance out as access to a foreign market became more commonplace, and that cross-border shopping would be limited to a handful of cheaper items or goods of higher quality. These assumptions, however, proved to be rather naïve in retrospect, particularly considering the imbalance of goods available in the GDR compared to Poland in this period.[30] As it became increasingly apparent that the tourist trade imbalance was here to stay—particularly considering the continued encouragement of it by the Polish government, which recognized a simple solution for economic woes when it saw one—some official voices of dissent began to appear. A 1976 issue of *Polityka* published a poem from eleven-year-old Hania Milewska, next to an article by Andrzej Wróblewski. Hania's poem read:

> On the bridge in Słubice, there is a lot of commotion
> You hear German and Polish.
> German kids eat Polish ice cream,
> And we munch on their candy.
>
> . . .
>
> Dietmar from Frankfurt,
> Jaś from Słubice
> Both know how to say
> Dzień dobry and Guten Tag

Although Hania evoked a child's world, it was firmly riveted in trade and exchange. The poem, placed on the cover page, gave Wróblewski the opportunity to comment snidely; reflecting on Hania's poem he elaborated that shopping was in fact *the* essential element of the open border for everyday Poles. "Today, when I went across the bridge," he wrote, "there was no commotion." People were not going to visit friends, but "to buy tomatoes."[31]

In East Germany, the increasing presence of empty shelves in the stores came to pose a "large physical and psychological strain" on store managers, the public, and worried state officials.[32] An East German official estimated that in a single year Polish buyers in one city bought up more than 25 percent of perishable goods, more than 60 percent of children's clothes, and more than 20 percent of women's shoes.[33] Clearly the scale of Polish consumption in East Germany was of concern. In 1976, at the same time that Polish leader Gierek raised prices on many goods, East Germany established a list of behaviors that needed to be extensively controlled:

- Criminal currency exchange and smuggling
- Secretive trade
- Violating different regulations within the residing country
- Violating moral and ethical norms (i.e., stealing or drunkenness)
- Engaging in paid employment (often without appropriate occupational qualifications); frequent extension of stay beyond the declared time frame [etc.][34]

At the same time, Poles threatened that, should prices be raised in their home-land, they would show their disdain by traveling to the GDR to purchase their vodka and gasoline there.[35]

While everyday Poles were learning how to use international agreements and the language of Borders of Friendship as a weapon against government policy, the Polish media took up the campaign to promote "rational" modes of travel consumption in East Germany. This tactic was common: through-out the Cold War (and, to some degree, on both sides of the Curtain) a typical instrument to discourage conspicuous consumption was caricature and derisive language. One way of reprimanding the Polish public about its "unsocialist" behavior was to poke fun at the absurdity of the goods bought. In his travel log, Mozołowski described the East German "Handelsmarkt" (trade market) on Saturdays in Zgorzelec and Görlitz. He was clearly unim-pressed by the "orgy of color," the "rich assortment" of bronze, porcelain, and wooden goods, the plates with pictures of Wrocław city hall, horses, and dogs. He was also not humored by the pidgin language spoken by Poles: "*Porceln, cwaj hundert, a to jest holc, tak samo cwaj hundert, egall*" ["Porcelain, *zwei hundert* (two hundred), and that is *Holz* (wood), *zwei hundert, egal* (what-ever)"]. One could not see beyond the stands with plates, he wrote, because of the terrible crowds. Later, he found an assorted variety of buttons and stickers: "Beatles, Locomotiv GT, ABBA and Frank Schöbel . . . unpretentious [buttons in English with phrases such as] 'I love you,' and, 'Kiss me,' ball caps with '*VM im Fussballspiel München 1974*'" ["WM football game Munich 1974"]. This last item he found particularly distasteful since "half of Görlitz" was already wearing it. From the trunks of cars, as he described, one could also buy "onions, apples and potatoes, 'Texas' jeans," and, to top it off, for 400 zloty, "neon sweaters" ("*'neonowe' sweterki*").[36] With his derogatory as-sessment of the East German Handelsmarkt, Mozołowski attempted to draw attention to the absurdity of paying so much money for what he considered East Bloc kitsch. In an article titled "Borders Without Complexes," Alekszan-der Paszyński and Marian Turski interviewed an inhabitant from a Polish border city:

> DO PEOPLE GO OVER THE BRIDGE [TO GERMANY]?
> No, what for? In the beginning there were more [German] marks, [and] the border guards were less stringent. . . . When they [the Germans] invited you, they put out sandwiches and you could sit the entire evening with just one glass of wine; not like here, where one does everything in order to lay the table with abundance [*by stół był zastawiony*], even when it's hard to buy things.

BUT SHOPS [OVER THERE] ARE STOCKED BETTER?

> It just seems that way, once [my] wife bought a blouse, [and] after
> the third wash—it's already a rag. In fact, all you have to do is look
> how we are dressed and how they are.[37]

In other words, the socialist German also had to deal with shortages, and the quality of GDR goods was perhaps not as good as originally thought. If the question of aesthetics did not prove to be persuasive enough, then the quality of goods might be.

Yet another solution to curbing cross border consumption was far more direct: border policing. Policing, seemingly amiss of brotherhood and unity, was justified in the Polish press as a prophylactic against the darker side of trader tourism—that is, speculation and smuggling. In answer to a reader's question about why there were customs controls and taxes, *Trybuna Ludu* (The People's Tribune) wrote that "even in the European Community" there were taxes on tourist goods, and the Polish customs guards were merely there to "protect" the public: "One of the tasks of the customs officers is to not allow the 'aiding' of state enterprises by private persons in foreign trade."[38] "Aiding state enterprises" was a euphemism used by smugglers for their activities, who were assumed to be the source of significant border abuse.

To some degree, public admonishment worked. A student and dissident, Wojciech Maziarski, explained his embarrassment when he was denied the appropriate stamp from the Polish police to travel abroad:

> The [officer] took my identification and examined it carefully. He
> count[ed] the number of pages in it. He finally ask[ed]:
>   "You sure you didn't tear out anything?"
>   "No, why would I tear anything out?"
> So the police officer [started phoning around]. . . .
>   "You won't get the stamp."
>   "Why?"
>   "I don't know," he replied, "you must have smuggled something."
>   *All people in the queue started staring at me, eyeing the smuggler* [em-
> phasis in original].[39]

Although official sources still encouraged people to buy in East Germany, significant stigma was placed on those who chose to "*handlować*" (deal). Official Polish sources continued to try to discipline their unruly trader tourist through subtle persuasion, but for the East Germans the answer to their Polish problem was increasingly clear.

Closing Time

As early as December 1972, in an effort to curb trader tourism, the East German government established limits on the amount of currency that could be exchanged by Poles. In June 1973, export of work and protective clothes was banned, followed by bans on exporting fine metals, fine stones, pearls, jewelry, recording tape, films, photographic chemicals, fine porcelain, stamps, bed sheets, shoes, children's clothes, synthetic window shades, knitted clothes, pantyhose, meat, and meat products.[40] By establishing exchange limits and export bans, the Central Committee reported in 1976 that the number of Poles traveling into East Germany was cut by four million.[41]

Poles, on the other hand, interpreted these controls as a condemnation not only of their shopping practices in Germany but also of their physical presence in the country, and they saw them as codification of perceived inequalities and hierarchies among Bloc-wide states and citizens. Indeed, Poles became perturbed by the German buying power that was also emptying the more meagerly stocked shelves on the Polish side of the border. At the start of one summer, *Trybuna Ludu* journalist Krystyna Kostrzewa noted that, "In particular areas, everything is already sold out for the entire summer, and to tourists from East Germany."[42] Furthermore, Wróblewski, in his 1976 article in *Polityka*, had reported that many wondered why the Germans did "not have any restrictions on their ability to buy in Poland."[43] If two brothers in socialism were to be treated equally, why should the East Germans have greater freedom than Poles?

The reason, clearly, was Polish smuggling and conspicuous consumption, which was never resolved. But though unresolved, it was, in essence, solved: in 1980, the East German government made the abrupt decision to completely close the border. Most historians explain this decision as the GDR's desire to contain Solidarity, the revolutionary trade union threatening communist power in Poland, but state documents consistently point to rampant consumption as the more influential factor in this dramatic decision.[44] In secret meetings before October 1980, Honecker and members of the GDR's Central Committee pointed not only to would-be "counter-revolutionaries" but also to widespread and consistent overconsumption on the part of Poles in East Germany. East Germany could not, and would not, risk overtaxing its model socialist republic with either counterrevolutionaries or shoppers from the East.[45]

The Polish government was caught between East German and Soviet expectations to control their subjects (both at home and abroad), and it also had to deal with a public demanding lower prices (following a long tradition of price-hike protests in communist Poland), as well as an independent trade union calling for greater political liberalization. The open border with the GDR (and Czechoslovakia) was widely considered to be a major mechanism for providing Polish citizens with hard-to-find goods. But the rising tide of East German restrictions that targeted Polish black market traders also impeded many average Poles from obtaining the sort of consumer goods (including powdered milk and lard) that belonged to a basic household. As a result, on September 10, 1980, just weeks before the East German border was sealed off, the Polish government moved to increase the maximum exchange from 350 to 400 marks in a last attempt to quell basic food shortages for at least part of the population.[46] Amid heightening political tensions, this was then followed by the more radical decision to offer ration cards at home for essential goods.[47]

On October 24, Stanisław Kania telephoned Honecker to speak of developments in Poland before traveling to Moscow. They spoke for nearly an hour. Outside of pressing concerns about the delivery of coal to the GDR (they had not received any since August), the main point of discussion was the upcoming decision to close the border and nullify the liberal travel legislation. Kania was distressed about those rumors, stating that "everyone in the [Polish] party [knew] that the agreement was an initiative of Comrade Erich [Honecker]." He pleaded with the East German leader, arguing that Borders of Friendship was not only about trade, and to end the agreement would simply "not be right." Honecker responded that since "the condition of [East German] retail trade was so fragile, it could not be put off any longer."[48] Three days later, the same stance was taken in a discussion between the secretary of the Central Committee and the Soviet Politburo. Secretary Joachim Hermann stated that Poles were "racketeering," a practice that needed to be halted:

> I would like to inform the [Soviet] comrades of the fact that the Politburo of our party has decided to change the agreement on pass- and visa-free travel between the GDR and People's Poland temporarily. This measure has become necessary because pass- and visa-free travel has been used for purposes in contradiction to its basic principles. Mass purchases and racketeering has reached an indefensible magnitude. This activity has come under increasing denunciation on the part of the population of the GDR.[49]

Clearly, from the German standpoint, Polish shopping practices, as well as illicit trade, were the central issue in forcing the border closure.

For their part, the Poles were understandably bitter about the unilateral decision to close down Borders of Friendship, and when the press reported the closure it squarely pinned the responsibility on Berlin. A short notice from October 31 informed Polish readers that limitations had been placed on individual travel, and that they were "limitations—initiated by the GDR."⁵⁰ This came just days following an editorial from the East German associated press to Poles, which praised the open border concept as a "step in serving friendly get-to-gethers between citizens." The editorial went on to note, however, that, "It has changed. . . . The decisions that have been taken are without doubt restrictive for the citizens of both countries. They are, nevertheless, necessary."⁵¹ Acting preemptively, the GDR seemed to be saying, unequivocally, "all's well that ends well."

Conclusion

Despite growing contradictions among socialist governments, Borders of Friendship was a project that, internationally speaking, was meant to prove the GDR and Poland were bona fide "brothers in socialism." Open borders were reflective of implicit trust between good friends. The degree of freedom accorded to the Polish and East German citizens was remarkable given that travel even between socialist states was generally tightly restricted during the communist period.

Even though both states had initial misgivings about the opening of the border, the problems for East Germany ended up being far more intractable. For the East Germans, the open border was meant to provide additional vacation-scapes in the hopes of boosting an East Bloc identity.⁵² Although East Germans also shopped on the Polish side, most traffic came from Poland to the GDR, whose government could not continue to promise a steady supply of goods and services to the millions of Poles arriving in its cities. GDR citizens were none too pleased to face their now-empty shelves, which they believed visiting Poles had emptied. The issue was more frequently aired in Poland, but East German readers were aware of trader tourist tensions from articles in *Neues Deutschland, Eulenspiegel,* and *Wochenpost.* The Polish shopper (and even more so the politically loaded Polish black market swindler) was an easy scapegoat for East German economic belt tightening, particularly once the ramifications of the global economic crisis (which hit the Bloc in the late 1970s) were clearly felt.

The interplay between the native (with limited abundance) and the foreigner (who was emptying shelves) was a common story across the Bloc. Even in hybrid countries—that is, socialist countries not officially aligned with Moscow, such as Yugoslavia—shopping tourism was a common feature. The social practice of shopping tourism was marked in the East since it aimed at mimicking Western models.⁵³ Western models of consumption were officially downplayed in the case of Borders of Friendship, but the economic efficacy of the international agreement was not. Scholars have shown how modes of consumption were tacitly accepted, that having citizens go abroad to quench the desire to shop was a critical part of a "formula of ambiguity."[54]

For Poland, its citizens, and the authorities, the open border project was an unambiguous economic necessity. Borders of Friendship served a practical function in a shortage economy and was seen as such by authorities who hoped the open border would serve as a safety valve to release steam from an otherwise insular kettle that all too frequently exploded in reaction to the lack (or high price) of consumer goods. Both populations exploited the availability of a second market; Poles were more active in achieving an almost free-market mentality toward the open border, judging quality and adjusting consumption on the basis of prices. This was in large part thanks to Poland's hobbled economy. As the current foreign minister of Poland recently remarked, anyone who traveled in the 1970s had "to trade . . . to pay for the holiday. Millions of people did it."[55]

State officials and the press actively condoned cross-border consumption; when it got out of control (which it did almost immediately), they began a parallel campaign of disciplining the consumer practices ignited by Borders of Friendship. Caricatures castigated conspicuous consumption, and travel reports ostracized ludicrous shopping practices. Whereas in 1972 the press on both sides was active in promoting tourism in the "*Freundschaftsland*" (with state-sponsored Polish courses, German-Polish information bureaus, hourly buses across the border, etc.), the tone was quick to change as East Germany instituted mechanisms to control consumption and Poland began to worry about the travel tourism of its own citizens.

Most scholars have portrayed this cross-border market as a hidden one, explicitly barred from the general public's attention, and denied by Party officials in public.[56] Existing literature tends to present the rampant consumption in terms of a Polish population that subversively instrumentalized liberal travel politics for their own profit.[57] What is clear from the official media on both sides, however, is that this black market was by no means invisible—neither to the daily press nor to its readers. Over the course of nine years, both regimes grew to acknowledge tourists from the other socialist state as *buyers*. The governments attempted to manage levels of travel consumption, but Polish authorities explicitly condoned consumption as long as their subjects did not export or import pornography—which was banned in all East bloc countries throughout state socialism—or social unrest. In many ways, in spite of official grumblings the open border was used as a secondary marketplace—where people filled gas tanks, bellies, and coffers with hard-to-find goods in both states—albeit under surveillance and censure. In the final analysis, Borders of

Friendship would have been a failure even without the antigovernment strikes in Gdańsk in 1980, but it took those events to finally legitimize its end.

NOTES

1. Hoover Archives, Biuletyn Informacyjny sekretariatu Komitetu Centralnego Polskiej Zjednoczonej Partii Robotniczej (henceforth HA), 272 VI from Oct. 30, 1976, 19. In the years from 1955 to 1971, there were 9,032,200 reported travels outside of Polish territory; in 1972 alone, there were 10,600,000. See *Rocznik Statystyczny* (Warsaw: Główny Urząd Statystyczny, 1973); Paweł Sowiński, *Wakacje w Polsce Ludowej*, (Warszawa: Wydawnictwo TRIO, 2005), 287.

2. See, for example, Alenka Švab, "Consuming Western Image of Well-Being: Shopping Tourism in Socialist Slovenia," *Cultural Studies* 16 (2002): 68; and Liviu Chelcea, "The Culture of Shortage During State-Socialism: Consumption Practices in a Romanian Village in the 1980s," *Cultural Studies* 16 (2002): 63–79.

3. See Chelcea, "Culture of Shortage," 63-79; and Mikołaj Morzycki-Markowski, "How People Crossed Borders in Socialism: The Polish Case," in *"Schleichwege," Inoffizielle Begegnungen sozialistischer Staatsbürger zwischen 1956 und 1989*, eds. Włodzimierz Borodziej, Jerzy Kochanowski, and Joachim von Puttkamer (Cologne: Böhlau, 2010), 55–66.

4. Národní Archív, KSČ-ÚV-02/1. KSČ—Ústřední výbor 1945–1989, Praha—předsednictvo 1971–1976, Sv. 24 ar.j. 25 b. 12, "Obchodně politické zásady zahraničního cestovního ruchu na rok 1972," 11.

5. See Monika Tantzscher, *Die verlängerte Mauer: die Zusammenarbeit der Sicherheitsdienste der Warschauer-Pakt-Staaten bei der Verhinderung von "Republikflucht"* (Berlin: Der Bundesbeauftragte für die Unterlagen des Staatssicherheitsdienstes der ehemaligen Deutschen Demokratischen Republik, 1998).

6. Christina Petrescu, "Entrepreneurial Tourism in Romania: A System-Stabilizing Factor?" in Borodziej et al. (eds.), *"Schleichwege,"* 115–34.

7. See Jonathan Zatlin, "Scarcity and Resentment: Economic Sources of Xenophobia in the GDR, 1971–1989," *Central European History* 40 (2007): 683–720.

8. See especially Borodziej et al. (eds.), *"Schleichwege."*

9. See Ludwig Mehlhorn, "Przyjaźń nakazana? Stosunki między NRD i Polską w latach 1949–1990," *Stosunki polsko-niemieckie 1949–2005. Wspólnota wartości i interesów?* eds. Basil Kerski and Wolf-Dieter Eberwein (Olsztyń: Borussia, 2005), 94–110.

10. See (no author identified) "East Germany, Poland OK Open-Border Pact," *Los Angeles Times* (henceforth *LAT*), Oct. 25, 1971, 2; James Feron, "East Bloc Opens Warsaw Parley," *New York Times* (henceforth *NYT*), Dec. 1, 1971, 15; Feron, "East Bloc Asks Step to Europe Parley," *NYT*, Dec. 3, 1971, 4; (no author), "East Germany, Czechoslovakia and Poland Drop Travel Curb," *NYT*, Jan. 2, 1972, 18.

11. *Sächsische Zeitung*, Dec. 31, 1971, 1; Halina Dylawerska, "Polen deckt den Touristen-Tisch!" *Wochenpost* 19 (1972), 27; Mark Keck-Szajbel, "The Politics of Travel and the Creation of a European Society," *Global Society* 24 (2010): 31–50.

12. Krystyna Kostrzewa, "Prywatny wyjazdy turystyczny do wszystkich krajów," *Trybuna Ludu* (henceforth *TL*), Jan. 1, 1972, 1, 4.

13. Mieczysław Rakowski, *Dzienniki polityczne 1972–1975* (Warsaw: Wydawnictwo ISKRY, 2002), 10.

14. "Ein Schritt von historischen Rang," *ND*, Jan. 10, 1972, 1.

15. Andrzej Kwilecki, "Badania socjologiczne na pograniczu Polski i NRD," *Sprawy Międzynarodowe* 7(8) (1973): 145–46; Kwilecki, "Problematyka socjologiczna ruchu granicznego i kontaktów ludnościowych Polska-NRD," *Przegląd Zachodni* 4 (1974): 399–404; Małgorzata Mazurek, *Społeczeństwo kolejki. O doświadczeniach niedoboru 1945–1989* (Warsaw: Wydawnictwo TRIO, 2010), 107–42.

16. HA, 219 VI from Feb. 4, 1972, 23; HA272 VI from Oct. 30, 1976, 23; see also n.a., "Treffpunkt Centrum," *Für Dich* 44 (1972): 32–35.

17. Jerzy Urban, "Przy drzwiach otwartych," *Polityka*, Jan. 15, 1972: 1, 5.

18. T. Filiatowski, "Drezno," *Światowid*, April 1978, 28–29; K. Konicki, "Lipsk," *Światowid*, January 1977, 24–25; Irena Pawełkowa, "Berlin," *Światowid*, August 1974, 26–28.

19. See Patrick Patterson, "Truth Half Told: Finding the Perfect Pitch for Advertising and Marketing in Socialist Yugoslavia, 1950–1991," *Enterprise and Society* 4 (2003): 683–720.

20. Interview with Peter Koehli, n.t., *Światowid*, Jan. 2, 1972, 3.

21. Andrzej Wróblewski, "Notacy," *Polityka*, Apr. 10, 1976, 5.

22. Jerzy Kochanowski, "Wir sind zu arm, um den Urlaub im eigenen Land zu Verbringen. Massentourismus und illegaler Handel in den 1950ger und 1960ger Jahren in Polen," in Borodziej et al. (eds.), *"Schleichwege,"* 135–52. Ludwig Mehlhorn, "Przyjaźń nakazana? Stosunki między NRD i Polską w latach 1949–1990," *Stosunki polsko-niemieckie 1949–2005. Wspólnota wartości i interesów?* eds. Basil Kerski and Wolf-Dieter Eberwein (Olsztyń: Borussia, 2005), 94–110.

23. HA295 III from Mar. 15, 1976, 16–17.

24. HA223 IV from May 2, 1972, 31.

25. Andrzej Mozołowski, "Notacy na granicą," *Polityka*, May 22, 1976, 3.

26. See Volker Zimmerman, *Eine sozialistische Freundschaft im Wandel. Die Beziehungen zwischen der SBZ/DDR und der Tschechoslowakei (1945–1969)* (Düsseldorf: Klartext, 2010), 393–98.

27. N.a., "Dzień dobry, Zielona Góra," *Wochenpost* 19 (1972): 18.

28. N.a., "Über meine Freundschaftsreise," *Eulenspiegel* 27 (1972): 8.

29. Maria Rogowiec, Tadeusz Szumowski, "Wpływ ruchu turystycznego między Niemiecką Republiką Demokratyczną a Polską na sytuację rynkową w wybranych rejonach naszego kraju," *Roczniki Instytutu Handlu Wewnętrznego* 68 (1973), 97–107; BArch, DL 203 20-00-44, Karton 357.

30. For work on smuggling, see particularly Karin Lenk, "Von Salamiwürsten und Salamanderschuhen. Schmuggel zwischen der DDR und der Volksrepublik Polen in den 1970er und 1980er Jahren" (M.A. thesis, Frankfurt/Oder, 2006).

31. Andrzej Wróblewski, op. cit.

32. Sächsiche Hauptstaatsarchiv Dresden, Signatur IV.C.2.18.756, Abteilung für Sicherheitsfragen, Dresden, Apr. 13, 1972, n.p.

33. SAPMO-Barch, DY 30, 2897, Auszug aus den Ausführung des Genossen Sindermann in der Beratung mit den Ministern, die Mitglieder und Kandidaten des

Zentralkomitees sind, am 13.10.1972, Bl. 125; also Zatlin, "Polnisches Wirtschaft," op. cit., 308.

34. HA 272 VI from Oct. 30, 1976: 21.

35. Instytut Pamięci Narodowej (IPN) 0038/39/1, Akcja specjalna krypt. "Turystyka." Tom I, 62–64.

36. Andrzej Mozołowski, "Handelsmarkt," *Polityka*, May 22, 1976, 3.

37. "Granice bez kompleksów," *Polityka*, May 28, 1977: 10–15.

38. Editorial, n.a., *TL*, Sept. 5, 1980, 5.

39. Wojciech Maziarski, "Z dziejów paszportu w PRL," *Gazeta Magazyn* 25 (June 18, 1996), n.p. For other examples of "spontaneous" declarations promising not to smuggle, see n.a., "Bruderbund DDR-Polen für immer unzerstörbar," *ND*, June 9, 1973, 1–2.

40. See Joachim Nawrocki, "Polens Spitzenführer in der DDR. Vertiefung der bilateralen Beziehungen," *Deutschland Archiv* 6 (1973): 681–86.

41. HA 272 VI from Oct. 30, 1976: 20.

42. Krystyna Kostrzewa, "Głód informacyjny," *TL*, June 20, 1972, 5; and "Niedziela w NRD," *TL*, June 7, 1972, 3.

43. Wróblewski, op. cit.

44. Zatlin, "Polnisches Wirtschaft," op. cit.

45. Mazurek, *Społeczeństwo*, op. cit.

46. Announcement, *TL*, Sept. 9, 1980, 2.

47. From Joachim Hermann, Anhang 1 zur Vorlage für das Politbüro, Arbeitsprotokoll 45/80 der Politbürositzung vom 11.11.1980, SAPMO-BArch ZPA, J IV 2/2/A-2361; "Hart und kompromißlos durchgreifen" in *Die SED contra Polen 1980/1981. Geheimakten der SED-Führung der polnischen Demokratiebewegung*, ed. Michael Kubina and Manfred Wilke (Berlin: Akademie Verlag, 1995), 97.

48. From [24.10.1980, Paraphe E[rich].H[onecker].], Arbeitsprotokoll 43/80 der Politbürositzung vom 28.10.1980, SAPMO-Barch ZPA, J IV 2/2/A-2358. In ibid., 91–96.

49. From Joachim Hermann, op. cit.

50. Polska Agencja Prasowa, Announcement, *TL*, Oct. 31, 1980, 6.

51. Allgemeine Deutsche Nachtrichtendienst, Announcement, *TL*, Oct. 29, 1980, 1.

52. Orvar Löfgren, *On Holiday: A History of Vacationing* (Berkeley: University of California Press, 1999).

53. Alenka Švab, op. cit.

54. Chelcea, op. cit.

55. See Radisław Sikorski, "The New Poland in a New Europe," at the World Affairs Council of North America, San Francisco, Aug. 5, 2009, http://wacsf.vportal.net/ (accessed Sept. 20, 2010).

56. Zatlin, op. cit.

57. Ironically, historians writing after the fall of state socialism have fallen in line with argumentation used by socialist planners. By depicting the growth of transnational consumption in terms of a society held captive in the shortage economy, they argue that citizens were subversive in their buying practices. Through nebulously defined smuggling (or, as central committee members called it, "racketeering"), citizens engaged in the pseudo-free market offered by cross-border consumption. As the story

goes, this was an effect of greater openness in late state socialism and was not intended by planners. See Małgorzata Irek, *Der Schmugglerzug: Warschau—Berlin—Warschau* (Berlin: Das Arabische Buch, 1998); Holger Seifert, "Der 'Nahhandel' über die 'Brücke der Freundschaft' in Görlitz," *INTER FINITIMOS. Jahrbuch zur Deutsch-Polnischen Beziehungsgeschichte* 3 (2005): 165–72; Paweł Sowiński, "Turystyka zagraniczna a czarny rynek w Polsce (1956–1989)," in *Socjalizm w życiu powszednim: Dyktatura a społeczeństwo w NRD i PRL*, eds. Sandrine Kott, Marcin Kula, and Thomas Lindenberger (Warsaw: Trio, 2006), 189–97; Paweł Sowiński, "Szlak kryształowy," *Polityka*, 12 (2006): 70; and Janusz Radomski, "Kształtowanie sie indiwidualnych zakupów turystów polskich w przygranicznych obszarach," *Przegląd zachodno-pomorski* 25 (1981): 41–57.

Index

quality of goods and, 145–46, 158,
160n24
response to, 145, 218
stimulation of, 326, 361, 363, 366
tracking, 380
consumer elites, 7, 21–24
conspicuous consumption of, 39
consumer golden age (1960s and
1970s), 12–13, 167
consumerism
consumption compared to, 4–5
socialist, 71, 192, 218, 244
United States' mission of
exportation of, 66n57
consumerist turn, 8–9, 120
consumer tourism, 308–9, 311–14,
319n27
consumption. *See also* communist
consumption; conspicuous
consumption; socialist
consumption; *specific countries
and products*
bourgeois, 8, 21
capitalism and, 5–6
consumerism compared to, 4–5
from egalitarian to self-managed,
353–59, 363
entrepreneurs, resistance and,
292–94
in framework of collective good,
12
good life and, 15, 88, 89, 94, 96,
119, 170, 179, 227
production and, 355
rational, 9, 230
in Stalinist period, 94, 336, 347n11
state-generated critiques of, 7
in West compared to Eastern
Europe, 5–7, 334, 387
youth and, 6

consumption and gender, 7
Ceauşescu, N., and, 231–35
lifestyle in Romania and, 226–45
cookbooks and recipes
advertisements and, 174–75, 175f, 177
Croatian, 189–90
foreign, 176–77, 186
the good life and, 170, 179, 184, 192
purpose and roles of, 170, 180–82,
185, 191–93
regional and national, 167, 185–91
Serbian, 190–91
substitutions in, 210, 242, 249n69
tourism and, 181
women and, 172–75, 178–85, 192
in Yugoslavia, 166, 167, 169–93,
175f
Cooperativa (village store), 258, 265
Corecom (hard currency institution),
29, 34–35, 101
Coresta (tobacco organization), 101,
106, 109
corruption
capitalism and, 45
housing and, 359
Corvin department store, 127–28,
129, 325
Council for Aesthetics of Industrial
Goods, 148
court system, 41–42, 41f
craftsmanship, 310, 320n30
crime
crackdown on hard currency
shops, 42, 47n52
criminalization of abortion, 228,
234, 247n29
criticism, 321–24
constructive, 322–23
of department stores, 130–32
self-, 321–22

consumer abundance in, 179
consumer elites in, 22
cookbooks and recipes in, 166,
167, 169–93, 175f
department stores in, 116, 120, 123,
125–26, 131, 138n18, 138nn20–21,
175
food and drink in, 166
housing in, 323, 351–69
new class of consumers in, 358–59,
371n33
Soviet Union's relations with, 171,
192, 321, 354

tobacco industry and, 106, 108–9,
114n49
trader tourism and, 251, 387
Western aesthetics and goods in,
89

Zhivkov, Todor, 148
Živković, Živorad, 357–60, 364
zones in occupied Germany,
199–201, 220n14
Bizone, 200–201
Soviet Occupied Zone, 199, 201,
204